TRANSFORMA
GOVERNANCE AND DEMOCRACY

National Academy of Public Administration

Terry F. Buss, Series Editor

Modernizing Democracy:
Innovations in Citizen Participation
Edited by Terry F. Buss, F. Stevens Redburn, and Kristina Guo

Meeting the Challenge of 9/11:
Blueprints for More Effective Government
Edited by Thomas H. Stanton

Transforming Public Leadership for the 21st Century
Edited by Ricardo S. Morse, Terry F. Buss, and C. Morgan Kinghorn

Foreign Aid and Foreign Policy:
Lessons for the Next Half-Century
Edited by Louis A. Picard, Robert Groelsema, and Terry F. Buss

Performance Management and Budgeting:
How Governments can Learn From Experience
Edited by F. Stevens Redburn, Robert J. Shea, and Terry F. Buss

Reengineering Community Development for the 21st Century
Edited by Donna Fabiani and Terry F. Buss

Innovations in Public Leadership Development
Edited by Ricardo S. Morse and Terry F. Buss

Innovations in Human Resource Management: Getting the Public's Work
Done in the 21st Century
Edited by Hannah S. Sistare, Myra Howze Shiplett, and Terry F. Buss

Expanding Access to Health Care: A Management Approach
Edited by Terry F. Buss and Paul N. Van de Water

Justice for All: Promoting Social Equity in Public Administration
Edited by Norman J. Johnson and James H. Svara

Transforming American Governance: Rebooting the Public Square
Edited by Alan P. Balutis, Terry F. Buss, and Dwight Ink

About the Academy

The National Academy of Public Administration is an independent, nonprofit organization chartered by Congress to identify emerging issues of governance and to help federal, state, and local governments improve their performance. The Academy's mission is to provide "trusted advice"—advice that is objective, timely, and actionable—on all issues of public service and management. The unique source of the Academy's expertise is its membership, including more than 650 current and former cabinet officers, members of Congress, governors, mayors, legislators, jurists, business executives, public managers, and scholars who are elected as fellows because of their distinguished contribution to the field of public administration through scholarship, civic activism, or government service. Participation in the Academy's work is a requisite of membership, and the fellows offer their experience and knowledge voluntarily.

The Academy is proud to join with M.E. Sharpe, Inc., to bring readers this and other volumes in a series of edited works addressing current major public management and public policy issues.

The opinions expressed in these writings are those of the authors and do not necessarily reflect the views of the Academy. To access Academy reports, please visit our Web site at www.napawash.org.

Transforming American Governance

Rebooting the Public Square

Editors
Alan P. Balutis
Terry F. Buss
Dwight Ink

NATIONAL ACADEMY OF
PUBLIC ADMINISTRATION

TRANSFORMATIONAL TRENDS IN
GOVERNANCE AND DEMOCRACY

M.E.Sharpe
Armonk, New York
London, England

Library of Congress Cataloging-in-Publication Data

Transforming American governance : rebooting the public square /   edited by Alan P. Balutis,
Terry F. Buss, and Dwight Ink.
   p. cm.—(Transformational trends in governance and democracy)
Includes bibliographical references and index.
ISBN 978–0–7656–2770–4 (hardcover : alk. paper) — ISBN 978–0–7656–2771–1 (pbk. : alk. paper)
   1. United States—Politics and government—21st century. 2. Federal government—United
States. 3. Political participation—United States. 4. Administrative agencies—United States—
Management. 5. Executive departments—United States—Management. 6. Administrative
agencies—United States—Reorganization. 7. Executive departments—United States—
Reorganization. I. Balutis, Alan P. II. Buss, Terry F. III. Ink, Dwight, 1922–

JK421.T825 2011
351.73—dc22   2011006072

Printed in the United States of America

The paper used in this publication meets the minimum requirements of
American National Standard for Information Sciences
Permanence of Paper for Printed Library Materials,
ANSI Z 39.48-1984.

♾

| IBT (c) | 10 | 9 | 8 | 7 | 6 | 5 | 4 | 3 | 2 | 1 |
| SP (p) | 10 | 9 | 8 | 7 | 6 | 5 | 4 | 3 | 2 | 1 |

Contents

Preface

Our nation faces a large—and growing—long-term fiscal imbalance driven by an aging population, which will dramatically increase health care and retirement costs. "The government is on an unstable path," says the recently released *Federal Government's Financial Health*. This report, prepared by the U.S. Department of the Treasury and Office of Management and Budget (with the assistance of the Government Accountability Office, or GAO), puts the challenge in stark terms:

> This year, 2008, is the year in which the first of the approximately 80 million baby boomers—those born between 1946 and 1964—become eligible to draw Social Security benefits. Scheduled Social Security and Medicare benefits together with other federal programs' projected long-term costs are much greater than the resources (revenue and borrowings) available to pay for them. Unless action is taken to bring program costs in line with available resources, the coming surge of entitlement spending will end in a fiscal train wreck that will have an adverse effect on the U.S. economy and on virtually every American.

In 2019, the Medicare Part A trust fund, which finances inpatient hospital services for elderly Americans, will not have enough money to pay full benefits. In 2080, the total cost of government will be more than three times the revenue.

Other Challenges

President Obama certainly faces other challenges: the continuing war on terror, increasing economic competition from emerging world powers like China and India, rising energy costs, environmental concerns, and unknown new problems and threats. As the baby boom generation retires and health care costs rapidly rise, Social Security, Medicare, and Medicaid programs—as well as interest on the national debt—will account for a growing portion of government cost, creating immense budget pressure on initiatives to fund the other challenges. Interest on the debt in FY2009 totaled $260 billion—about what was spent by the U.S. Departments of Education, Energy, Health and Human Services, Homeland Security, Housing and Urban Development, Interior, and Justice combined.

Any one of the challenges would be a large enough agenda for a new administration. Their convergence creates an environment of unparalleled complication for the president and government management. Just look at the partial list of 21st-century challenges prepared by the GAO:

- Large and growing long-term fiscal imbalance
- Evolving national and homeland security policies
- Increasing global interdependence
- The changing economy
- Demographic shifts
- Science and technology advances
- Quality-of-life trends
- Diverse governance structures and tools

The administration, then, has no shortage of problems to solve. The question is whether it will adapt new approaches to the management of government to meet the challenges it faces. Facing these challenges will require a "changed" government, a 21st-century government transformed to operate on demand. With confidence in government at an historic low, the time for action is now.

Moving Toward a Transformed Government

In the aftermath of September 11 and Hurricane Katrina, we heard again and again that government needs to be better managed. "Everything has changed" was the constant refrain. "Never has American history seen a time when management has been more important but the stock of new ideas has been so low," argues professor Donald Kettl of the University of Maryland.

What characteristics would a transformed "21st-century" government have? Although the outline of such a government is becoming clearer, the literature has yet to describe a real model or even it's key characteristics. What are some of the elements of such a government? In the past few years, several texts—the Internet Business Solutions Group study, *The Connected Republic 2.0;* Elaine C. Kamarck's *The End of Government . . . as We Know It;* Donald F. Kettl's *The Next Government of the United States;* and others from the IBM Center for the Business of Government—have offered various visions:

- Several trends are transforming government: (1) the "rules of the game" are changing in human capital, financial management, and organization structure; (2) performance management is increasingly used; (3) governments are taking market-based approaches, such as competition, choice, and incentives; (4) government is moving from business as usual to performing on demand; (5) citizens are becoming more engaged; and (6) governments are using collaborative networks and partnerships to deliver services and solutions.
- These trends—and the formidable challenges facing the nation—will drive government to reconfigure itself to serve the needs of its citizens in the 21st

century. As Professor Kettl has put it, "At the core is a fundamental problem: the current conduct of American government is a poor match for the problems it must solve." Thus, Kettl notes five imperatives for the performance of government in the 21st century: (1) a policy agenda that focuses more on problems than on structures; (2) political accountability that works more through results than through processes; (3) public administration that functions more organically through heterarchy than rigidly through hierarchy; (4) political leadership that works more by leveraging action than by simply making decisions; and (5) citizenship that works more through engagements than remoteness.

- A new, transformed, on-demand government would have different characteristics than today's government has. It would be responsive, agile, resilient, flexible, dynamic, flatter, more connected, less hierarchical, seamless, more personalized, and transparent.
- Such a transformed government might deliver services by three different approaches to policy implementation: reinvented government, government by network, and government by market.
- Finally, regardless of the transformations that occur, greater attention must be given to effective management and proper implementation of the systems and structures put in place.

These trends will drastically affect what it is like to work in the public sector. New forms of coordination and control will evolve. Governments will place a premium on the skills of orchestration and facilitation and the ability to recognize the credibility and authority of sources of policy insight and advice outside the formal structures of the public sector. New accountability methods will be developed to match the radically dispersed and collaborative nature of public purpose work. Governments will need to make their own workplaces flatter, more connected, and less hierarchical, more in tune with the values and behavior of the talented people that need to be attracted to the public sector.

That is the general conclusion of the experts assembled in this volume; they have come at this issue from different perspectives. Our contributors view the question from the perspective of public administration theory and the administrative state. They discuss it within the framework of such current policy challenges as the nation's fiscal crisis and our ongoing war on terrorism. They debate it as it affects state and local governance and ponder the question, "Whither American Federalism?" They speculate about exactly how government will respond, while some assert that the answers already exist in past—or current and emerging—changes and reform models. And they ponder the future—as a new Millennial generation enters public service, powerful 2.0 social networking, collaborative technologies become more prevalent, and new models of citizen engagement, and even co-production—change the very nature of government itself and/or government management.

It has been a challenging and exciting task to produce this volume, one of the

National Academy of Public Administration's series with M.E. Sharpe, "Transformational Trends in Governance and Democracy." Our thanks go to the Academy. This has been a true collaboration and in the tradition of public administration we list the editors in alphabetical order.

We hope this volume can begin an important dialogue about new and different models of government and of governance. If that dialogue begins, we at the Academy will have achieved our ends.

Alan P. Balutis
Senior Director and Distinguished Fellow,
Internet Business Solutions Group,
Cisco Systems

Terry F. Buss
Executive Director and
Distinguished Professor of Public Policy,
Carnegie Mellon University,
Australia

Dwight Ink
Fellow, National Academy of Public Administration

Transforming American Governance

1

American Governance 3.0

Issues and Prospects

TERRY F. BUSS, ALAN BALUTIS, AND DWIGHT INK

Governance in America is undergoing a great transformation. For some, this is a crisis. For others, it's a welcome evolution. No one knows for certain how all this will end up: better, worse, or perhaps just different from the past. The transformation is driven by events, movements, information technology, national public policy, and institutional change, all interacting and all taking governance in different, often contradictory, directions, and into unknown territory (see Figure 1.1). Some are calling for a new "social contract" to govern America. Others see no need for change. Others believe this is all business as usual.

Consider these competing drivers of change in governance over the past two decades:

1. Events. The Republican Party takeover of Congress in 1994, the Clinton scandal in 1998, and the George W. Bush/Al Gore election controversy in 2000; the dot.com bust and recession of 2001; terrorist attacks on New York and Washington in 2001; ongoing prosecution of wars beginning in Afghanistan in 2001 and Iraq in 2003; the response to the Katrina hurricane disaster of 2005; the global financial crisis of 2008; the election of President Barack Obama in 2008, along with the Republican loss of control of Congress; and in 2010 the Republican takeover of the House of Representatives and the narrowing of the Democratic Party control of the Senate.

2. New Public Management movement. The pervasiveness of performance management and budgeting and the ascendency of the New Public Management (NPM) movement, a movement based on business management principles, market approaches, efficiency, and effectiveness; and the backlash to NPM from its critics and opponents.

3. Information technology. The ascendency of information technology (IT), fostering e-government, open government, social media, collaboration, and knowledge management.

4. Public policy. Out-of-control budget deficits and debt under Presidents Bush and Obama; economic recovery and management of the economy and monetary policy; government intervention in and management of private business in the form

Figure 1.1   **Determinants of American Governance**

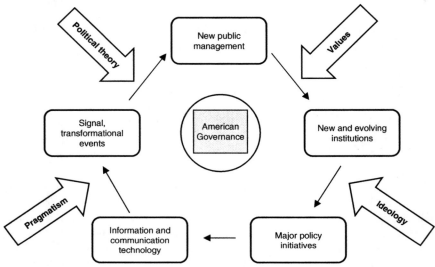

of public ownership, bailouts, subsidies, and regulation; reemergence of regulatory policy generally; and upheavals in health care, carbon emissions, energy, immigration, and foreign policy.

5. *Institutions.* Congress and executive relations and balance of power; intergovernmental relations and federalism; new organizational models in international affairs; networked government, both formal and informal; new forms of collaboration; expansion and contraction of authority in international organizations; and the rise of nongovernmental organizations (NGOs)—the so-called third sector.

How these factors influence governance—or are influenced by it—is now a matter for debate. Causality may go in either direction: public policies are developed in response to events and public policies produce events. Factors are not mutually exclusive: a public policy, for example, creating the Department of Homeland Security, can be viewed as a policy initiative and also as an event. There are many more critical factors influencing government than can be adequately dealt with here. Our treatment is by necessity selective.

Now is a propitious time to look at governance anew. We need to describe how governance is different now from the way it was in the past. We need to understand how governance will likely evolve and transform in the future. We should immediately begin a national dialogue concerning whether our democracy will be improved or diminished as governance changes. H. George Frederickson, in Chapter 2, lays out a possible role for the National Academy of Public Administration (the Academy)—the sponsor of this volume—in working on a national governance agenda for public administration. And we need to put into place mechanisms to keep government on the right course, whatever that turns out to be. This chapter lays out the issues.

Whether American governance is hopelessly broken or simply needs reengineering remains an open question. But few would disagree with our assessment about what ought to be addressed, stated in the form of questions:

- Is attempting to radically transform governance following every presidential election necessary for the renewal of the country? Or is it unnecessarily disruptive and divisive? What is the role of consensus building and compromise?
- Has partisanship become exponentially worse, further reducing effective governance? Or has this always been characteristic of the political system? How has this partisanship played out in Congress and the executive branch? Is basic civility a casualty?
- How has the balance of power between the executive, legislative, and judicial branches changed governance? Is the balance intended by the Founding Fathers out of whack?
- Is our Federalist model transforming? Or is the model in place since the Reagan administration alive and well?
- Has government lost its ability to tackle big problems (Eggers and O'Leary 2010)? Or has it always been ineffective and inefficient in the design and implementation of policies and programs?
- Has the United States given up too much of its national sovereignty to international organizations? Or should it play an even greater part in a global governance system?
- Has performance-based management and budgeting and civil service reform improved governance? Or have they been largely irrelevant?
- Will social media and collaboration with Internet-based technologies transform governance? Or will they turn out to be just another fad in the public arena? Could these technologies actually make governance worse?
- Has networked government—both formal and informal—improved governance or impeded it? Has it transformed governance in significant ways?

A number of books have appeared over the past decade calling for new institutions, models, or approaches to inform or improve governance (e.g., Cooper 2003; Denhardt and Denhardt 2007; Goldsmith and Eggers 2004; Kamarck 2007; Kettl 2008; Morse, Buss, and Kinghorn 2007; Newbold and Terry 2008; Noveck 2009; Stanton 2006). Most of these books suggest the need for a smaller, more nimble government, oriented toward efficient and effective service provision through performance- and evidence-based policy and management. They call for increased use of partnerships, collaboration and networking, and reliance on IT, especially social networking and knowledge management—in short, American Governance 2.0. As we began putting this volume together, we accepted as a premise this view of governance in transformation. But with the unfolding of patterns in the past two years, governance may be different from anything anyone could possibly have imagined. Perhaps the nation has skipped to Governance version 3.0.

Before addressing these issues, it might be useful to define what we mean by governance and why it is always evolving.

The Essence of Governance

Governance Defined

Governance is a pivotal concept in public management; yet, surprisingly, there is little consensus among researchers, practitioners, and educators about its meaning (Frederickson and Smith 2003). By governance we mean:

> A system of values, laws, policies, processes, and institutions through which society articulates and aggregates competing interests; compromises and reaches consensus; manages resources; exercises power and authority; and resolves conflict to promote fairness, human rights, and growth and development for the public good.

Governance also applies at the organizational level in government. According to the Australian Public Service Commission, governance is "the set of responsibilities and practices, policies and procedures, exercised by an agency's executive, to provide strategic direction, ensure objectives are achieved, manage risks and use resources responsibly and with accountability" (Australian Government 2008).

A Clash of Values and Ideologies

Governance structures reflect a society's competing values, political ideologies, philosophies, and theories. America is a society deeply divided along political, social, cultural, ethnic, racial, class, religious, generational, and economic lines. The past two decades have become a battleground where factions clash or unite around alternative visions, self-interest, and expectations. Factions disagree about the causes, appearance, and resolution of governance issues. Because no single faction prevails for long in the political system, governance at times becomes curiously transient, fragmented, incongruent, and inconsistent. In short, it's very messy. Nevertheless, it mirrors society. Although this is the essence of democracy, many believe that governance is getting exponentially more dysfunctional, threatening the very foundations of the nation. Of course, some might argue, every period in history reflects this sense of impending doom. Then, over time, people forget and worry about something else. Durant, in Chapter 3, places these factional divisions in historical context.

Two Competing Factions

In the United States there are two major factions and a myriad of minor ones, occupying countervailing positions. Frederickson reviews both in the context of public administration in Chapter 2. One espouses social welfare values, which hold that the state is responsible for protecting individuals from economic distress, guaranteeing an acceptable standard of living, and compensating individuals when they are harmed. The other believes in a market-based society where individuals are responsible for their own lives. Thus, the government exists to enforce laws, referee disputes, and create an equal playing field, but not to guarantee successful or egalitarian outcomes. When these extremes clash in the political system, neither side overwhelms the other. Each side gets something, but not everything. These factions are unstable: people, groups, and political parties shift sides on many issues. The result is that governance becomes a hybrid, with elements from both extremes, as well as inputs from factions at the center.

Consider the financial crisis of 2008. The social welfare faction blamed the financial crisis on business—excess, greed, corruption. Social welfare proponents push for more government regulation of the private sector, business bailouts to protect jobs, and social programs such as unemployment insurance, public health insurance, job retraining, and the like. They favor corporatism—that business exists to serve the interests of the people (workers and state), not management (owners and shareholders). Free-market proponents blame financial crises on government intervention, especially in the form of stultifying regulation, excessive taxation, and invasive public policy. Free marketers favor laissez-faire policies and individual responsibility. Hybridization occurs in governance when free-market advocates approach government for favors that limit competition or protect private interests. So, for example, according to many economists, the Federal Reserve System was created by private financiers to protect their interests, when economies threaten them, by spreading or sharing risk with taxpayers. Hybridization also occurs when government creates government-sponsored enterprises (GSEs) to influence public policy through market manipulation: for example, creating Fannie Mae and Freddie Mac to securitize home mortgages to promote homeownership. Ink, in Chapter 15, calls for cooperation across party lines as the only way to resolve the nation's factional differences.

Often policymakers attempt to find common ground on factious issues by creating a bipartisan or nonpartisan task force to build consensus. Redburn, in Chapter 4, provides insights into the role of experts on task forces working on the federal deficit and debt in the aftermath of the financial crisis.

Renegotiating the Social Contract

For several decades many have been calling for a new social contract between government, business, and the American public. "During and after the Great Depression, workers, employers and the government entered into an implied social contract that afforded Americans a basic level of economic security if they worked hard and took responsibility for their families" (Rodin 2008, p.1; see also Brooks 2007 and Kochan and Shulman 2007). This movement had little traction until the financial crisis of 2008 (Sunstein 2007). Low unemployment rates, rising housing values, easy credit, unprecedented returns on investment, and "unquenchable exuberance" created massive wealth over several decades, causing many to believe economic good times would never end. The 2008 financial crisis changed this perception for many, setting up the potential for another round of confrontation (Saporito 2008).

Change occurs not only at the national level but at the organizational level as well. Christopherson, in Chapter 14, proposes a model and strategy for overcoming barriers and resistance. Change management is often overlooked in the context of governance. At the microlevel, in Chapter 20, Blanchard and his colleagues look at the role of leadership in the context of governmental organizations and governance.

Signal Events of the Past Two Decades: 1990–2010

Numerous events from 1990 through 2010 have been nominated by various commentators as emblematic of, setting the stage for, or precipitating the transformations in governance.

Musical Chairs in National Leadership and Political Scandals

George H. W. Bush was elected president in 1988, succeeding two-term president Ronald Reagan.[1] The Bush administration focused on foreign policy issues—interventions in Panama and the first Gulf War—but was perceived by many as ineffective in managing an economic downturn. Bush pledged no new taxes, but then reneged under pressure from a Democratic Party–controlled Congress. Some believe this not only contributed to Bush's subsequent electoral defeat but also inspired Republicans, accustomed to being in the minority, to try to regain control of Congress. Politics swirling around the tax issue may have contributed to increasingly souring relations with Congress. In 1991 the nomination to the Supreme Court of Clarence Thomas, a conservative African American, created a great deal of acrimony among Democrats and Republicans which carried over into the Clinton presidency (and continues even today).

Bill Clinton won election to the presidency in 1992, defeating George H. W. Bush and billionaire Ross Perot, an Independent advocating a business approach to government. Democrats had ended 12 years of Republican control of the White House and enjoyed majorities in the Senate and the House. Clinton supporters took the victories as a mandate—even though having received only 43 percent of the vote—for his "Third Way" philosophy of governance. Many Clinton opponents believed that had Ross Perot not run, Bush might well have won a second term. Some critics also argue that Clinton's campaign leadership needlessly created bad feelings among opponents. At any rate, the country was deeply divided over a recession and the burgeoning budget deficit and national debt, not to mention a new liberal vision for the country. Clinton complicated the start of his presidency with a poorly managed, slow-moving transition to office, which some believe contributed to a perceived crisis in governance and subsequent Republican victories.

In 1994, the Republican Party, running under the banner "A Contract with America," won control of Congress, ousting the Democratic Party which had held power in the House for 40 years. The Contract called for smaller, more responsible, more efficient government and reform of "welfare state" programs. In 1995, Republicans went so far as to temporarily shut down the federal government by withholding approval of appropriations in an effort to slow government spending. In 1996, Clinton, in his State of the Union address, apparently joining the Republicans, declared that the "era of big government was over." Earlier, Clinton launched the National Performance Review (NPR) to make government more efficient and effective (Gore 1993). Also in 1996, Congress passed the Welfare Reform Act (employing several procedural mechanisms which would come to the fore in the Obama Congress), limiting long-term participation in the program and requiring welfare recipients to look for work. Some Democrats viewed this as an assault on their hard-won agenda.

In 1998, the Republican-controlled Congress impeached President Clinton on perjury and obstruction of justice charges arising out of a scandal with Monica Lewinsky, an intern at the White House. At the time, a special prosecutor, Ken Starr, was undertaking rigorous investigations into several other Clinton scandals— Whitewater, Filegate, Travelgate. Although Clinton was acquitted by the Senate, his second term was in shambles. Also in 1998, reeling from what turned out to be unfounded charges of wrongdoing levied in retaliation over attacks on Clinton, loss of Republican seats in Congress, and a revolt of conservatives in the House, Speaker Newt Gingrich resigned. That left the Republican Party in the hands of new leaders, who would subordinate Congress to President Bush and his agenda, and were to become, in the view of naysayers, much more polarizing.

In November 2000, George W. Bush defeated then vice president Al Gore for the presidency. In Florida, only a handful of votes separated the candidates, prompting Gore to contest the election and call for a recount. A series of court decisions by the U.S. Supreme Court and the Florida Supreme Court, as well as administrative decisions by Florida's secretary of state, gave the election to Bush.[2] To this day, many see Bush as having stolen the election from Al Gore. Building on Clinton's NPR, Bush launched a comprehensive management reform agenda to make government more efficient and effective. Bush reached out to Senator Ted Kennedy, D-MA, to shepherd the No Child Left Behind Act of 2001, which enjoyed widespread bipartisan support for its standard-based education reforms. Kennedy later became furious when Bush failed to adequately fund the initiative. Bush was immediately confronted by a recession, the September 11 terrorist attacks, Hurricane Katrina, wars in Afghanistan and Iraq, and budget deficits, all issues that were highly divisive and transformative. Bipartisanship suffered.

In November 2004, Bush handily defeated Democratic Party candidate Senator

John Kerry to secure a second term as president. This election was acrimonious, with groups on both the Left (Moveon.Org) and the Right (Swift Boaters) pulling out all the stops in trying to elect their candidate. Internet politics and cable news exacerbated the acrimony (T. F. Buss and N. J. Buss 2006), further dividing people and parties. In November 2006, the Democratic Party regained control of the House. Polling data showed the American people to be dissatisfied with the Afghan and Iraq wars, gridlock and lack of progress in Congress, and numerous scandals plaguing Republicans. Among them were Jack Abramoff's lobbying activities, Abu Ghraib prison, Halliburton Company, Blackwater security, and widespread fraud in Iraq; as well as scandals—later proved unfounded—involving Tom DeLay, majority leader of the House, and Scooter Libby, Vice President Cheney's chief of staff. For many out of power in Washington, Vice President Dick Cheney's and Secretary of Defense Donald Rumsfeld's approach to governance represented an ongoing source of antagonism.

Barack Obama's election in November 2008 not only shifted the presidency to control of the Democratic Party, but also created Democratic control of the Senate and the House, seemingly giving the new president carte blanche to enact his agenda. Initially, it appeared that voters were responding negatively to Bush and the Republicans by aligning with Obama and the Democrats. But polls showed that Obama's message of hope, reconciliation, and change hit a responsive chord. President Obama took his election as a mandate, launching perhaps the most ambitious agenda since Franklin Roosevelt's in the 1930s and Lyndon Johnson's in the 1960s. The Democratic Party–controlled Congress, seemingly able to ramrod the president's agenda through both houses, appeared to many commentators to be employing much the same strategy as had the Republicans upon taking charge. For many, the implications for American governance would be staggering if accomplished.

Obama's first two years in office proved disappointing to some, with strong opposition from a more unified Republican Party as well as dissent from liberals and conservatives in the Democratic Party, which dampened the initial enthusiasm for an era of hope. Democrats lost a key Senate seat once held by the late Ted Kennedy in a special election in January 2010, denying in the process the Democratic supermajority in the Senate. In addition, two Democratic governorships (New Jersey and Virginia) were won by Republicans. A new movement, the Tea Party, arose ostensibly to oppose both parties, but especially the Democrats. In the early days of the Obama administration, several political appointees were never confirmed, or were forced to resign over tax evasion scandals, while others decided not to go into government for fear of jeopardizing their reputations. Two senators, Al Franken, D-MN, and Roland Burris, D-IL, came to the Senate by what many considered dubious means, weakening the credibility of the deliberative body. Congress is, at this writing, in gridlock. Obama's ambitious health care reform agenda, passed in March 2010, deeply divided the country, shaking the very foundations of governance. Congress is reshuffling yet again. Senator Evan Bayh, D-IN, announced he would not run for reelection. Senators Chris Dodd, D-CT, Byron Dorgan, D-ND, and Roland Burris, D-IL, as well as Representative David Obey, D-WI, announced retirements when it became clear they likely would not be reelected. Senator Kay Bailey Hutchinson, R-TX, left the Senate to run for the Texas governorship, then returned after her primary election defeat. And venerable Senator Robert Byrd, D-WV, passed away in June 2010. Scandals, most notably involving congressional representatives Charles Rangel, D-NY, Maxine Waters, D-CA, and Eric Massa, D-NY, plagued Congress throughout 2010.

In midterm elections in 2010, the Democratic Party ascendancy came to a screeching halt as the electorate returned control of the House of Representatives to the Republican Party and the emerging Tea Party. Democrats also lost their supermajority in the Senate. This was the worst midterm electoral defeat in generations. The pendulum of power has dramatically swung once more, and once again changes in governance will follow in its wake. Although there are many reasons for the Obama defeat, many cite lack of progress in repairing and growing the economy on the one hand, and the growth of big government and "European socialism" on the other. Now it remains to be seen how the Republican Party and the Tea Party will work together.

Recession and Budget Surpluses

In March 2001 an economic recession lasting about eight months ended an unprecedented expansion of the economy under President Clinton. The relatively mild recession has been blamed on the dot.com bust in which stocks in IT companies precipitously fell because of overexuberant speculation in the stock market, excessive availability of venture capital funds, excessively low interest rates, and even the Y2K crisis (which never occurred). During this period, the Federal Reserve lowered interest rates six times, minimizing the damage caused by the downturn. Former chairman of the Federal Reserve Board Alan Greenspan suggested that the successful management of the economy in crisis lulled the financial community and policymakers into a false sense of security in which they were willing to take ever greater risks (Greenspan 2010). Terrorist attacks on September 11, 2001, also slowed the economic recovery, but did not stop it. At the same time, the federal budget was in surplus and the national debt was "relatively" modest.

The Clinton administration's "halcyon days," at least with respect to the economy and budget, teed up the Bush administration for trouble when the economy declined and budget deficits soared. Bush's attempt to rally the economy through tax cuts in 2001 and 2003 only served to inflame his opponents, who would blame the decline in tax revenues (along with uncontrolled spending) for budget deficits under Obama. The tax cuts were also passed through legislative procedures that would serve as a model for the Obama health care legislation (see Robert 2005). The wars in Iraq and Afghanistan, both going badly, and a Congress exercising little restraint on spending, did not help. Obama ran on a platform pledging to fix these problems, but like his predecessor has had great difficulty in doing so. For many informed observers, the economic fortunes of Bush I, Clinton, Bush II, and Obama have been largely misrepresented by all concerned. However, as concerns the economy, the constant blaming and credit taking affects governance, often in inappropriate ways as we shall see.

Terrorist Attacks, 2001 to the Present

On September 11, 2001, al-Qaeda terrorists launched attacks against the World Trade Center in New York and the Pentagon in Washington, D.C., killing 2,973 civilians representing 90 countries. Subsequent hearings and investigations concluded that the country did not have adequate intelligence-gathering capacity and that bureaucratic barriers in some 16 or so intelligence agencies prevented their working together either to share intelligence or to organize a coordinated response to thwart terrorism (National Commission on Terrorist Attacks 2004). In response to the attacks, the United States immediately retaliated against the Taliban in Afghanistan. In 2001 the United States had declared a "War on Terror." Americans seemed to come together in this time of national emergency, and goodwill was shown around the world. But this was not to last. In 2003 the United States invaded Iraq, to prevent dictator Saddam Hussein from employing weapons of mass destruction (WMDs). No WMDs were found, and policy goals shifted to restoring Iraqi freedom, promoting democracy, and fighting terrorism (Woodward 2008). The Iraq War, costing more than 5,000 American lives to date, turned out to be grounded in bad intelligence, and certainly in politics. In addition, the war damaged U.S. relations with its allies, and some prominent political leaders lost their jobs. In both political parties many felt betrayed. The country had gone to war on flimsy intelligence, a situation bitterly dividing the country. The "clash of civilizations" (Huntington 1998) between the West and radical Islam shifted into high gear. Republicans blamed Clinton for emasculating the intelligence services and "wishing away" the threat of terrorism rather than addressing it.

The War on Terror markedly transformed American governance. Consider the Patriot Act of 2001. The act gave sweeping powers to the federal government to combat terrorism. This, of course, divided the country into those who supported civil liberties and those who supported a crackdown on terrorism. The act was always contentious and divisive from a governance perspective, but became even more so when those supporting civil liberties saw a chance to repeal the law under Obama and a Democratic Congress. They were wrong: Congress voted to extend the act as it was until February 2011. Obama signed the subsequent act, essentially postponing the issue. This fractured the Democratic Party further into right and left, making governance problematic.

The Patriot Act is emblematic of a broader schism between political factions that cuts across political parties, ideologies, and national defense. The Bush administration had imprisoned war fighters (indigenous and foreign terrorists, nationalists, extremists, opportunists, and others opposing coalition armies in Afghanistan) in a military prison in Guantanamo Bay, Cuba. Obama promised to try these individuals in civilian courts and to close the prison because it gave the United States a bad image and may have fueled further terrorism. He then backed down on these pledges once elected. Under the Bush administration, prisoners held in Baghdad at Abu Ghraib prison were tortured by U.S. military personnel and CIA contractors, causing that facility to be closed. Terrorists apprehended in various places were moved around the globe to secret CIA jails or placed in prisons in countries where jails are not governed by human rights conventions. But these facilities and operations have remained largely secret. Suicide bombers continue to strike at the United States. One terrorist tried to explode a bomb in Times Square, New York City, while another tried to blow up a U.S. aircraft over Detroit. Governance issues have enveloped the terrorism issue. Some question the extent of the threat. Some refuse to acknowledge that there is a threat. Some question whether the response to the threat is worse than the threat itself, or that it breeds further threats. Others believe that the values of the nation are being sacrificed. Others believe that terrorism is an existential trend and must be met full out. Others want to extend the rights of citizens to terrorists. Others want to give back punch for punch. All of this creates chaos in the courts, foreign affairs, military operations, national security, and the like. Decision making is based on shifting sands.

Hurricane Katrina, 2005

In August 2005, Hurricane Katrina hit the Gulf Coast, killing 1,836 people and inflicting $100 billion in damages on the region. Federal, state, and local governments, with some exceptions, were grossly unprepared and responded poorly in both the short- and long-term recovery efforts. Many in the private sector responded much more effectively (Sobel and Leeson 2007). Some might excuse the poor governmental response as understandable given the unprecedented nature of the disaster. Unfortunately, race became an issue as many of the neighborhoods destroyed by flooding were populated by poor African Americans. The implications for governance, not just under disaster scenarios, were enormous. Consider two.

A little-noticed issue outside Washington was the U.S. Small Business Administration's (SBA) response during Hurricane Katrina and its aftermath. SBA's Disaster Loan Program makes loans to businesses and homeowners immediately following a disaster. SBA was overwhelmed by Katrina (Buss and Thompson 2009). After Katrina, the program received 422,000 loan applications totaling $10.6 billion. The Northridge, California, earthquake of 1994 was the next largest disaster event at 250,000 applications and $4 billion in loan requests. Before that, Florida's Hurricane Andrew of 1992 yielded 46,000 applications and SBA lent $700 million. SBA was caught in the middle of a total reorganization of the disaster program, including relocating offices nationwide, reengineering its computer system, trying to redo its business processes, and attempting to reorganize its disaster volunteer workforce. The program literally collapsed under the weight of Katrina.

Admiral Thad Allen, then chief of staff of the U.S. Coast Guard, probably single-handedly changed the notion of how important leadership is in crisis management (Marek 2006). In the initial response to Katrina, government virtually shut down. Disaster management was in disarray. No one seemed in charge, and a number of decisions appeared to a stunned nation to be nonsensical. For example, government could not provide water to people across the devastated city of New Orleans, yet turned away trucks laden with drinking water provided by Walmart. Much of the disaster response amounted to blaming everyone else for failures. Michael Chertoff, Secretary of Homeland Security, appointed Admiral Allen to take charge of the rescue and recovery operations, replacing the ill-suited director of the Federal Emergency Management Agency (FEMA), Michael Brown. Allen's success lay in not accepting bureaucratic inertia, stovepiping, and risk aversion as givens. Rather, he understood that leadership was called for.

Global Financial Crisis, 2008 to the Present

Throughout 2008, the U.S. financial system began to show serious signs of distress, eventually collapsing at year's end. The Bush administration tried to address the crisis in February 2008 through the Economic Stimulus Act of that year which offered $150 billion in tax rebates and incentives to spur spending. In October the administration authored the Emergency Economic Stabilization Act of 2008 to bail out financial institutions and stimulate lending. The U.S. crisis soon enveloped the entire global financial system. Many observers have offered different opinions on the causes of the crisis, but surprisingly few have discussed its governance implications.

The Financial Meltdown's Impact on Governance

There is more than enough blame to spread around concerning the causes of the financial crisis. Setting aside charges of greed and deception on Wall Street which many believe precipitated the crisis, just from a governance perspective, the issues appear to be:

Fannie Mae and Freddie Mac. Fannie Mae, a stock-owned corporation, was chartered by Congress to purchase and securitize mortgages to ensure that lenders had sufficient capital to make loans. Freddie Mac purchases mortgages in the secondary market, then packages and resells them as mortgage-backed securities. In his seminal book *Government-Sponsored Enterprises* (1991), Tom Stanton tried to persuade policymakers that a new federal regulator was necessary to regulate Fannie Mae and Freddie Mac because of their weak financial supervision and low capital standards. Fannie and Freddie held 70 percent of mortgages in the market. In 2002, Stanton again sounded an alarm, warning that the government had allowed Fannie and Freddie to grow so big that it could neither regulate (or control) them effectively nor privatize them. Both imploded during the crisis. Because both are GSEs, many rightly believed that there was an implicit taxpayer guarantee against default to keep them viable, even though they are owned by private shareholders. Thus far, they have been bailed out to the tune of $126 billion and have been promised whatever additional funds might be needed. Critics believe this created a moral hazard in that GSE executives could behave recklessly without consequence.

Financial Market Regulation. Financial market regulation has increasingly unraveled over the past two decades. Regulators have struggled and failed to mitigate the systemic risks posed by large financial institutions. In financial markets regulators have had to address problems produced by less-regulated financial institutions and have been unable to stay ahead of innovative investment instruments in play. They have not kept pace with accounting and auditing standards and have imposed rules that for some observers make no sense. Regulators have been unable to cope with the globalization of financial markets. Moreover, they are fragmented, often unable to work together. Under the Bush administration, a philosophy of deregulation prevailed. Critics suggest that everyone ignored the potential downside of deregulation because they were making money, including the government itself through tax revenues.

Homeownership Policy. Expanding homeownership has been a policy goal of every administration and Congress for over 20 years. Private lenders and GSEs were encouraged to lend more to a broader spectrum of ever-more-high-risk borrowers. The U.S. Department of Housing and Urban Development (HUD), for example, significantly increased housing goals for Fannie and Freddie from 2001 to 2004. Opponents claim that this, and other policies, helped launch bad loan practices as lenders waived or ignored the standard lending requirements and financial markets began to engage in risky practices in securitizing mortgages.

Federal Reserve Bank Policy. In Fall 2008, a little more than a year after the Bank for International Settlements (a Switzerland-based organization that fosters cooperation between central banks) warned that "years of loose monetary policy have fuelled a giant credit bubble, leaving us vulnerable to another 1930s slump," the combustive concoction of free market fundamentalism, corporate-dominated globalization, stagnant wages, growing inequality, greed, excessive leverage, and financial innovations such as securitization finally exploded (Levinson 2009).

Alan Greenspan (2010) recently explained his thoughts on the Fed: he could not fathom that the private sector would risk survival of their firms and even the market to make a profit.

Federal Responses to the Financial Meltdown

In responding to the financial crisis, which turned into a full-blown economic catastrophe, government has intervened in unprecedented ways in financial markets and the economy (Gravelle et al. 2009). Durant, in Chapter 3, places the financial crisis in historical perspective. Government now is all but managing several large banks, an insurance company, two automobile manufacturers, and two GSEs. Government, through the Federal Reserve System, the Department of the Treasury, and the Federal Deposit Insurance Corporation (FDIC), is controlling the economy. In July 2010, Congress reached consensus on a financial industry regulatory bill. In true compromise fashion, at least to critics across the political spectrum, it failed to reform Fannie Mae and Freddie Mac, merge disparate regulatory agencies into a smaller number, and stem the possibility of future financial institution bailouts (*Economist* 2010). The government is busy prodding and demanding that companies, especially those receiving bailout money, hold down executive pay and performance compensation.

Federal intervention has also appeared in noneconomic sectors. Some actions are likely temporary—tax credits, Social Security and Supplemental Security Income (SSI) payments, "cash for clunkers," business taxes, and state/local infrastructure spending. Whereas others may have a long tenure—education and training programs, health care, food stamps, Head Start, and child care development.

Each intervention has its own legacy for the nation. Some will fundamentally change the country; others will have fleeting, temporary impacts. Taken together, government interventions will greatly expand annual budget deficits for decades as well as the national debt. Because of their magnitude, it is important for the American people to understand how the Obama administration intends to extricate itself from these interventions. As of November 2010, citizens still do not know how, when, or whether the Federal Reserve, Treasury, and FDIC will exit. Equally painful is that these institutions had no contingency plans for dealing with crisis and were slow to respond to it.

Recent debates about financial system regulation show that solutions will not be easy: there is little consensus on how regulation failed and what should be done to reengineer the regulatory system so that future financial crises are mitigated. There are basically two schools of thought. One is that financial markets are essentially self-regulating, and right themselves eventually. The other is that actors in financial markets cause failures as they skirt regulation and behave to excess. The self-regulatory school refuses to accept that markets were not self-regulating in the current crisis, citing government policy and intervention as culprits. Nearly everyone agrees that the regulatory institutions, created largely during the New Deal, are too antiquated to perform their intended function. Whether or not they are underfunded and understaffed is a subject of debate. Some want international bodies to take a greater regulatory role, and would like to see greater cooperation between regulatory bodies in countries with a strong financial presence in the global economy. A major issue concerns how prudent it is to try to reengineer the regulatory system as the country emerges from the financial crisis, as we have not yet seen the extent of the problems to be managed. All this aside, Congress passed a Financial Regulation Reform bill in July 2010 that appeared to many critics not to have pleased anyone.

In addition to regulatory policy, others question the role of the Federal Reserve, FDIC, and the Department of the Treasury in managing the economy (Miller 2009). Proponents and opponents of federal intervention in the economy agree that these institutions failed to anticipate crisis, likely contributed to it, seemed to over- and underrespond, lacked coherent strategies, and appeared all too often to be befuddled. Experts are unsure whether this assessment represents a one-off event that will not recur—the Black Swan theory—or whether these institutions need to be rethought (Taleb 2007).

A worry now as it relates to governance is that government has created moral hazards across the economy. Because government is blamed for the crisis and is responsible for its resolution, private sector business and individuals "expect" to be rescued.

Obama's First Two Years in Office, 2009–2010

In addition to managing the financial crisis, the Obama administration has launched a large number of initiatives intended to change American governance in significant ways. Opponents question the wisdom of undertaking such an expansive reform agenda without laying the groundwork and building consensus during a major economic crisis. Proponents claim that federal government spending, even in a time of deficit, is the only way to stimulate recovery; once spending works its way through the system, deficits will decline precipitously. Kettl, in Chapter 17, lays out how the following initiatives listed constitute a new form of governance, smuggled into the political arena by stealth:

- Health care reform
- Stimulus package
- Climate change
- Energy policy
- Regulatory activism (EPA)
- Proliferation of czars

Health Care Reform

Health care reform has been the bane of presidents over the past two decades (see Buss and Van de Water 2009). It also, for many critics, reflects the very worst in American governance. Presidents Clinton and Bush failed to achieve it. Obama has succeeded. In 1993, First Lady Hillary Clinton developed a universal health care plan, mandating employers to cover workers through a system of regional alliances of health care providers, with cost caps, subsidies, and regulation. A Democratic Congress rejected the plan, proposing several other competing options. No health care reforms issued from the Congress for a decade until the Bush administration's Medicare prescription drug program in 2004.

The Hillary Clinton initiative, in her words, failed because it neglected to take into account the legislative process (imposing instead an executive branch solution), neglected to build bipartisan support for the plan, and was too comprehensive to have worked in practice. The Health Care Task Force, spearheading the plan's development, chose an exclusionary approach, conducting much of its business behind closed doors.

Bush's Medicare prescription drug program, the largest expansion of Medicare since its creation in 1965, was pushed through a compliant Republican Congress with only lukewarm bipartisan support. Initially, the costs of the program were misrepresented by the administration and then ignored (according to critics), in hopes that funding could be found. It was not. Democrats were not happy with the program.

The Obama administration, according to some commentators, perceived the Clinton failure as occurring because Clinton tried to force health care reform on Congress. Obama allowed Congress to take the lead on health care, while he stayed above the fray. Congressional leaders in the House and Senate were only too happy to take the lead, trying to enact legislation that would replace the predominant private-market, employer-based health insurance system with a public one. To accomplish this, congressional leaders excluded Republican input into the process and either strong-armed opponents in the Democratic Party or bought them off with incentives. The proposed legislation was not widely shared with Republicans, or even many Democrats, before votes were taken, as a way to stifle opposition. This created a crisis in both parties and the American people turned against Congress.

When it appeared that health care reform had failed, Obama entered the fray and the reforms gained new life. Democrats considered using technical procedures (outside the scope of this chapter), reconciliation, and "deem and pass," also used by past Republican Congresses to enact the reforms (Robert 2005). The current state of affairs is that, in the foreseeable future, everything will be highly partisan. There will be little compromise or consensus building. No Senate or House Republican voted for either the Senate or the House bill. And, eventually, as Democrats lose control of the reins of power, their work will be undone or blocked by a Republican House. Some have dubbed this the beginning of a hundred years' war.

To add fuel to the fire, in July 2010 Obama appointed Donald Berwich to head the federal Medicare/Medicaid health insurance programs, bypassing congressional hearings that likely would have derailed Berwich's nomination. Berwich is a staunch proponent of health care rationing, one of the most contentious parts of the health care reform bill.

Stimulus Package

In February 2009, Congress passed the American Recovery and Revitalization Act, authorizing expenditure of $787 billion to stimulate the economy. The Recovery Act provides tax benefits ($288 billion), contracts, loans and grants ($275 billion), and entitlements ($224 billion). Entitlement spending includes education, unemployment compensation, food stamps, health care insurance, and other social programs. About $114 billion went to state and local governments for "fiscal relief." Obama's Recovery Act followed on the heels of two Bush stimulus packages, the Economic Stimulus Act of 2008 ($168 billion, February 2008) and the Emergency Economic Stabilization Act of 2008 ($700 billion, for financial institution bailouts, October 2008).

The Obama stimulus package has precipitated numerous governance issues. No House Republicans and only three Senate Republicans voted for the bill. Understandably, the Obama administration wanted to jump-start the economy quickly to avoid further disaster, so it did not tolerate opposition. Democrats argued that Bush had also promoted a stimulus package under considerable opposition. Nevertheless, many in opposition could see huge problems. There was considerable disagreement among economists about whether this stimulus would improve the economy and, even more important, whether other methods might not work better. Many questioned why 30 percent of funding went to education, health, and social programs, part of Obama's long-term domestic agenda. Others questioned how spending on preservation of state government jobs could stimulate recovery, as it simply substitutes federal taxpayer for state taxpayer monies.

Funding under the bill since February 2009 raised further issues. Only 31 percent of funding had been spent overall, whereas half of social program funding had been spent. Again critics asked, how can this be the best way to stimulate the economy? Many questioned the job creation claims for the Recovery Act. When proposed to Congress, the bill was cast as a job creation/job retention initiative. As it became clear that jobs were neither being created nor retained, the administration added a new criterion. Instructions to stimulus-fund recipients were: "It does not matter if the hours were worked by a person who was newly hired, a person whose job was saved by the Recovery Act, or a person who is in an existing position that is now being funded by the Recovery Act" (Recovery.gov 2010).

The stimulus packages of both Bush and Obama raise serious, legitimate questions about whether government spending works to stimulate recovery, and whether these spending packages are the best way to stimulate recovery. The political elite are so seriously fractured that it is impossible to debate the issue in Congress or have a national dialogue.

Climate Change

Environmentalism has been a major force in American politics for years. Environmentalists have protected endangered species, curtailed offshore drilling, stopped construction of nuclear power plants, improved the quality of the nation's air and water, and protected wetlands, national parks, and natural resources (Congressional Budget Office 2010b): in our view, all for the better.

Now, the issue is global warming, or climate change, that advocates assert is threatening the planet (see the UN Intergovernmental Panel on Climate Change 2011). The Clinton administration launched the first serious attempt to address climate change by reducing carbon emissions when it committed the nation to the Kyoto Protocol in 1997. The protocol called for "first world" industrial nations to set targets to drastically reduce carbon emissions by 5 percent of 1990 levels. The treaty undergirding the protocol was never approved by the Senate. Critics were concerned that the targets were too costly to U.S. business and that developing countries like China and India were not obligated to cut emissions, giving them an economic advantage. The Bush administration did not pursue the protocol.

After suffering defeat in the 2000 elections, Al Gore took up the climate change question, releasing a documentary film, *An Inconvenient Truth*. This rekindled the issue in the United States and earned him a Nobel Prize.

The Obama administration tried to recommit the United States to reducing carbon emissions at an international conference in 2009 in Copenhagen, but no agreement was reached. The same issues about emission targets, costs, and cooperation were still unresolved. The House passed "cap-and-trade" legislation before the conference, but it died in the Senate. As an alternative, Obama pursued carbon emission regulation through the Environmental Protection Agency (EPA). EPA had been granted authority to regulate carbon emissions because its studies had found such emissions to be carcinogenic. Opponents of EPA believe that such far-ranging regulation during an economic crisis is ill conceived. The EPA regulations are opposed in Congress by members of both parties.

Recently, the Obama administration was embarrassed when it promoted the creation of green jobs in the wind turbine industry as a mechanism for reducing carbon emissions from fossil fuels. Senator Sherrod Brown, D-OH, complained about a "$450 million federal stimulus grant to a Texas wind farm that will be built with Chinese wind turbine components." Brown and three other senators said the project would generate 3,000 jobs in China and 330 in the United States, all but 30 of which would be temporary (Eaton 2010).

With the electoral crisis in November 2010, Obama seems to have shelved any ambitious plans for climate change policy.

Energy Policy

In an effort to stem criticism of the negative economic effects of climate change policy and to appease Republicans and the business community, the Obama administration announced a plan both to increase energy resources by increasing the number of nuclear power plants and to expand offshore oil drilling on the Atlantic Coast and in the eastern Gulf of Mexico region and in Alaska, where it had been prohibited. Shortly after this announcement, on April 1, 2010, the worst oil spill in history occurred in the Gulf of Mexico. An oil rig leased by British Petroleum (BP) exploded, killing 11 workers and producing an environmental and economic disaster in the billions of dollars. BP was unable to contain the oil surging into the gulf for months and the U.S. government appeared to critics as feeble in its response. When it sued to have a six-month moratorium on offshore oil drilling in June 2010, it lost in federal court. The Obama administration is now using this disaster as evidence of the need to wean the country off of carbon-based fuel and to move toward alternative energy. Be that as it may, the government's poor response to the crisis reignited concerns about the ability of the country to effectively govern during crisis—à la Hurricane Katrina and the financial crisis of 2008.

Regulation

Under George W. Bush, government regulation was reduced through decreases in funding and policy decisions. Under Obama, nearly all regulatory agencies received healthy budget increases in the 2011 budget request to Congress. Among them are the EPA, Food and Drug Administration (FDA), Occupational Safety and Health Administration (OSHA), Federal Trade Commission (FTC), Securities and Exchange Commission (SEC), Commodities Future Trade Commission (CFTC), and Federal Communications Commission (FCC). The long-running era of deregulation appears to have stalled and a regulatory agenda across the board seems to be evolving. Critics wonder why regulatory policy should be increasingly ramped up when businesses are struggling under the country's economic woes.

Czars

The Obama administration has chosen to create an unprecedented number of high-level political appointment positions to execute its far-reaching domestic and foreign agendas. These individuals report only to the president and are not approved by the Senate (see Table 1.1).

The late Senator Robert Byrd, D-WV, complained that the proliferation of czars in the Obama administration represents an attempt to expand the power of the president over Congress:

> As presidential assistants and advisers, these White House staffers are not accountable for their actions to the Congress, to cabinet officials, or to virtually anyone but the president. . . . They rarely testify before congressional committees, and often shield the information and decision-making process behind the assertion of executive privilege. In too many instances, White House staff has been allowed to inhibit openness and transparency, and reduce accountability. (Kossov 2010)

Patterson, in Chapter 16, looks closely at the role of White House advisers in the context of governance. Redburn's Chapter 4 on outside experts contrasts nicely with Patterson's analysis of insiders.

Table 1.1

Czars Initially Appointed Under the Obama Administration

Afghanistan Czar	Richard Holbrooke
AIDS Czar	Jeffrey Crowley
Auto Recovery Czar	Ed Montgomery
Border Czar	**Alan Bersin**
Car Czar	Ron Bloom
Central Region Czar	Dennis Ross
Domestic Violence Czar	Lynn Rosenthal
Drug Czar	**Gil Kerlikowske**
Economic Czar	Paul Volcker
Energy and Environment Czar	Carol Browner
Faith-Based Czar	Joshua DuBois
Great Lakes Czar	Cameron Davis
Green Jobs Czar	Van Jones (resigned on Sept. 6)
Guantanamo Closure Czar	Daniel Fried
Health Czar	Nancy-Ann DeParle
Information Czar	*Vivek Kundra*
International Climate Czar	Todd Stern
Mideast Peace Czar	George Mitchell
Pay Czar	Kenneth Feinberg
Regulatory Czar	**Cass Sunstein**
Science Czar	John Holdren
Stimulus Accountability Czar	Earl Devaney (statutory position)
Sudan Czar	J. Scott Gration
TARP Czar	**Herb Allison**
Terrorism Czar	John Brennan
Technology Czar	**Aneesh Chopra**
Urban Affairs Czar	Adolfo Carrion Jr.
Weapons Czar	**Ashton Carter**
WMD Policy Czar	Gary Samore

Source: Staff, "President Obama's 'Czars'," Politico.com, September 8, 2009, http://www.politico.com/news/stories/0909/26779.html.

Note: Bolded names = confirmed by Congress; italicized name = statutorily required.

The New Public Management

Since the early 1900s, successive administrations have attempted to improve public management and budgeting; to make the civil service more efficient, effective, and economical; or to make the civil service more (or less) responsive to or more (or less) independent of elected officials and political appointees (for an overview see T. F. Buss and N. J. Buss 2011; and Kettl, Chapter 17). The most comprehensive efforts occurred under the Clinton and the Bush administrations. The Obama administration, at least during Obama's first year in office, has not initiated major management or civil service reforms.

Reinventing Government

In the 1990s, two books by David Osborne, *Laboratories of Democracy* (1988) and *Reinventing Government* (1992), along with efforts by Congress and the Clinton administration, elevated performance management to a full-fledged movement, the New Public Management (NPM), intent on bringing private sector practices into government (see also Durant, Chapter 3). A UK House of Lords report, *The Public Service (1997–98),* summed up the movement well:

> NPM involves a focus on management, performance appraisal and efficiency; the use of agencies which deal with each other on a user-pay basis; the use of quasi-markets and contracting out to foster competition; cost-cutting; and a style of management which emphasizes, among other things, output targets, limited term contracts, monetary incentives and freedom to manage.

Upon taking office in 1993, President Clinton announced the National Performance Review (NPR), later the National Partnership for Reinventing Government (1998). Clinton described it as a call for "reinventing government," based on similar reforms he had championed as governor of Arkansas and similar to the Texas Performance Review. Initially, NPR, under the direction of Vice President Al Gore (1993), focused on administrative initiatives such as reducing red tape by streamlining processes, eliminating unnecessary regulation, improving customer service, creating marketlike dynamics, decentralizing decision-making processes, empowering employees, and other measures. NPR's organizing principle was the promotion of high-quality customer service.

Congress, in passing the Government Performance and Results Act (GPRA) in 1993, the Chief Financial Officers Act of 1990, the Government Management Reform Act of 1994, and the Information Technology Management Reform Act of 1996, also took a more aggressive role in promoting performance management. GPRA's intent was "to shift the focus of federal management and accountability from what federal agencies are doing to what they are accomplishing." GPRA employs a classic business strategic planning model that is mission driven and results oriented.

The newly elected Bush administration was unhappy with NPR and GPRA because they did not make government more efficient or effective in their view. They did not reduce the size of government either through program termination or outsourcing to the private sector. They did not encourage formal evaluations that could be used in budget decisions.

President's Management Agenda

Under the Bush administration, emerging NPM approaches came into full swing across the federal system. The Bush administration's President's Management Agenda (PMA) was a "whole of government" approach, explicitly linking program performance, evaluation, management, and budgeting in the same system. Stanton discusses issues involved in federal agency collaborating in the context of PMA in Chapter 5. PMA also tried to improve performance in e-government, procurement, financial management, human capital, and competitive sourcing. Policymakers grounded PMA in producing program results based on evidence and evaluations and tying budgetary decision making to goal attainment and results. To drive performance, the agenda launched a variety of strategic human capital initiatives, such as the Human Capital Assessment and Accountability Framework (HCAAF), a system that builds capacity in the civil service to undertake "results-oriented management." Because government was believed to be less efficient and effective than the private sector, "competitive sourcing" was expanded.

Human Capital Management

NPM spurred renewed policy and management interests in improving the efficiency and effectiveness of the civil service and in reducing the size of government. Under NPM, managing the civil service gradually moved from the old personnel system based on transactions (i.e., tracking vacation and sick days, providing health and life insurance, computing retirement eligibility, and the like) to a new system that made the federal workforce a focus of government, igniting concerns over recruitment, development, performance, and strategy.

In addition to performance, the human capital movement focused on the need to implement strategies to replace the army of civil servants—as many as 30 percent in some agencies—expected to retire from government over the next 10 years. Few agencies had "succession" plans or initiatives in place to address the "retirement tsunami."

Seven activities encapsulate the issues in human capital management (HCM) under the Bush administration:

- GAO high-risk list—2001
- HCAAF—2001
- Department of Homeland Security—2002
- Chief Human Capital Officers—2002
- Volcker Commission—2002
- OPM reorganizations, 2002, 2009
- Defense Authorization Act—2004, 2009

GAO High-Risk List. In 2001, The U.S. Government Accountability Office (U.S. GAO) placed federal strategic HCM on its high-risk list—a list of management challenges that must be addressed if the government were to function properly (U.S. GAO 2010). GAO found in its assessments that characteristics of a well-functioning HCM system, common in the private sector, were not widely found in the federal government. Federal managers were not (1) exerting leadership, (2) integrating HCM into other management contexts, (3) acquiring, developing, and retaining talent, or (4) promoting a results-oriented organizational culture. GAO retains HCM on its high-risk list still.

GAO not only tried to ignite interest in the HCM approach, the agency also reengineered itself in the spirit of the model. At first, the agency appeared a model of reform. Later, reforms seemed to stall as large numbers of employees began to protest performance pay and the redefinition of their work responsibilities.

Human Capital Assessment and Accountability Framework. Drawing on the work of GAO, in 2001 the Office of Personnel Management (OPM) developed a checklist that would allow (require) managers to assess their HCM operations against a state-of-the-art set of standards, criteria, and best practices: strategic alignment, leadership and knowledge management, results-oriented performance culture, talent management, and accountability (U.S. OPM 2010a). Although the checklists have been judged by many to be excellent management tools, others believe they did not make much difference in improving the performance of the federal workforce.

Department of Homeland Security. According to critics, the Bush administration, in a hurry to get the new department in place, did not provide much detail about what the agency was supposed to accomplish and how it would be structured (see also Chapter 6). This was left to policymakers forced to address issues on the fly. For example, little thought was given to how the different management, personnel, and financial systems and the policies, missions, and strategies of the 22 constituent agencies would be reconciled into one department. Policymakers tried to reengineer the Department of Homeland Security (DHS) workforce by abrogating union contracts in favor of broad labor classifications, performance pay, and flexibilities in hiring and firing. In 2008, after several years of court cases, unions prevailed over management, and DHS abandoned its new human capital management plans (Brook and King 2009).

Chief Human Capital Officers. One problem in creating a federal HCM system was that agency personnel offices lacked the status, authority, and knowledge to lead such an effort. Policymakers used the Homeland Security Act of 2002 which created DHS to require agencies to have a Chief Human Capital Officer (CHCO) on their senior management team. Critics point out that CHCOs still do not participate in managing agencies and programs. As evidence, they note that HCM plans rarely interface with agency or program strategic plans, budgeting, IT, or other planning efforts.

Volcker Commission II. Also in 2002, the National Commission on the Public Service (the Volcker Commission) issued its report (2003), *Urgent Business for America: Revitalizing the Federal Government for the 21st Century,* calling for civil service reforms that would align pay and job descriptions to today's labor markets; replace the 15-grade general schedule pay and classification system, which results in advancement based primarily on longevity, with broader pay bands and advancement opportunities based on performance; adopt best practices of human capital management in private industry; improve recruitment outreach; and reward performance.

More specifically, the report called for "revitalizing federal operations required wholesale reorganization, giving the president fast-track authority to rearrange federal agencies and departments as needed, realigning congressional committees to match agency missions and more personnel flexibilities" (Ballard 2003). Many of the commission's recommendations were used to support Bush administration programs.

Reorganizing OPM. In 2002, the Bush administration reorganized OPM to make it more effective in the new human capital management framework (U.S. Office of Personnel Management 2010b). The reorganization separated policy and operations—creating a policy, advisory and technical assistance, and fee-for-service function. Many observers applauded the reorganization. For decades, OPM had been viewed by many as ineffective; and most administrations either ignored it or tried to reform it. Also over this period, more and more HCM functions were devolved to federal agencies rather than retained in OPM.

In 2009, the Obama administration added a new office to OPM to focus on the Senior Executive Service, once seen as a major initiative to improve management performance among senior civil servants.

Defense Authorization Act—National Security Personnel System. Following on the extensive efforts of the Bush administration to develop a DHS workforce from its disparate component agencies, the Defense Department launched the National Security Personnel System (NSPS). NSPS created a paybanding performance system that removed the narrow job classification system that rewarded workers for longevity and replaced it with a broader classification scheme that gave management much more flexibility in rewarding performance pay (Sistare, Shiplett, and Buss 2009). Congress repealed the system in the Defense Authorization Act of 2009. Some say this was because of labor union pressure.

Criticizing PMA

With the Bush administration out of office, the Program Assessment Rating Tool, or PART, has attracted much criticism (see Redburn, Shea, and Buss 2008). Obama's head of management at OMB, Jeffrey Zients, summed up the problems with PART in testimony before the Senate Committee on Homeland Security and Government Affairs on October 29, 2009 (pp. 1–2):

> The test of a performance management system is whether it is used. Despite the extent and breadth of these historic efforts, the current approach fails this test.

Congress doesn't use it. Agencies don't use it. And it doesn't produce meaningful information for the public. Most metrics are process-oriented and not outcomes-based. We do not track progress on goals that cut across agencies. Overall, too much emphasis has been placed on producing performance information to comply with a checklist of requirements instead of using it to drive change.

Other critics variously suggest that the Bush administration was using the NPM approach not so much to downsize government, but to control the federal workforce so that it would better do its bidding (see, e.g., Singer 2005). Pay for performance, performance contracts, and weakened civil service job classifications forced the civil service to pursue the president's agenda, and weakened public sector unions. Likewise, massive outsourcing allowed the administration to control the government through the procurement process by transferring responsibilities to the private sector.

Callahan and Lyles, in Chapter 12, argue that decision making needs to be based on evidence, grounded in public debate, sensitive to contingency, supported by audits and action reports, buttressed with resources, and executed over longer-term time horizons.

Frederickson, in Chapter 2, briefly discusses the rise of NGOs in the context of downsizing government through outsourcing.

The Obama Administration

The Obama administration appears intent on undoing Bush's PMA, if only in a modest way.

On the PART performance management system, in "A New Era of Responsibility: Renewing America's Promise," the administration announced:

> The Administration will fundamentally reconfigure the PART. We will open up the insular performance measurement process to the public, the Congress and outside experts. The Administration will eliminate ideological performance goals and replace them with goals Americans care about and that are based on congressional intent and feedback from the people served by Government programs. Programs will not be measured in isolation, but assessed in the context of other programs that are serving the same population or meeting the same goals.

In spite of the rhetoric against PMA and PART, some have criticized the Obama administration for being the first in almost a century not to come into office with a management reform strategy. With the other problems facing the administration— financial crisis, health care crisis, wars in Iraq and Afghanistan—some believe that the era of performance management and management reform in the United States may be over. In any case, the Obama administration got off to a slow start with its performance initiative, when the person chosen to lead the government-wide effort withdrew because of tax issues. The new performance "czar" did not assume the position until one year into the new administration.

The Obama administration's FY2011 budget proposal includes several minor initiatives. The administration announced that it wanted each agency to focus on priority performance goals for its programs. The so-called High Priority Performance Goal Initiative requires policymakers to develop high-level goals that require no new legislation or resources and can be completed in 24 months. The FY2011 budget funds 23 major program evaluations in priority areas, rather than requiring periodic, ongoing program evaluations. The budget creates a Performance Improvement Council (PIC), made up of performance improvement officers representing every federal agency. PIC will function as a performance management network and community of practice. And the budget emphasizes the use of benefit-cost analysis in assessing performance.

Obama has called for a reduction in outsourcing, requiring agencies to attempt to bring back in house those functions outsourced by Bush. As part of this initiative, agencies are experimenting with ways to reform the federal procurement system in a series of pilot projects. Critics see this as an attempt by Obama to appease federal labor unions whose members had feared for their jobs under Bush.

Evidence-Based Policy and Management

As a natural outgrowth of performance management and budgeting, many policymakers, practitioners, researchers, theorists, and commentators over the past two decades have called for reforms that would improve policymaking and public management by marshalling sound evidence for decision making (see Shillabeer, Buss, and Rousseau 2011). Clinton's National Performance Review opined:

> Unfortunately, few of these studies helped us design solutions. Few of the investigating bodies had studied success stories—organizations that had solved their problems. And without studying success, it is hard to devise real solutions. For years, the federal government has studied failure, and for years, failure has endured. Six of every ten major agencies have programs on OMB's high-risk list, meaning they carry a significant risk of runaway spending or fraud. NPR approached its task differently. Not only did we look for potential savings and efficiencies, we searched for success. We looked for organizations that produced results, satisfied customers, and increased productivity. We looked for organizations that constantly learned, innovated, and improved. We looked for effective, entrepreneurial public organizations. And we found them: in local government, in state government, in other countries—and right here in our federal government.

In launching the Bush administration's PMA in 2002, OMB explained:

> Federal programs should receive taxpayer dollars only when they prove they achieve results. The federal government spends over $2 trillion a year on approximately 1,000 federal programs. In most cases, we do not know what we are getting for our money. This is simply unacceptable. Good government—a government responsible to the people whose dollars it takes to fund its opera-

tions—must have as its core purpose the achievement of results. No program, however worthy its goal and high-minded its name, is entitled to continue perpetually unless it can demonstrate it is actually effective in solving problems. In a results-oriented government, the burden of proof rests on each federal program and its advocates to prove that the program is getting results. The burden does not rest with the taxpayer or the reformers who believe the money could be better spent elsewhere.

The Obama administration has incorporated evidence-based policy in many of its initiatives. In launching his $4.35 billion education program, Race to the Top, Obama stated (Editorial 2009, A16):

> This competition will not be based on politics, ideology or the preferences of a particular interest group. Instead, it will be based on a simple principle—whether a state is ready to do what works. We will use the best data available to determine whether a state can meet a few key benchmarks for reform, and states that outperform the rest will be rewarded with a grant.

The evidence-based policy (EBP) movement is quite fractious, so much so that it is unclear whether the movement will ever become institutionalized in government or academe. EBP in practice has been problematic. Unresolved issues include what is evidence?, what standards must research or analysis satisfy to be considered evidence?, and what role does evidence play in making policy in juxtaposition with politics and other factors? EBP tends to drag along with it all of the methodological issues unresolved in social sciences.

Policymakers and public managers have not embraced the movement: according to the GAO, many public managers did not use performance information in program decision making and policymakers have not used it to terminate or shrink programs. There is some movement to apply evidence-based approaches to the practice of management, as is now done for policy. But this emerging field has been slow to materialize (Shillabeer, Buss, and Rousseau 2011).

Consider climate change. Recent policy debates on climate change seem to have politicized the EBP enterprise for the worse. Both sides of the debate are accusing one another of employing "junk science," misrepresenting or falsifying research findings, engaging in ad hominem attacks in attempts at one-upmanship, keeping dissenter opinion and research out of publication, and otherwise suppressing opposition.

Once the sciences become politicized, policymakers lose access to "objective" information to inform policy decisions, forcing everyone to rely exclusively on politics to decide outcomes. Losing science in policymaking will have a deleterious effect on governance.

Connecting Citizens and Government

Increasing citizen engagement has been a goal of every administration. Regardless of innovations through the years, much more could be done (Buss, Redburn, and Guo 2006). Over the past decade, engagement has coincided with efforts to promote e-governments.

As part of its e-government initiative, the Bush administration promulgated a policy calling for government to be citizen-centric—that is, designed and implemented to serve the needs of people, not government. Bush's e-government initiative substantially advanced the use of IT to better serve citizens.

The Obama administration, in January 2009, took e-government in a different direction (see Ginsberg 2010). Under his Open Government Initiative, Obama directed all federal agencies to become more transparent, participatory, and collaborative. Information that was classified under Bush would be declassified. Citizens would be offered greater opportunities to see how government was performing by having access to a variety of websites. And federal, state, and local government would be encouraged to work together more closely. Federal agencies have implemented the directive to varying degrees. For critics, it is unclear how much real change has occurred; the reason: the directive has no penalties for noncompliance.

Redburn discusses the role of citizen engagement in the context of informing expert opinion on budget deficits and debt in Chapter 4. In Chapter 10 Shark offers a governance agenda to convert who he believes are enraged citizens into engaged citizens.

Social Media

Social networking employs a wide variety of collaborative technologies—Facebook, Flickr, YouTube, My Space, Second Life, Twitter, Delicious, RSS, blogging, wikis, and even e-mail—that allow individuals to interact in a virtual world. Government or citizens can post information to the Web to inform one another or seek feedback. Government does those same things on restricted access websites limited to federal employees. Social networking sites allow people and government to amass unprecedented amounts of information, process it, and use it.

Some federal agencies have been quick to embrace and exploit new technology and applications. Quoting from the Collaboration Project, a website devoted to the furtherance of social networking in government, one finds the following examples:

> Since the initiative was announced in August 2008, the Coast Guard has branched into existing social media platforms on the Internet, including creating a "celebrity" page for the Commandant and Coast Guard page on Facebook; launching a Coast Guard channel on YouTube to post videos and responses from service members; posting photos from Coast Guard events on Flickr; and offering news and opinions through podcasts. All these platforms are updated very frequently, sometimes daily. The Commandant also manages his own blog (iCommandant Journal), where service members can post messages and directly access Commandant Allen. The initiative has been made a central feature of the Commandant's Corner 2.0 page. The Coast Guard also has plans to launch in December 2008 more extensive internal tools, including a new "Coast Guard Central" platform with blogging and wiki capability. (The Collaboration Project 2010b)

Specifically the NOAA Earth Research Lab created the virtual island within Second Life allowing the NOAA to educate people about the Earth's Oceanic and Atmospheric features. In order to accomplish this goal they created two islands, Meteora (dealing with the atmosphere) and Okeanos (dealing with the ocean). Users are able to use the program to take a ride on a plane through the atmosphere, tell when a tsunami will be coming and see the effects of global climate change (ice caps melting). (The Collaboration Project 2010c)

In September of 2006, the Office of eDiplomacy created Diplopedia. Diplopedia is a part of the Transformational Diplomacy plan, and under this it will utilize Web 2.0 technologies such as blogs and wikis to smooth the progress of information sharing. Diplopedia is similar to wikipedia in the sense that it is an encyclopedia for the Department of State. All information pertains to all employees and members are allowed to add or edit articles. Users can access a plethora of information pertaining to diplomacy and international relations. The program provides intranet access for registered members of the department. Within the program there are communities and work groups. Communities have the ability to read and make contributions to articles, and work groups are selected groups who are able to access a specified type of restricted information. Diplopedia is also available to foreign affairs agencies as well as members of the intelligence community. (The Collaboration Project 2010a)

Trudeau, in Chapter 21, examines the evolution of technology-enabled collaboration in government with the aim of capturing what works and suggesting what might be next. Childs and colleagues, in Chapter 19, observe that technology is no longer just enabling us to do our work, it is driving us to create new models to communicate, facilitate, and reengineer work. For the Millennials (those born between the late 1970s and 2000), approaching problems using a web of digital collaborative tools has become common. They want to be connected, to interact, and, as part of this interaction, to be continually stimulated. For the baby boomers (born between 1946 and the mid-1960s), this approach to problems is foreign. But it is becoming all too familiar, forcing seniors to adapt. The government finds itself between these two very different generational approaches in its workforce and its interactions with citizens.

Social networking has the potential to redefine and expand the role of citizen participation in government affairs and in interaction between management and the workforce, as well as among the workforce. Communications are instantaneous, ubiquitous, and exciting.

But social networking in the governance context has potential downsides. Social networking is difficult for government to control, and opens government not only to worthwhile interactions, but also to frivolous, malicious, or even criminal activities. Attempts to rein in social networking typically lead to charges of censorship, cover-up, or bias. Social networking excludes those who do not have access to the required technology or who do not know how to use it. Social networking can be used to overwhelm the system with undue praise or criticism. And we lack laws and regulations appurtenant to social networking.

Use of social networking or social media as noted is a way to encourage collaboration within and across federal agencies. But Stanton reminds us in Chapter 5 how collaboration might be improved generally.

Institutions

A Dysfunctional Congress

> There are many causes for the dysfunction: strident partisanship, unyielding ideology, a corrosive system of campaign financing, gerrymandering of House districts, endless filibusters, holds on executive appointees in the Senate, dwindling social interaction between senators of opposing parties and a caucus system that promotes party unity at the expense of bipartisan consensus.
> —Evan Bayh on why he left the Senate, February 21, 2010 (Bayh 2010)

The balance-of-power relationship between the Congress and the executive branch is a pendulum that swings back and forth. With former Speaker of the House Nancy Pelosi's management of the health care reform bill, the pendulum may be swinging back toward Congress.

Nonetheless, Gallup polls conducted in 2010 show Congress with its lowest approval rating yet, 14 percent. Norm Ornstein and Thomas Mann, in their book *The Broken Branch: How Congress Is Failing America and How to Get It Back on Track* (2008), offer some insights about why this is so. Congressional members have foregone many of the norms that made the institution great, especially the sense of institutional pride and patriotism. Members seem to be focused on job retention. Congress has evolved from a decentralized, committee-based institution into a centralized one where party trumps committee. Congress has begun to mirror parliamentary systems of government in this respect. Congress is no longer a civil body, but one of acrimony, contempt, and distrust. In passing the health care reform bill, the process was delayed because House Democrats did not trust Senate Democrats to keep their word in passing alternative versions of the bill. Bipartisanship is dead. Congressional members do not meet with one another as they did in the past, preferring instead to meet in closed caucuses. Increasingly, Congress has become a mechanism for revenge and "payback" against the opposition, reminiscent of a blood feud. Congressional oversight of the executive branch has virtually disappeared. The administration has appointed an army of "czars" not subject to congressional oversight and Congress has been silent. Congressional members acknowledge the need for reform—earmarks, ethics, campaign finance, and so on. Yet efforts to enact such reforms have repeatedly failed. "Logrolling" and "horse trading" have always been features of the legislative system, but they are being done at the expense of the country. Exempting Nebraska from Medicaid taxes in exchange for a senatorial vote on health care reform infuriated even the most jaded political operatives. Congress exempts themselves and congressional staff from legislation they impose on others.

Networked Government

Astute observers of governance have long noted the rise of informal networks in government that parallel and often displace more formal, hierarchical systems (Goldsmith and Eggers 2004). Networks are nonhierarchical, self-organizing, transitory, collaborative, and fragile. Hurricane Katrina and the attacks of September 11 exposed these networks in a very public way, compelling observers to acknowledge their implications for governance. At the same time, both catastrophes spontaneously produced new networks out of necessity. Durant discusses networked government in Chapter 3.

Informal networks have had some notable successes. In a study of the emergency management response to tornados in Orlando, Florida, for example, emergency food and beverage supply to first responders did not come from government or even nongovernmental organizations, but from the private company Starbucks.

In spite of the successes of informal networks, there are critics. Some worry over the implications for public accountability. Because there is no accountability of the electorate over government, actors in informal networks, even government ones, cannot be easily controlled, monitored, or held accountable. Others fear that informal networks might clash with formal structures, causing still more problems. Others fear wasteful duplication and inefficiency. And there are those who fret about the diminution of government. Many of these criticisms echo those of the social media. Our knowledge of networks is in its infancy, and may always be so given their fluidity.

Federalism

Relationships between states and the federal government since the 1980s have been deemed the New Federalism—a philosophy of government wherein powers and responsibilities residing in the federal government are devolved to the states. Examples of New Federalism activity include:

- The Unfunded Mandates Reform Act of 1995, requiring that the Congressional Budget Office analyze legislation making
- Congress's awareness of the existence and cost of unfunded mandates imposed on the states
- The Social Security Act authorizing multiple waiver and demonstration authorities (including research and demonstration projects to encourage innovation, and managed care/freedom of choice waivers) and home- and community-based service waivers to allow states flexibility in operating Medicaid programs

The financial crisis, the terrorist attacks of September 11, and Hurricane Katrina have called into question some of the basic tenets of the New Federalism. Some suggest that many federal agencies established in the distant past have outlived their usefulness because states are now much more capable of managing than they were decades ago. For example, states now plan and fund infrastructure projects on their own and no longer need the Economic Development Administration (EDA) or parts of the Department of Housing and Urban Development (HUD). The role of the federal government could be downsized to funding and policy guidance to achieve national goals, rather than managing large federal programs. Many states have taken the lead and exceed federal efforts on the environment, education, and health care.

Others suggest that the powers of the federal government be expanded. Critics have called into question the wisdom of allowing states to offer a patchwork of health care programs with different eligibility requirements, benefits and options, health service outcomes, and social equity issues (Johnson and Svara 2011). Some argue that state regulation allows financial institutions too much autonomy, leading to economic instability. States are unable to meet responsibilities for unemployment compensation, Medicaid funding, and other federal matching-fund requirements during economic downturns, necessitating subsidies and bailouts. Kincaid offers an alternative view of Federalism in Chapter 7.

As the economy begins to recover over the next decade and national debt and budget deficits continue to be problematic, the governance implications of Federalism will more clearly emerge: less federal, more state responsibility; less responsibility for both; more responsibility for both; or a mixed bag of changing responsibilities.

We have selected several chapters that tie together networks, collaboration, and technology in the context of Federalism. Reilly and Tekniepe, in Chapter 8, have identified collaborative regional networked structures that affect the viability of economic development. Urahn and Thompson, in Chapter 9, point out the intersection of Federalism and technology with collaboration in multistate, multijurisdictional strategies for political reform. Shark, in Chapter 10, argues that local government services are more highly valued than either state or federal services and explains how the social media plays into new models of Federalism. Jacknis, in Chapter 11, introduces the concept of globally shared, or "cloud," services as a new model for delivering services. Johnston and Hansen, in Chapter 13, show how smart, connected communities rely on smart governance infrastructures that can return more power to the people. And Johnston and Stewart-Weeks, in Chapter 18, show that governance based on centralized or decentralized models is giving way to more distributive models that operate at the edge of traditional structures.

New Institutions and Organizations

In addition to the creation of DHS, numerous new organizations have appeared that seek to redefine governance (see also Chapter 6). One is the Millennium Challenge Corporation (MCC). In 2002, responding to pressure from the international donor community at an international conference in Monterrey, Mexico, on foreign aid, President Bush pledged to substantially expand U.S. aid commitments under a radically different foreign assistance model. Bush proposed an independent agency that would allocate aid based on a developing country's progress in attaining good governance standards (e.g., rule of law), on its capacity to manage aid, and on its likelihood of achieving results (Buss and Gardner 2008). The Millennium Challenge Act of 2002 launched the new, independent, performance-based agency—MCC. The rationale for the new agency was that the Bush administration believed aid allocated under the U.S. Agency for International Development (USAID) was ineffective. Because USAID proved difficult to reform or terminate, policymakers created MCC to work in parallel with it. At the same time, USAID was folded into the State Department, losing much of its independence.

In addition to dramatically increasing foreign assistance, and investing it in countries that seemed to be making progress in their own governance, MCC was designed to run like a business. Had congressional support been in place, there is little doubt that the administration would have eliminated USAID in favor of the MCC model.

MCC's first two years of operation compelled Congress, in a bipartisan attack under Republican leadership, to de-fund the agency. MCC, when brought into existence, was at best an idea. No one in the administration had done serious work on design and implementation. Policymakers made serious errors in judgment about how agency management would work. Only a handful of procurement officers, for example, were taken on board to write complex performance contracts with developing country governments. Few policies, procedures, and controls were in place at start-up. MCC did not provide aid to any government during its first two years in operation. A new MCC director was brought in to redesign the agency and manage its way out of the crisis.

MCC now appears, according to most observers, to be on track. Interestingly, the Obama administration has not only retained MCC but substantially increased its budget in FY2011.

Budget Deficits and Debt

Under the Clinton administration, the nation had a balanced budget and manageable public debt. Under the Bush administration, budget deficits and public debt began to rise dramatically as a result of tax cuts in 2001 and 2003, the Medicare prescription drug program, steady growth in Medicare, Medicaid, and Social Security, and out-of-control congressional spending. The Afghan and Iraq wars added to the budget deficits. Now, under the Obama administration, budget deficits and public debt remain out of control, and are unsustainable (Congressional Budget Office 2010a).

In spite of calls to address the deficit/debt issue by the Government Accountability Office, Congressional Budget Office, and numerous foundations and think tanks (e.g., National Academy of Science/National Academy of Public Administration 2010), both political parties, the Congress, and the Bush and Obama administrations ignored the issue. President Obama, at a meeting of global powers in June 2010, even called on other nations to increase debt spending to stimulate economic recovery. With Greece embroiled in economic crisis, other nations demurred putting into place deficit reduction schemes. Apologists suggested the country could grow its way out of the problem.

Budget deficits and the growing national debt are the most long ranging governance issues. Redburn, in Chapter 4, reports on what the MacArthur Foundation concluded about the issue. Is it appropriate for recent Congresses and administrations to mortgage the country's long-term future? The burgeoning debt and budget deficits threaten not only the economic security of the United States but also national security and the sustainability of social programs.

Governance into the Future

Having reviewed governance issues at a high altitude and in a narrow scope, we now offer a prognosis for the future. Attempting to launch major domestic and foreign policy initiatives without adequate consensus building and compromise apparently leads to chaos and gridlock. Ironically, some consensus and compromise does emerge eventually, but it tends to set the stage for a repeat performance with each new administration. From a change management perspective this is simply crazy: putting the country through a perpetual agitation cycle is counterproductive. Competing forces perpetually line up against one another. And because the stakes are so high, each faction treats everything as a zero-sum game. The result is incivility.

Notes

1. We could have begun our review at the start of the Reagan administration, or the administration of Carter, Nixon, or Johnson for that matter. The effects on governance would have been equally transformational.

2. In response to the issues with voting machines in the Bush/Gore election, Congress passed the Help America Vote Act of 2002 (HAVA). The act offered election reform grants used to fund new voting machines and upgrades, pay for college students hired as poll workers, and support implementation of HAVA-mandated voter registration databases.

References

Australian Government. 2008. "Building Better Governance. Part One—What Is Public Sector Governance?" February 1. http://www.apsc.gov.au/publications07/bettergovernance1.htm.

Ballard, Tanya N. 2003. "Panel Backs Restructuring, Reorganization of Agencies." *Government Executive,* January 7. http://www.govexec.com/dailyfed/0103/010703t1.htm.

Bayh, Evan. 2010. "Why I'm Leaving the Senate." *New York Times,* February 20. http://www.nytimes.com/2010/02/21/opinion/21bayh.html.

Brook, Douglas A., and Cynthia L. King. 2009. "Legislating Innovations in Human Capital Management." In *Innovations in Human Resource Management,* ed. Hannah Sistare, Myra Howze Shiplett, and Terry F. Buss, pp. 277–291. Armonk, NY: M.E. Sharpe.

Brooks, David. 2007. "The New Social Contract." *New York Times,* September 7.

Buss, Terry F., and Nathaniel J. Buss. 2006. "The Internet, Politics and Democracy." In *Modernizing Democracy,* ed. Terry F. Buss, F. Stevens Redburn, and Kristina Guo, pp. 263–331. Armonk, NY: M.E. Sharpe.

Buss, Terry F., and Nathaniel J. Buss. 2011. "Evidence in Public Management: A Comparative Perspective." In *Evidence-Based Public Management: Practices, Issues, and Prospects,* ed. Anna Shillabeer, Terry Buss, and Denise Rousseau, pp. 119–153. Armonk, NY: M.E. Sharpe.

Buss, Terry F., and Adam Gardner. 2008. "The Millennium Challenge Account." In *Foreign Aid and Foreign Policy,* ed. Louis Picard, Robert Groelsma, and Terry F. Buss, pp. 329–355. Armonk, NY: M.E. Sharpe.

Buss, Terry F., F. Stevens Redburn, and Kristina Guo (eds). 2006. *Modernizing Democracy: Innovations in Citizen Participation.* Armonk, NY: M.E. Sharpe.

Buss, Terry F., and Joseph Thompson. 2009. "Building Surge Capacity in the Disaster Workforce." In *Innovations in Human Resource Management,* ed. Hannah Sistare, Myra Howze Shiplett, and Terry F. Buss, pp. 55–76. Armonk, NY: M.E. Sharpe.

Buss, Terry F., and Paul N. Van de Water (eds). 2009. *Expanding Access to Health Care: A Management Approach.* Armonk, NY: M.E. Sharpe.

The Collaboration Project. 2010a. "Diplopedia."http://www.collaborationproject.org/diplopedia/.

———. 2010b. "Coast Guard Social Media Initiative." http://www.collaborationproject.org/coast-guard-social-media-initiative/.

———. 2010c. "NOAA Virtual World." http://www.collaborationproject.org/noaa-virtual-world/.

Congressional Budget Office (CBO). 2010a. *Analysis of the President's Budgetary Proposals, FY2011.* March. Washington, DC: CBO.

———. 2010b. *Federal Climate Change Programs.* March. Washington, DC: CBO.

Cooper, Phillip J. 2003. *Governing by Contract.* Washington, DC: CQ Press.

Denhardt, Janet, and Robert Denhardt. 2007. *The New Public Service.* Armonk, NY: M.E. Sharpe.

Eaton, Sabrina. 2010. "Senator Sherrod Brown Steps into Controversy." *Cleveland Plain Dealer,* March 4.

Economist. 2010. "Not All on the Same Page." July 1.

Editorial. 2009. "Obama's Race to the Top." *New York Times,* July 31, p. A16.

Eggers, William D., and John O'Leary. 2010. "Can the U.S. Still Tackle Big Problems?" *Washington Post,* March 21, p. B01.

Frederickson, H. George, and Kevin Smith. 2003. *The Public Administration Theory Primer.* New York: Rawat.

Ginsberg, Wendy. 2010. *The Obama Open Government Initiative.* Congressional Research Service, August 17, #7–5700. Washington, DC: Government Printing Office.

Goldsmith, Stephen, and William Eggers. 2004. *Governing by Network.* Washington, DC: Brookings Institution Press.

Gore, Al. 1993. "From Red Tape to Results." *National Performance Review,* September 7. Washington, DC. http://govinfo.library.unt.edu/npr/whoweare/historypart1.html.

Gravelle, Jane, et al. 2009. *Economic Stimulus: Issues and Policies.* Congressional Research Service, February 27, #7–5700/R40104. Washington, DC: Government Printing Office.

Greenspan, Alan. 2010. *The Crisis.* Washington, DC: Greenspan Associates.

Huntington, Samuel. 1998. *The Clash of Civilizations.* New York: Simon and Schuster.
Johnson, Norman, and James Svara (eds). 2011. *Justice for All: Responsibilities and Actions to Promote Social Equity in Public Administration.* Armonk, NY: M.E. Sharpe.
Kamarck, Elaine. 2007. *The End of Government as We Know It.* Boulder, CO: Lynne Rienner.
Kettl, Donald. 2008. *The Next Government of the United States.* New York: Norton.
Kochan, Thomas, and Beth Shulman. 2007. "A New Social Contract." Briefing Paper, No. 184, February 22. Washington, DC: Economic Policy Institute.
Kossov, Igor. 2010. "Byrd Calls Obama Czars Dangerous." *CBS News,* February 25. http://www.cbsnews.com/blogs/2009/02/25/politics/politicalhotsheet/entry4828759.shtm.
Levinson, Mark. 2009. "The Economic Collapse." *Dissent* 56 (1) Winter: 61–66.
Marek, Angie. 2006. "Always Ready for the Storm." *US News and World Report,* March 19.
Miller, Rick, et al. 2009. "The New Fed." *Business Week,* November 7.
Morse, Ricardo S., Terry F. Buss, and C. Morgan Kinghorn (eds). 2007. *Transforming Public Leadership for the 21st Century.* Armonk, NY: M.E. Sharpe.
National Academy of Science (NAS)/National Academy of Public Administration (NAPA). 2010. *Choosing the Nation's Fiscal Future.* Washington, DC: NAS/NAPA. http://www.ourfiscalfuture.org/wp-content/uploads/fiscalfuture_full_report.pdf.
National Commission on the Public Service. 2003. *Urgent Business for America: Revitalizing the Federal Government for the 21st Century.* Washington, DC: Brookings Institution Press.
National Commission on Terrorist Attacks. 2004. *The 9/11 Commission Report.* Washington, DC: author.
Newbold, Stephanie, and Larry Terry. 2008. "From the New Public Management to the New Democratic Governance." In *Innovations in Public Leadership Development,* ed. Ricardo Morse and Terry F. Buss, pp. 33–49. Armonk, NY: M.E. Sharpe.
Noveck, Simone. 2009. *Wiki Government: How Technology Can Make Government Better, Democracy Stronger, and Citizens More Powerful.* Washington, DC: Brookings Institution Press.
Recovery.gov. 2010. "How Jobs Are Calculated." January 15. http://www.recovery.gov/News/featured/Pages/Calculator.aspx.
Redburn, F. Stevens, Robert J. Shea, and Terry F. Buss (eds). 2008. *Performance Management and Budgeting: How Governments Can Learn from Experience.* Armonk, NY: M.E. Sharpe.
Robert, Keith. 2005. "The Budget Reconciliation Act." Congressional Research Service, RL33030. Washington, DC: Government Printing Office, August 10.
Rodin, Judith. 2008. "The New Social Contract." *Time magazine,* July 17.
Saporito, Bill. 2008. "85% of U.S. Unhappy with Economy." *Time magazine,* July 16.
Shillabeer, Anna, Terry F. Buss, and Denise Rousseau (eds). 2011. *Evidence-Based Public Management: Methods, Issues, and Prospects.* Armonk, NY: M.E. Sharpe.
Singer, Paul. 2005. "Bush and the Bureaucracy: A Crusade for Control." *Government Executive,* March 25. http://www.govexec.com/dailyfed/0305/032505nj1.htm.
Sistare, Hannah, Myra Howze Shiplett, and Terry F. Buss (eds). 2009. *Innovations in Human Resource Management: Getting the Public's Work Done in the 21st Century.* Armonk, NY: M.E. Sharpe.
Sobel, Russell S., and Peter Leeson. 2007. "The Use of Knowledge in Natural Disaster Relief Management." *The Independent Review* 11(4): 510–532.
Stanton, Thomas H. 1991. *Government-Sponsored Enterprises.* Washington, DC: Brookings Institution Press.
———. (ed.). 2006. *Meeting the Challenge of 9/11: Blueprints for More Effective Government.* Armonk, NY: M.E. Sharpe.
Sunstein, Cass. 2007. *The Second Bill of Rights: FDR's Unfinished Revolution.* New York: Basic Books.
Taleb, Nassim. 2007. *The Black Swan.* New York: Penguin.

UN Intergovernmental Panel on Climate Change (IPCC). 2011. *The Fifth Assessment Report.* New York: IPCC http://www.ipcc.ch (accessed March 4, 2011).

U.S. Government Accountability Office (U.S. GAO). 2010. *GAO High Risk and Other Major Government Challenges: Strategic Human Capital Management.* Washington, DC: U.S. GAO. http://www.gao.gov/highrisk/risks/efficiency-effectiveness/strategic_human_management.php.

U.S. Office of Management and Budget. 2004. "FY2004 Budget Submission to Congress" (chapter introducing PART). http://www.gpoaccess.gov/usbudget/fy04/pdf/budget/performance.pdf.

U.S. Office of Personnel Management (OPM). 2010a. *Human Capital Assessment and Accountability Framework.* Washington, DC: OPM. http://apps.opm.gov/HumanCapital/tool/index.cfm.

———. 2010b. *OPM Reorganizes.* Washington, DC: OPM. http://www.opm.gov/news/opm-reorganizes-to-better-meet-the-needs-of-its-customers,1500.aspx.

Woodward, Bob. 2008. *The War Within.* New York: Simon and Schuster.

2

Administration in the Coming Public Era

H. GEORGE FREDERICKSON

In this chapter I choose to speak on the subject of "administration in the coming public era." The burden of my argument is that history moves back and forth in sweeping arcs of change and that public administration is swept up along these epochs of change, both changing each epoch and being changed by it. In broad terms, the arc of change moves from an individualistic, corporate, market, and private ethos at one pole to a collective or public ethos at the other pole. We are, I shall argue, at the ending point of an individualistic or corporate era, which began at about the middle of the 20th century, and are just now entering a new era characterized by a distinctly strengthening public ethos. The theories and practices of public administration are, I shall argue, central to this emerging public era.

Modern American public administration traces its origins to problems of incompetence and corruption at all levels of government in the late 19th and early 20th centuries. The American Progressive Era and the reform movement formed the seedbed in which public administration grew, expressions of our disappointment with government corruption and corporate excess. The reform architecture of the American Progressive Era included merit-based civil service systems as well as the creation of instruments for the firm regulation of business. It worked. By the middle of the 20th century the United States had successfully fought two world wars and pulled itself out of the Great Depression. We look back on this period as an era of positive and effective government and historical evidence that professional public administration is a key to honest, ethical, and effective government.

But by mid-20th century a different kind of disappointment had set in. This was disappointment with large, expensive, slow, unresponsive government bureaucracies and with what many believed to be excessive control of business. The deregulation of business then came into fashion as did cutting back the civil service, replacing it with contractors doing much of the administrative work of government. Over the next 40 years, in an arc from that time until this, we have witnessed continuing problems of government effectiveness and steadily increasing corporate power and debt.

Looking out across the great contemporary landscape of ethical disappointment one sees the general meltdown of the public accounting business, the business that is supposed to protect the interests of corporate stockholders; the brazen use of government funds for policy propaganda; so much money in politics that the old joke—that we have the best government money can buy—is no longer a joke; the relentless accumulation of corporate scandals and failures—Enron, WorldCom, Tyco, Weststar, Freddy Mac, Fannie Mae, Bear-Stearns, AIG; and now the credit crisis.

The revolving door of jobs, money, information, and access between the federal government and large contractors swings freely. The Project on Government Oversight estimates that approximately 300 former senior government officials have, since 1997, taken top positions in the defense contracting industry or with their lobbyists.

It is interesting to review the standard garden-variety list of things wrong with contemporary government. As I review this list, please note what is left out, including:

1. the pervasive influence of money in politics;
2. the power of interest groups and lobbyists;
3. legislative gridlock;
4. the growing legacy of debt being passed on to our children;
5. the portion of federal obligations that are fixed and continuing, so-called nondiscretionary spending;
6. the growth of earmarked pork barrel spending;
7. growing corruption;
8. declining regard for the United States (not for Americans) abroad;
9. ever more coarse and shrill partisan politics.

It seems that all the items on the list are amplified in the harsh light of an unpopular war, anxiety over global terrorism, and now the credit-driven recession.

What is missing from the list? Missing are contemporary claims, either by elected officials or by serious followers of public affairs, that bureaucracy, or ineffective management, or poor policy implementation is a central element of what is wrong with government. When compared with the serious cracks and fissures in the national government, problems of public management are minor. These days elected officials get little traction running against the bureaucracy because the people now understand that bureaucracy is not the primary problem. Because of this lack of traction, elected officials are actually running against one another and even campaigning on actual policy issues. Can you imagine it? Indeed, it is even fashionable for elected officials to be full of praise toward the military.

Reconsider two political mantras of the 1980s. First, remember this one: "the era of big government is over." That turns out to be true. The era of big government is over, having been replaced by "the era of really big government." Second, remember this one: "government is not the solution, government is the problem." Well, it appears to the investment banks, to the automobile industry, to those holding bad mortgages, to state and local governments, and to firms lined up to be bailed out that government is the solution. How things have changed!

We may be witnessing the beginning of the end of the long era of bureaucrat bashing, of tearing down the managerial capacity of the national government, and the beginnings of re-regulation. It is evident that one of the things the country needs is the restoration of many of the traditional values of public administration. It is now clear how much we need substantive competence. At the upper ranks of federal agencies we need nonpartisan, nonpolitical officials who are experienced, technically knowledgeable, and managerially capable. We need equally good neutral competence at the middle and line levels of federal hierarchies. And we need a much brighter line, a much stronger firewall, between politics on one hand and the details of agency management and policy implementation on the other.

The beginning of the end of the era of bureaucrat bashing comes with one delicious irony. When one opens the kit for fixing government what does one find? Voilà! Public Administration!

The era of radical individualism and market dogma is winding down and a new era of public regardedness is in sight. Indeed, it is argued by columnist David Brooks that the coming of a new and stronger public sector is nested in a confluence of three changing epochs. We are, Brooks claims, at the end of an economic era, a political era, and a generational era. The allure of living beyond our means and of relying on the invisible hand of the market is waning. The politics of being antigovernment and antibureaucratic has caught up with us. And, as the baby boom generation steps away from power, it is their children who are left to clean up the mess. American public administration is nested in this confluence of changing epochs, and if we do it right, these changing epochs hold great promise to bring about an era of competent and ethical public administration.

We are, I believe, at that tipping point. Building a robust public administration as part of the emerging new public era will require great imagination and creativity. We will need to build new bridges between public problems on the one hand and public institutions on the other. We will need to invent a new public language. We will need to build new public management narratives and metaphors. Because the world is greatly changed, we cannot simply return to that old-time public administration religion. We cannot put Humpty Dumpty together again.

A Possible Role for NAPA in the Coming Public Epoch

At this time the National Academy of Public Administration (the Academy) has a unique and special responsibility, a responsibility to conceptualize the vital place of administration in the emerging public era, and a particular responsibility to advocate for a newly conceptualized public sector and public service. These responsibilities can only be met by a NAPA reconfigured to better take on the big issues of modern public administration, a willingness to take positions on these issues, to speak forcefully for those positions, and to work for them. This is not the time for NAPA to be timid.

We have in the membership of the Academy a remarkable accumulation of public administration expertise and wisdom. Through the funded project panels and occasionally through the work of the standing panels, the Academy has responded to requests for advice and has brought some of its horsepower to bear on issues of federal public administration and governance. Much of that work has been very good. However, in my opinion, because of the way the project panels are organized and financed, much of that work has been reactive rather than proactive. The Academy has not managed to harness its impressive resources in such a way as to exercise sustained leadership on the big public administration issue of the day, let alone work on the coming challenges in the field. Nor has the Academy responded as effectively as it might to the objectives and purposes spelled out in our congressional charter. Although the congressional charter is 25 years old, please note how directly the statement of objectives and purposes in that charter speak to the pressing public administration challenges of our time. The Academy should be:

1. "evaluating the structure, administration, operation, and program performance of Federal and other governments and government agencies, anticipating, identifying, and analyzing significant problems and suggesting timely corrective action;
2. foreseeing and examining critical emerging issues in governance, formulating practical approaches to their resolution;
3. assessing the effectiveness, structure, administration, and implications for governance of present or proposed public programs, policies, and processes, recommending specific changes;
4. demonstrating by the conduct of its affairs a commitment to the highest professional standards of ethics and scholarship."

With words like "foreseeing," "anticipating," and "emerging issues," I am struck by how strongly our congressional charter calls upon the Academy to be bold and forward looking.

To more fully meet the expectations of our charter and to further the prospects that the Academy could become the authoritative voice of public administration in the coming public era, I suggest a new Academy program. For purposes of discussion, let it be called the Academy Vital Issues Program or VIP. Established by the Board of Trustees, the Vital Issues Program would engage groups of Academy fellows in the study of agreed-upon vital issues; invite them to prepare reports with recommendations for the consideration of the Board. After deliberation on a given report and with possible modification, the Board may choose to issue an Academy Position Paper. An Academy Position Paper would be designed to be an informed review of the state-of-the-art of a particular organizational or managerial issue and an authoritative statement of appropriate and effective practices. Once adopted by the Board of Trustees, an Academy Position Paper would be exactly that, the formal position of the Academy. In a similar way the excellent reports of panels should be the subjects of Academy Position Papers.

It is recommended that the Vital Issues Program establishes and takes responsibility for a new annual publication, the *Annals of the National Academy of Public Administration,* and that Academy positions be published in the *Annals.* The recommended Vital Issues Program would serve to engage many more of our Fellows in the work of the academy, particularly our academic Fellows. Furthermore, the Vital Issues Program should enliven and sharpen our deliberations. Finally, the implementation of these recommendations would, in time, cause NAPA to look and act more like the other congressionally chartered academies. I am not recommending that any present Academy programs or initiatives be discontinued. And I am aware that recommending the Vital Issues Program raises questions of Academy finances, organization, and position taking.

Studies That Could Tip Public Administration Toward a More Effective Public Sector in the Future

Having completed this detour, let me return to the main road and to the challenges associated with building a robust public administration in the context of the coming public era. In doing this I will, from time to time, refer back to the Academy and to the proposed Vital Issues Program.

At the risk of oversimplification, let me briefly describe four possible Academy studies that could help public administration tip American affairs toward a vital public ethos. All of these proposed studies have to do with third party government.

First, Woodrow Wilson and our early founders wisely chose to call our field and profession "public" administration and not "government" administration. That was a critically important choice and one that matters especially today. "Public" is a broad pregovernmental concept. The public manifests itself in many ways as "patterns of purposeful human association"—neighborhoods, tribes, clans, voluntary associations, churches, clubs, businesses and corporations, nongovernmental organizations, and, yes, governments. Note that governments are but one type of public. We teach and practice not just government administration but public administration. It is not the National Academy of Government Administration, it is the National Academy of Public Administration. The differences are not trivial. The public is the greater subject. Governments float in a vast public sea.

This point is vital to the contention that we are at a tipping point toward greater competence in public policy implementation and more ethical governance. The primary reason is that "the public sector" is now understood to include not just government but all of those businesses, institutions, and other nongovernmental organizations doing "public administration" via governmental grants and contracts. At the same time that the ranks of the civil service were being depleted, the ranks of the third party bureaucracy were being dramatically increased. It is now clearly evident that the huge shadow federal bureaucracy is the way the national government is doing business and will continue to do business. Using contemporary beltway parlance, corporate and nonprofit contractors are agency *partners* in the implementation of public policy. As Lester Salamon (1995) wisely puts it, modern federal public administration is now primarily third party government.

Whatever we call it—third party government, the hollow state, the shadow bureaucracy, the blended public workforce, articulated chains of third parties, public programs and their partners, steering rather than rowing, or governance—it is *the* public administration challenge of our time.

Federal third party government is here to stay and, therefore, the face of federal public administration is forever changed. Over the next decade it is essential that public administration specialists invent the arrangements whereby civil servants and their third party partners can effectively and accountably implement public policy together. These arrangements will need to be much more than simple contract management and agency oversight. The reason public administration specialists, both academic and practicing, must invent these arrangements is that we must insist that such arrangements be arms length from elected officials and politics. History teaches us that when politics, elected officials, and government contracts are brought together they form the seedbeds for favoritism, pork barrel earmarking, and corruption. So, building firewalls between contractors and elected officials is up to us.

To conclude this first point, I insist that public administration be understood to include governments *and* all other persons and organizations doing the public's work. Taking action on the conceptual and practical aspects of this subject seems to me an ideal topic for the proposed Academy Vital Issues Program. I cannot think of any organization with the expertise and experience on this subject that even comes close to the Academy. As the leading voice on this vital issue, the Academy should take a principled position on it.

A *second* possible study, which would engage public administration in the emerging public ethos, is to acknowledge that we are worn out by the normative arguments over whether contracting out and privatization is good or bad. Third party government is here to stay, and as young folks say, deal with it. Contracting and privatization are the means by which Americans can appear to have it both ways: the illusion of smaller government on the one hand with little actual diminution in government services on the other.

Public management via contracting out and grant making has grown so rapidly that the contracting practices of modern governance have gotten far ahead of our capacity to build either explanatory theory or concept that helps government officials manage more effectively. As Todd LaPorte, a faculty member at George Mason University, is fond of saying, "Public administration by contracting out and grant making may work in practice but it doesn't work in theory."

As a starting point, it is essential to sort out some core public administration concepts and practices in light of the rapid growth of third party government. What was traditionally thought to be public administration—service delivery, human resources management, budgeting, IT, and so forth—is now mostly exported to grantees or contractors. If the contractors are doing the management, what, exactly, are those who let the contracts and oversee the contracts doing? Is this public administration by spreadsheet? Is this the new form of delegation? Is this antiseptic management? Is this management by remote control, or administration on autopilot? I think of when we learned to ride a bicycle and would shout, "look ma, no hands." Third party government sometimes thinks like that. Finding the right words to describe and theoretically "name" this new form of "management" and make conceptual distinctions between kinds of public management would be an important practical and conceptual contribution.

To conclude this second point, the development of a useful language of third party governance, complete with categories and types, examples, and empirical evidence, would be an important contribution to the field of public administration. It would be especially impressive if an authoritative statement of principles of effective and ethical third party government were developed by the Academy, and put forward as the formal position of the Academy on the subject. In this way the Academy would be the authoritative voice in American public administration.

The *third* suggested study designed to engage public administration in the emerging public era is not profound, but it would still be helpful. We have an ongoing problem of a misinformed public, a misinformed media, and many misinformed public officials regarding the size and characteristics of the modern public sector. A couple of examples will do. We are regularly told of the "American presence in Iraq," usually described as about 130,000 pre-surge troops. And that information has informed our policy debates on the subject. But the actual American presence, or "footprint," in Iraq is approximately twice that, when so-called force augmentation contractors are factored in. A less contentious example would be the National Institutes of Health (NIH). NIH has approximately 11,000 employees. But when NIH research grantees are factored in, the full-time equivalent workforce is about 60,000. Essentially the same story is true for most federal agencies. It is very difficult to describe, let alone understand, modern federal public administration if only federal civil servants are thought to be the subject. As Paul Light (2006) so eloquently has described for us, the nonuniformed federal workforce is not about 1.8 million people. The actual federal public sector workforce is somewhere in excess of 10 million people.

A formal review of the subject and the formulation of a statement of the position of the Academy on this subject would be helpful. I am not talking about a normative statement, but an informed description of the dimensions and characteristics of the subject and a language by which the modern federal workforce can be more accurately described. Again, the Academy could be the source of an authoritative position on this subject. Such a position statement would be especially helpful with the media. It could help the media start to ask the right questions.

A *fourth* suggested study that would help public administration tip the country toward a more effective public sector would be taking up, in a broad sense, some legal questions associated with third party government. In many ways third party government is in a legal space between business law and regulation on one hand and civil service laws and regulations on the other. Consider, for example, the matter of transparency. As a matter of principle, should corporations implementing government contracts fall under the same transparency requirements that the agencies letting the contracts are required to meet? I am not suggesting that the Academy begin to act like a law firm. But I am suggesting that among its Fellows the Academy has the horsepower to consider legal issues such as transparency in third party government and to develop principled positions on those issues. And I like to think that once adopted, these Academy positions would be taken seriously in quarters far beyond the Academy.

Some Conclusions

Let me turn now to a brief conclusion. We are, I suggest, winding down a 50-year era of the dominance of individual, private, corporate, and market concerns and beliefs. That private and individualistic era followed the earlier Progressive Era and the so-called reform movement. There is, I argue, a public-private cycle, a cycle driven by disappointment. First there was disappointment with government graft and corruption in the late 19th century. This was followed by the Progressive Era of the early 20th century, which was followed by disappointment with bureaucracy and big government. There followed from that disappointment a 50-year period of the dominance of private concerns and market ideology. Now we are again disappointed with corporate greed and corruption and we see all around us evidence of an emerging and strengthening public ethos, and the coming of a new public era. If this proves to be the case, the present period of government bailouts, re-regulation, and the growth of government by contracting will prove not to be a blip but a longer cycle of public regard and interest, in short, a new public era.

If that prediction is right, I suggest there are important implications, opportunities, and responsibilities for the National Academy of Public Administration. We should, I suggest, turn to our congressional charter for guidance. That charter tells us to be about the business of "anticipating, identifying, and analyzing significant problems," to be "foreseeing and examining critical emerging issues in governance," and to have "a commitment to the highest professional standards of ethics and scholarship." This suggests a bolder NAPA. We should, I suggest, consider implementing a program of studies under the auspices of a Vital Issues Program. Under the direction of the Academy Board of Directors, the Vital Issues Program would, for example, establish a study group to take up a particular pressing issue of public administration, summarize the state of knowledge on that issue, draft a report with recommendations that include principles of effective administrative practice, and a statement of the Academy position on that issue. At its discretion, the Board of Directors may accept the study and may adopt the position proposed in it. And, at its discretion the Board of Directors may authorize the publication of the study, with the attendant Academy position, in the *Annals of the National Academy of Public Administration*. Such an Academy enterprise would place the Academy more nearly in a position to shape the emerging public era and establish the Academy as the principled authoritative voice in public administration.

Author's Note

This chapter was originally presented as the Elmer B. Staats Lecture at the Fall 2008 meeting of the National Academy of Public Administration in Washington, D.C. It has been revised and updated for this book.

References

Light, Paul. 2006. "The New True Size of Government." New York: The Wagner School, Organizational Performance Initiative, New York University.
Salamon, Lester. 1995. *Partners in the Public Service.* Baltimore: Johns Hopkins University Press.

3

Crises, Governance, and the Administrative State in a Post-Neoliberal World

ROBERT F. DURANT

The past three decades in the United States have seen especially virulent debates over how societies can deal best with the public problems they face. Through the mid-1970s in the United States, what has been called the "positive state" philosophy had triumphed since the Progressive Era of the early 20th century. This is the idea that government is—and ought to be—the ultimate promoter, provider, and guarantor of essential goods, services, and opportunities to its citizenry. Government was the *solution* to market failures and a countervailing force against large-scale socioeconomic forces that were beyond their control or ability to deal with alone. Proponents of this *interventionist* philosophy favored (1) centralization and planning of policy in Washington; (2) creation of agencies organized on the basis of function, staffed with public interest–oriented experts in problem areas, and managed on the basis of the principles of administration; (3) use of largely regulatory (command-and-control) policy tools to make things happen; and (4) taking politics out of administration (depoliticization) by means of civil service reform. Nor was it a coincidence that this growth of federal-centric government arose in an era of two major world wars, followed by a nearly half-century-long Cold War that saw the United States on a permanent war footing. Historically, the power and prowess of the federal government has evolved with the ebb and flow of national military challenges (Arnold 1998).

By the end of the 20th century, however, astute observers of the administrative state in Washington saw a pronounced change in its nature, focus, and relevance. They began referring to a "contract" state, a "hollow" state, a "disarticulated" state, a "third-party" state, a "networked" state, an "enterprise" state, and a "neomanagerialist" state. Others referred to an emergent "marketized public administration" as a fourth tradition in public administration, one added to the managerial, political, and legal traditions of the field (Rosenbloom 1993). Regardless of the term used to characterize it, however, all shared the notion that "governance" had replaced "government" as the central animating principle of public administration practice and theory building as the 20th century ended.

The apogee of interventionism in markets, the positive state philosophy was turned on its head by Thatcherism and Reaganism. Theirs was a *noninterventionist* view of the role of the state, with proponents viewing it as the source of, rather than the solution to, societies' ills. Their mantra was the exact opposite of that offered by positive state proponents: (1) decentralization (within agencies); (2) devolution of responsibilities to the states, localities, and nongovernmental actors; (3) debureaucratization and a commensurate turn to market-based service delivery; (4) reintroduction of politics into administration, with policy set by appointees and merely implemented by the career civil service; and (5) deskilling of the career bureaucracy that remained, with a downsized workforce of professionals turned into contract monitors overseeing the kinds of work they were originally hired to do. Moreover, as embraced typically by minimal state proponents, this new public management (NPM) accorded no special role for either the public service (in Washington or elsewhere) or the public interest, aside from what market forces allowed or dictated. Nor was it a coincidence that this turn to markets and effort to attenuate federal-centric government through devolution of responsibilities upward to international bodies, downward to state and local governments, and outward to private and nonprofit organizations reached its apogee in the post–Cold War era and prior to the tragedy of September 11 and the new semi-war-footing against terrorism.

By the end of the first decade of the 21st century, however, some had begun reconsidering the power of this neoadministrative state to deal adequately—technically, politically, and philosophically—with this nation's formidable challenges. And once again, perceptions of crises—real, contrived, or imagined—have stimulated such thinking, along with perceptions of government failure. The former include global warming, the war on terror, precarious economic security in light of a spiraling national and foreign debt and the economic meltdown in 2008–2009, and underfunded and still-growing entitlement programs exacerbated by an aging population. Many, for example, agreed with Polanyi's (2001) scornful indictment in the midst of World War II of the "utopia of a self-adjusting market" and called for greater government intervention in markets.

Here, traditional positive state interventionists have seized a window of opportunity to tout the virtues of a return to government activism in Washington. Indeed, and as will be discussed in this chapter, much as the failures of the associationalist movement in the 1920s laid the groundwork for Roosevelt's New Deal and its accompanying administrative state in the 1930s (Durant 2009), perceptions of the lackluster performance of critical government agencies led to cries in the United States for an increased national administrative focus in the 21st century. Problems included contracting scandals, service delivery fiascos (e.g., Hurricane Katrina), the need for international cooperation of security agencies worldwide, and the "dark side" of networks. Again echoing Polanyi, they countered claims of the classic economic liberalism of the 1990s by stating that "regulation both extends and restricts freedom; only the balance of the freedoms lost and won is significant" (2001, p. 254).

Importantly, positive state activists were joined in this perception by so-called big government, or "heroic" conservatives who saw the national government as a means for addressing the crises they perceived as threatening the United States (e.g., declining moral standards, a coarsening of the culture, the AIDs epidemic, spreading democracy around the world, and especially the war on terror). Not the least of those proponents was George W. Bush. The president did not choose this label for his efforts. Rather, it was coined by various supporters and opponents to characterize Bush's efforts to build a permanent conservative electoral coalition, one that adapted Reaganism to changed conditions (demographic, cultural, and philosophical changes speeding up in America) (Brooks 2004; Gerson 2008). As Brown notes, Bush "was socially and economically conservative, but he was also a government activist" in pursuing those aims (2009, p. 80).

As a heroic conservative himself, columnist David Brooks captured it best early in the Bush presidency: "Bush understood that the simple government-is-the-problem philosophy of the older [Reagan] Republicans was obsolete . . . [and he grasped] the paradox that if you don't have a positive vision of government, you won't be able to limit the growth of government" (2004, paragraphs 19–20). Put differently, Bush understood that government could be used to advance conservative principles. As Gerson (2008, p. 175) puts it, Bush defined a series of traditionally liberal goals: better education for minority children, help for addicts and the homeless, and prescription drugs for the elderly. This, in his view, required a strong, energetic executive to break up existing bureaucratic arrangements in the domestic policy arena—use of federal power to push power beyond government.

In the wake of these events, Hill and Hupe (2009) argue that we are seeing a "selective interventionist" model of governance emerging in response to crises worldwide. Their observation, moreover, occurred during the Bush years before the 2008 Troubled Asset Relief Program and other market interventionist policies tried to right a sinking economy, and before the similarly inspired initiatives of the Obama administration. Indeed, contrary to the deregulatory image of the Bush administration, the federal government selectively mandated nearly $30 billion in new regulatory costs on U.S. industry and citizens, $11 billion in FY2007 alone (Gattuso 2008). Then came Obama's health care initiative, with government intervention in nearly a sixth of the economy, followed by bipartisan efforts to re-regulate housing and financial markets. Further calls came for the federal government to deal aggressively with a massive oil spill in the Gulf of Mexico and to ensure safety standards on offshore drilling. Thus, while both the Bush and Obama administrations followed the typical pattern of issuing spates of regulations during the last year (Bush) and first year (Obama) of their terms, the pace, aggressiveness, and scope of the Obama administration's regulatory efforts represented a qualitative shift upward in stringency (Lipton 2008).

Obama and the liberal Democratic leadership in Congress have experienced a backlash among independents against their selective interventionist policy efforts on health care reform, cap-and-trade, and the greening of industry policies, culminating in their defeat in the House of Representatives in the 2010 midterm elections. Even if neointerventionism on the scale that Obama envisions occurs, however, associationalism will prevail if one takes as a measure the kind of implementation structures created by this revival of government activism. What is more, it is a picture that has played itself out repeatedly in American political development since 1789. More precisely, implementation structures characterized by public-private-nonprofit partnerships, or what was called the associationalist state in the 1920s, informed the Obama administration's efforts—as it had his predecessors dealing with crises. In practice, and regardless of effectiveness or the challenges they pose to accountability and coordination, these networks are the way that America's otherwise disparate economic liberalism and civic republican values have been reconciled by politicians.

With this in mind, this chapter addresses whether, why, and with what implications contemporary crises will lead to the resurgence of the positive state, federal agency capacity building, or the neoadministrative or networked state. Its arguments are threefold: (1) the persistent turn to the private and nonprofit sectors is rooted in America's classic conflict between economic liberalism and civic republicanism; (2) path dependency and the constitutive effects of policy and administration in American political development have persistently produced networked governance in the face of crises in America and are likely to do the same in the face of today's crises; and (3) consequently, the challenges of networked governance in a democratic republic are likely to increase rather than diminish in any crisis-driven return to a neointerventionist state. The chapter concludes by discussing what this continuing need to network in the shadow of hierarchy means. Public agencies will have to continue to reconceptualize their purpose in light of this selective intervention, reconnect with citizens, redefine administrative rationality, recapitalize assets, reengage resources, and revitalize democratic constitutionalism in the 21st century.

Continuity Amid Discontinuity: The Dynamics of Crisis-Driven Governance Reform

Because of the early cultural primacy of classic economic individualism and civic responsibility as predominant, albeit competing, philosophies that the United States has struggled to reconcile, public-private-nonprofit partnerships have proven throughout the nation's history to inform large-scale administrative reform movements stimulated by crises. Classic economic liberalism embraces such American exceptionalist values as antistatism; faith in markets, technology, and rationality; states' rights; and individual rather than group egalitarianism (Lipset 1996). In contrast, civic republicanism is community oriented rather than individual oriented: "In the [civic] republican view, the colonial and Revolutionary ideal lay, not in the pursuit of private matters, but in the shared public life of civic duty, in the subordination of individual interests to the *res publica*" (Morone 1990, p.16).

The Founding Century as Prologue

As these two values—classical liberalism and civic republicanism—are negotiated by actors within the American political system, building a "government out of sight" was the default option of American leaders in the wake of crises in the 18th and 19th centuries (Balogh 2009; Howe 1979; Wilentz 2005). During the nation's first century, they did so by, among other things, relying on tariffs collected at U.S. ports rather than internal taxes, depending on the decentralized nature of local government with its watchful eye on the judiciary, subsidizing and giving tax-free deals for settling and developing western lands, and not recognizing a distinction "between state and civil society or, for that matter, public and private roles for citizens" (Balogh 2009, p. 24). In this sense, while republicanism fostered antistatist values, it also embraced energetic government through the talents of all sectors (public, private, and nonprofits) rather than reforms dominated by the national government.

Wrought also in the 19th century was a linkage between markets and citizenship that helped further put the United States on a networked governance path. That made the predominant administrative business practices in any given historical period the default option for administrative reform. Social historians argue that during the first three decades of the 19th century the notions of democracy and capitalism themselves became linked in Americans' minds to create an enduring "myth of national identity." Appleby portrays that linking as Americans "convinc[ing] themselves that government had little or nothing to do" with the rising prosperity the nation experienced (2000, p. 257).

Even after the Civil War and its establishment of the power of national authority, corporate and political party interests benefiting from a nonprofessional or "clerical state" (Carpenter 2001) that dispensed succor to them in the form of land grants and subsidies fought successfully to maintain and expand its power. Moreover, this occurred despite several major economic "shocks" to the American system (e.g., economic depressions in 1873 and 1993). In fact, these made national governance authority more powerful because of the parallel "social service" state that the parties and voluntary associations became in the absence of a welfare state (Skowronek 1982). As Skocpol notes, even the Civil War did not leave as its legacy a "permanent autonomous federal bureaucracy" (1992, p. 68).

Because of what American political development scholars call "lock in" (Clemens 2006), or what Light (1999) calls "layering without learning," administrative reforms responding to crises are layered upon each other without finding out what works and what does not work. All this typically means that prior reform efforts often appear in recycled guises (Light 1999). That is, while still grounded in business approaches, these reforms reflect the latest iteration of management thinking about best business practices (BBPs; e.g., zero-based budgeting and partnering). Disappointed again because reforms work in some situations (e.g., the Planning, Programming, and Budgeting System [PPBS] in the Pentagon) and not others (PPBS in social agencies), citizens again become more open to appeals for non-governmental solutions, for different tools and less-direct delivery of government actions for addressing public problems (e.g., tax expenditures), and for downsizing of the government agencies that remain.

Ironically, these only further, gradually, and ironically erode citizen confidence and faith in government as citizens see less direct connection between government and the meeting of their needs. Lost, in turn, is reliable citizen support for or participation in coalitions necessary to pressure Congress for administrative capacity building. This then sets the stage for further governance failings, which inspire new calls for reform predicated on corporate, nongovernmental, and market-based solutions. This occurs as critics argue that existing administrative structures are not up to the changes confronting society.

What are the underlying causal mechanisms driving these dynamics? They occur partially because private, nonprofit, and cross-sectoral governance networks are an easier "sell" in the political market, resonating as they do with American exceptionalist values. They also occur because of what scholars working in American political development—in particular, those taking a historical-institutionalist perspective—call the amplifying effects of path dependency and the constitutive effects of earlier administrative reforms. The former refers to the tendency for prior decisions to limit the range of possible policy alternatives in the future, with apparently small early changes leading to qualitative changes in the longer term. The latter—constitutive effects—refers to the process by which prior reforms and policies create legislative and administrative structures that produce biases within the system, privileging some policies and interest groups and marginalizing others.

In the case of administrative governance reforms, this bias involves the ability of corporate interests to ensure that their capacity to influence the discretion that agencies exercise is institutionalized in governance (and agency) structures. Thus, once these interests believe that something is going to happen in the way of legislative or administrative reform, they prefer implementation of rules by public agencies because they can influence discretion through relatively opaque subsystem politics rather than in the fishbowl of Congress. They also prefer fragmented implementation structures by the states or by networks of cross-sectoral actors. Unless corporations prefer national standards, the former means less opposition to their initiatives in some states, that the costs of lobbying go up for opponents who must organize coalitions in 50 state capitals rather than just the nation's capital, and that generosity and equity of services is less likely (Mettler 1998). Networks, in turn, create resource dependence, monitoring, and accountability challenges that are less tractable when programs are housed within agencies (Frederickson and Stazyk 2010)—thus creating additional leverage for private and nonprofit providers over policy implementation.

The Search for Order and the Progressive Era

As the eminent historian Gordon Wood has written, the "emergence of the liberal, individualistic, commercial, and interest-ridden world of early 19th century America" remains today "part of the nation's understanding of itself" (2008, p. 255). A critical juncture of claims that existing administrative structures were not up to the task of contemporary problems combined with enduring cultural predilections to launch the Progressive reform movement of the late 19th and early 20th centuries (1880–1928). Among a litany of factors that reformers of governance pointed to as crises were the transition from a rural agricultural to an urban industrial society, international business competition, the rise of professions stimulating a broader middle class, small business animosity toward contracting arrangements benefiting larger businesses, the increasing migration into cities in southern Europe, and political corruption.

Progressives saw existing governance structures as unable to cope, for example, with health and safety problems in urban areas where immigrants congregated or as incapable of ending the corruption of political machines dependent on immigrants for electoral support. Likewise mismatched were state regulatory authorities with a burgeoning industrial system that crossed state lines, along with international economic, industrial, and foreign policy threats that reformers said only professionalization and executive-centered government could allay. Madisonian checks and balances were too cumbersome, slow, and amateurish to cope with these challenges and would put the United States at a commercial and military disadvantage.

As Waldo (1984) describes, the administrative theory regnant in the Progressive (and later the New Deal) Era to address this capacity gap married the "Great Society" (i.e., civic republican) vision of Graham Wallas, the Progressive "social gospel" of government activism articulated by Herbert Croly, and the corporate model of scientific management as a means for planning, administering, and regulating societies for the public good. In addition, proponents saw business competition as inherently inefficient, sought cooperation and coordination among firms in given industries as a means to eliminate inefficiency, and placed their faith in the ability of scientifically derived data applied by experts to eliminate waste in organizations (Hofstadter 1989).

Privileged were professional and technoscientific skills that uneducated immigrants did not have. This was, as Progressives famously aimed at "running government like a business," a position that eventually decentered a civic republican form of administration because of the asymmetric power of the business coalition touting it.

One also sees the first of repeated signs throughout American history of a business sector under assault from many quarters grasping for new administrative institutions that eventually would bring order, stability, and predictability to their operations before stricter restraints—most notably trust-busting—were applied to them. What typically were seen as progressive reforms creating independent regulatory commissions (IRCs)—such as the Interstate Commerce Commission and the Chemistry Bureau (charged with implementing the Pure Food and Drug Act of 1906)—reining in the "malefactors of wealth" actually were lobbied for by industry associations.

Kolko chronicles, for example, how "any measure of importance in the Progressive era was not merely endorsed by key representatives of businesses involved; rather, such bills were first proposed by them" (1963, p. 283; see also Hofstadter 1989; Wiebe 1967). This "political capitalism" (Kolko 1963) produced agencies that were soon captured by the industries they were designed to regulate.

Infinitely less appreciated by public administration today, however, was another faction within the Progressive reform movement: the associationalists. Dubbed the "associative state" (Hawley 1974), this alternative model of progressive administrative reform was championed most notably by Herbert Hoover. Associationalism as a public philosophy was premised on government-stimulated voluntary cooperation to address public problems, with direct government intervention a last resort if private and civic volunteerism failed (Kennedy 2005). For associationalists, properly educated and self-governing businesses, state and local governments, voluntary organizations, and professional associations informed by data analyses provided by federal agencies would willingly tackle any problems identified (Hofstadter 1989). Thus, the role of federal agencies was solely to "stimulate the private sector to organize and govern itself" in the public interest (Clements 2000, p. 128). As such, associationalism was an early 20th-century variant of today's infatuation with "emergent" networks "work[ing] out bureaucratic arrangements that would nourish individual, community, and private effort rather than supplant them" (Hawley 1974, p. 116).

A Bilateral World, the Neoassociationalist Prescription, and Building the Enterprise State

Conventional wisdom accurately portrays the associationalist bubble bursting rapidly in the aftermath of World War II contracting scandals and in the wake of the Depression and Hoover's failed policies during his presidency. Absent federal government pressures to form associations, these presumably self-emergent and public-interest–oriented partnerships floundered: major industries refused to partner with one another, the trust necessary between business and labor waned amid a worsening economy and scandals, and associations quickly turned into self-serving oligopolies. Then, after Hoover's presidency was discredited, perceptions of yet another major capacity gap arose, with the FDR administration putting distance between itself and associationalism and expanding the bureau-centered administrative state that would continue unimpeded through the Johnson administration's "Great Society."

Beginning in the early 1970s, however, historians began noting that the networking aspects of the associationalist model actually got marbled into the emerging administrative state during the New Deal (e.g., Barber 1985; Burner 1978; Hawley 1974). They also found that this continued under both Republican and Democratic presidents and Congresses during the remainder of the 20th century (Hart 1998). Hart, for example, argues that the "associative undercurrents of the conservative

Barber, William J. 1985. *From New Era to New Deal: Herbert Hoover, the Economists, and American Economic Policy, 1921–1933.* Cambridge, UK: Cambridge University Press.

Baumgartner, Frank R., Jeffrey M. Berry, Marie Hojnacki, David C. Kimball, and Beth L. Leach. 2009. *Lobbying and Policy Change: Who Wins, Who Loses, and Why.* Chicago: University of Chicago Press.

Brooks, David. 2004. "How to Reinvent the G.O.P." *New York Times,* August 29, A20. http://www.nytimes.com/2004/08/29/magazine/29REPUBLICANS.html?pagewanted=all.

Brown, Laura M. 2009. "Reactionary Ideologues and Uneasy Partisans: Bush and Realignment." In *Judging Bush,* ed. Robert Maranto, Tom Lansford, and Jeremy Johnson, pp. 77–95. Stanford, CA: Stanford University Press.

Burner, David. 1978. *Herbert Hoover: A Public Life.* New York: Knopf.

Carpenter, Daniel P. 2001. *The Forging of Bureaucratic Autonomy: Reputations, Networks, and Policy Innovation in Executive Agencies, 1862–1928.* Princeton, NJ: Princeton University Press.

Clemens, Elisabeth S. 2006. "Lineages of the Rube Goldberg State: Building and Blurring Public Programs, 1900–1940." In *Rethinking Political Institutions: The Art of the State,* ed. Ian Shapiro, Stephen Skowronek, and Daniel Galvin, pp. 187–215. New York: New York University Press.

Clements, Kendrick A. 2000. *Hoover, Conservation, and Consumerism: Engineering the Good Life.* Lawrence: University Press of Kansas.

Durant, Robert F. 2009. "Theory Building, Administrative Reform Movements, and the Perdurability of Herbert Hoover." *American Review of Public Administration* 39(4): 327–351.

Frederickson, H. George, and Edmund C. Stazyk. 2010. "Myths, Markets, and the *Visible Hand* of American Bureaucracy." In *The Oxford Handbook of American Bureaucracy,* ed. Robert F. Durant, pp. 349–371. Oxford, UK: Oxford University Press.

Gattuso, James. 2008. *Red Tape Rising: Regulatory Trends in the Bush Years.* The Heritage Foundation, March 25. http://www.heritage.org/research/reports/2008/03/red-tape-rising-regulatory-trends-in-the-bush-years (accessed May 13, 2010).

Gerson, Michael J. 2008. *Heroic Conservatism: Why Republicans Need to Embrace America's Ideals.* New York: HarperOne.

Hart, David M. 1998. "Herbert Hoover's Last Laugh: The Enduring Significance of the 'Associative State' in the United States" (speech presented at the annual meetings of the Society for the History of Technology, Lowell, MA, 1998, March and the Northeastern Political Science Association, Providence, RI, 1994, November). *Journal of Policy History* 10(3): 419–444.

Hawley, Ellis W. 1974. "Herbert Hoover, the Commerce Secretariat, and the Vision of an 'Associative State,' 1921–1928." *Journal of American History* 61(1): 116–140.

———. (ed.). 1981. *Herbert Hoover as Secretary of Commerce: Studies in New Era Thought and Practice.* Iowa City: University of Iowa Press.

Hill, Michael, and Peter Hupe. 2009. *Implementing Public Policy: Governance in Theory and in Practice,* 2d ed. Thousand Oaks, CA: Sage.

Hofstadter, Richard. 1989. *The American Political Tradition: And the Men Who Made It.* New York: Vintage Books.

Howe, Daniel W. 1979. *The Political Culture of the American Whigs.* Chicago: University of Chicago Press.

Kennedy, David M. 2005. *Freedom from Fear: The American People in Depression and War, 1929–1945.* Oxford, UK: Oxford University Press.

Kolko, Gabriel. 1963. *The Triumph of Conservatism: A Reinterpretation of American History, 1900–1916.* New York: Free Press.

Koppell, Jonathan G. S. 2003. *The Politics of Quasi-Government: Hybrid Organizations and the Dynamics of Bureaucratic Control.* Cambridge, UK: Cambridge University Press.

Landler, Mark, and Edmund L. Andrews. 2008. "For Treasury Dept., Now Comes Hard Part of Bailout." *New York Times,* October http://www.nytimes.com/2008/10/04/business/economy/04plan.html (accessed October 3, 2008).

Light, Paul C. 1999. *The True Size of Government.* Washington, DC: Brookings Institution Press.

Lipset, Seymour M. 1996. *American Exceptionalism: A Double-Edged Sword.* New York: Norton.

Lipton, Eric. 2008. "With Obama, Regulations Are Back in Fashion." *New York Times,* May 12. http://www.nytimes.com/2010/05/13/us/politics/13rules.html?ref=consumerproduct safetycommission.

Meacham, Jon, and Evan Thomas. 2009. "We Are All Socialists Now." *Newsweek,* February 16, pp. 23–27.

Mettler, Suzanne. 1998. *Dividing Citizens: Gender and Federalism in New Deal Public Policy.* Ithaca, NY, and London: Cornell University Press.

Morone, James A. 1990. *The Democratic Wish: Popular Participation and the Limits of American Government.* New York: Basic Books.

Mullins, Daniel R., and John L. Mikesell. 2010. "Innovations in Budgeting and Financial Management." In *The Oxford Handbook of American Bureaucracy,* ed. Robert F. Durant, pp. 738–765. Oxford, UK: Oxford University Press.

Pear, Robert. 2010. "Health Insurance Companies Try to Shape Rules." *New York Times,* May 16. http://www.nytimes.com/2010/05/16/health/policy/16health.html.

Perry, James L., Debra Mesch, and Laurie Paarlberg. 2006. "Motivating Employees in a New Governance Era: The Performance Paradigm Revisited." *Public Administration Review* 66(4): 505–514.

Polanyi, Michael. 2001 [1943]. *The Great Transformation,* 2d ed. Boston: Beacon Press.

Rosenbloom, David H. 1993. "Have an Administrative Rx? Don't Forget the Politics!" *Public Administration Review* 53(6): 503–507.

Skocpol, Theda. 1992. *Protecting Soldiers and Mothers: The Political Origins of Social Policy in the United States.* Cambridge, MA: Belknap Press.

Skowronek, Stephen. 1982. *Building a New American State: The Expansion of National Administrative Capacities, 1877–1920.* Cambridge, UK: Cambridge University Press.

Waldo, Dwight. 1984. *The Administrative State: A Study of the Political Theory of American Public Administration,* 2d ed. New York: Holmes and Meier.

Wiebe, Robert H. 1967. *The Search for Order, 1877–1920.* New York: Hill and Wang.

Wilentz, Sean. 2005. *The Rise of American Democracy: Jefferson to Lincoln.* New York: Norton.

Wood, Gordon S. 2008. *The Purpose of the Past: Reflections on the Uses of History.* New York: Penguin Press.

Part I

Challenges for a
21st-Century Government

4

Experts and the Fiscal Challenge

Strategies of Influence

F. Stevens Redburn

An understudied aspect of governance is the role of expert groups in promoting and shaping action to address tough political problems. Experts are most likely to become engaged when issues have an important technical or scientific dimension. The long-term fiscal challenge facing the United States (as well as many European countries) provides an opportunity to examine this phenomenon, describe different strategies being employed, and consider how well matched the strategies pursued by these groups are to the politics of this or similar issues.

Experts are consulted and employed by governments to provide professional advice or assistance on a wide variety of tasks requiring specialized knowledge or synthesis of research findings. However, these typically are tasks performed at the direction of government agencies as they implement policy. The activities of expert groups examined here are distinguished from government-initiated consultations by the experts' self-motivation to leverage their expertise and scientific/technical analysis to influence public policy, that is, by the experts' self-initiated attempt to influence policy outcomes and thereby take a role in governance. In these cases, expert groups have put themselves into the field with organized interests and other potential opinion leaders, many with substantial economic backing and all attempting to increase support for particular policies, either by directly influencing the actions of leaders or less directly by shaping broader public opinion. Their work typically begins with formal study, whether original or a synthesis and interpretation of others' research; and their influence relies heavily on the perceived quality, balance if not neutrality, and clarity of their scientific findings and report. However, at a later stage the groups examined here also have attempted to leverage their scholarly work to mobilize "grass tops" (local opinion elites outside the beltway) and sometimes to reach and influence even broader groups of voters. At this stage they may deploy a wide variety of standard tools of influence—including books and film, media interviews and events, and newer methods of social networking—to gain attention and support for their positions. Using the U.S. long-term fiscal challenge as its focus, this chapter will describe the primary actors and their interactions, characterize the policy space in which they operate, analyze their strategies and styles, assess their prospects, and specify criteria by which they and others can judge their success. It represents a first, very preliminary effort to analyze the determinants of their effectiveness and to assess their prospects in this case.

The Main Actors

Within the past two or three years, several groups of privately sponsored or self-organized experts have pursued a set of roughly parallel efforts to develop and communicate a better understanding of the U.S. fiscal challenge, its implications, and possible responses. The groups include the joint National Research Council/ National Academy of Public Administration Committee on the Fiscal Future of the United States, the Concord Coalition, the Committee for a Responsible Federal Budget (which also operates the Peterson-Pew Commission on Budget Reform), the Debt Reduction Task Force of the Bipartisan Policy Center, and the Taking Back the Fiscal Future project of the Brookings Institution and Heritage Foundation (sometimes referred to as the "gang of 16"). Major funders include the Peter G. Peterson Foundation, the John D. and Catherine T. MacArthur Foundation, and the Pew Charitable Trusts. The groups have overlapping memberships, generally mixing people with academic and other professional government backgrounds and people of different partisan and ideological perspectives. Their expertise is not only scientific and technical but in many instances a product of their practical experience as government officials or politicians. The groups and their funders are in close communication, although not necessarily closely coordinating. Their actions can be seen as largely complementary, but with differences in strategy, focus, tone, and substance that raise the potential for conflict.

• The Committee for a Responsible Federal Budget (CRFB 2010a) was established in 1980 by former congressmen Robert Giaimo (D-CT) and Henry Bellmon (R-OK), and incorporated in 1981. Mr. Giaimo served as chairman of the House Committee on the Budget. Mr. Bellmon was the ranking Republican on the Committee on the Budget from its inception in 1975. The two convened a group including other former Budget Committee chairmen, former directors of the Office of Management and Budget, leading economists, and businesspeople. The group concluded that the country needed an organization outside government committed to sound budget process. Since 2003 the Committee has been housed at the New America Foundation. It runs a number of ongoing projects. Its U.S. Budget Watch (CRFB 2010c), funded by Pew Charitable Trusts, has reported on important fiscal issues during and after the 2008 presidential election. With support from the Peter G. Peterson Foundation and Pew Charitable Trusts, the Committee also runs the Peterson-Pew Commission on Budget Reform. CRFB also monitors the federal government's response to the current economic crisis (CRFB 2010b). Through Stimulus.org CRFB puts out regular reports and releases on various budgetary issues and runs the Fiscal Roadmap project, created to help policymakers navigate the country's economic and fiscal challenges.

• The Concord Coalition (Concord Coalition 2010) was formed in 1992 and originally chaired by the late former U.S. senator Paul Tsongas, a Massachusetts Democrat, former senator Warren Rudman, a Republican from New Hampshire, and former U.S. secretary of commerce Peter Peterson. Former senator Bob Kerrey (D-NE) was named a co-chair of the Concord Coalition in January 2002. The Concord Coalition is dedicated to educating the public about the causes and consequences of federal budget deficits, the long-term challenges facing America's unsustainable entitlement programs, and how to build a sound economy for future generations. Its staff and volunteers have emphasized outreach to the attentive public—holding lectures and interactive exercises, conducting classes, giving media interviews, and briefing elected officials and their staffs. Some would question the extent to which its agenda is guided by experts, although few would question the budget expertise and experience of many on its board.

• The Taking Back Our Fiscal Future group (Antos et al. 2008) is an informal alliance of people across a broad ideological spectrum and affiliated with a diverse set of organizations and funding foundations. Since 2007, under the auspices of the Brookings Institution and the Heritage Foundation, it has worked to define the dimensions and consequences of the looming federal budget problem, examine alternative solutions, and reach agreement on what should be done. Despite diverse philosophies and political leanings, the group has agreed that (1) unsustainable deficits in the federal budget threaten the health and vigor of the American economy; and (2) the first step toward establishing budget responsibility is to reform the budget decision process.

• The Committee on the Fiscal Future of the United States was jointly appointed in 2008 by the National Academy of Sciences and the National Academy of Public Administration, with funding from the John D. and Catherine T. MacArthur Foundation, to produce baseline projections of the federal budget, deficit, and debt, based on its analysis of the nature and extent of the nation's long-term fiscal challenge; to develop a framework and set of guiding principles that leaders and the public could use to address the fiscal outlook, taking into account information on values, preferences, and concerns of the American public; to develop policy scenarios and estimates of the effects of selected budget options; to demonstrate what combinations of policy options would yield a sustainable federal budget; and to identify and evaluate options to improve fiscal transparency and discipline in the federal budget process. Its broadest purpose is to provide a framework for constructive public debate about the options, leading to constructive action. The Committee's study report (National Research Council and DBASSE 2010) was issued in January 2010.

• The Debt Reduction Task Force of the Bipartisan Policy Center (BPC) (Bipartisan Policy Center, 2010) was launched in January 2010, and is co-chaired by former OMB and CBO director Alice Rivlin, a Democrat, and former Republican senator Pete Domenici. BPC is a nonprofit organization that was established in 2007 by former Senate majority leaders Howard Baker, Tom Daschle, Bob Dole, and George Mitchell to develop and promote solutions that can attract public support and political momentum in order to achieve real progress. The BPC acts as an incubator for policy efforts that engage top political figures, advocates, academics, and business leaders in the art of principled compromise. This task force is just now organizing itself and defining its role and strategy.

In February 2010, President Obama established by executive order (The White House 2010) a bipartisan fiscal commission charged with developing a set of proposals to eliminate the primary deficit (the gap between revenues and spending other than for interest on the debt) by 2015. Six of its 18 members were appointed by the president, the rest in equal numbers by the Democratic and Republican leaders of the U.S. House and Senate. Fourteen members agreed in December of 2010 on a package of proposals to meet this fiscal target, but congressional leaders have yet to vote on it. Its official status should give the work of this commission prominence and potential for influence that set it apart from the privately sponsored expert groups, and therefore it should be placed in a separate category for analysis.

The Governance Challenge

The rapid buildup of government debt in the United States and many other industrial countries since 2008, combined with a large long-term gap between the cost of honoring current and future public commitments and revenue collections projected under current policies, presents these nations with a novel and profound governance challenge. That is, leaders and citizens alike must confront and address a difficult and unavoidable set of choices that will affect everyone deeply. If they cannot do so, the familiar institutions and relationships that define roles of leaders, voters, and organized groups (including those made up of various categories of experts) may be forced to change in unforeseen ways.

Recent events surrounding the Greek debt crisis of early 2010 dramatize not only the economic risks and political challenges facing individual nations, but also the challenges to established modes of international governance within the European Union and more broadly. Leaders must respond in ways that are acceptable if not pleasing to a public, deeply divided as always by interests and values, at a time when the bonds of trust between leaders and experts are frayed and political discourse is often angry and ugly. Into this fray come self-designated experts seeking to influence the outcome of the public debate. If they are successful, then perhaps the fiscal crisis can be met without profound consequences for governing institutions and the relationship between leaders and the public. If not, then either a resulting crisis or prolonged period of economic stagnation could have profound consequences for the legitimacy and operation of our governing institutions.

To understand the size of the political challenge the expert groups face and the potential role they could play, it is necessary first to examine the magnitude and character of the fiscal challenge itself. This will highlight the political difficulty of finding agreement on necessarily painful policy adjustments. The magnitude of the challenge is measured not only by the current size of publicly held government debt (e.g., U.S. federal debt is now about 65 percent of its GDP and rising rapidly) but also by the width of the "fiscal gap" between projected revenues under current law and obligations and spending commitments built into current policies projected over several decades. In other words, it is not only the size and immediate growth of the debt but the implied long-term mismatch between resources and commitments that fully measures the scale of the challenge. The embedded promises to citizens and the structure of interests and political relationships that surround and defend these make it extremely challenging to alter policies in the short run to the extent needed to close the fiscal gap. Moreover, in a nation of any size, it takes a long time to slowly turn the fiscal ship without disruption to the economy and to personal plans and circumstances.

An International Monetary Fund (IMF) report helps quantify the size of the fiscal challenge facing the United States and others (IMF 2010). IMF estimated that to lower the average country debt to the pre-crisis median of about 60 percent of GDP would require an adjustment of the cyclically adjusted primary budget balance (i.e., the deficit excluding interest on debt) of 8.7 percentage points of GDP, from a projected deficit of 4.9 percent of GDP in 2010 to a surplus of 3.8 percent of GDP in 2020 (2010, p. 28). The size of the adjustment facing the United States is similar. Whereas these adjustments would be quite large if corrective action were taken soon, with delay they will grow and become more difficult. Changes will affect a broad range of policies and interests, touching nearly everyone. And although the pain of adjustments would be felt soon, their potential benefits are long-range and uncertain.

The consequences could be avoidance of a market crisis such as Greece and other countries experienced when holders of their debt demanded greater yields or fled to safer investments; or it could take the form of a prolonged period of economic stagnation such as Japan has experienced over more than a decade following a downturn and pileup of public debt. Japan has no trouble financing its debt, which is held mostly by its own citizens, but the drag exerted on its economy has eroded its performance. Based on a range of econometric techniques, the IMF estimates that on average a 10-percentage-point increase in a nation's initial debt-to-GDP ratio is associated with a slowdown in annual real per capita GDP growth of around 0.2 percentage points per year (2010, p. 29). Carrying a larger debt requires that a larger portion of the public budget be devoted to debt service, either squeezing program spending or forcing higher revenues to compensate. This can lead to a self-reinforcing downward spiral that is difficult to reverse and escape.

A defining characteristic of the fiscal challenge is that delay is both costly and risky. Delayed action would result in higher near-term deficits, which would result in a higher debt. This higher debt, in turn, would require more interest to service it, adding further to deficits and debt. For example, if action to correct course begins in 2017 rather than 2012, the debt-to-GDP ratio will have risen to 72.1 percent by 2016, rather than 64.9 percent had remedial action begun five years earlier. The consequences of a delay of 10 years are more than twice as severe as those for a delay of 5 years, for two reasons (NRC/NAPA 2010). First, because of compound interest on the additional debt, doubling the years of delay more than doubles the addition of debt. A doubled delay to attain a sustainable debt-to-GDP ratio would thus require more than twice as large an increase in revenue, even with everything else unchanged. Second, during those 10 years the number of Social Security, Medicare, and elderly Medicaid beneficiaries would have been augmented by retirement of additional baby boomers. Thus, such a delay would put program spending on a permanently higher trajectory even when the same specific policy reforms are eventually introduced.

The consequence of delay that cannot be modeled is the heightened risk that the nation's creditors—especially, those abroad—will recognize that the United States has no credible plan to restore fiscal stability and so will demand higher interest rates on their loans or even broader economic changes. Carrying a higher debt is like sailing closer to the reef. With more of the budget thus devoted to debt service, the revenues available for programs shrink, and the options for corrective action on the spending side become still more difficult. The longer the period over which the United States carries a high debt, the greater the likelihood that an unanticipated shock—requiring emergency spending and possibly coupled with financial or economic disruption—will push the debt to a tipping point from which both economically and politically it will be difficult to recover.

The longer a nation exposes itself in this way, the more likely an adverse economic gust or current will push it onto the rocks. The United States occupies a unique position because of the size and vitality of its economy and because it finances its borrowing in its own currency. Investor anxieties about other economies' problems have, if anything, caused them to seek safety in U.S. treasuries, sending a possibly false signal that there is no concern about the ability of the United States to manage its fiscal affairs. But markets will not wait indefinitely for the United States to address its fiscal challenge. U.S. bond spreads widened in 2008 and 2010 and could do so again quickly if there is no policy agreement to change fiscal course or if a common belief arises that no such agreement is possible. The uncertainty and potential swiftness of market reaction to the absence of action, or to a plan to address the fiscal challenge, is a source of great uncertainty, as well as a wild card politically that complicates the political challenge for leaders and experts seeking to influence the course of public debate.

There are two possible ways to err in the face of such uncertainties and the implications of delay. One kind of error—overreacting—is readily reversible; the other—underreacting—may not be. That is, the risks of error in dealing with the fiscal challenge are asymmetric. Some observers believe that the political risks of tough choices needed to correct the fiscal course and stabilize the publicly held U.S. debt are so high that only an economic crisis will compel leaders to change course. And history suggests that political leaders rarely step forward to lead such an effort as long as there are no obvious and compelling short-term economic or political consequences of current policies.

If the expert groups' analysis is correct, then remedial action is needed soon if not immediately, and therefore today's voters must be convinced to make sacrifices in current consumption and to accept reductions in promised government benefits—to reduce the probability of a future crisis and to improve the living standards of the next and future generations. The pain of cutting spending, increasing taxes, or both, is immediate, whereas the gain of avoiding a fiscal train wreck—and its devastating consequences—is in the future. Because all fiscal projections are inherently uncertain, the long-term benefit that will result from the short-term pain cannot be precisely specified. A rough analog may be the political challenge of addressing climate change, another problem with a long fuse, surrounded by uncertainty, and requiring painful near-term actions. Although climate change could precipitate an eventual environmental crisis, the fiscal challenge seems to hold even greater potential for sudden instability because of the forward-looking assessments made by financial markets. This could mean that disruption of normal governance and options for orderly adjustments arrive in the very near future and with little warning, but there is no way of knowing. Even more than remedial action to limit global warming, addressing the fiscal challenge will affect virtually every part of the budget and therefore every economic interest.

Given the magnitude of the fiscal challenge facing the nation and the costs of delay in meeting it, action would seem to be urgent. Yet the uncertainties, the difficulty of the choices required, the nature of the U.S. political system, the record of most recent efforts to address the nation's fiscal health, and continuing pressures for higher spending and lower taxes all suggest that early and decisive action will be difficult. Even if everyone becomes convinced soon of an urgent need to act, differences in values and perceptions of what government should do and how to pay for it will constrain and delay possible agreement on what to do. Policy disagreements will be intensified by the need to limit what government will be able to do in the future.

Expert Group Politics

In their attempts to address the long-term fiscal challenge, the groups previously listed (as well as many individual scholars and teams affiliated with think tanks and academic institutions) share a common policy space that has become increasingly crowded, especially within the last five years. Several prominent scholars, former budget office heads, and former elected congressional leaders with budget expertise have participated in more than one group's efforts. Not surprisingly—given overlapping memberships, a shared body of experience, and frequent interaction— they share a common perspective on the nature and causes of the long-term fiscal challenge and, less completely, on possible political strategies to address it.

There is much less agreement across or within the groups on what specific policy changes—such as tax increases or reductions in spending for particular programs or functions—are desirable to stabilize the fiscal outlook. This is not surprising given differences in ideology and partisanship within and across the groups. To some extent this divergence also reflects substantive disagreements about policy priorities and the urgency of action.

The role of expert groups has been explored in other policy domains. In a classic work, Walter Lippmann stressed the role of insiders and experts in guiding and shaping the public debate, including their role in helping prepare a distracted public to deal with major national challenges (Lippmann 1927). He feared the bewildering complexity of the modern world combined with the electoral potential of mass publics, largely uninformed and intellectually unsophisticated. He saw a possible role for technical experts and other insiders to check and guide the less-engaged mass of voters. More recently, some have stressed the limits of expert influence on policy outcomes, while others believe experts can under some conditions and for some policy problems contribute in ways that other influential actors cannot, especially where neutral analysis is vital either to building public and leadership understanding of the problem and available policy options or to informing wise choices (Posner 2006; Weiss 1979). As Posner notes, it has been hypothesized that expert views are more likely to be used when there is a research consensus, interest group opposition is weak or absent, and expert judgments are widely discussed and debated over an extended period (Rich 2004).

Posner puts particular emphasis on the contribution of experts in helping leaders address policy challenges early on, before they become hard-to-manage crises. This "policy foresight" function seems particularly applicable to the U.S. fiscal challenge as characterized by the expert groups looking at it now. Their contribution can be measured in part by the degree to which the problem has gained saliency with the public and led to public, media, and leadership attention. These intermediate effects, while not sufficient to achieve remedial action, are probably prerequisites to it.

Given the characteristics of the fiscal challenge and the political context in which it will be addressed, can experts help leaders and voters come to grips with it? Both self-nominated experts and funders of expert study groups have thought so. As noted above, funded studies and related outreach efforts on the fiscal challenge have recently multiplied. The different groups and their funders have taken different, but potentially complementary, approaches.

The approaches taken by different study groups and funders differ somewhat in their (1) strategies to achieve policy change; (2) communications targets; and (3) communications methods. Strategies may be implicit or ill defined. They encompass differences in the way the problem is framed and in the methods of attempting to influence the actions of political leaders.

The initial near-term aim of the groups examined was to raise the saliency of this set of issues, which had previously peaked with the candidacy of H. Ross Perot in 1992. The saliency of the federal budget deficit and debt is now high, with 74 percent of the public saying in January 2010 that "the federal budget deficit" is either "extremely" or "very important" to them personally (AP/Gfk survey, cited in Public Agenda 2010). The Pew Center survey that month found 60 percent saying that "reducing the budget deficit" should be a "top priority" of the president and Congress, an increase of 7 percentage points in the past year and 25 percentage points in the past six years (Public Agenda 2010).

Apart from efforts by the groups themselves, the economic and financial crisis, by ballooning deficits and raising debt rapidly, has raised the saliency and perceived urgency of the fiscal challenge. In 2010, most of the expert groups examined here seemed to be shifting or had shifted their emphasis from raising awareness of the long-term fiscal challenge and its potential consequences to advocating for early policy changes—including reforms of the budget process to facilitate and sustain those changes—to put the federal government on a sustainable fiscal path.

Expert groups can contribute at the next stage by, as the NRC/NAPA committee explicitly attempted to do, *framing* the problem in terms that foster constructive debate and give leaders more potential political support for proposed corrective policies. The framing of public debate about policy questions is an art that has emerged in recent decades from cognitive psychology (Chong and Druckman 2007; Entman 1993), has been deployed on behalf of parties and interest groups, and more recently has been practiced by consulting firms interested in broader reshaping of public debate, citizenship, and democratic dialogue between citizens and leaders. These groups are addressing the limits and distortions typical of most public issues debates, seek to improve the quality of debate, and aim to transcend the limitations of standard methods of registering public opinion. This places them therefore at the leading edge of efforts to deepen and modernize the U.S. democratic process (cf. Barber 1984; Redburn and Buss 2006). Leading practitioners of the art of public engagement include Public Agenda (through its Center for Advances in Public Engagement), America Speaks, the Kettering Foundation, and the FrameWorks Institute. Most of these have received foundation support for projects that either study how framing of the fiscal challenge affects public attitudes and responses or structure active engagements with groups of U.S. citizens and/or leaders on the fiscal problem and choices to address it. Given the enormous political difficulty of forging policy agreement sufficient to put the U.S. budget on a sustainable course in a highly polarized and intensely partisan political environment, the contribution of self-conscious efforts to framing and structuring of the debate may prove crucial to the outcome.

Strategy choices at least loosely imply choices of who to target with communications and what communications tools to employ. The communications targets and means pursued by the study groups and commissions, their funders, and public engagement consultants concerned with the fiscal challenge seem to be targeted at segments of the public with different levels of political engagement or different roles in governance, ranging from grassroots to "grass tops" to national elected officials. Communications strategies are highly varied, and may or may not be matched to either the change strategy or the communication target. Of the groups examined here, the Concord Coalition—which has led the "fiscal wake-up tour" of budget experts from Brookings, Heritage, and other institutions—is the most explicitly interested in shaping broader public opinion, and many of its public activities are aimed at audiences outside Washington and attracting media coverage of "town hall" style events that can attract a cross-section of the public. Activities of the Committee for a Responsible Federal Budget and the Taking Back the Fiscal Future Group are aimed largely at a Washington-based leadership audience and national media, although the former has deployed a range of social networking techniques to reach a broader segment of the public. Following on and leveraging the NRC/NAPA study, the MacArthur Foundation has initiated a set of new projects aimed at both opinion leaders and a broader interested group of voters. From the outset, their sponsorship of the NRC/NAPA study was explicitly aimed at framing and fostering an informed public debate about ways to address the fiscal challenge; this orientation led the funders to explicitly charge the study committee with developing a range of policy options and stabilizing long-term budget scenarios *without* recommending a particular path to stability. At a later stage, MacArthur worked with public opinion experts to define a multifaceted influence strategy as a basis for selecting its follow-on projects.

In addition to raising the saliency of the fiscal challenge and helping to frame the issue for constructive discussion, the set of expert groups examined here are explicitly interested in early action to turn the fiscal ship from what they all see as an unsustainable and increasingly dangerous course. And two of the expert panels, joined by others, have recommended the formal adoption of a medium-term fiscal goal to stabilize the federal government's publicly held debt within a few years at a specified percentage of U.S. GDP (NRC/NAPA 2010; Peterson-Pew 2009).

As they move beyond efforts to raise the saliency of the fiscal challenge and to frame the issue, what strategies might the groups pursue with a plausible expectation of success, and what strategies of influence do their statements and actions imply? At this stage, success requires the groups to communicate a more complex message that includes the importance of early action, the magnitude of required changes, and the consequences of failing to take bold steps soon. To decide whether to support painful remedial action, leaders and voters also need at least a broad understanding of the range of policy choices available to them. For the expert groups, success at this stage therefore will require communicating messages that demand more prior knowledge or additional education regarding details of the federal budget, the constraints and available choices, and how the budget interacts with the economy.

One plausible influence strategy at this stage might be to create more political space or freedom of action for leaders by continuing to help spread understanding of the issue and choices among a broad group of activists and informed voters. This targeting of "grass tops" would be an extension of the groups' prior efforts and would be based on the same claims to expert judgment and analysis as the groups' initial efforts to raise and frame the issue. Its messages could be communicated through the same channels, including media and online social networks of attentive segments of the public, who could in turn influence the less attentive. The goal at this stage would be to increase the public's tolerance for proposals that might impose new costs or reduce promised benefits based on recognition that the alternative of staying the course could result in even greater future losses for them and others. Seeing evidence of increased tolerance among voters for such actions, leaders might be prepared to act.

A second strategy the expert groups and their funders could pursue would be to even more directly address the legitimate fears of leaders that advocating the kinds of policies necessary to close the fiscal gap could amount to electoral suicide. One way to do this is with formal structured forums conducted with representative groups of voters. These would be designed to show that, with proper framing and information, people with a diversity of ideologies and interests can over time develop a sophisticated understanding of the fiscal challenge and, working with the problem, the choices, and each other, find themselves in agreement on at least some significant elements of required policy change. One of several initiatives funded by the MacArthur Foundation following release of the NRC/NAPA study is organizing a national discussion to find common ground on tough choices about our federal budget. Americans from across the country will be brought together to weigh in on strategies to ensure a sustainable fiscal future and a strong economic recovery. As a part of this national discussion, on June 26, 2010, thousands of Americans participated simultaneously in a National Town Meeting (AmericaSpeaks 2010). A general model for such policy forums is presented in Redburn and Buss (2006, pp. 42–43). A formal demonstration showing how to safely and constructively approach the fiscal challenge with voters might give leaders both the confidence and the template they need to use in developing public agreement on difficult choices.

A third strategy that the groups might pursue is to reach over the heads of leaders and the media to the mass of voters with a message that it is in their interest to accept the required painful changes and to trust and reward leaders who step forward to advocate for these changes. Mounting this kind of public campaign strategy would require new skills on the part of expert groups, and certainly require a much higher level of resources than the first two strategies. It is expensive because of the costs of production of film or similar media, advertising, books and popular articles, or postings that can command wide viewing and communicate complex messages to a wide and often inattentive audience. It is expensive also because the volume of competing messages and information is so great that any message, especially one of this nature, can easily be drowned out. This third strategy may be the riskiest strategy as well because it places experts in settings where their messages are more vulnerable to distortion, highjacking, or attack by others with competing or conflicting political goals. If it were successful, a mass communications campaign would swing public opinion toward the need for early, painful actions to stabilize the debt, and seeing this swing, leaders would follow.

The strategies being pursued at this stage by the expert groups and their funders do not conform neatly to any one of the three models previously outlined. They contain elements of all three, in varying degrees. For example, the Committee for a Responsible Federal Budget is talking regularly to elected leaders and communicating its message to the most attentive part of the public through a variety of online media. Its members regularly appear, often alongside members of one or more of the other groups, in televised panels or other widely watched forums discussing the challenge and possible remedial action. And it has developed a budget simulation that can be used either by individuals or in representative town-hall-style events to develop, test, and explore policy alternatives. This "mixed" strategy may reflect a conscious judgment to pursue a variety of channels and targets of influence, perhaps experimentally to see which will be most successful, or it may reflect a degree of uncertainty about the best way for expert groups to move leaders to an early decision to lead in the direction they believe the situation demands.

The groups' individual or collective success at the next stage will require not only greater awareness and a proper framing of the fiscal problem but also their ability to increase the willingness of both leaders and voters to consider painful choices needed to stabilize the debt. Early action to this end will require of elected leaders both a willingness and an ability to shape agreements that by their nature will involve difficult trade-offs and sacrifices across a broad range of policies and interests. The economic downturn of 2008–2009 may have both dampened the immediate prospects of gaining action on the fiscal challenge and at the same time reduced the amount of time remaining for developing and adopting plans to deal with it. By rapidly expanding the federal government's deficits and debt, it has raised new doubts about the budget's sustainability and by the same process increased the difficulty of the choices required to stabilize the budget. This, in turn, has sharpened the required trade-offs and may have further polarized debates on many issues. Even prior to the downturn, many leaders of the two major parties had taken firm positions against one or more likely components of a potential policy agreement—on one side refusing to consider tax increases and on the other rejecting proposals that would significantly slow the growth of spending for health and pensions. And as if these obstacles to agreement were not enough, the proportion of the public willing to trust government and its elected leaders is at a low point, further reducing leaders' freedom of action. Thus, it is hard to exaggerate the political difficulty and dangers facing politicians prepared to take on this challenge. They are properly fearful of the personal political risks of leading in this direction, even when or if they grasp the problem's full implications. This is the context in which the expert groups and funders seeking early, bold actions to stabilize and reduce the federal debt must devise strategies to foster this result.

Criteria for Judging Success

As noted earlier, in the near term, the groups' success can be measured by their success in (1) helping raise the salience and understanding of the fiscal challenge, and (2) framing the issue in terms that foster support for constructive debate and remedial action. At the next stage, measures of success will include whether leaders and key elements of the public adopt the groups' views of the seriousness of the fiscal challenge, the urgency of major policy changes, and the need to forge proposals that can find broad support in a polarized, highly partisan political environment.

Most of the groups discussed here have endorsed a broad policy goal of stabilizing the publicly held federal debt within a few years at a specified percentage of GDP (and some prefer to state the goal in terms of reduced annual deficits). Their proposals differ in specifying either the ratio or the year when it would be achieved. These differences, while they may seem small arithmetically, would require quite different magnitudes of short-term policy adjustment, reflecting different views about the dangers of waiting too long to adjust and the importance of reducing debt relative to preserving current patterns of spending and revenues. An expert consensus on the level of debt considered prudent and how quickly that level should be reached would multiply the groups' joint influence, but despite its possible importance as a guide to fiscal policy, agreement on such a target may prove elusive. If in the interest of preserving their unity on other questions the groups choose to blur their differences on the degree of fiscal discipline required now, they will have passed up an opportunity to shape the actions of leaders on what may prove to be the pivotal policy decision facing them in the next year or two.

Given the experts own lack of consensus on the set of policies to be adopted—including limits on the growth of major entitlements for health care and Social Security, new revenues and possibly tax reform, and reductions in other spending—it may be unfair to judge the influence of expert groups by whether public support is increased for such dramatic changes. Moreover, building on some initial success in raising and framing the fiscal challenge probably depends on whether the groups can maintain a bipartisan and ideologically broad position in favor of early remedial action without endorsing a specific set of remedial policies.

A pessimist might say that in a polarized political environment where many see every policy problem as an opportunity to fashion a new weapon with which to beat their opponents, and few organized interests have enthusiasm for fiscal discipline if applied to themselves, the limits of expert groups' influence may have been reached. However, one area of potential policy agreement, and one that may even be a prerequisite for more substantive agreement, is reform of the federal budget process. Most of the expert groups have identified reform of the budget process as essential to adoption of and disciplined adherence to the difficult policy path needed to first stabilize the debt in the medium term and then align spending and revenues over coming decades. So, adoption of significant budget reforms will be another near-term indicator by which to judge the groups' success in advancing their common agenda.

Finally, the ultimate test of the groups' success will be whether, partly as a result of their efforts, the federal budget is placed on a sustainable course, and whether this is accomplished before or following a highly disruptive fiscal and financial crisis and without prolonged damage to prospects for economic growth.

Analysis and Propositions for Further Study

Indirect evidence indicates that the combined efforts of the expert groups have helped highlight the nature and seriousness of the fiscal challenge. As noted earlier, the latest public opinion research suggests that the groups may have contributed to raising the saliency of the fiscal challenge. It is impossible from this evidence alone to isolate the influence of the expert groups on issue salience, but they have certainly contributed to the volume and visibility of analysis and media attention.

In part, the groups' analysis of the fiscal problem merely elaborates and reinforces what leaders and official government agencies are saying at the same time about the long-term fiscal outlook. Their contribution may in part be to help validate official views by identifying them with panels composed of people with expert reputations and a claim to being either neutral or bipartisan. However, as a price for embracing people of different parties and diverse ideology, they are also limited in what they can agree on. Therefore, their influence is likely to be greatest in identifying the importance and nature of the fiscal challenge, but much less on when and whether to address it, still less on how to address it.

The next ambition of the expert groups is to help convince leaders that it is both economically necessary and politically safe to act. Some would argue that the expert stream of policy influence will have diminished importance at this and subsequent stages of the policy process (cf. Kingdon 1984). To succeed, the groups' work and its publicity and use must help convince leaders and voters to act in a timely way to change direction. Beyond this, the experts hope to convince leaders to enact and adhere to a medium-term fiscal goal and perhaps to adopt disciplining process reforms to help them reach and maintain a stable, long-term relationship between spending and revenues. If they cannot agree among themselves on even these broad policies, they will not likely contribute to broader agreements among leaders or voters on how to address the fiscal challenge.

Any endorsement of more specific policies immediately opens the groups to accusations that their efforts are a smokescreen for attacks on specific programs or policy objectives. For example, several groups have highlighted the rapid growth of spending on the large federal entitlements for pensions and health—Social Security, Medicare, and Medicaid—as major drivers of the long-term imbalance between spending and revenues. Defenders of these programs have now formed their own campaign, charging one foundation funder of fiscal challenge study groups with waging a propaganda campaign and "fanning the flames of deficit hysteria" (see, e.g., Hickey 2010).

This and similar reactions suggest that the role of expert groups in contributing to a solution to the fiscal challenge is limited, and may be approaching an end. Moreover, the same credentials that experts bring to policy debates make their efforts vulnerable to assault by people with other interests. Many are suspicious of experts and scholarship. Just how these suspicions can be used to quickly delegitimize scientific and technical sources was illustrated in recent months by the controversy surrounding published scientific assertions about the effects of carbon emissions on climate. A latent distrust of scientific expertise, combined with concern about the short-term costs of addressing the problem, has helped drive down U.S. public support for "dealing with global warning" as one of the top priorities of the president and Congress; it is now placed in this category by just 28 percent of the public, a drop of 10 percentage points in three years (Peterson-Pew Commission 2009; Public Agenda 2010). A strain of anti-intellectualism, which may be stronger in the United States than in many European countries, contributes to the vulnerability of scientific claims advanced by scholars and experts to assertions or evidence that they have been manipulated for nonscientific reasons.

This analysis leads to the following propositions about the potential role of expert groups in achieving their common goal of fostering broad support for early, major changes in the federal budget to put it on a sustainable course:

1. The influence of expert groups will be greatest in raising the salience of the problem and fostering public support for making it a high priority.
2. The influence of expert groups in increasing public support or leadership attention to the problem is limited by their own diversity of views and lack of agreement on solutions.
3. The influence of expert groups is further limited by their vulnerability to claims of manipulation, heightened by widely held suspicions of technical experts.
4. The influence of expert groups at the stage of developing policy responses may be primarily through their ability, if any, to mobilize other groups with more resources and with direct economic interest in the outcome to enter the fray with their own solutions.

The success of the expert groups at the next stage will depend in part on whether they choose a strategy that will influence leaders to take the required actions, either by talking to them directly or by campaigning to build broader public understanding and support, or can demonstrate to leaders how they can themselves talk to the public about the issue in ways that are both safe for them and constructive in shaping broad public acceptance for the required painful adjustments. In the current U.S. political environment, it is unclear that any such strategy can succeed. However, the consequences of a collective failure to stabilize the U.S. government's finances would represent a failure of governance and political will that could have profound consequences hard both to imagine and to contemplate.

The potential role of expert groups in helping shape public and leadership understanding and response is a source of hope and may prove critical to the outcome. If these groups are successful in shaping a constructive debate and wise choices, they may validate Lippmann's expectation and hope that this small slice of the public can play an important role in moderating and guiding a broader public opinion. In the process, not only would they help put the nation on a sustainable fiscal course, but would also help mend the frayed relationships between government and the governed.

Author's Note

An earlier version of this chapter was presented at the Sixth Transatlantic Dialogue, "Rethinking Financial Management in the Public Sector," University of Siena, Siena, Italy, June 24–26, 2010. The author thanks Paul Posner, Alan Balutis, Terry Buss, and other readers for their comments. The views expressed are the author's alone.

References

AmericaSpeaks. 2010. "AmericaSpeaks: Our Budget, Our Economy Highlights." http://usabudgetdiscussion.org/.
Antos, Joseph, et al. 2008. "Taking Back Our Fiscal Future." The Brookings Institution and the Heritage Foundation, April. http://www.brookings.edu/~/media/Files/rc/papers/2008/04_fiscal_future/04_fiscal_future.pdf.
Barber, B. 1984. *Strong Democracy, Participatory Politics for a New Age.* Berkeley: University of California Press.
Bipartisan Policy Center. 2010. "Bipartisan Policy Center Domenici-Rivlin Task Force Begins Exploring Solutions to Debt Crisis." Press release, February 26. http://www.bipartisanpolicy.org/news/press-releases/2010/02/bipartisan-policy-center-domenici-rivlin-task-force-begins-exploring-sol.
Chong, D., and Druckman, J. N. 2007. "Framing Theory." *Annual Review of Political Science* 10: 103–126.
Committee for a Responsible Federal Budget (CRFB). 2010a. http://crfb.org/.
———. 2010b. Stimulus.org. http://stimulus.org/.
———. 2010c. "U.S. Budget Watch." http://usbudgetwatch.org/.
The Concord Coalition. 2010. http://www.concordcoalition.org/.
Entman, R. M. 1993. "Framing: Toward Clarification of a Fractured Paradigm." *Journal of Communication* 43(4): 51–58.
Hickey, Roger. 2010. "URGENT: Stop CNN from Airing Deficit Propoganda." Campaign for America's Future, April 9. http://www.ourfuture.org/blog-entry/2010041409/urgent-stop-cnn-airing-deficit-propaganda.
International Monetary Fund (IMF). 2010. "Navigating the Fiscal Challenges Ahead." *Fiscal Monitor,* May 14.
Kingdon, J. W. 1984. *Bridging Research and Policy: Agendas, Alternatives, and Public Policies.* New York: HarperCollins. (Second edition published in 1995.)
Lippmann, W. 1927. *The Phantom Public.* New York: The Macmillan Company.
National Research Council and Behavioral and Social Sciences Education Database (DBASSE). 2010. *Choosing the Nation's Fiscal Future.* Washington, DC: National Academies Press. http://www.nap.edu/catalog.php?record_id=12808.
Peterson-Pew Commission on Budget Reform. 2009. *Red Ink Rising: A Call to Action to Stem the Mounting Federal Debt.* Washington, DC: Peterson-Pew Commission on Budget Reform.
Posner, P. 2006. Policy experts in the policy process: Reclaiming a vital role. Paper prepared for delivery at the annual meeting of the Midwest Political Science Association, Chicago, April 20.
Public Agenda. 2010, February. "Summing Up Public Opinion on Federal Debt and Deficits." New York: Public Agenda.

Redburn, F. S., and Terry F. Buss. 2006. "Expanding and Deepening Citizen Participation: A Policy Agenda." In *Modernizing Democracy,* ed. Terry F. Buss and F. S. Redburn, pp. 29–48. Armonk, NY: M.E. Sharpe.

Rich, A. 2004. *Think Tanks, Public Policy, and the Politics of Expertise.* New York: Cambridge University Press.

Weiss, Carol. 1979. "The Many Meanings of Research Utilization." *Public Administration Review* 5: 426–431.

The White House, Office of the Press Secretary. 2010. "Executive Order—National Commission on Fiscal Responsibility and Reform." Press release, February 18. http://www.whitehouse.gov/the-press-office/executive-order-national-commission-fiscal-responsibility-and-reform.

5

Improving Collaboration by Federal Agencies

Thomas H. Stanton

Collaboration among government agencies and across networks is essential for government to be effective. Katrina and the recent BP oil spill are two major examples of problems that exceed the capacity or jurisdiction of any single organization. In one realm of government after another, such as national security, homeland security, public health, and delivery of government benefits, organizations must collaborate with others to meet their responsibilities. As organizational development expert Michael Maccoby (2007) contends, transformation of government bureaucracies into collaborative organizations is imperative if government is to keep pace with developments in the private sector.

Technology makes collaboration easier than ever before. The electronic delivery of Food Stamp benefits—requiring collaboration among multiple federal and state agencies and for-profit and nonprofit private organizations—is a good example of interorganizational collaboration that became possible only because of improved technology (Stanton 2006).

While technology made that electronic system feasible at reasonable cost, organizational culture also likely played an important role. Collaboration between the Food and Nutrition Service (FNS) of the U.S. Department of Agriculture, which administers Food Stamps, and the Department of Health and Human Services, which administered the former AFDC (Aid to Families with Dependent Children) welfare program, had been necessary since the inception of the Food Stamp program, since AFDC eligibility conferred automatic Food Stamp eligibility. Also, states provided the delivery of food stamps to beneficiaries. That history of necessary collaboration facilitated a culture that made FNS particularly open to participating with other stakeholders to move Food Stamps to an electronic delivery system.

While collaboration with other organizations has become both more necessary and easier, organizational resistance to collaboration remains a major problem. It is time now to change the cultures of federal organizations to embrace greater collaboration and to facilitate the rise of collaborative leaders and managers to positions of authority.

The Office of Management and Budget (OMB) will be critical for the success of a new administration in this effort. To promote a culture of collaboration by federal agencies, OMB should expand the application of available tools, such as interagency councils and agency performance rating systems, to increase incentives of federal managers to collaborate with those outside of their agencies' boundaries. Individual departments and agencies should adopt such rating systems as part of their department- or agency-wide strategic and performance plans and should incorporate such ratings into the performance evaluations of senior executives and other managers. OMB will need to exercise its leadership systematically over many years so that federal agencies internalize collaboration into their organizational values and cultures.

The Need to Solve Problems Beyond Organizational Boundaries

In many areas of governmental endeavor, the number of actors needed to achieve effective results has always been large. Federal highway programs, delivery of housing benefits, federal loan guarantee programs, and delivery of Medicare and Medicaid benefits are examples.

In recent years the context in which government programs operate has become even more complicated. While agencies have long operated through third parties, as Lester Salamon (1981) pointed out in his seminal article many years ago, staffing and budget constraints and pressures for outsourcing have increased this dependence. Constantly evolving technologies produce multiple effects, including forcing an unbundling of previously combined goods and services, and recombining them in new ways. Technology also creates new opportunities for joint delivery of services, such as common portals or data systems that support multiple programs. More problems than ever before have acquired global dimensions that require cooperation across international boundaries.

Policymakers increasingly take a government-wide view of the goods and services that agencies should provide. The Debt Collection Improvement Act of 1996, for example, requires federal agencies to cooperate to assure that federal debts are repaid and that people and businesses with defaulted federal debts do not receive tax refunds, new federal loans, or other federal benefits. Federal agencies must be more nimble than ever before; problems that they attack may involve more and different actors.

Examples abound of the need for improved collaboration across organizational boundaries. The delivery of emergency benefits to disaster victims should be possible electronically once applicant eligibility and availability of funds have been determined; however, except for Food Stamps and various state benefit programs, the country still lacks an interoperable national system for delivering most benefits. Creating interoperable systems for program delivery is a major category where collaboration can create a result that is superior to each agency or private organization trying to go it alone (Stanton 2007).

Until recently, the Federal Housing Administration (FHA) lost market share to the private sector, in part because of its lack of technology systems to facilitate more effective underwriting, risk management, and loan processing. With enactment of legislation expanding the role of FHA in the current troubled housing market, this shortcoming will become even more significant. Collaboration between FHA and Ginnie Mae, the government corporation responsible for providing a secondary marker for FHA loans, could help to replicate private sector advances in underwriting and processing mortgage loans electronically. Enhanced collaboration among the major federal housing program agencies also would lead to improved financial risk management.

Collaboration in the Federal Agency Context

It is useful to distinguish *coordination* from *collaboration* of multiple organizations. Interagency coordination might be defined as a specific form of collaboration that applies to particular cases or operations. By contrast to collaboration, when multiple agencies may perceive mutual benefit in working together, coordination often is more of a top-down exercise. It takes place when a leader with authority over multiple organizations directs them to collaborate to achieve a specified joint purpose. The effort to induce federal intelligence agencies to share information with one another and with state and local governments is an example of attempted coordination. As Seidman (2004) points out, coordination is not easy to achieve, despite its importance. Indeed, it is quite difficult to persuade intelligence agencies even to share information, much less to coordinate joint action, with other organizations.

With the Government Accountability Office (U.S. GAO), this chapter accepts Eugene Bardach's definition of collaboration as "any joint activity by two or more organizations that is intended to produce more public value than could be produced when the organizations act alone" (Bardach 1998, p. 8). Whereas this chapter recommends the application of top-down authority to help create incentives for collaboration, agencies often can select the areas where they expect to produce the greatest benefits. This contrasts with coordination, where the top-down exercise specifies the area where coordination must occur. It can be seen that the concepts of coordination and collaboration can overlap in some significant applications.

One example of the difference between coordination and collaboration, as the terms are used here, is the evolution of the President's Management Council (PMC), an OMB-led council composed of the second ranking official at each executive department and some major agencies. In the 1990s, the council was a major source of collaborative efforts. Top political appointees, generally responsible for managing their departments or agencies, would exchange information and work together to solve common problems. As former OMB official Margaret Yao (2000) has written, the PMC successfully adopted a "member-owned, member-operated" culture. This contrasts with the top-down approach to coordination, rather than collaboration, which is usually the practice in the current administration. Thus, the PMC was responsible for implementation of PMA during the Bush administration.

The lack of emphasis on collaboration is explained in good part, says one former OMB official, by the fact that the PMA mostly addresses chronic, internal administrative management issues, such as accounting systems, workforce planning, and so forth. Thus, there is little call for collaboration in these areas and considerable room for an OMB-led agenda because most efforts require new systems and additional resources.

By contrast, collaboration is a cooperative effort by multiple organizations to work together to achieve a common objective. As Seidman (2004, p. x) points out, "Agencies are most likely to be willing to collaborate and network when they are agreed on common objectives, operate under the same laws and regulations, and do not compete for scarce resources." Collaboration is the subject of this chapter. An example of collaboration would be the development of interoperable standards that allow organizations to pool their activities to achieve common goals. Federal and state agencies, nonprofits, and private organizations developed interoperable standards, governing critical factors such as card format and content, to permit the electronic delivery of food stamps.

Another good example is the PMC's development in 2000 of FirstGov.gov, a common portal (see www.FirstGov.gov) that users of multiple government programs can access to obtain information through use of an effective search engine. "The PMC recognized the need to think differently about the opportunities afforded by technology and wanted to make government services and transactions available, not by the traditional stove-piped agency or department, but by need—in a fast, reliable way" (Yao 2000, 1).

As Dwight Ink has written, the recovery effort for the Alaska earthquake of 1964 provides a striking contrast to the slow and disjointed post-Katrina recovery effort some 40 years later. The Alaska recovery relied on leadership rather than special legal or procedural devices. The use of collaborative councils, which themselves had no independent authority but were charged with facilitating collaborative solutions, contributed to the quick decision making and rapid actions that characterized the recovery (Ink 2006).

The Department of Housing and Urban Development (HUD) has built a small and effective collaborative system called CAIVRS, the Credit Alert Interactive Voice Response System. CAIVRS provides a model of interorganizational collaboration with potential application to other parts of government such as homeland security watch lists. HUD developed CAIVRS in the 1980s as a database that FHA lenders could check to determine whether a borrower had defaulted on a previous FHA loan. The FHA lender would enter basic identifying information and receive notification that there either was or was not a match with the HUD database of defaulted borrowers. In the early 1990s, working under the auspices of the Federal Credit Policy Working Group, an interagency council chaired by the OMB Deputy Director for Management, HUD expanded CAIVRS to permit other agencies to report delinquent nontax debt and, ultimately, to access CAIVRS to assure that they were not extending credit to defaulted debtors from other programs. This interagency collaboration is essential to assure that defaulted debtors from one federal program do not receive funding from a different federal agency without settling their outstanding debts first. HUD reports that CAIVRS has helped HUD and other agencies to avoid billions of dollars in potential losses on loans to defaulted borrowers who sought to obtain new federal credit.

In improving collaboration among federal agencies and with other organizations, the accountability of any new arrangements must be considered. Interorganizational collaboration must be done without weakening or blurring the accountability of government agencies to spend public resources wisely to carry out their missions. Problems created by increased interagency collaboration in undertaking federal procurement, which the U.S. GAO has placed on its high-risk list, stand as warnings in this regard. Whereas the idea of developing specialized procurement centers to serve multiple agencies is attractive in the abstract, the contracting agencies too often failed to maintain proper accountability of the contractors that they hired this way.

Laws to Mandate Improved Collaboration

Some legislation has successfully mandated interorganizational collaboration. The Goldwater-Nichols Department of Defense Reorganization Act of 1986 transformed the Joint Chiefs of Staff (JCS) from a weak coordinating body into a source of influence that could promote serious interservice cooperation. The act accomplished this by (1) increasing the JCS chairman's authority, (2) improving JCS staff quality by requiring joint service for promotion to flag or general officer rank, and (3) granting unified and specified combatant commanders (CINCs) increased autonomy and authority over their joint field commands. Observers attribute a significant increase in United States military capabilities, from combined service operations in the Persian Gulf War to the 1986 Goldwater-Nichols Act and the reform of the JCS (Zegart 1999).

Pursuant to the mandate of Section 1011 of the Intelligence Reform and Terrorism Prevention Act of 2004, the Director of National Intelligence, who is responsible for promoting cooperation among Intelligence Community (IC) agencies, adopted the personnel mobility requirements of the JCS. In June 2007, the Office of the Director of National Intelligence (ODNI) announced that ODNI would implement the Intelligence Community's Civilian Joint Duty Program (ODNI 2007, p. 1):

> Joint IC duty is a civilian personnel rotation system similar to joint duty in the military. The implementing instructions require joint duty as a prerequisite for promotion to senior civilian rank in order to encourage and facilitate assignments and details of personnel to national intelligence centers, and between elements of the IC.

The theory of increased mobility is that it both fosters an understanding of the perspectives of other organizations and also creates the interpersonal relationships that can facilitate more effective collaboration.

Although both the 2004 Act and the Goldwater-Nichols Act were difficult to enact, such legislation can greatly improve collaboration across organizational boundaries. Another type of legislation that may promote collaboration across agencies is a law that permits or mandates pooling of budget resources. The U.S. GAO notes one such example, where a 2002 law required the Departments of Defense (DoD) and Veterans Affairs (VA) to make a minimum contribution of $15 million annually for four years to fund a joint program to share health resources. That effort continues, but the process of conforming DoD and VA health systems so that soldiers can make a seamless transition from one system to the other continues to progress only slowly. A more comprehensive legislative approach is the establishment of a Joint Planning and Development Office to coordinate and plan for a transition from today's air traffic control system to a next-generation air transportation system. That legislation includes provisions for interagency pooling of resources in ways that are still being developed.

There are positive examples, but many government-wide efforts at promoting collaboration have not fared well over time. The Senior Executive Service (SES) was expected to permit and encourage development of a cadre of professional managers who would rotate among multiple federal agencies. That would facilitate adoption of improved practices from other agencies and also would contribute to a broader perspective for senior federal managers. However, this did not happen. A 1999 survey by the U.S. Office of Personnel Management (OPM) in conjunction with the Senior Executive Association showed that over 90 percent of all SES members had not moved between agencies since becoming senior executives. Two-thirds had not moved between components of a single agency (OPM 1999).

Policymakers sometimes try to use reorganization to promote improved collaboration. Reorganization is a clumsy tool, at best, for this purpose. Problems of poor collaboration often affect agencies within the same executive department, such as the Department of Homeland Security (DHS). When he studied problems of communications across the boundaries of organizations within DHS, Maccoby (2006) found that the "easy part was to install communication technology. The hard part was getting people to communicate in a timely way." Maccoby contends that effective collaborative leadership and a culture of collaboration are far more important than mere structural approaches such as reorganization. DHS would benefit from developing a culture that values collaboration and from training and growing leaders and managers based on collaboration as a core value and performance criterion.

An Agenda for Improved Collaboration Across Organizational Boundaries

How can federal agencies gain incentives to collaborate with others? Many budget and personnel tools already exist, but leadership from the top of government is needed to make them work.

OMB could create and lead new interagency councils, for instance. These could be similar to the Federal Credit Policy Working Group, to promote collaborative efforts to address common problems. After the Gulf of Mexico environmental disaster, there is a clear need for improved interagency collaboration both to address the current reconstruction effort and to plan for a future catastrophe. Such councils also may need to include representatives from state and local governments, nonprofits, and for-profit companies.

The councils could bring together multiple agencies that would benefit from collaboration, sometimes along with state, local, and private partners, under the auspices of an OMB that could exercise persuasion to foster such collaboration; the drawback is that councils require continuing OMB leadership to maintain momentum. The demise of the Federal Credit Policy Working Group stands as a warning: although the council achieved significant results, it disappeared as other priorities attracted OMB's leadership. Council leadership places demands on time and attention from OMB officials effective as collaborative leaders. To be effective across multiple councils, OMB would need to increase staff, and especially senior OMB managers effective as collaborative leaders, available to the deputy director for management. They then could establish, maintain, and lead (or support the leadership of) the councils.

An additional approach would be for OMB to rate agencies perhaps annually, or maybe even quarterly, according to their collaboration across organizational boundaries. Such a rating might be based on criteria such as the following:

1. The extent to which the agency adopts promising practices from other agencies, state and local government, or the private sector.
2. The extent to which the agency shares promising practices and other support (such as HUD's sharing of CAIVRS) with other organizations.
3. The extent to which the agency adopts and applies effective performance measures for collaboration in its strategic and performance plans and in performance criteria for senior executives and other managers.
4. The results of an annual 360-degree review of the agency—including the views of other agencies, state and local governments, and private organizations—as to the perception that the agency collaborates willingly and usefully.

To avoid gaming of the system, OMB will need to scrutinize agency claims to assure that collaboration is taking place in high-priority areas that actually produce more public value than when the agency and its partners act alone. OMB examiners also will need to exercise restraint so that agencies that collaborate do not fear that OMB will reduce their budget resources to reflect putative savings.

A rating system similar to that implemented under PMA could provide the vehicle, or at least a good model, for rating agencies and reporting results. Agencies were rated on five indicators: human capital, competitive sourcing, financial performance, e-government, and integration of budget and performance. These are administrative areas where individual agency action, rather than interagency collaboration, is often called for.

To help build collaboration into each agency's culture, it is important to build a set of measures for collaboration into the Standard for Executive Excellence that is used to rate the performance of each agency's senior executives. PMA used this approach, to promote implementation for senior executives. OPM, backed up by OMB, will need to play a role in assuring effective implementation of collaborative measures applied to senior executives and other federal managers.

Another interesting idea comes from Michael Morris of the Burton Blatt Institute of Syracuse University. Similar to some other academics, he believes that the Program Assessment Rating Tool (PART), administered by OMB, manifests significant shortcomings. In particular, even though PART in fact has led to changes in management and operation of programs rather than in changed or redirected funding, he is concerned that PART may reflect the interagency competition for scarce federal resources that is inherent in the budget process. Why not use PART to encourage collaboration across organizational boundaries?

In contrast to the PMA, which focuses largely on administrative management matters, PART applies directly to programs and program performance. PART question 3.5 does ask, "Does the program collaborate and coordinate effectively with related programs?" However, the way that PART currently addresses collaboration is quite limited, and thus not as useful as it could be if collaboration were given a higher priority.

There is one likely exception to the spectrum of agencies that might improve collaboration on the basis of leadership from OMB. These are the national security agencies. OMB does not appear to play nearly as significant a role with respect to the national security agencies as it does on the domestic side of government. In her careful analysis of the establishment and evolution of major national security agencies, including the Joint Chiefs of Staff, National Security Council, and Central Intelligence Agency, Amy Zegart does not refer even once to OMB (1999). Whereas the National Security Council, thanks to its position in the Executive Office of the President (EOP), may have some ability to lead collaboration among the national security agencies and with outside organizations, the potential effectiveness of such leadership is not as apparent as for OMB vis-à-vis domestic agencies.

Changing Organizational Cultures to Promote Collaboration

My thesis is that increased collaboration is an essential part of building more capable government to respond to a plethora of changing circumstances that raise problems that a single federal agency cannot address by itself. There are good reasons why many agencies neglect collaboration. The pressure of competition for jurisdiction among congressional committees and subcommittees and their constituencies is a major influence on the organizational culture of federal agencies that depend on these committees and constituencies for their resources. As Bernie Martin, an experienced observer, noted to me:

> Agencies have specific legislative mandates which are policed by powerful interest groups and often very narrowly focused congressional committees and subcommittees. If they believe that in attempting some form of collaboration, the agency is neglecting its prime purposes, the agency will soon hear about it in no uncertain terms, often in the context of threats to reduce resources.

Also, collaboration often requires longer-term activity, including the development of relationships with people outside of one's own agency, than may be possible for the many officials who find their time consumed by crises or the possibility of crisis. In addition, agency administrative stovepipes that separate financial operations, information technology, human capital, and other functions can impede the ability of managers to collaborate effectively within the same department or agency.

Legislation also plays a role to the extent that it reflects intent of opponents of particular governmental activities to fragment agency jurisdiction and prevent effective implementation (Moe 1989). Some agencies have operated as rivals for so long that it may be difficult to bring them to collaborate. Difficulties at DHS in integrating customs and immigrations functions for "one face at the border" reflect deep cultural and policy differences that can take years to overcome.

For administrators who share a common culture, such as chief financial officers, chief information officers, chief human capital officers, or inspectors general, collaboration can come naturally. It can be difficult, and sometimes much more difficult, to obtain collaboration among program managers from different organizations. That is the big challenge.

On the other hand, there are increasing pressures for improved program collaboration. Especially with the development of a national and global economy, many private interest groups have gained an increased stake in collaboration by federal agencies across organizational boundaries. Federal agencies frequently lag behind the private sector in this respect. The electronic delivery of food stamps, and current efforts to expand electronic delivery of other federal and state benefits, have been driven in part by the urging of private financial institutions that seek to serve an interoperable national market rather than by a fragmented congeries of smaller programmatic and geographic jurisdictions.

Federal agencies also may lag behind state and local governments, which have collaborated for years. Thus, states responded to Katrina by invoking the Emergency Management Assistance Compact (EMAC), a mutual aid agreement that allowed the affected states to request assistance from other states for National Guard resources, law enforcement personnel, medical team support, search and rescue services, and commodities such as ice and water, and to provide reimbursement once the emergency was over. Some localities have begun to copy the EMAC model, which applies only to the states, for their own collaborative relations.

Some pressures that induced agencies to hoard resources and support today are giving way to an environment where increased collaboration is welcome if not required. Unfortunately, agency cultures may not have changed appropriately to reflect the often-changed context. How, then, can agency organizational culture be changed to promote the value of collaboration?

The application by OMB of a combination of tools—interagency working groups and monitoring agency collaboration across organizational boundaries, preferably linked to performance goals and objectives for each federal agency and to performance measures for senior executives and managers—will be an important beginning. An important tool will be for OMB to reward collaboration and recognize managers and agencies that collaborate well. The OMB deputy director for management will need to prevent premature budget cuts and designate areas where revenue sharing among agencies can be a high priority.

Just as important will be careful oversight by OMB and OPM of the way that application of these tools improves the organizational culture at each agency and promotes a collaborative outlook. As Dwight Ink wrote me in 2007:

> I regard the statutory restoration of some sort of management capacity in the EOP (either in or out of OMB) as a critical step toward effective and sustained attention to interagency and intergovernmental coordination and collaboration. I have been unable to think of something that can replace it. One can develop all sorts of policies, and issue all kinds of directives without it, but making the diverse governmental machinery function effectively is a different matter, especially as the number of political appointees increases.

In other words, while application of the recommended tools by OMB can help to improve collaboration by federal agencies, it is only with a dedicated strategy of leadership and promoting cultural change that OMB can use the next administration effectively to change the fundamental dynamics of interorganizational collaboration by federal agencies and managers.

Several factors can work together to promote a culture of collaboration across organizational boundaries:

- A new wave of federal employees, schooled in the Internet age and more open to collaboration than many of their predecessors, coming into government.
- Senior executives whose hiring, promotion, and retention would be based in part on measures of their collaborative skills (what Maccoby [2007] calls "soft skills").
- The practice of agencies, with leadership from OMB, to increase collaboration in areas that perceptibly benefit their individual missions.

Conclusion

Improved collaboration of federal agencies with state and local governments and private sector organizations has become imperative. Agencies that fail to collaborate may lack critical information that partners may be able to provide. These agencies risk finding, in today's technology-driven and complicated environment, that the way they perform their missions has become obsolete.

OMB stands at the apex of the executive branch. It is the only agency that currently has the capacity and clout to foster improved collaboration by federal agencies. Both through a government-wide rating system and by establishing new councils to promote collaboration in critical areas, as well as leadership that expresses itself more generally, the next administration should use OMB to assure that government agencies collaborate effectively across organizational boundaries.

Acknowledgments

This chapter has benefited from insights contributed by numerous friends and colleagues, including Cora Beebe, Rick Cinquegrana, Steven Cohen, Murray Comarow, George Frederickson, Gerry Gingrich, Dan Guttman, Dwight Ink, Herbert Jasper, Frederick Kaiser, Al Kliman, Michael Maccoby, Bernard Martin, Bruce McDowell, Chris Mihm, Ken Ryder, Robert Shea, Myra Shiplett, Tom Stack, Harold Steinberg, Bernice Steinhardt, Andrew Uscher, Barbara Wamsley, and Robert Worley. None of them can or should be held responsible for this chapter; while grateful for their collaboration, the author takes sole responsibility for the final product.

References

Bardach, Eugene. 1998. *Getting Agencies to Work Together.* Washington, DC: Brookings Institution Press.
Ink, Dwight. 2006. "Managing Change That Makes a Difference." In *Meeting the Challenge of 9/11: Blueprints for Effective Government,* ed. Thomas H. Stanton, pp. 166–198. Armonk, NY: M.E. Sharpe.
Maccoby, Michael. 2006. "The Many Cultures of Government." In *Meeting the Challenge of 9/11: Blueprints for Effective Government,* ed. Thomas H. Stanton, pp. 219–229. Armonk, NY: M.E. Sharpe.
———. 2007. *The Leaders We Need.* Cambridge, MA: Harvard Business Review Press.
Moe, Terry M. 1989. "The Politics of Bureaucratic Structure." In *Can the Government Govern?* ed. John E. Chubb and Paul E. Peterson, pp. 267–330. Washington, DC: Brookings Institution Press.
Office of the Director of National Intelligence (ODNI). 2007. "Director McConnell Signs Instructions to Implement Joint Duty." ODNI News Release No. 17–07, June 26.
Salamon, Lester M. 1981. "Rethinking Public Management: Third Party Government and the Tools of Government Action." *Public Policy* 29(1): 255–275.
Seidman, Harold. 2004. "Foreword." In *Making Government Manageable,* ed. Thomas H. Stanton and Benjamin Ginsberg. Baltimore, MD: Johns Hopkins University Press.
Stanton, Thomas H. 2006. "Improving Federal Relations with States, Localities, and Private Organizations on Matters of Homeland Security: The Stakeholder Council Model." In *Meeting the Challenge of 9/11: Blueprints for Effective Government,* ed. Thomas H. Stanton, pp. 315–332. Armonk, NY: M.E. Sharpe.
———. 2007. *Delivery of Benefits in an Emergency: Lessons from Hurricane Katrina.* Washington, DC: IBM Center for the Business of Government.

U.S. Government Accountability Office (US GAO). 2005. October. *Results-Oriented Government: Practices That Can Help Enhance and Sustain Collaboration Among Federal Agencies.* GAO-06–15. Washington, DC: U.S. GAO.

U.S. Office of Personnel Management (OPM). 1999. "1999 Survey of the Senior Executive Service." http://www.opm.gov/fedregis/2000/65–38442-a.txt (accessed August 16, 2010).

Yao, Margaret L. 2000. *The President's Management Council: An Important Management Innovation.* Pew Center Endowment for the Business of Government, December. Washington, DC: Pew Research Center.

Zegart, Amy B. 1999. *Flawed by Design: The Evolution of the CIA, JCS, and NSC.* Stanford, CA: Stanford University Press.

6

Governance Implications of the Bush Administration's War on Terror

NATHANIEL J. BUSS

The events of September 11, 2001, shattered the national security policy equilibrium in the United States. Even with its formidable intelligence community, law enforcement capabilities, military supremacy, and extensive global presence, the United States was caught off guard by weaknesses in deterrence, prevention, and response to terrorism. The George W. Bush administration in response to threats of terrorism launched a portfolio of new initiatives that have helped move Governance 2.0 into the relatively unknown territory of Governance 3.0, the theme of this book:

- Created the Department of Homeland Security
- Reengineered the Federal Bureau of Investigation
- Created the Office of the Director of National Intelligence
- Created the Africa Command

Taken together, the Bush administration's counterterrorism initiatives constitute perhaps the most extensive reorganization of government ever (National Academy of Public Administration 2003b). They represent a unique opportunity to assess the Bush administration's approach in executing large-scale change. Rather than look at specific policies related to terrorism, I focus instead on how the initiatives were developed and launched to ascertain their effectiveness from a governance perspective.

Creation of the Department of Homeland Security

In 2001, before September 11, the congressional Commission on National Security in the 21st Century issued a report calling for the creation of a Department of Homeland Security (DHS). Even with broad congressional support, the recommendation, lacking a sense of need or urgency, was not enacted. In 2002, President Bush proposed his version of the new department, which Congress approved. The legislation folded 22 separate agencies and around 200,000 employees into DHS, most notably the Federal Emergency Management Agency (FEMA), the

Coast Guard, the Customs Bureau, the Immigration and Naturalization Service, and the Transportation Security Administration. This became by far the largest organizational reengineering effort since the formation of the Defense Department, National Security Council, and Central Intelligence Agency under the National Security Act of 1947.

For many critics, the development and implementation of DHS became a case study in how not to launch a new agency. In fairness, a major dilemma for the administration was to choose between acting quickly to address terrorism or taking a more circumspect approach to make sure they got it right. They chose the former. Choosing the latter would have left the United States too exposed to the new, unprecedented threat, and, they argued, delays in crafting a response would not necessarily have produced a better response. Immediately following are some of the problems experienced during the development and implementation phases of DHS, followed by a closer look at the Transportation Security Administration (TSA).

Mission

In its haste to focus on counterterrorism in its early stages of development, DHS all but ignored its natural disaster mission. Some believe that the country paid a heavy price for this decision when Hurricane Katrina caught the country unprepared for a megadisaster in 2004. The BP petroleum company's oil spill in June/July 2010, producing the worst environmental disaster in history, suggests that the emergency response mechanisms for megadisasters are still not in place.

Organizational Structure

Looking back at the organizational structure for DHS in the legislation, it seems that policymakers had only the roughest sketch in mind about how 22 agencies would be combined so that they eliminated duplication, fragmentation, and gaps. Early on, DHS found the initial organizational structure unworkable, which led to several years of reorganizations in which organizations were moved from one place to another and functions within them were reassigned. One senior civil servant remarked that he had given up printing business cards for his program, as it was continually being reengineered.

Federal Workforce

Merging together 22 agencies having different workforces was a daunting task. Many of the agencies, for example, had employees who were authorized to carry weapons, but the when, where, how, and why of the use of these weapons varied greatly, as did the job classifications and salaries of workers. The Coast Guard has different kinds of personnel and authorities from those working in immigration and customs, yet they often have similar missions. The question was, how to make these consistent across DHS? Rather than address the issue at the micro level, the administration decided to broadly classify workers into job classifications that would remove these difficulties, then allow managers a great deal of authority to manage. This approach would solve the issue, but in the process greatly reduce the power of federal unions. Attempts to impose flexibilities and authorities in managing the workforce led to lawsuits that nullified the administration's efforts (Brooks and King 2009).

Intergovernmental Relations

The key to making DHS work is the extent to which federal, state, and local government, along with nongovernmental organizations (NGOs) and the private sector, can work as a system (NAPA 2004). In the field of counterterrorism and natural disaster responses, the system was highly fragmented. Organizations were unable to communicate across the system and in many cases within their own part of the system. To complicate matters, governance had evolved from a command and control hierarchical system to one that is networked and collaborative. So, care needed to be taken to bring these disparate actors together. The administration decided to mandate a system and force nonfederal entities to go along. At a congressional hearing on intergovernmental relations a DHS representative, when asked by a congressman why his department had not apparently consulted with states and cities in setting up its intergovernmental model, replied that states and cities were argumentative and obstructionist, and therefore had been excluded (U.S. House Committee on Government Reform 2004). This prompted the director of homeland security for the state of Massachusetts to respond that it neither needed nor wanted any federal help. The necessary consultations and consensus building that should have gone on did not. As a consequence, the model had to be redone several times until the various actors came on board.

DHS Operations

Federal agencies have legislative mandates requiring them to produce strategic and human capital management plans, among other things, so that Congress and the administration can perform their oversight function in promoting transparency and accountability. As a new agency, DHS was not in a good position to prepare these documents, so it took years before any appeared. This meant that policymakers and legislators who should have had information did not.

Congressional Relations

Both the administration and Congress were controlled by Republicans, yet they did not, on occasion, work well together. For example, Congress appropriated money and charged FEMA to work with the National Academy of Public Administration (NAPA)—a congressionally chartered organization that conducts management studies for Congress and executive agencies—to assist it in planning and management. Congress was concerned about agency management. FEMA refused, precipitating a crisis that lasted nearly a year, at which point it ended up participating in the assessment anyway.

After eight years, many issues still remain unresolved at DHS. (I hasten to note that these criticisms do not apply to the federal workforce charged with keeping the nation safe. Indeed, they are the best at what they do.)

Launching TSA

TSA is one of the 22 agencies merged into DHS. Its launch provides a vivid example of just one aspect of the complexity of creating DHS: outsourcing or contracting out federal responsibilities. Consider this overview presented in a NAPA report on TSA contracting out (NAPA 2003a, p. 1):

> Faced with a congressionally mandated deadline of January 1, 2003 to replace contract passenger and baggage screeners at the nation's 429 commercial airports with federal employees, the government turned to a private contractor to do the job. A year before the deadline, the fledgling TSA (then part of the Department of Transportation) had only 18 employees on board to administer what was to become the largest peacetime mobilization in the nation's history. TSA outsourced the task of federalizing the airport security workforce, awarding a $100 million-plus contract to a single firm: Pearson. The contract required applicant screening; assessment; health, security, and other checks; interviewing; and day-to-day human capital management services on behalf of TSA. Between the contract award in February 2002 and November 19, 2002, Pearson
>
> - Assessed more than 430,000 prospective applicants.
> - Qualified more than 125,000 candidates.
> - Assisted TSA in hiring 62,192 screeners and 2,433 administrative staff.
>
> Changes in requirements (e.g., more than doubling the targeted number of hires and going from staged to single-day candidate processing) delayed the beginning of actual recruitment until June 18, 2002. The contractor delivered more than 67,000 screeners by the end of the year.

Contracting out or outsourcing what were once federal responsibilities to the private sector is a huge governance issue. Under the Bush administration, policymakers favored outsourcing as much government activity as possible (see Cooper 2003). Under Obama, it appears that outsourcing is gradually being "clawed back." There are not very many studies that offer conclusions about which is most effective, efficient, and economical—outsourcing or government production of services. Some believe that the issue is largely ideological. The TSA experience illustrates that private companies can produce spectacular results, but that outsourcing would be subject to the same governance problems had the government undertaken the initiative. Changes in contract specifications, accompanied by changes in policy directions, imposes inefficiencies in the private sector that are characteristic of some of the new initiatives handled by government within DHS.

Reengineering the Federal Bureau of Investigation

The FBI, since September 11, 2001, has come under pressure to transform its operations from traditional criminal investigation and law enforcement to a new focus on counterterrorism. To critics, this transformation proved problematic, but not nearly on the scale that the transformation to DHS did. The FBI had a specialized workforce, one neither hired nor trained for counterterrorism, and data systems not designed for work in the new field. Its working relationships with the intelligence community were hopelessly stovepiped. The FBI's transformation required engagement in new hiring, training, career development, IT, and management initiatives on a large scale. All things considered, the FBI has been commended for its efforts at transforming the workforce (NAPA 2005). But other things have gone wrong.

Consider information technology, or IT. The FBI, realizing that its antiquated IT systems would greatly impede its effectiveness, launched the Trilogy Program to replace computer equipment, develop better networks, and improve IT case management systems. The FBI, just after September 11, tried to develop a new IT system, a Virtual Case File that would transform the agency from a paper-based system to one that would allow intelligence officers and investigators to share information and conduct analyses. In 2005 the new system, costing over $100 million to develop, had to be abandoned because it did not work. The inspector general at the Justice Department found that the most publicized IT system failure in history resulted from: "poorly defined and slowly evolving design requirements; overly ambitious schedules; and the lack of a plan to guide hardware purchases, network deployments, and software development for the bureau" (Goldstein 2005). A private IT vendor and the FBI, according to the FBI's inspector general, shared the blame.

Office of the Director of National Intelligence

The process by which foreign intelligence is collected and analyzed for policymakers has been extremely controversial since the modern intelligence community was established in the early stages of the Cold War. While the specific disagreements fluctuated, a fundamental dilemma is ever present. The National Security Act of 1947 established several mechanisms to coordinate intelligence activities under the authority of the Director of Central Intelligence (DCI). There are more than 20 intelligence agencies in the U.S. government. However, the various departmental organizations with intelligence missions must retain relative autonomy from a central authority to serve their unique missions. Consequently, proprietary agencies have been reluctant to surrender resources and information collection and reporting procedures. This proved to be a major issue in the September 11 terrorist attacks on the United States. So, how can "stovepiping" or "siloing" in the intelligence community be eliminated? The administration's answer, facetiously offered by critics: create another intelligence agency to watch over the rest!

In response to the multiagency intelligence coordination issue, Congress passed the Intelligence Reform and Terrorism Prevention Act of 2004, creating the Office of the Director of National Intelligence (ODNI) to head the nation's intelligence agencies and oversee implementation of the National Intelligence Program. ODNI also was a centerpiece of the *9/11 Commission Report.* Creation of the office had been proposed by different Congresses and administrations since the 1950s, each noting the fragmentation issue.

As many commentators predicted, ODNI faces major management challenges as it attempts to coordinate and direct the intelligence community, a collective that seems unwilling to fully cooperate (Office of the Inspector General 2008). Some critics believe that the same problems that existed before ODNI still exist. Consider two high-profile cases from 2010. One, on December 24, 2009, acting on behalf of an al-Qaeda sect operating from Yemen, Umar Farouk Abdulmutallab purchased a ticket with cash for Northwest Flight 253 headed for Detroit with intentions of detonating explosives on board. Department of Homeland Security Secretary Janet Napolitano infamously said, "the system worked." Though his attempt was thankfully unsuccessful it was primarily because of the terrorist's own incompetence and not government intervention or deterrence. Officials became aware of Abdulmutallab on November 11, 2009, when British officials alerted American authorities that he had spoken with Muslim lecturer and suspected al-Qaeda recruiter Anwar al-Awlaki, and pledged his support for the global jihad. What is more, Abdulmutallab's father approached the CIA via the U.S. Embassy in Abuja, Nigeria, and reported his son's extremist views and that he might be in Yemen. Acting on the report, authorities added Abdulmutallab's name to the 550,000-name Terrorist Identities Datamart Environment (TIDE), a database of the U.S. National Counterterrorism Center. It was not added, however, to the FBI's 400,000-name Terrorist Screening Database, the terror watch list that feeds both the 14,000-name Secondary Screening Selectee list and the U.S.'s 4,000-name No Fly List, nor was Abdulmutallab's U.S. visa revoked.

Additional flags were raised throughout the process, but the information was not adequately transmitted to the appropriate parties. The State Department was also aware that he had a multiple-entry visa, but the nature of his threat was not adequately communicated. The National Security Agency had intercepted communications indicating that the Yemen-based branch of al-Qaeda was planning an attack, and that a Nigerian was being readied to carry it out. Later reports suggested it might happen during the holiday season. That advice is fairly ambiguous, but when the information is coupled with the advice from the British and from Abdulmutallab's father, the connection becomes clearer.

The second attack is equally troubling; however, the success after the fact shows the progress of law enforcement in investigating and tracking terror suspects. Faisal Shazhad was arrested just 53 hours after he left a crudely developed and assembled car bomb in New York's Times Square (*New York Times* 2010). As of this writing, it appears he was working for the Pakistani Taliban. The failed attempt once again was the result of poor planning and execution by Shazhad and not by government intervention. The aftermath was an impressive effort by law enforcement to track and apprehend Shazhad after he boarded an Emirates flight headed for Pakistan.

One issue poses a barrier to an effective ODNI: that is, it may lack teeth when attempting to manage the intelligence system. It has no budgetary authority over the component agencies, according to critics. As such, some wonder whether the initiative was real.

Creating the Africa Command

The importance of Africa to U.S. interests—in both the areas of counterterrorism and the encroachment of the Chinese on the continent—prompted the Bush administration to create a new military presence in Africa, operational in 2008 (see Buss et al. 2011; Buss, Buss, and Picard 2011). With the rise of terrorist threats, faltering economic development, political instability, and frequent armed conflict and civil war, but with the need to respect African sensitivities to their independence and self-determination, the Bush administration launched AFRICOM.

AFRICOM offers an interesting model in the context of national security. AFRICOM is a major counterterrorism initiative that has remained off the national radar screen attracting little attention except from specialists. AFRICOM does not have occupying forces or fixed bases, but rather one that combines security, diplomacy, and development in new ways. AFRICOM is headed by a general and a diplomat, has only a small contingent of troops in Djibouti, fosters coordination between USAID, state, and other federal agencies, and is headquartered in Nairobi, Kenya. The model has several appealing aspects for those interested in "soft power" (see, e.g., Center for Strategic and International Studies 2010).

While AFRICOM is well intentioned, it opened up the United States to more criticism. Many in Africa question the motivations of U.S. policymakers and use this to further cleavages on the continent—paranoia and suspicion reign for many. This was exacerbated by AFRICOM's failure to fully consult with African governments before launching the scheme. Some advocates for Africa want the United States to take the budget it has for defense and spend it on economic and social development instead; while others decry the loss of mission in USAID. They refer to AFRICOM as "armed social work." It's too soon to tell whether this model will work. Nonetheless, the Obama administration has cut AFRICOM's budget.

Implications for Governance

> The problem is not our system. By design, democracy is slow to change course; new ideas always face a lengthy struggle. Rather, the problem is that the ways in which we have come to use this system—how we develop ideas, test them and put them into action—need repair. (Eggers and O'Leary 2010)

In this chapter I take no position on the public policy implications of counterterrorism as reflected in the Bush and, to some extent, the Obama administrations' initiatives. Rather, I focus exclusively on the governance perspective, narrowing this down to the launch of major new initiatives. While there is no silver bullet to resolve the governance difficulties apparent in the counterterrorism initiatives discussed earlier, there are some issues that ought to be addressed by every administration.

Lesson 1: Spend time not only on design and development issues, but also on implementation

Often, policymakers do not have time to fully develop initiatives, especially in crisis situations requiring immediate action. But all too often, policymakers fail to consider implementation issues, apparently believing that these will resolve themselves as an initiative is rolled out. As Pressman and Wildavsky (1973) pointed out long ago, this is the Achilles' heel of public management. Ron Moe, former researcher at the Congressional Research Service, has argued that enabling legislation that creates or reengineers programs should include implementation criteria. Others are not so sure that Congress has the knowledge to offer such direction. Regardless, implementation is just as important as development.

Lesson 2: Do not exclude those who have opposing views from deliberations

It seems to some critics that policymakers are increasingly excluding those who hold opposing views from deliberations on new initiatives, likely because they believe they know best or do not wish to take on the challenge of building compromise and consensus. Hillary Clinton's failed health care reform initiative, many of the Bush administration's policies, and much of Obama's undertakings are highly exclusionary, even among their supporters. In June 2010, Prime Minister of Australia Kevin Rudd was literally deposed as PM because he began making decisions on virtually everything after consultations with only a select few. Democratic governance requires the clash of ideas to make policymaking better (Eggers and O'Leary 2010). There is increasing evidence that "two heads are better than one" (Howe 2006). Those who decide to go it alone typically regret the failures that result.

Lesson 3: Build consensus

In addition to excluding opposition views—which may originate not only from members in opposing political parties or in different branches of government, but also from within—policymakers should take care to build wide coalitions in support of change (see also Chapter 14). Mostly, they do not. Policymakers prefer, so it seems, to put together "minimal winning coalitions" (usually thought of in the electoral context) to get things accomplished. The Obama administration's health care reforms were, for many critics, an example of this approach. The problem with this is that opposition forces, particularly in the United States, are able to marshal resistance to initiatives until they overturn or greatly modify them. This makes even the best initiatives unsustainable and creates chaos in the political system.

Lesson 4: Do not pursue megainitiatives requiring sweeping change; rather, decompose them into doable subparts

All of the cases I have described are efforts to execute global changes that massively restructure entire systems. The probability that these will lead to failure increases dramatically as the complexity of the task at hand increases (Simon 1996). Those in IT fields know this principle all too well. As a consequence, technicians break tasks down into manageable chunks that can be executed by individual "agents," then assemble them into a system that is much more likely to work. The policy sciences in the 1960s understood systems thinking quite well, yet this may have been forgotten in recent decades (e.g., Easton 1965).

References

Brooks, Douglas A., and Cynthia King. 2009. "Legislating Innovation in Human Capital Management: Lessons from the Department of Homeland Security." In *Innovations in Human Resource Management,* ed. Hannah Sistare, Myra Shiplett, and Terry Buss, pp. 277–291. Armonk, NY: M.E. Sharpe.

Buss, Terry, Joseph Adjaye, Donald Goldstein, and Louis Picard (eds). 2011. *African Security and the African Command: Viewpoints on the U.S. Role in Africa.* Alexandria, VA: Kumarian Press.

Buss, Terry F., Nathaniel J. Buss, and Louis A. Picard. 2011. "Al-Queda in Africa: The Threat and Response." In *African Security and the African Command: Viewpoints on the U.S. Role in Africa,* ed. Terry Buss, Joseph Adjaye, Donald Goldstein, and Louis Picard. Alexandria, VA: Kumarian Press.

Center for Strategic and International Studies. 2010. "Smart Power Initiative." http://csis.org/program/smart-power-initiative.

Cooper, Phillip J. 2003. *Governing by Contract.* Washington, DC: CQ Press.

Easton, David. 1965. *A Framework for Policy Analysis.* New York: Wiley.

Eggers, William D., and John O'Leary. 2010. "Can the U.S. Still Tackle Big Problems?" *Washington Post,* March 21, B01.

Goldstein, Harry. 2005. "Who Killed the Virtual Case File?" *IEEE Spectrum Magazine,* September.

Howe, Jeff. 2006. "The Rise of Crowdsourcing." *Wired,* June. http://www.cm/wired/archive/14.06/crowds.html (accessed March 17, 2007).

National Academy of Public Administration (NAPA). 2003a. *Advancing the Management of Homeland Security.* Washington, DC: NAPA.

———. 2003b. *Protecting the Homeland: Lessons from Past Reorganizations.* Washington, DC: NAPA.

———. 2004. *Managing Intergovernmental Relations for Homeland Security.* Washington, DC: NAPA.

———. 2005. *Transforming the FBI: Progress and Challenges.* Washington, DC: NAPA.

New York Times. 2010. "Times Square Bomb Attempt" (May 1, 2010). NYTimes.com, May 24. http://topics.nytimes.com/top/reference/timestopics/subjects/t/times_square_bomb_attempt_may_1_2010/index.html.

Office of the Inspector General. 2008. "Critical Intelligence Community Management Challenges." Washington, DC: Office of the Director of National Intelligence, Office of the Inspector General.

Pressman, Jeffrey and Aaron Wildavsky. 1973. *Implementation.* Berkeley: University of California Press.

Simon, Herbert A. 1996. *Sciences of the Artificial.* Cambridge, MA: MIT Press.

U.S. Congress. House. Committee on Government Reform. 2004. *Hearings on Homeland Security.* March 24, Washington, DC: Government Printing Office.

Part II

Whither American Federalism?

7

Effective Governance

Withering Without Federalism

JOHN KINCAID

Symptomatic of the problems of government hierarchy that have emerged was the plaintive cry of Congressman David R. Obey (D-WI), chairman of the House Appropriations Committee, upon announcing his retirement in May 2010 from the U.S. House of Representatives after 40 years of service: "I hate to do it. There is so much that needs to be done. But frankly, I am bone tired" (quoted in Young and Giroux 2010, p. 1149). The congressman's tenure, like that of other senior incumbents, witnessed an unprecedented decline of public trust in the federal government, rise of public debt, and proliferation of the governance problems that occasioned this volume. Public confidence in government's ability to do great things dropped, too. In 1965, for instance, most Americans believed that the War on Poverty would "help wipe out poverty"; now, most believe that "poor people have become too dependent on government assistance" (Hetherington 2006). Yet the congressman wishes he could stay in Washington to do even more, obliviously unaware that his statement is not noble but ignoble.

Absent from this solipsism are echoes of Cincinnatus and Publius, models for the founders, who really were historically indispensable, but who recognized the importance of rotation in office for republican vitality. Modern governance elevates the indispensable man or woman—the career bureaucrat, career lobbyist, career contractor, and, most important, career legislator reelected repeatedly from a gerrymandered district who expects "the American people" to be grateful that he worked himself to the bone for them. "What's missing on Capitol Hill are signs of shame" (Cook 2010, p. 72) for creating a dysfunctional, crisis-prone government. Instead, legislators immortalize themselves by earmarking taxpayers' money to erect "monuments to me," such as the David R. Obey Center for Health Sciences, Bud Shuster highway, John Murtha Johnstown-Cambria County Airport, Carl Albert Congressional Research and Studies Center, and Charles B. Rangel Center for Public Service.

The concentration of power and wealth in Washington, DC, where, now, "ten cents of every federal procurement dollar spent anywhere on Earth is spent in

Virginia" (Helderman 2010), was long advocated by progressive reformers. They sought to marshal the federal government's seemingly superior fiscal resources and intellectual talent to enact enlightened, well-planned, and highly coordinated policies in the public interest based on national visions of a great society. Much good came from the rise of federal power, not the least of which was the Civil Rights revolution. But as Abraham Lincoln noted in his July 10, 1858, campaign speech in Chicago, wielding federal power against slavery did not mean that it would also be beneficial "to interfere with the cranberry laws of Indiana, the oyster laws of Virginia, or the liquor laws of Maine." Yet, the centralization of power, however incremental, attracts ambitious individuals with vested interests in expanding centralization so as to intrude into every nook and cranny of state and local government, even to points of dysfunction. Consequently, the federal government is highly fragmented, poorly coordinated, ideologically polarized, and lacking in planning acumen. These dysfunctional features of federal power also get passed onto state and local governments in the forms of nearly 800 grant-in-aid programs, hundreds of conditions of aid, preemptions, mandates, and revolving door policies.

Events of the 2000s—from the dot-com bust to 9/11, the wars in Afghanistan and Iraq, Hurricane Katrina, the great recession that began in 2008, and the 2010 BP oil spill in the Gulf of Mexico—suggest, as well, that the federal government is ill-equipped to anticipate and respond to the catastrophic and global events that were most often said to require centralized governance. A strong, centralized, national government was seen as necessary to act as the "countervailing power" to big business (Galbraith 1952) and the forces of a globalizing world and to defend the nation, protect the environment, and respond to disasters.

By contrast, Canada, a smaller and much less centralized federal polity than the United States, where provincial governments account for about 55 percent of public expenditures, weathered the 2008–2011 global economic crisis much better than did the United States, even though it is highly dependent on the U.S. economy. Its financial regulations proved more effective. In the key housing sector, Canada has a higher rate of homeownership (68 percent) than the United States and a negligible rate of foreclosures without the panoply of national programs, tax deductions, and quasi-governmental institutions such as Fannie Mae, Freddie Mac, and the Federal Housing Administration that mark the fragmented U.S. housing policy scene (Kincaid 1993). Switzerland also has weathered the global financial crisis comparatively well, again belying the proposition that bigger, more centralized governments are better able to deal with modern problems. Unlike the United States, moreover, Canada and Switzerland rely heavily on intergovernmental consultation and negotiation among elected federal and constituent-government policymakers to formulate and implement policies.

Yet, more often than not, proposed solutions to governing problems in the United States advocate more centralization and more coercion of state and local governments. This is inevitable, because the well-institutionalized interests that benefit from federal power have strong incentives to maintain centralization and, quite often, are unable even to think in terms of noncentralization. A major flaw of the centralization thesis was its failure to recognize that centralization would attract powerful interests whose centrifugal effects on policymaking would defeat the very objectives of centralization. What results, therefore, is not high-minded, well-planned, and coherent public policies "but simply a potpourri of parochial claims proffered by private interests parading in governmental dress" (Stockman 1986, p. 33).

Given that centralization will not surrender its prerogatives easily, reforms need to be oriented toward making it more benign, more cognizant of federalism, and more cooperative with elected state and local officials across the country. Indeed, one of the ironies of contemporary centralization is that it arose in part to defeat the northern political machines and southern white courthouse gangs that had so corrupted government. However, the reformations and resurgence of state and local governments (Bowman 1986) have not yet enabled those governments to act as a countervailing power to federal corruption or to restore a more equitable and productive balance of state-federal power.

Reconsidering Some Conventional Paradigms

At a basic level, the stickiness of centralization is abetted by the language of "levels" of government routinely used to describe the federal system today. This language denotes a hierarchy of layers of government in which the federal government sits at the top of the pyramid, while local governments lie on the bottom and state governments are sandwiched in the middle. This conception has no foundation in the federal Constitution (because the supremacy clause applies only to the federal government's constitutionally limited field of delegated powers), nor does the notion of "levels" appear in *The Federalist*. This language also spawns absurd phrases such as state-level officials, state-level governor, and local-level mayor. Most important, this language connotes a single, unitary system of multilevel government.

Dropping "levels" from the lexicon would facilitate fresh thinking about the federal arrangement. For those who need generic terms, "orders" of government (often used in Canada) or "arenas of government" would suffice as nonhierarchical alternatives.

The concept of "governance," now dominant in public administration, also is congenial to centralization. Despite governance theory's emphasis on horizontal networking and conjunct governance, hierarchy is its operational essence (Hill and Lynn 2005). The concept also is dismissive of state and local governments. It subsumes intergovernmental relations under a unitary conception of a multitude of public and private actors interacting in networks as more or less equals, even though within these networks, state and local government officials, along with their federal counterparts, are the only actors elected by the people. They are not merely stakeholders. Whatever one's opinion of the governor of California, he or she was elected to govern 37 million people and preside over the world's ninth largest economy. The governor should not have to stand in line behind thousands of for-profit and nonprofit interest groups in order to get attention in Washington, D.C. Furthermore, by embracing the host of nongovernmental actors who influence policy formulation and implementation, the governance concept contributes to the fragmentation of the federal government. The concept may accurately describe reality, but it is not a prescription for good government.

In contrast to Harlan Cleveland's 1972 rallying cry—"What the people want is less government and more governance"—what is needed today is more government and less governance. Namely, what is needed is representative government in which elected officials make decisions with less interest group retribution, nongovernmental actors are clearly subordinate to elected officials, elected state and local officials play important partnership roles in national policymaking, and important government functions are carried out by public servants rather than by some 7.5 million federal contract workers who also have vested interests in centralization and government expansion.

Innovation is another popular paradigm. It creates opportunities for interest groups to propose changes in benign guises. But innovation is not uniformly beneficial and is especially problematic for government. It is often said that the private sector is highly innovative and that government should follow suit. Yet, innovation in the private sector is not always successful, let alone beneficial. In the financial world, for example, ATMs, index funds, and junk bonds, among others, proved to be beneficial innovations. But such innovations as credit-default swaps, subprime loans, and structured investment vehicles had catastrophic consequences for the global economy. Innovation in the private sector also is subject to "creative destruction" (Schumpeter 1950). But transferring this concept to the public sector is problematic, given the stability and continuity needed in most government institutions. Instead of bad policies experiencing creative destruction, moreover, they ordinarily experience longevity because innovations create new vested interests. Consequently, yesterday's innovation can be today's white elephant or perverse budget drain. Innovations also emerge to circumvent bad policies, thus adding to the proliferation of policy fragmentation. Innovation is driven acceptably in the private sector by self-interest. But innovation driven by self-interest in the public sector is not necessarily conducive to the public interest. Furthermore, in the contemporary federal system, there is a strong tendency to further centralization by nationalizing state and local innovations. As President Bill Clinton put it: "If something is working in a state, I try to steal it [and] put it into federal law" (1999, p. 26).

Possible Foundational Reforms: Redistricting and Primaries

One of the most salient characteristics of federal policymaking today is party polarization, which has reached its highest level in both houses of Congress since Reconstruction (McCarty, Poole, and Rosenthal 2006). During the most active period of modern centralization (from about 1932 to 1980), party polarization was at an historical low point, fostering bipartisanship. But numerous socioeconomic, policy, and institutional changes during the 1960s, especially the spread of primary elections and the rise of partisan gerrymandering after the U.S. Supreme Court's "one person, one vote" reapportionment decisions, fostered polarization in Washington. Centralization also fostered polarization. By sucking up issues previously diffused among the states and subject to diverse policies, it vastly increased the political stakes involved in winning or losing in the national arena, making it ever more important for more interests to capture the federal government in order to nationalize their policy preferences. This polarization further fragments policymaking, rendering it less analytical, less well planned, less coherent, and less high minded. This gives rise to highly dysfunctional government, which, under conditions of centralization, infects the entire federal system with severe consequences.

Gerrymandering

A foundational factor in this polarization is partisan gerrymandering. It is now on steroids because innovative mapping software has vastly improved legislators' ability to select the voters they want to represent. Such redistricting not only fosters polarization but also hardens it by creating safe districts whose representatives have no incentives to compromise with others. Reform of redistricting is essential to reducing this polarization.

One long-standing proposal is to create bipartisan or nonpartisan redistricting commissions. In 2008, California voters approved the creation of an independent, nonpartisan Citizens Redistricting Commission. These institutions can likely increase party competition and, thereby, nudge candidates more toward the middle of the political spectrum. But creating truly nonpartisan bodies charged with such a fundamentally crucial political task as redistricting is very difficult. A safer alternative would be to program a computer to do the redistricting. A computer would need to be instructed only to create districts that are equal in population, geographically compact, and congruent with county and municipal boundaries as much as possible. This process would remove partisan temptations, restore jurisdictional communities as key arenas for representation, and, thereby, enhance the role of local elected officials in federal elections. It would also reduce incentives for incumbents to manipulate federal policymaking and appropriations in efforts to influence redistricting, leave incumbents uncertain as to whether they will survive decennial redistricting, and ensure that districts reflect in-state population changes even when there is no change in the number of a state's house seats.

Primary Elections

Primary elections are another foundational factor in partisan polarization because the die-hard partisans on the left and on the right are more likely to vote in primaries. Turnout during nonpresidential primaries is very low (15–30 percent). Primaries were a Progressive innovation of the early 20th century. But up until 1968, no more than 12 states used presidential and congressional primaries. After 1968, primary elections became widespread, marking the rise of polarization. Numerous proposals have been made to reform or abolish primary elections. Louisiana and Washington have essentially abolished traditional primaries. The new (2006) Washington system is a "fully open/top two" primary in which all would-be candidates run in a qualifying election; then the top two vote-getters appear on the November ballot. In June 2008, California voters had to decide whether to adopt this system. California's Proposition 14 had garnered substantial public support. But it was opposed by the Green Party and other third parties who believed that the top-two system will eliminate third parties from general elections.

An alternative approach would focus on increasing voter turnout for primary elections to blunt the impacts of the die-hard leftists and rightists. Turnout could be increased if states adopted (a) three to four rolling regional primaries that would produce more media coverage and political advertising needed to stimulate voters, and (b) semi-open primaries that would allow independents to participate. Furthermore, for presidential and congressional primary elections, states should establish concurrent primaries, one for rank-and-file party members and independents and one for currently elected state and local officials. In order to win a party's nomination, a candidate would need to win the rank-and-file vote as well as the elected-officials' vote. This system would partially restore the role of state and elected officials in the party system, further counteract the polarized extremes of each party, reduce the impacts of national interests operating in local primaries, and at least loosely re-tie the electoral fortunes of federal officials to state and local government officials. The confederated party system that had existed from the 1820s to 1968 fostered intergovernmental consultation and cooperation. But the rise of the media, partisan gerrymandering, and primary elections cut federal officials loose from their state and local government moorings and tied them more closely to national interest groups.

In summary, changes in redistricting and primary elections, which could be carried out by the states themselves, would likely reduce polarization, foster more intergovernmental cooperation, and mitigate some of the deleterious effects of centralization on the federal system.

Ameliorating Coercive Federalism

Centralization has displaced cooperative federalism in the policymaking domain, giving rise since the late 1960s to an era of coercive federalism. This term describes an era in which

1. the federal government is the dominant policymaker in the federal system,
2. the federal government can assert its policy will unilaterally over states and localities in virtually any policy field,

3. elected state and local officials are more often lobbyists than partners in intergovernmental policymaking,
4. interactions between federal officials and elected state and local officials are more often polite consultations than substantive negotiations,
5. there are few constitutional limits on the exercise of federal power,
6. cooperative policymaking when it occurs is most often due to the influence of interest groups operating outside the intergovernmental system than to state and local officials operating inside the intergovernmental system,
7. all important arenas of state and local decision making are infused with federal policy rules.

The principal characteristics of coercive federalism are

1. a shift of federal aid from places to persons,
2. conditions of aid that compel states to comply with policies that often fall outside of Congress's constitutional ambit,
3. federal mandates on state and local governments,
4. federal preemptions of state powers,
5. restrictions on state and local tax powers,
6. the nationalization of criminal law,
7. the demise of intergovernmental institutions,
8. a decline of intergovernmental political cooperation,
9. federal-court litigation (Kincaid 1990, 2008).

Federal Grants-in-Aid

Federal aid has shifted sharply from places to persons since 1978 (Kincaid 2001). In contrast to 1978, a high point in federal aid, when only 31.8 percent of aid was dedicated to payments for individuals (i.e., Medicaid and other social welfare), 54.7 percent of aid was dedicated to payments for individuals in 1988 and 65.2 percent in 2008. In 2015, about 70.9 percent of aid will go to payments for individuals.

This shift has six major consequences for state and local governments. *First*, it has reduced aid for place-based functions such as infrastructure, criminal justice, economic development, environmental protection, and government administration. Medicaid alone accounts for more than 45 percent of all federal aid. As the Government Accountability Office (GA) noted, because of Medicaid especially, "other federal grants—including those for education, highways, weatherization, housing, and other programs—are projected to decline as a percentage of GDP after 2010" (GAO 2010, p. 6). Thus, a long-term socioeconomic impact of this shift is likely to be reduced state and local spending on infrastructure, higher education, and other core functions that traditionally defined the states' raison d'être.

Yet such place-based functions are vital for the nation and for the development of human capital. They provide benefits and opportunities for everyone, not just special interests. As a recent Canadian government report also put it: "We are rediscovering that economic competitiveness, social well-being, and ecosystem resilience depend, in large part, on collective behaviour in specific places. . . . the complexity of today's problems requires more collaborative and integrated approaches, . . . policy decisions are interconnected, and . . . looking at place may help make sense of these connections. 'Place' is where the impacts of decisions are felt, whether they are made in other countries" (Shugart and Townsend 2010, pp. 4–5), Washington, D.C., or a state capital.

Second, this shift has wedded state budgets to social welfare programs susceptible to escalating federal regulation, cost-shifting, and matching state and sometimes local costs. Social welfare programs entail substantial federal regulation, even if they permit administrative discretion. On average, moreover, states spend about 17 percent of their general funds on Medicaid alone (with the federal match, about 22 percent of their budgets), making Medicaid the second largest category of state spending after K–12 education. By 2020, moreover, states will pay a rising portion of the costs stemming from the 2010 health care reform. Because of an aging population, Medicaid's long-term care component will become especially burdensome.

Third, the shift has heightened the role of states as administrative agents of the federal government, delivering services to individuals, historically a classic state role.

Fourth, the shift of aid from places to persons is the major factor in the decline of federal aid for local governments since the mid-1970s. States are the primary recipients of federal aid for social welfare. Local governments will likely experience further reductions in federal aid, with municipal governments being affected most acutely because they perform the fewest social welfare functions. In turn, though, states will have less revenue to send to local governments; state aid for K-12 education will take precedence over aid for most other local functions. Yet, local governments also face rising social welfare costs because they are welfare providers of last resort (e.g., county hospitals and municipal homeless programs) and because state and federal mandates have imposed costs on them (e.g., special education, which accounts for about 20 percent of school budgets). In addition, all school districts, most county governments, and many municipal and township governments face escalating personnel costs. For municipalities that have employees, the costs of wages, salaries, benefits, and pensions often consume well over 60 percent of the local budget.

Fifth, the growing scarcity of federal aid for non-social-welfare and non-Medicaid functions will likely increase competition among all the stakeholders in the contemporary governance system. This competition will militate against consolidations of the federal government's 800-some grants into block grants because interest groups will defend all programs that benefit them.

Sixth, this shift partly explains why, despite the huge increase in federal aid since 1987, this aid has not significantly alleviated long-term state-local fiscal stress. The infusion of $87 billion for Medicaid through the American Recovery and Reinvestment Act of 2009 still left most states with large budget shortfalls.

The negative consequences of this change in federal aid could be alleviated substantially if the federal government brought all senior citizens covered by Medicaid into the Medicare program (Scheppach and Shafroth 2008). This policy reform would probably enable states to fund all the costs of health care for the nonelderly poor, and still leave money for education, infrastructure, and other place-based functions. However, the federal government recently moved in the opposite direction by expanding Medicaid as part of its health care reform. In the long run, this will place more strain on state and local budgets. Even before this Medicaid expansion, the Government Accountability Office (GAO 2010) projected a steady fiscal decline for state and local governments through 2060, with revenue growth as a percentage of GDP likely remaining flat. If state and local governments wish to stem this decline, they will have to reduce spending by about 12.3 percent annually or increase revenues by 12.3 percent annually for the next 50 years. These are untenable policy paths.

Another coercive aid characteristic is the increased use of crosscutting and crossover conditions since the mid-1960s (ACIR 1984), such as speed limits, the 21-year-old alcoholic-beverage-purchase age, and drunk-driving blood-alcohol level attached to surface-transportation aid. These conditions advance federal policy objectives, and extract state and local spending on those objectives. Although the emergence of block grants during the era of coercive federalism led to predictions of a devolution revolution (e.g., see Conlan 1998; Nathan 1996), block grants account for only a small portion of federal aid. Congress has regularly reconditioned block grants, and block grants foster administrative discretion in federal policy implementation, not devolution of policymaking authority. This was evident in the Personal Responsibility and Work Opportunity Act of 1996, which gave states considerable discretion in how they achieved detailed federal policy objectives (Kincaid 1999). A survey of city officials reported that the "programmatic results of federal devolution policies . . . have been marginal at best" (Cole, Hissong, and Arvidson 1999).

A subcategory of conditional aid is congressional earmarking. Earmarks in appropriations bills increased from 1,439 in 1995 to 13,997 in 2005, thereafter dropping to 11,610 in 2008 (costing $17.2 billion) and 10,160 in 2009 (costing $19.6 billion) according to Citizens Against Government Waste (CAGW 2009). Faced with declining federal aid for place-based functions, members of Congress seek money for tangible public projects for which they can claim credit. In turn, state and local officials are compelled to lobby for earmarks as second-best sources of place-based funding, although members of Congress frequently earmark money for projects that conflict with state and local plans and needs.

Overall, Congress ought to eliminate earmarks and move toward more less-conditioned block grants rooted in intergovernmentally negotiated policy priorities. States beseech the Supreme Court to reconsider its 1988 *South Dakota v. Dole* ruling in which it acknowledged that conditions of aid could, in principle, become so coercive as to violate the Constitution.

Federal Mandates on State and Local Governments

Federal mandates, of which only two were enacted before 1964, increased significantly under coercive federalism until enactment of the Unfunded Mandates Reform Act of 1995 (UMRA). This law is one of the few restraints on coercive federalism. Since 1995, only 11 mandates have been enacted with costs above the act's threshold (Congressional Budget Office 2009, p. 2). However, UMRA covers only a narrow portion of federal actions that impose costs on states and localities and does not include conditions of aid, preemptions, and some other policies. Congress ought to amend UMRA to include such cost-inducing measures. The National Conference of State Legislatures (2010) estimated that federally induced costs for the states equaled at least $130 billion from 2004 to 2008. However, it also is estimated that during 2002–2008, the federal government promulgated an average of 527 rules per year regulating state governments and 343 regulating local governments, the costs of which are unknown (Crews 2009).

In UMRA's wake, Congress appears to be shifting from de jure to de facto mandates. One example is the REAL ID Act of 2005. States complain that it is underfunded and, in its original form, could have cost states about $13 billion to produce compliant driver's licenses. States can opt out of the act's rules. But if they do, their residents' licenses will not be accepted for any federal government purpose, including boarding an airplane, riding Amtrak trains, opening a bank account, purchasing a firearm, applying for federal benefits, and entering a federal building. Thus, while not technically a mandate, REAL ID puts states in such an untenable position with their citizens as to constitute a de facto mandate.

Mandates reflect the constant temptation for Congress to offload costs onto state and local governments to avoid the pain of asking federal taxpayers for more revenue. Fiscal discipline and accountability would be enhanced if the federal government were required to pay for its policy choices.

Federal Preemptions of State Powers

Another major characteristic of coercive federalism is preemption. From 1970 to 2004, Congress enacted some 320 explicit preemptions, compared to about 200 explicit preemptions enacted from 1789 to 1969 (National Academy of Public Administration, 2006). That is, 62 percent of all explicit preemptions in U.S. history have been enacted since 1969, a period accounting for only 15.8 percent of U.S. constitutional history (as of 2004). In addition, there is a vast but uncounted field of implied preemption embedded in federal agency and federal court rulings. Although some preemptions are beneficial to the states (Zimmerman 2010), the historically unprecedented leap in preemption since 1969 has irrevocably established the federal government as the top dog in the federal system.

Congress has thus far declined to enact preemption notification legislation proposed by the Advisory Commission on Intergovernmental Relations in 1988. Such legislation would notify the states of proposed preemptions. Galloping preemption of state economic regulatory powers should be reconsidered, too, especially in light of the financial crisis of 2008–2011. State regulators were not sufficiently equipped to check and balance lax and nonexistent federal regulation. The federal government's deregulatory trend, which began in 1978, was almost always accompanied by preemptions preventing the states from regulating what the federal government had deregulated. In light of the financial crisis and the likelihood of continuing economic volatility, it is vital that redundancy be restored to the federal system so that states can act more effectively in the face of federal inaction or neglect. When it must preempt, Congress should do so explicitly and with plain language; and it should employ partial preemption as much as possible. Partial preemption establishes national rules or standards but leaves certain state powers standing or allows states to establish rules or standards that are more rigorous than those enacted by Congress.

Restrictions on State and Local Tax Powers

Federal intrusions into state and local tax powers also characterize coercive federalism. Prominent examples are the Supreme Court's restriction on state sales-taxation of out-of-state mail-order sales (*Quill* 1992). In October 2007, President George W. Bush signed the Internet Tax Freedom Act Amendment Act, a seven-year extension of the moratorium on state-local taxation of Internet access. In response to *Quill,* some states have joined the Streamlined Sales and Use Tax Agreement; however, Congress has not approved the agreement. Consequently, the federal government is distorting state revenue systems and introducing inequities. In today's world, it is essential that states be able to collect sales taxes on out-of-state purchases and on computer-downloaded products.

A looming threat to state-local tax systems is the proposal to enact a federal value-added tax (VAT). A federal VAT would put tremendous downward pressure on state and local sales taxes and on state and local taxes generally, especially if a federal VAT were not offset by reductions in federal income taxes. Most other federal countries have a VAT, but those federations share their VAT revenue with their constituent governments, usually in the form of fiscal equalization. Thus far, discussions of a U.S. federal VAT have not featured promises to share that revenue with state and local governments.

Nationalization of Criminal Law

In the Kentucky Resolutions of 1789, Thomas Jefferson wrote that the U.S. Constitution "delegated to Congress a power to punish" four sets of crimes "and no other crimes whatever." Now, there are about 4,500 federal criminal laws, including about

50 capital offenses. This development (since the Omnibus Crime Control and Safe Streets Act of 1968) prompted Arthur Maass in 1987 to warn that "the most serious and politically disabling federal intrusion of recent years into the independent political status of state and local governments" was the rising federal campaign "to prosecute elected state and local officials . . . for local corruption" under vague and broadly drawn federal statutes not aimed at such officials (1987, p. 196).

Only recently have commentators, both left and right, awakened to the civil liberties dangers of this nationalization (Liptak 2009; Silverglate 2009), another feature of coercive federalism. Business interests are concerned, for example, about the federal theft-of-honest-services statute, which is frequently used to prosecute business executives and state and local officials. Civil libertarians worry about rights deprivations occurring under federal drug laws, such as longer sentences for black users of crack than for white users of powdered cocaine. The repressive potential of such statutes as the federal anti-riot act, which makes it a felony to cross state lines to "organize, promote, encourage, participate in, or carry on a riot," also elicit anxiety. Of particular concern are federal laws that are overly broad, vague, and punitive. Furthermore, some significant federal laws lack requirements to prove traditional types of criminal intent, allow federal prosecutors to shop for a conviction-friendly venue, and produce disproportionately large private property seizures compared to alleged offenses.

Demise of Intergovernmental Institutions

Coercive federalism also produced the demise of executive, congressional, and independent intergovernmental institutions established during the era of cooperative federalism. Most notable was the death of the Advisory Commission on Intergovernmental Relations in 1996 after 37 years of operation. Congress no longer has important committees devoted to federalism and intergovernmental relations. And federal departments have either no intergovernmental office or a highly political one. President Ronald Reagan dismantled the intergovernmental unit in the Office of Management and Budget. The GAO's intergovernmental unit was phased out in the early 1990s. The White House office currently called Intergovernmental Affairs and Public Engagement is an important political and favor-dispensing office but not a vital node for state and local influence over presidential policymaking.

Congress and the executive branch should consider reestablishing institutions able to improve intergovernmental relations, especially cooperation and coordination.

Decline of Political Cooperation

The old saying that "if you want a friend in Washington, D.C., get a dog" applies to intergovernmental relations as well. Absent political incentives, federal officials do not have altruistic motives to cooperate with state and local officials. As Senator

Carl Levin (D-MI) commented to this author in 1989, "there is no political capital in intergovernmental relations."

Since the collapse of the South as the bastion of states' rights, the disintegration of the New Deal Democratic coalition, and the decline of the traditional party system in the 1960s, there have been fewer incentives for federal officials to embrace intergovernmental political cooperation. This is another reason why reforms of gerrymandering and primaries are important to create incentives for federal officials to become more intergovernmentally attentive.

Federal Court Litigation

Coercive federalism has been marked as well by unprecedented numbers of federal court orders and a huge increase in lawsuits filed against state and local governments in federal courts. In terms of the Court's incorporation of the U.S. Bill of Rights, moreover, 59 percent of the selective incorporations occurred during the 1960s. Although federal court orders dictating major and costly changes in such institutions as schools, prisons, and mental health facilities have declined since the early 1990s, state and local governments are subject to high levels of litigation in federal courts. Furthermore, numerous judicial consent decrees, some of which can last more than 20 years, are another constraint on state and local officials. Decrees have become a major means to guarantee state or local government compliance with federal rules in many intergovernmental policy areas, such as education, environmental protection, and Medicaid. The U.S. Supreme Court resurrected the Eleventh Amendment in the 1990s to restrain some types of litigation, but the reach of the Court's decisions has been quite limited.

Litigation is costly for state and local governments; consequently, more emphasis should be placed on alternative-resolution mechanisms. And Congress and the courts should modify federal laws that create excessive incentives, including lucrative bounties, for interest groups to sue state and local governments.

Conclusion

This chapter's focus on federalism is not meant to imply that there are no other domains in need of reform, or that state and local governments are not also in need of reform. Instead, the chapter's contention is that federalism reform is necessary, though not sufficient, to achieve the objectives implied in the title of this volume.

References

Advisory Commission on Intergovernmental Relations (ACIR). 1984. *Regulatory Federalism: Policy, Process, Impact and Reform*, A-95. Washington, DC: ACIR February.

Bowman, Ann O'M. 1986. *The Resurgence of the States*. Englewood Cliffs, NJ: Prentice-Hall.

Citizens Against Government Waste (CAGW). 2009. *2009 Congressional Pig Book Summary*. Washington, DC: CAGW.

Cleveland, Harlan. 1972. *The Future Executive: A Guide for Tomorrow's Managers.* New York: Harper and Row.

Clinton, Bill. 1999. "Address by William Jefferson Clinton." *Publius: The Journal of Federalism* 29 (Fall): 23–32.

Cole, Richard, Rodney V. Hissong, and Enid Arvidson. 1999. "Devolution: Where's the Revolution?" *Publius: The Journal of Federalism* 29 (Fall): 99–112.

Congressional Budget Office. 2009. "Intergovernmental Mandates in Federal Legislation." Economic and Budget Issue Brief (July 14), Washington, DC.

Conlan, Timothy J. 1998. *From New Federalism to Devolution: Twenty-Five Years of Intergovernmental Reform.* Washington, DC: Brookings Institution.

Cook, Charles. 2010. "The Anti-Everything Mood." *National Journal* 42 (May 8): 72.

Crews, Clyde Wayne. 2009. *Ten Thousand Commandments.* Washington, DC: Competitive Enterprise Institute.

Galbraith, John Kenneth. 1952. *American Capitalism: The Concept of Countervailing Power.* New York: Houghton Mifflin.

Helderman, Rosalind S. 2010. "Virginia's Love-Hate Relationship with Federal Spending." *Washington Post,* May 6, B1.

Hetherington, Marc J. 2006. *Why Trust Matters: Declining Political Trust and the Demise of American Liberalism.* Princeton, NJ: Princeton University Press.

Hill, Carolyn J., and Laurence E. Lynn Jr. 2005. "Is Hierarchical Governance in Decline? Evidence from Empirical Research." *Journal of Public Administration Research and Theory* 15: 173–196.

Kincaid, John. 1990. "From Cooperative to Coercive Federalism." *Annals of the American Academy of Political and Social Science* 509 (May): 139–152.

———. 1993. "From Cooperation to Coercion in American Federalism: Housing, Fragmentation, and Preemption, 1780–1992." *Journal of Law and Politics* 9 (Winter): 333–433.

———. 1999. "De Facto Devolution and Urban Defunding: The Priority of Persons Over Places." *Journal of Urban Affairs* 21 (Summer): 135–167.

———. 2001. "The State of U.S. Federalism, 2000–2001: Continuity in Crisis," *Publius: The Journal of Federalism* 31 (Summer): 1–69.

———. 2008. "Three Faces of Contemporary American Federalism." In *The Federal Nation: Perspectives on North American Federalism,* ed. Iwan W. Morgan and Philip J. Davies, pp. 63–81. New York: Palgrave Macmillan.

Liptak, Adam. 2009. "Right and Left Join to Take on U.S. in Criminal Justices Cases." *New York Times,* November 24, A1, A22.

Maass, Arthur. 1987. "U.S. Prosecution of State and Local Officials for Political Corruption: Is the Bureaucracy Out of Control in a High-Stakes Operation Involving the Constitutional System?" *Publius: The Journal of Federalism* 17 (Summer): 195–230.

McCarty, Nolan, Keith T. Poole, and Howard Rosenthal. 2006. *Polarized America: The Dance of Ideology and Unequal Riches.* Cambridge, MA: MIT Press.

Nathan, Richard P. 1996. "The Devolution Revolution: An Overview." *Rockefeller Institute Bulletin 1996,* pp. 5–13. Albany, NY: Rockefeller Institute of Government.

National Academy of Public Administration (NAPA). 2006. *Beyond Preemption: Intergovernmental Partnerships to Enhance the New Economy.* Washington, DC: NAPA.

National Conference of State Legislatures (NCSL). 2010. *State Budget Update.* Lexington, KY: NCSL, November.

Quill Corp. v. North Dakota, 504 U.S. 298 (1992).

Scheppach, Raymond C., and Frank Shafroth. 2008. "Intergovernmental Finance in the New Global Economy." In *Intergovernmental Management for the 21st Century,* ed. Timothy J. Conlan and Paul L. Posner, pp. 42–74. Washington, DC: Brookings Institution Press.

Schumpeter, Joseph A. 1950. *Capitalism, Socialism and Democracy.* New York: Harper and Row.

Shugart, Ian, and Thomas Townsend. 2010. "Bringing 'Place' On—Exploring the Role of the Federal Government in Place-Based Approaches." *Horizons* 10 (March): 4–6.

Silverglate, Harvey A. 2009. *Three Felonies a Day: How the Feds Target the Innocent.* New York: Encounter Books.

Stockman, David. 1986. *The Triumph of Politics: How the Reagan Revolution Failed.* New York: Harper and Row.

U.S. Government Accountability Office (GAO). 2010. "State and Local Governments' Fiscal Outlook: March 2010 Update." GAO-10–358. Washington, DC: U.S. GAO.

Young, Kerry, and Greg Giroux. 2010. "After 40 Years, Tired but Still Blunt." *CQ Weekly* (May 10): 1149.

Zimmerman, Joseph F. 2010. *Congress: Facilitator of State Action.* Albany, NY: SUNY Press.

8

Collaborative Regional Networked Systems

Thom Reilly and Robert J. Tekniepe

Traditional city and county governments are being replaced by new collaborative approaches to governance: regional structures with complex networks of local governments, limited-purpose regional authorities and taxing districts, and private, civic, faith-based, and nonprofit organizations participating in local governance simultaneously are becoming far more common (Foster 2000). Over the last couple of decades, there has been a proliferation of these regional governance structures and arrangements both to provide a regionwide platform for economic development and regional planning (Luger 2007; Ye 2009), and to address the ever-growing number of cross-boundary, complex, and large-scale problems affecting local communities (Frahm and Martin 2009; Kettl 2000; Laslo and Judd 2006). However, barriers to effective regional cooperation remain high. Muro (2008) recently proclaimed: "While leaders may want to promo megascaled responses to megascale problems, they are frequently hobbled because they lack the super-scaled governance and networks needed to shape their futures" (p. 6). Many regional institutions are weak, and federal and state program, policy, agency, and funding structures often impede effective cross-jurisdictional problem solving (Berube 2007; Muro et al. 2008; NAPA 1998).

The United States is essentially a metropolitan nation. And there is a growing recognition that its 363 metropolitan areas are the key to national prosperity and home to much of its economic, cultural, and social life (Berube 2007). Over 65 percent of the U.S. population, and 77 percent of its ethnic minority population, live in the 100 largest metro regions. Two-thirds of all U.S. jobs and three-quarters of the nation's output are also generated by the 100 largest metro regions (Muro et al. 2008). The operations and effectiveness of regional networks and local governance are critical to the American economy and to the ability of the United States to continue to recover from the Great Recession. This chapter examines the need for and current state of collaborative regional networked systems; explores barriers to establishing effective cross-jurisdictional problem solving; outlines key features necessary for these structures to become effective, efficient, and economically viable; and outlines the type of federal policy agenda needed to support these structures.

Traditional Public Service Delivery Models

For the better part of the 20th century, hierarchical government organizations were the predominant service delivery model used to distribute regional public services and execute public policy goals and objectives (Goldsmith and Eggers 2004). These traditional structures were typified by their pyramid shape and top-down configuration, and could be characterized in two ways. In the first, the lower levels of the pyramid are fully included in the higher levels. In the second, the lower levels are superseded by the higher levels (top-down) (van Dijk and Winters 2009).

Near the turn of the century, researchers began to view shared services systems or "networks" as the new organizing model for the delivery of public goods and services (Agranoff and McGuire 2001a; Frederickson and Smith 2003). In many respects, the new framework associated with the term "networks" embodies the contemporary analyses and practices of public administration (Heinrich, Hill, and Lynn 2004). One reason for the recent focus on networks is the newfound relationship between public service providers and the populations they serve (Kettl 2002). The contemporary view of networks suggests that governmental institutions will no longer act in the role of direct service providers; instead, they will become producers of public value within the web of multigovernmental relationships that increasingly characterize modern government (Goldsmith and Eggers 2004). This new perspective also suggests that the traditional view of hierarchical government structures as best suited for the delivery of public services is falling by the wayside, with the idea networks—public service providers operating within a setting of multiple shared forces—taking its place (Stoker 1998).

Most recently, regional delivery systems have caught the attention of many researchers. These systems, which are synergetic alliances of local governments, describe shared services delivery models between area and regional governments, such as municipalities and counties, and nongovernmental partners. Where municipalities and counties once acted as the predominant overseers of local public service delivery, regional delivery systems are now being viewed as a more appropriate method of delivery (Agranoff and McGuire 2001b). Regional delivery systems of the 21st century will require greater recognition of the dispersion of local jurisdictional authority as well as the increasingly complex governmental boundaries (Goldsmith and Eggers 2004).

Trend Toward Shared Service Delivery Models, or "Networks"

To most researchers, it is quickly becoming apparent that public service delivery by means of hierarchical government bureaucracies is coming to an end. Emerging in its place are shared service delivery models, or networks, designed to provide more integrated services across multiple governmental boundaries. A shared service delivery model simply implies a separate and distinct entity whose focal point is on shared responsibility for an end result that exemplifies a high level of service and public satisfaction. Recent actions among local community stakeholders toward decentralizing vertically integrated, intergovernmental partners, as well as private and not-for-profit agencies that operate on more horizontal levels, are leading this revolution of change (DeGroff 2009).

The need to horizontally integrate multiple hierarchical government structures and private/not-for-profit agencies in the delivery of a shared public service is considered a primary driver toward the use of networks. The increased emphasis on decentralization, combined with an increased dependence on independent third parties as service delivery focal points, has contributed vastly to the expansion of the contemporary network model (Milward and Provan 2004). Some researchers have gone as far as suggesting that particular policy tools encourage the utilization of network models (Agranoff and McGuire 2001b; Salamon 2002).

Another major factor contributing to the emergence of shared service delivery structures is their ability to effectively maintain the collaborative interactions necessary to address complex problems (Agranoff and McGuire 2001b; Keast et al. 2004; O'Toole 1997). Coordinated efforts encompassing a multitude of governmental and nongovernmental agencies, as well as various levels of government, ensure a high degree of integration and efficiency in the delivery of public services (Agranoff and McGuire 2001a).

Further contributing to the trend toward creating networked delivery models is the emergence of more difficult and complex social problems, problems that necessitate the involvement of many stakeholders (Agranoff and McGuire 2001b; O'Toole 1997). DeGroff (2009) suggests this is certainly the case when problems reflect the collision of economic, social, physical, and environmental factors.

Finally, in a federal grant-funding environment exemplified by a "stovepiped" grant submission and award mechanism, networked delivery models offer a more holistic solution to the regional delivery of public services. In fact, more and more federal grant-funding opportunities are requiring regional and/or statewide alliances as a factor (Wandersman, Goodman, and Butterfoss 1997).

Given this fact, it is easy to see why many researchers view the 21st-century networked delivery system as one that will involve not just one agency, with sole responsibility, accountability, and authority over the delivery of public services, but an interdependent network of governmental, private, and not-for-profit agencies working in unison (Frederickson and Smith 2003; Kettl 2002; Milward and Provan 2006).

What Are Collaborative Regional Networked Systems?

A central feature of regionally shared service delivery systems, or collaborative regional networked systems, is their ability to coexist between traditional hierarchical government structures and horizontal, voluntary associations (Hill and Lynn 2005). Collaborative regional networked systems also incorporate horizontal relationships designed to increase the efficiency of delivering shared public services by partnering governmental agencies with nongovernmental agencies.

Milward and Provan (2006) cite a slightly different definition by McGuire that more clearly recognizes the relationships that are the foundations of networked systems: networks are organizational structures involving multiple nodes—governmental and nongovernmental agencies and organizations—with multiple linkages. Such network systems can be formal or informal, and are typically intersectional, intergovernmental, and based functionally in a specific policy or public service delivery arena.

Collaborative regional networked systems can also be defined as an interdependence of governmental and nongovernmental structures involving multiple entities in which a single stakeholder or unit is not merely the formal subordinate of the others in a larger hierarchical arrangement (O'Toole 1997). As O'Toole suggests, the institutional fastener that solidifies networked bonds may include a stakeholder's authoritative power, exchange relations, and shared public service needs based on common interest.

Salamon (2002) suggests that all shared service delivery systems possess four key characteristics: pluriformity, self-referential, asymmetric interdependencies, and dynamics. *Pluriformity* refers to the involvement of a diverse range of governmental and nongovernmental agencies, each exhibiting a limited amount of experience in collaboration as well as an understanding of each other's styles of operation. *Self-referential* denotes independent interests in the organizations participating in the networked system, each with its own unique set of perspectives and incentives. *Asymmetric interdependencies* simply mean that all network stakeholders depend on each other, but in asymmetric ways. *Dynamics* indicates that a network's features constantly transform in response to the various conditions of stakeholder repositioning, leadership changes, and strategy shifts.

Most recently, Milward and Provan (2006) put forth the viewpoint that collaborative regional networked systems of the 21st century will most likely fall into one of four categories. The first category is termed "service implementation networks," and consists of intergovernmental programs often funded by federal grants, for example, services programs for the disadvantaged. The second category is "information diffusion networks," which governmental and nongovernmental agencies use to develop the means to share information across jurisdictional boundaries. The third category is "problem-solving networks," which are designed to help policymakers set agendas in regard to regional problems. The fourth category is "community capacity-building networks," which is intended to build social capital to help regional institutions better handle the ever-increasing multitude of complex problems, for example, economic development and crime abatement.

Why There Is a Need for Collaborative Regional Networked Systems

Whereas many allude to fiscal responsibility as the principal factor in implementing collaborative regional networked systems, local governmental agencies that seek high performance will take a more value-oriented viewpoint toward adopting networked systems. For example, a local governmental agency may seek to leverage the full potential of regionally shared service delivery systems by recruiting fellow governmental entities, as well as private and not-for-profit agencies, in an effort to improve public-sector value and the delivery of public services (Kamarck 2007).

DeGroff (2009) builds upon Kamarck's perspective on the need for collaborative regional networked systems, that governmental agencies are finding it difficult to address a myriad of complex horizontal service delivery problems with traditional vertical solutions. DeGroff sees the role of the 21st-century governmental agency quickly being transformed from a direct service provider to a generator of public value. Public value, according to Chrislip and Larson (1994), includes the collaborative regional networked systems' ability to achieve tangible results, generate new processes that lead to solutions where in the past traditional approaches have failed, empower citizenry and nongovernmental stakeholders and groups, and fundamentally change the way regional government institutions address complex problems and issues (in the conjunctive).

De Sanctis and Fulk (1999), on the other hand, suggest a slightly different explanation for the expansion and need of collaborative regional networked systems: the combination of horizontal and vertical control and coordination. According to van Dijk (2006), this is the secret of the potential benefits that collaborative regional networked systems, as flexible organizational forms, can yield. Collaboration among governmental entities and/or private and not-for-profit agencies at various levels of the structures is, obviously, a fundamental transformation of how local governments attempt to fulfill their responsibilities of delivering public services.

Goldsmith and Eggers (2004) propose that the advantages attributed to the 21st-century regional networked system are fourfold. *First,* flexibility is enhanced because collaborative regional networked systems are apt to be more lithe and nimble than their traditional hierarchical counterparts. *Second,* innovation improves because more-novel solutions to complex problems are encouraged in a collaborative environment, free of the rule-bound setting inherent in traditional hierarchical governments. *Third,* specialization is nurtured, because collaborative regional networked systems allow a government to concentrate on its core mission by leveraging the expertise of "best-of-breed" providers. *Fourth,* reaction speed improves because the decentralized, fluid form of a regional networked system and the independence of each stakeholder allow for decision making at the local level.

The Current State of Collaborative Regional Networked Systems

It comes as no surprise that regional governmental institutions are in the midst of transforming the fundamental ways in which they provide public services, with improved overall system efficiency and effectiveness in mind (Robertson and Speier 1998). In fact, most local governmental agencies are considering, planning, implementing, or have recently implemented collaborative regional networked systems in one form or another (Bryson, Crosby, and Stone 2006; Milward and Provan 2006).

The heightened interest in collaborative regional networked systems—entities that rely upon synergetic alliances between not only local governmental and nongovernmental institutions, but a wide range of special interest groups and concerned citizens as well—has generated a variety of new and innovative organizational structures, such as partnerships, coalitions, alliances, strategic alliances, consortiums, and networks (McGuire 2006; O'Toole and Meier 2004; Thomson and Perry 2006; Vigoda 2002).

Some of the reforms have been aimed at new forms of bureaucratic management, while others have called for a departure from traditional monocentric bureaucratic structures to alterative forms of network coordination (Svensson, Trommel, and Lantink 2008). Governmental reorganization, such as merging different levels of government into one consolidated unit, has been difficult to implement, and has not been very popular in the United States (Ye 2009). As Leland and Thurmaier (2005) found, only 34 city-county consolidations have actually occurred since 1805, and approximately 85 percent of consolidation campaigns have failed. This is largely due to the constitutional design of American government and public choice theory (Ye 2009). Local government structures extend to the suburbs where they have the political power to resist increases in taxes to support regional-wide services. And smaller governmental structures can be seen as more efficient because they can tailor their services and taxes to their individual residents.

In a recent report from the National League of Cities, researchers Parr, Riehm, and McFarland (2006) identified 17 regional organizational approaches, organized along a continuum of implementation difficulty ranging from easier to harder, which could offer benefits when local governmental agencies embark on creating a regional networked system. Each approach presents its own unique set of opportunities for advancing regional-scale public service delivery.

What follows is short explanations of the nine most popular, widespread organizational approaches currently in use, beginning with the simplest approach and ending with the most difficult. Examples of communities using each approach illustrate the real-life applications of collaborative regional networked systems.

1. *Informational Cooperation* is an approach that typically involves two or more local jurisdictions that offer reciprocal actions to each other, such as the St. Louis Regional Chamber and Growth Association (RCGA), a regional network that represents a 16-county, bi-state area. The RCGA has three primary roles: to serve as the regional chamber of commerce for over 4,000 member companies; to serve as the bi-state region's lead economic development organization; and to investigate and support public policy initiatives that help the region thrive and grow.

2. *Joint Powers Agreement* is an agreement between two or more local governments to provide shared planning, financing, and service delivery

to residents of all involved jurisdictions. An example would be the Metropolitan Transportation Commission for the nine-county San Francisco Bay Area, which is tasked with transportation planning and acts as the coordinating and financing agency for the Bay Area.

3. *Council of Governments* are organizations formed by counties and cities to service local governments and residents in a region through government cooperation, such as the North Central Texas Council of Governments. These involve voluntary association of, by, and for local governments to assist in planning for common needs, cooperating for mutual benefit, and coordinating for sound regional development.

4. *Federally Encouraged Single-Purpose Regional Bodies* are organizations formed to administer some federal aid programs. Today, single-purpose regional bodies are primarily formed for transportation planning and funding activities, such as the Metropolitan Area Planning Council (MAPC) for metropolitan Boston. The MAPC is a regional planning agency serving the people who live and work in metropolitan Boston; its primary purpose is to promote smart growth and regional collaboration.

5. *Local Special Districts* is an approach for providing single services or multiple related services to a number of jurisdictions, for example, water reclamation. One example is the Snyderville Basin Water Reclamation District, which provides state-of-the-art wastewater collection and reclamation services for Park City, Utah, and the surrounding area.

6. *Transfer of Functions* is a method used to permanently change who provides specific services, with one government releasing authority to another. A good example is the Erie County Central Police Services, an administrative criminal justice agency established to provide centralized countywide support services to law enforcement and criminal justice agencies in Erie County, New York, including enhanced 911 and police radio communications, a forensic laboratory, computerized systems, and law enforcement education.

7. *Special Districts and Authorities* are entities designed to address single issues, such as mass transit, pollution control, hospitals, airports, or water supply, on an areawide basis. The Las Vegas Valley Water District (LVVWD) in Nevada, for example, is a not-for-profit water supply agency that has provided water to the Las Vegas Valley since 1954. The LVVWD helped build the area's water delivery system and now provides water to the city of Las Vegas and the unincorporated areas of Clark County.

8. *Metro Multipurpose Districts* are districts established to perform many diverse functions, not just one set of related services (as special districts and authorities are). One example is the Multi-Purpose Community Action Agency (MPCAA), which serves Bullitt, Shelby, and Spencer

counties in Kentucky. The MPCAA is designed to help citizens meet basic needs such as health, safety, food, and shelter; it primarily serves individuals and families seeking a road out of poverty into self-sufficiency, and elderly citizens seeking assistance in maintaining independent living arrangements.

9. *Regional Asset Districts* are special tax districts used to fund regional resources, such as arts and cultural institutions, entertainment venues (like sports stadiums), and parks and libraries. One example of a regional asset district would be the Allegheny, New York, Regional Asset District, a special-purpose areawide unit of local government designed to support and finance regional assets in the areas of libraries, parks and recreation, cultural activities, and sports and civic facilities and programs.

Collaborative regional networked systems are not unknown in most local jurisdictions. In fact, an increasing number of local public administrators and elected officials are sensing the need for furthering these systems within their own communities. How and why local organizations choose a specific structure may have to be carefully weighed to achieve a balance between flexibility and stability (Edgar and Chandler 2004; Goldsmith and Eggers 2004; Milward and Provan 2000).

Principal Factors That Influence the Success of Collaborative Regional Networked Systems

Addressing all the factors that influence a successful outcome of any regional networked system can be challenging, considering the vast amount of research performed in this arena and the various views and opinions this research has spawned (Linden 2010). Despite these conditions, there seems to be general agreement that 20 key factors (in one form or another) nestled within six general categories are necessary for collaborative regional networked systems to succeed (Agranoff and McGuire 2003; Fischer 2006; Fung and Wright 2001; Goldsmith and Eggers 2004; Mattessich, Murray-Close, and Monsey 2001; Ray 2002; Salamon 2002; Sorenson 2006; Winer and Ray 1994).

Category 1: Environment

Factors 1 through 3 reside in the first general category, labeled "environment." These factors include:

1. *a history of past collaboration* between key local entities such that representative stakeholders can gain an understanding of their roles and expectations as participants of the networked system;
2. a view that local entities represented in the networked system are *reliable and competent;*

3. *general support* from local entity public administrators and/or elected officials toward the system's mission, goals, and objectives.

Category 2: Member Characteristics

Factors 4 through 7 make up the second general category, "member characteristics." These factors are:

4. members share *mutual respect, understanding, and trust* toward each other and the local entities they represent;
5. the networked system includes an *appropriate cross-section of stake-holders;*
6. stakeholders see real benefits from their participation in the process;
7. stakeholders are willing to *negotiate to affect compromise,* knowing that one resulting course of action will not fit the exact preferences of each stakeholder.

Category 3: Process and Structure

Factors 8 through 13 relate to the third category, titled "process and structure." Within this category, the factors are:

8. stakeholders feel a sense of ownership such that they mutually share in the network system's processes and outcomes;
9. a multiple-layered representation scheme exists within each of the participating entities' management hierarchies;
10. the networked system remains flexible in organizing itself and accomplishing its mission;
11. stakeholders have a clear understanding of their respective roles, rights, and responsibilities;
12. stakeholders are able to adapt to changes to ensure the sustainability of the system;
13. the networked system is allowed to evolve over time at a reasonable pace that does not impede its capabilities.

Category 4: Communication

Factors 14 and 15 constitute the fourth category, called "communication." These two factors are:

14. stakeholders *interact and update each other on a regular basis* with regard to important issues related to the networked system;
15. stakeholders maintain not only formal lines of communication, but *informal lines of communication* as well.

Category 5: Purpose

Factors 16 through 18 make up the fifth category, labeled "purpose." These factors include:

16. *realistic goals and objectives* that are clear to all stakeholders and obtainable;
17. a *shared purpose or vision* among stakeholders;
18. a sense that the *mission of the system is sufficiently different from that of the participating entities.*

Category 6: Resources

Factors 19 and 20 constitute category 6, labeled "resources." These factors are:

19. *sufficient resources* exist, such as funding, staffing, time, and materials, to accomplish the networked system's mission;
20. the networked system has in place *skilled leadership.*

Barriers to Establishing Collaborative Regional Networked Systems

While many local governmental agencies are currently considering, planning, or implementing collaborative regional networked systems, others are taking a more guarded view. This cautious stance by local governmental entities is principally due to perceived and/or real barriers to a networked system's success.

For example, in *21st Century Local Government,* the April 2008 report of the New York State Commission on Local Government Efficiency and Competitiveness, researchers found that local public administrators and elected officials expressed grave concerns about turning over control of local governmental services. Their concerns included apprehension over the possible loss of control of public service deliveries over time and the reduced level of responsiveness provided by networking the service; trepidation over the potential loss of local identity; alarm that larger governmental agencies will be favored over smaller, less influential ones; and suspicions that at a later point, overall costs will increase as employee wages and benefits rise to the level offered by the highest-paying community.

Barriers to establishing collaborative regional networked systems have also sometimes been categorized as either external or internal impediments. External impediments may include conflicting or competing policies of participating entities and/or conflict within the networked system due to the different organizational views of the stakeholders. Internal impediments may consist of political or strategic resistance of participating entities; a lack of necessary manpower, skills, capacity, and information necessary to accomplish the networked system mission; various cultural backgrounds; conflicting objectives; and stakeholder concerns about the extent to which collaborative regional networked systems can offer real and significant savings.

Collaborative regional networked systems, by virtue of their organizational structure and mission, also reflect the propensity for difficult outcomes, both individual and organizational, because they must result from the actions of a multitude of stakeholders addressing complex problems in unity (van Dijk and Winters 2009). In a shared decision-making environment, leaders must effectively foster collaboration of stakeholders that once aligned themselves with different types of governmental entities, as well as nongovernmental and not-for-profit agencies (Abramson, Breul, and Kamensky 2006). This raises a potential barrier that Milward and Provan (2004) term the "joint production problem"—an impediment that results when program synchronization and execution occurs across a decentralized service network.

Other barriers that may impede the establishment of an effective collaborative regional networked system fall into the category of legal issues. These can include state, county, and municipal statutes, codes and regulations, union labor agreements, collective bargaining, and arbitration awards.

Features Necessary for Structures to Become Effective, Efficient, and Economical

Berube (2007) and Muro et al. (2008) argue that the United States and its economy are metropolitan, and this is where the nation's future economic competitiveness, social health, and environmental sustainability will be decided. The term "metropolitan areas" has been used to define new urban spaces connected by transportation networks and widespread economic and social activity (Lang and Dhavale 2005). These spaces share a physical geography and a political and structural history, and they exist throughout the United States. Geographer Jean Gottman used the term "megalopolis" in the late 1950s to describe the growing economic, cultural, and political corridor from Boston to Washington, D.C. (Lang and Dhavale 2005). More recently, Lang, Sarzynski, and Muro (2008) from the Brookings Institution have coined a new urban form, "mountain megas," to describe a super-region or "urban agglomeration" of five southern Intermountain West states connected by transportation networks and widespread economic, social, political, and urban activity. These authors have suggested that there is a need in the United States to have a "a purposeful, supportive, and effective body of federal, state, and local policies and stances that can help unleash the full potential of America's 363 varied engines of prosperity" (Muro et al. 2008, p. 5).

Effective regional governance systems will largely depend on producing a new breed of leaders who are skilled in managing networks; replacing the functional budgeting and personnel systems that dominate local governments and do not lend themselves to cross-jurisdictional problem solving; focusing on community indicators and organizational performance standards to determine success or failure;

and bringing in a federal government that works with local communities to create more deliberate, coherent, and strategic policies that support quality places to live and allow for productive and sustainable economic growth.

New Leadership to Manage Networks Effectively

To be effective at cross-jurisdictional problem solving, government needs a new breed of leaders at the local and regional level who promote collective action to advance the public good by engaging government, general-purpose entities, quasi-public and nonprofit organizations, private industry, and citizens. Instead of delivering the service themselves, local government managers need to become facilitators, conveners, and brokers who engage the community's talents to solve difficult and complex problems (Goldsmith and Eggers 2004; Laslo and Judd 2006; Reilly 2007).

Local governments need an array of employees who not only can perform traditional duties, such as planning, budgeting, and deploying staff, but also are trained in boundary-scanning skills—such as facilitation and negotiation, contract negotiation and management, and risk analysis—and the ability to manage across boundaries (Goldsmith and Eggers 2004; Salamon 2002; Thomas 2007). Frahm and Martin (2009) have suggested, in addition, activation/enabling skills to bring public, private, nonprofit, and other agencies to the table to jointly address issues; framing skills to arrange and facilitate agreement on respective roles; orchestration skills to keep everyone working cooperatively; mobilization skills to build and maintain support; synthesizing skills to create cooperative environments; and modulation skills to successfully use rewards and penalties to solicit and maintain cooperative interactions between various players.

Public managers not only must effectively manage people inside government, but also must focus on outward negotiating shared purposes, coordinating services, mobilizing resources, and forging political coalitions that benefit the entire community. The key is to be able to influence the strategic actions of other actors, as well as to be able to effectively manage resources that belong to others. It is critical that universities include these skills in their undergraduate and graduate curriculums and broaden the curriculums' perspective to include the emerging tools of collective action. As well, public, private, and nonprofit agencies need to build these competencies into their recruitment and hiring practices, in-house training courses, and job performance standards.

Budgeting and Personnel Systems That Do Not Lend Themselves to Cross-Jurisdictional Problem Solving

As previously discussed, local governments are dominated by organizational structures that still operate under the assumption that they will deliver services directly, even though services are increasingly being delivered through multiple and often nongovernmental partners. The challenge is to build an organization that can structure itself hierarchically for some problems and nonhierarchically for others (Nalbandian and Nalbandian 2003). According to Kettl (2000), "government's structure is function based, at a time when more of its problems are area based" (p. 495). As seen earlier in this chapter, a number of regional network systems and shared service delivery models are emerging across the United States in an attempt to be more creative and responsive to boundary-spanning problems. However, the functional budgeting and personnel systems that dominate local governments often prevent the cross-jurisdictional problem solving that is needed. The budgeting systems seldom have the ability to track community-wide expenditures and capture the number and dollar volume of contracts awarded; they are apt to be focused on single agencies. Likewise, the civil service system is organization focused, hierarchical, and built on the assumption of direct service delivery (Kettl 2000). Increased unionization of the public sector has produced labor agreements and rigid job classifications focused on single governmental entities. Collective bargaining units differ from local government to local government, making it difficult to craft job classifications and performance rewards that allow cross-boundary work with multiple actors. New regional institutional arrangements are needed, with their own fiscal and administrative powers that are focused on the community or region. Involvement of the private and nonprofit sectors may contribute to or facilitate these institutional arrangements and offer additional accountability measures, along with flexible and creative tools for collective action.

Focusing on a Measurement System That Incorporates Program and Community Outcomes

As traditional governmental service delivery systems are replaced by more horizontal, collaborative regional networked systems, there will be a greater need to put in place mechanisms that are capable of gauging the successes and/or failures of the new systems. Given this situation, networked system leaders may want to strongly consider implementing a comprehensive measurement system that is capable of monitoring both program and community outcomes (Kelly 2002; Poister 2003).

Program outcomes sometimes represent performance indicators, such as financial/nonfinancial, internal/external, or short-/long-term conditions of the system, to measure the efficiency and effectiveness of an organization (Henri 2006; Neely 1999). Performance measurement systems—coupled with program outcome indicators that express the dynamic characteristics of the organization—help provide an accurate and measurable picture of what an organization looks like and the direction in which it is heading (Carrier and Wallis 2005).

Community outcomes, on the other hand, measure the impact that program outcomes have on the community. They are not program visions or goals, but the networked system's destination. When selecting community outcomes, it is important to choose results that are achievable. Selecting community outcomes often involves reducing the networked system's vision or goal to a more specific change or benefit to the community, for example, for a select geographic area or population group.

Comprehensive measurement systems have been widely used at the federal level, and to a lesser extent at the regional and local levels. The practice has primarily been based on measuring program outputs in the traditional view of bureaucratic hierarchy, where the formal lines of command and control—or responsibility, accountability, and authority—are customarily straightforward (Frederickson 2003; Frederickson and Frederickson 2006; Perrin 1998, 2006).

There are many collaborative regional networked systems in existence today, with many more in the planning stage. Each networked system is unique because of its size, location, structure, scope, participant makeup, fiscal capability, and community purpose. While each networked system may have a different purpose, their principal focus is still the same: efficient and effective delivery of public services (Carrier and Wallis 2005). Measurement systems provide network system leaders with a tool to not only measure program and community outputs but enhance the efficiency and effectiveness of current or future programs (Jennings and Haist 2004; Wholey 1999).

A Federal Policy Agenda That Supports Local Governance

The role of the federal government in prompting collaborative regional network systems is critical; however, instead of promoting cross-jurisdictional problem solving, the federal government often impedes (or does not adequately support) these efforts because of its program, policy, and funding structures. Furthermore, according to Lang, Sarzynski, and Muro (2008), the federal government has mostly withdrawn from its past efforts in the 1960s and 1970s in supporting regional problem solving. In 1998, the National Academy of Public Administration (NAPA) commissioned a report on how the federal government could help build stronger regional communities and concluded that money, flexibility in federal rules and requirements, increased public debate, and the provision of information were essential. These requests are still relevant and needed today. Ten years later, the Brookings Institution embarked on a multiyear initiative called "The Blueprint for American Prosperity" to promote an economic agenda for the United States that builds on the strengths of metropolitan areas (Berube 2007; Lang, Sarzynski, and Muro 2008; Muro et al. 2008).

The Brookings report offers a compelling federal agenda geared toward empowering local communities to respond effectively and realistically to mega-sized and messy issues. It calls for the federal government to spur innovation, grow human capital, create state-of-the-art infrastructure, and develop innovative quality places by (1) leading where it must because of the need to match the scale and geographic reach of key current challenges, (2) empowering metro areas where it should to reflect the variety of metropolitan experiences and unleash the potential for innovation and experimentation that resides closest to the ground, and (3) maximizing performance and fundamentally altering the way it does business in a changing world (Muro et al. 2008).

The "ask" from Washington is as much that the federal government provide the right framework as that it write more checks. Like the NAPA report, the Brookings report calls for *information via better data and modeling* and *assistance in facilitating creative, collaborative regional agreements.* The report even goes so far as to suggest that the federal government could not only promote, but incentivize, regionalism and regional planning. At the very least, it strongly urges the federal government to take a more active and constructive role by encouraging and promoting bolder cross-boundary collaboration. The federal government could accomplish this by (1) rewarding the most path breaking proposals for connecting regional and superregional governance areas in transportation planning, land use, and housing; (2) awarding money to partnerships between states, localities, regional business alliances, and other groups that focus on the boldest, multijurisdictional proposals for improving cross-boundary coordination, service, and program integrations or regional decision making; and (3) providing seed funding for regionally scaled and regionally tailored public-private partnerships (Lang, Sarzynski, and Muro 2008).

Requests for monetary assistance would mostly involve *compensating state and local governments* for the impacts of immigrant populations, boosting the wages of lower-income workers and their families by expanding and modernizing the Earned Income Tax Credit program, and forging partnerships with private and philanthropic organizations to provide access to higher education. Such assistance would help address uneven prosperity levels in many metropolitan areas.

Finally, Katz (2010) suggests a need to "connect macro vision to metro reality" and calls for the federal government to establish a new National Infrastructure Bank to invest in regionally and nationally significant high-value projects for the future, as well as a National Innovation Foundation to bring under one roof efforts to boost commercial innovations in such areas as manufacturing, information technology, and clean energy.

The work contained in "The Blueprint for American Prosperity" offers a focused roadmap and obtainable agenda for empowering local communities to address large-scale issues. The call to action is not just a request for a handout from the federal government. Instead, the report argues that the federal government should simply provide the kind of basic rules, tools, and resources that will allow local entities to prosper.

Conclusion

Considerable attention has been given to the need for local communities to transform the roles, responsibilities, and configurations of the institutions that govern civil society. Development in many metropolitan areas is widely believed to be outstripping regions' local governance structures and their ability to influence events, raising the need for a new governance arrangement that supports solutions on critical large-scale issues like infrastructure, education, energy, immigration, and economic development (Muro 2008).

The reality is that creating effective governance for today's interconnected web of cities, counties, and suburbs will require bold approaches and new institutional arrangements that rely on dynamic and rich networks of governmental and nongovernmental actors. It is essential that local leaders be skilled in managing networks and that traditional governmental service delivery systems be replaced by more horizontal, collaborative regional networked systems. Furthermore, measurement systems must incorporate program and community outcomes. Finally, the federal government must implement an aggressive, supportive partnership that empowers local communities in addressing large-scale, cross-jurisdictional problems in an efficient, effective, and economically viable manner.

References

Abramson, Mark. A., Jonathan. D. Breul, and John M. Kamensky. 2006. *Six Trends Transforming Government.* Washington, DC: IBM Center for the Business of Government.

Agranoff, Robert, and M. McGuire. 2001a. "American Federalism and the Search for Models of Management." *Public Administration Review* 61(6): 671–681.

———. 2001b. "Big Questions in Public Network Management Research." *Journal of Public Administration Research and Theory* 11(3): 295–326.

———. 2003. *Collaborative Public Management: New Strategies for Local Governments.* Washington, DC: Georgetown University Press.

Berube, A. 2007. *MetroNation: How U.S. Metropolitan Areas Fuel American Prosperity.* Washington, DC: Brookings Institution Press.

Bryson, James M., B. C. Crosby, and M. M. Stone. 2006. "The Design and Implementation of Cross-Sector Collaborations: Propositions from the Literature." *Public Administration Review* 66(1): 44–55.

Carrier, A., and A. Wallis. 2005. *Regional Indicators: Telling Stories, Measuring Trends, Inspiring Action.* Denver: Alliance for Regional Stewardship.

Chrislip, D. D., and C. E. Larson. 1994. *Collaborative Leadership: How Residents and Civic Leaders Can Make a Difference.* San Francisco: Jossey-Bass.

Commission on Local Government Efficiency and Competitiveness. 2008. *21st Century Local Government.* Report of the New York State Commission on Local Government Efficiency and Competitiveness, April. New York: State of New York.

DeGroff, A. S. 2009. New Public Management and Governance Collide: Federal-level Performance Measurement in Networked Public Management Environments. PhD diss., Georgia State University.

DeSanctis, G., and J. Fulk. 1999. *Shaping Organizational Form: Communication, Connection and Community.* Thousand Oaks, CA: Sage.

Edgar, L., and J. Chandler. 2004. *Strengthening Social Policy: Lessons on Forging Government-Civil Society Policy Partnerships.* Ottawa, Ontario, Canada: Institute on Governance.

Fischer, F. 2006. "Participatory Governance as Deliberative Governance: The Cultural Politics of Discursive Space." *American Review of Public Administration* 36(1): 19–40.

Foster, K. 2000. *Regionalism on Purpose.* Cambridge, MA: Lincoln Institute of Land Policy.

Frahm, K., and L. Martin. 2009. "From Government to Governance: Implications for Social Work Administration." *Administration in Social Work* 33(2): 407–422.

Frederickson, D. G. 2003. Performance Measurement and Third Party Government: A Study of the Implementation of the Government Performance and Results Act in Five Health agencies. PhD diss., Indiana University.

Frederickson, D. G., and H. George Frederickson. 2006. *Measuring the Performance of the Hollow State.* Washington, DC: Georgetown University Press.

Frederickson, H. George, and K. B. Smith. 2003. *The Public Administration Theory Primer: Essentials of Public Policy and Administration.* Boulder, CO: Westview Press.

Fung, A., and E. O. Wright. 2001. "Deepening Democracy: Innovations in Empowered Local Governance." *Politics and Society* 29(1): 5–41.

Goldsmith, Stephen, and William D. Eggers. 2004. *Governing by Network: The New Shape of the Public Sector.* Washington, DC: Brookings Institution Press.

Heinrich, C. J., C. J. Hill, and Lawrence E. Lynn Jr. 2004. "Governance as an Organizing Theme for Empirical Research." In *The Art of Governance: Analyzing Management and Administration,* ed. A. I. Patricia and L. E. Lynn Jr., pp. 3–19. Washington, DC: Georgetown University Press.

Henri, J. F. 2006. "Management Control Systems and Strategy: A Resource-Based Perspective." *Accounting, Organizations and Society* 31: 529–558.

Hill, C. J., and L. E. Lynn Jr. 2005. "Is Hierarchical Governance in Decline? Evidence from Empirical Research." *Journal of Public Administration Research and Theory* 15(2): 173–195.

Jennings, Edward, and M. P. Haist. 2004. "Putting Performance Measurement in Context." In *The Art of Governance: Analyzing Management and Administration,* ed. A. I. Patricia and L. E. Lynn Jr., pp. 152–194. Washington, DC: Georgetown University Press.

Kamarck, Elaine. 2007. *The End of Government—As We Know It: Making Public Policy Work.* Boulder, CO: Lynne Rienner.

Katz, Bruce. 2010. Restoring prosperity: Repositioning Southern Nevada for the next economy, Speech presented at the Brookings Institution, Washington, DC, April 5. http://www.brookings.edu/speeches/2010/0405_nevada_katz.aspx.

Keast, R., M. Mandell, K. Brown, and G. Woolcock. 2004. "Network Structures: Working Differently and Changing Expectations." *Public Administration Review* 64(3): 363–371.

Kelly, J. M. 2002. "Why We Should Take Performance Measurement on Faith (Facts Being Hard to Come By and Not Terribly Important)." *Public Performance and Management Review* 25(4): 375–380.

Kettl, D. F. 2000. *The Global Public Management Revolution.* Washington, DC: Brookings Institution Press.

———. 2002. *The Transformation of Governance: Public Administration for Twenty-first Century America.* Baltimore: Johns Hopkins University Press.

Lang, R., and D. Dhavale. 2005. *Beyond Megalopolis: Exploring America's New Megapolitan Geography.* Alexandria, VA: Metropolitan Institute, Virginia Polytechnic Institute and State University.

Lang, R., A. Sarzynski, and M. Muro. 2008. *Mountain Megas: America's Newest Metropolitan Places and a Federal Partnership to Help Them Prosper.* Washington, DC: Brookings Institution Press.

Laslo, D., and D. Judd. 2006. "Building Civic Capacity Through an Elastic Local State: The Case of St. Louis." *Review of Policy Research* 23(6): 1235–1255.

Leland, S. M., and K. Thurmaier. 2005. "Metropolitan Consolidation Success: Returning to the Roots of Local Government Reform." *Public Administration Review Quarterly* 2(24): 202–213.

Linden, R. 2010. *Leading Across Boundaries: Creating Collaborative Agencies in a Networked World.* San Francisco: Jossey-Bass.

Luger, M. 2007. The role of local government in contemporary economic development(working paper, Lincoln Institute of Land Policy, Cambridge, MA). https://www.lincolninst.edu/pubs/dl/1254_Luger%20Final.pdf.

Mattessich, P. W., M. Murray-Close, and B. R. Monsey. 2001. *Collaboration: What Makes It Work.* St. Paul, MN: Amherst H. Wilder Foundation.

McGuire, M. 2006. "Intergovernmental Management: A View from the Bottom." *Public Administration Review* 66(5): 677–679.

Milward, H. B., and K. G. Provan. 2000. "Governing the Hollow State." *Journal of Public Administration Research and Theory* 10(2): 359–379.

———. 2004. The public manager's guide to network management. Paper presented at the annual meeting of the American Political Science Association, Chicago.

———. 2006. *A Manager's Guide to Choosing and Using Collaborative Networks.* Washington, DC: IBM Center for the Business of Government.

Muro, M. 2008. *Mountain Megas: America's Newest Metropolitan Places and a Federal Partnership to Help Them Prosper: A Profile of Colorado's Front Range.* Washington DC: Brookings Institution Press.

Muro, M., B. Katz, S. Rahman, and D. Warren. 2008. *MetroPolicy: Shaping a New Federal Partnership for a Metropolitan Nation.* Washington, DC: Brookings Institution Press.

Nalbandian, J., and C. Nalbandian. 2003. "Contemporary Challenges in Local Government." *National Civic Review* 92(1): 83–91.

National Academy of Public Administration (NAPA). 1998. *Building Stronger Communities and Regions: Can the Federal Government Help?* Washington, DC: NAPA.

Neely, A. 1999. "The Performance Measurement Revolution: Why Now and What Next?" *International Journal of Operations & Production Management* 19(2): 205–228.

O'Toole Jr., L. J. 1997. "Treating Networks Seriously: Practical and Research-Based Agendas in Public Administration." *Public Administration Review* 57(1): 45–52.

O'Toole Jr., L. J., and K. Meier. 2004. "Public Management in Intergovernmental Networks: Matching Structural Networks and Managerial Networking." *Journal of Public Administration Research and Theory* 23(1): 31–47.

Parr, J., J. Riehm, and C. McFarland. 2006. *Guide to Successful Local Government Collaboration in America's Regions.* Washington, DC: National League of Cities.

Perrin, B. 1998. "Effective Use and Misuse of Performance Measurement." *American Journal of Evaluation* 19(3): 367–379.

———. 2006. *Moving from Outputs to Outcomes: Practical Advice from Governments Around the World.* Washington, DC: IBM Center for the Business of Government.

Poister, T. H. 2003 *Measuring Performance in Public and Nonprofit Organizations.* San Francisco: Jossey-Bass.

Ray, K. 2002. *The Nimble Collaboration: Fine-Tuning Your Collaboration for Lasting Success.* St. Paul, MN: Amherst H. Wilder Foundation.

Reilly, Thom. 2007. "Management in Local Government: An Evolving Landscape." *Administration in Social Work* 3(2): 49–65.

Robertson, P. J., and J. V. Speier. 1998. "Organizing for International Development: A Collaborative Network-Based Model." *The International Journal of Technical Cooperation* 4(2): 166–187.

Salamon, Lester M. 2002. "The New Governance and the Tools of Public Action: An Introduction." In *The Tools of Government: A Guide to the New Governance,* ed. L. M. Salamon, pp. 1–47. New York: Oxford University Press.

Sorenson, E. 2006. "Metagovernance: The Changing Role of Politicians in Democratic Processes." *American Review of Public Administration* 36(1): 98–114.

Stoker, G. 1998. "Governance as Theory: Five Propositions." *International Social Science Journal* 50(1): 17–28.

Svensson, J., W. Trommel, and T. Lantink. 2008. "Reemployment Services in the Netherlands: A Comparative Study of Bureaucratic, Market, and Network Forms of Organizations." *Public Administration Review* 68(3): 505–515.

Thomas, P. 2007. "The Challenges of Governance, Leadership and Accountability in Public Service." In *Managing Change in Public Services,* ed. M. Wallace, M. Forting, and E. Sheller, pp. 116–135. Malden, MA: Blackwell.

Thomson, A. M., and J. L. Perry. 2006. "Collaboration Processes: Inside the Black Box." *Public Administration Review* 66: 20–32.

van Dijk, J. 2006. *Network Society: Social Aspects of New Media.* Thousand Oaks, CA: Sage.

van Dijk, J., and A. Winters. 2009. "The Perspective of Network Government." In *2008 ICTs, Citizens & Governance: After the Hype!* ed. A. Meijer et al. Amsterdam and Fairfax, VA: IOS Press.

Vigoda, E. 2002. "From Responsiveness to Collaboration: Governance, Citizens, and the Next Generation of Public Administration." *Public Administration Review* 62: 527–540.

Wandersman, A., R. M. Goodman, and F. Butterfoss. 1997. "Understanding Coalitions and How They Operate." In *Community Organizing and Community Building for Health,* ed. M. Minkler. New Brunswick, NJ: Rutgers University Press.

Wholey, Joseph S. 1999. "Performance-based Management: Responding to the Challenges." *Public Productivity and Management Review* 22(3): 288–307.

Winer, M., and K. Ray. 1994. *Collaboration Handbook: Creating, Sustaining, and Enjoying the Journey.* St. Paul, MN: Amherst H. Wilder Foundation.

Ye, L. 2009. "Regional Government and Governance in China and the United States." *Public Administration Review* 69(1): 116–121.

9

Will New State Government Management Models Emerge from the Economic Crisis?

SUSAN URAHN AND W. FREDERICK THOMPSON

In the aftermath of the global financial crisis of 2008, the 50 states face a fiscal crisis as great as any in their history. Those that were well managed and well prepared for normal economic cycles are as challenged and threatened financially as those that did not plan or manage well. In most cases, responses to date have been measured and incremental and have not always been commensurate with the magnitude of the crisis. However, some states (such as Michigan) have seen the recession come at a time when the state economy was already under pressure from economic restructuring. Michigan may be the first (but not the last) to ask basic questions about what the role of a state should be and whether or not there needs to be a fundamental change in what citizens should expect from it. Basic functions and governing approaches are under examination in radical and historic ways. Looking forward, each of the states faces major challenges and few politically attractive ways to address them. We see at least three possible approaches, depending on the length and severity of the fiscal crisis: (1) they may just hand power back and forth between parties as each finds its solutions and strategies and each party in turn loses popular support in successive elections; or (2) they may "spread the pain" and do everything a little less fully and a little less well; or (3) they may follow the lead of states like New Jersey and Michigan and restructure their roles vis-à-vis the federal government, each other, local governments, and nonprofits and fundamentally change how they respond to major social issues.

The path ahead will be determined less by what states want to do than by how the underlying economy does. If there is full and rapid national economic recovery, incremental responses of the type made to date may forestall an economic day of reckoning long enough to put longer-range remedies in place. However, if this crisis proves to be deep and protracted, either states will have to reconsider their roles, governing scope, and style, or they will be faced with the specters of bankruptcy and inadequate program delivery. That path will lead to social and political unrest that will threaten the health, safety and security of citizens.

The Scope of the Economic Challenge

Just as the rain falls on the just and the unjust, the economic crisis brought on by the Great Recession has fallen on the prepared and the unprepared and the well managed and the poorly managed states. Now, as all of the states face the need to operate within static or declining budgets, they run the risk of becoming part of the nation's economic problem themselves. Cutbacks in spending and personnel (necessary to balance their budgets) could put the brake on economic recovery and result in increased unemployment. States are also finding it difficult to provide the services needed to help drag the nation out of recession. States have reduced payroll costs by reducing workweeks, furloughing staff, and, more recently, making permanent reductions to payroll. They have postponed infrastructure investments. States are key to delivering emergency services such as unemployment assistance, Medicaid health services, and education and retraining. When they cut back on these programs or deliver them less effectively, they prolong the recession and stall our national economic comeback.

Rainy Day Fund Protections

Protection mechanisms for less-prolonged crises, like state "rainy day funds," have proven inadequate to respond to the current economic crisis. It would be unrealistic to expect them to be adequate for shortfalls of the magnitude experienced; they are not a reasonable long-term strategy for creating a buffer for economic support. To address this crisis, they would have been so large that they would be subject to political pressures to reduce taxes or provide tax rebates. States need enough funds to operate and prepare for predictable risks. Rainy day funds are not an appropriate remedy for extraordinary national financial risk; the current recession demonstrates that. However, in states that had these funds in place, they have had some "extra" time to sort out longer-range responses and delay unattractive cuts while trying to form political consensus on how to respond to budget pressures.

Revenue and Spending

Only Montana and North Dakota avoided shortfalls in their 2010 fiscal year budgets. Their economies have been cushioned (as have those to a lesser degree in Texas and West Virginia) by the strength of the natural resources sector of the economy. Overall, across all of the states, the gap between revenue and expenditures has been large and growing. Tax collections in all 50 states were down in the first quarter of FY2009 by a record 11.8 percent. Some states have been hit harder than others, but all have been hurt. While spending projections understated needs (costs have increased, for instance, in Medicaid benefits), revenue projections are out of date with the current national economic climate.

Debt

Some have compared the condition of American states like California to troubled European countries like Greece. Those parallels are overstated. Since most states have constitutional requirements to balance their operating budgets, they are on a sounder footing for long-term debt even though they face immediate pain in balancing their operating budgets. American state and local debt in 2009 was $2.4 trillion: about 16 percent of U.S. Gross Domestic Product. Although this is a large number, as the *Economist* points out, most states have fees or assets earmarked for paying this debt back, and state debt funded by general revenues is only about 5 percent of GDP (compared, for instance, to 115 percent in Greece) (*Economist* 2010, p. 31). However, some states have essentially borrowed from themselves by not making investments in their public pension plans. Unlike businesses, they have flexibility in what funds they put aside for these plans. These investment shortfalls create another long-term liability and will prolong the economic challenges they face even after the economy recovers.

The bottom line is that the current crisis will affect states even after an economic recovery begins to take hold. The National Governors Association (NGA) projected that states may face a "lost decade" of fiscal health as they struggle to rebuild their infrastructure and finance their commitments even if a financial recovery begins in the next couple of years (Thomasian 2010). NGA suggests that states consider establishing advisory bodies or commissions that could examine "fundamental changes to state government," including policy decisions about what states do and how they should best structure their resources to meet needs. NGA emphasizes the need to involve "state legislators, the private sector, outside groups and citizens" and suggests that this will take a considerable period of time.

The State Budget Response to Core Missions

When one examines state budgets it becomes clear that the biggest expenditures are for education, transportation, public safety (including prisons), health (with Medicare being a major component), and public payrolls and pension costs. None of these costs is trending in the right directions; major challenges loom on the horizon.

Education, Transportation, and Health

Kindergarten through high school education, plus state university systems, can make up 40 percent or more of all state spending. The federal stimulus programs enacted in 2009 brought $280 billion to state governments. Much of this supported Medicaid, stabilization for education and public safety, and infrastructure repair. This covered nearly 40 percent of state budget gaps (Pew Center on the States 2009a). But this was a temporary fix; the day of reckoning will come in 2011 and beyond as stimulus money becomes less generous and less available. With the current climate in Congress, states will not see another stimulus program to help them fund these programs. Instead, cutbacks and restructuring plans will need to be developed and implemented.

Prison and Correction Systems

Over the last twenty years, states have tripled their correction system budgets to a total of $50 billion each year (Pew Center on the States 2009a). This is unsustainable given the dwindling revenues states are faced with. The Pew Center on the States has made proposals to reduce the jailing of nonviolent offenders and to invest in counseling and other programs aimed at reducing recidivism. States need to find a way to change the political calculus that "being tough on crime" means putting more lawbreakers behind bars. To save money and still reduce violent crime, states need to come up with different criteria for imprisoning citizens and find different means of oversight and rehabilitation of those who are not imprisoned. They also need to reduce the costs of the prison facilities they retain. This mix of operational efficiencies, program redesign, and new measures of performance needs to be formulated into a political discussion, and a set of meaningful alternatives that resonate with taxpayers.

Public Payrolls and Pensions

States face a trillion-dollar gap in funding pension, health care, and other retirement benefits as of 2008, according to the Pew Center on the States (2010a). This likely underestimates the gap today. In 2000, more than half the states had fully funded pensions. Now, only Florida, New York, Washington, and Wisconsin can make that claim. And they also are under extreme economic pressure. As noted earlier, states are borrowing from underfunded pension programs by postponing their contributions. States have a political challenge in fully funding these programs, and that challenge is likely to grow over time. States argued that submarket pay for employees could be offset through pension programs and still attract quality employees. As long as there were large companies with robust and comprehensive pension plans, this argument could resonate politically. However, when some of the largest companies in the United States eliminated pension plans (e.g., IBM, FedEx, U.S. Steel) it became harder to make the case that state retirees deserve defined benefit retirements when the rest of the country is supported by 401(k)-type plans. The issue for states will be more fundamental than funding. It will be a question of whether or not to phase these plans out and how to pay for that if new workers are not contributing to help offset current costs.

Revenue

States have differentiated themselves from one another by how they collect revenue and pay for their operations. For instance, Florida attracted retirees not only because of its sand and sun, but also because of its decision not to impose an income tax. The Great Recession has had a disproportionate impact on "low-tax" states like Florida because it has affected real estate values and liquidity. This, in turn, is affecting real estate appraisals and tax assessments. The so-called sand states (Arizona, California, Florida, and Nevada) are paying a high price for their reliance on real estate assessments to fund programs. States will need to consider abandoning taxing traditions and precedents to diversify revenue sources. If some sectors fail (like real estate), others (personal or corporate income or mining taxes) might offset these losses. Some reexamination might be necessary to maintain stability in revenue and program support.

Fundamental change needs to be made in the way state programs are funded and in how they are administered. The questions go beyond how do we pay for what we are doing and enter the realm of whether or not states should even be doing what they are doing and whether or not the status quo will ever be affordable in the future.

The Michigan Existential Crisis

Michigan was rated by the Pew Center on the States as one of the best managed states in government. In theory, it should have been well positioned to respond to the current financial crisis. However, Michigan had to face the crisis within a longer and more persistent industrial downturn. Its reactions are important because they illustrate the challenges a state and its governor may encounter when the crisis is major and prolonged and when revenues do not recover. Michigan's revenue fell by $2.4 billion (more than 25 percent) over just two years. No amount of planning or rainy day funds could possibly cushion a state from that readjustment.

Governor Jennifer Granholm's approach to this challenge emphasized efficiency. She eliminated five state departments and 300 boards and commissions and managed a $10 billion shortfall over her term as governor. She noted that, adjusted for inflation, state revenues are at a 45-year low (Granholm 2010). However, the governor has argued for strategic priorities and minimized cuts in education programs. She has argued that education and training are key to grow new industries and restore vitality in light of the decline of the auto industry. However, this can have severe consequences for other programs. If 30 to 40 percent of the budget is taken off the table, cuts must be draconian in other sectors. One indication of the severity of Michigan's budget shortfalls is that the state has not been able to agree to spend the $80 million necessary to get $475 million in matching federal road funds.

Governor Granholm's reward for tackling the financial crisis has been plummeting approval ratings. According to a *Detroit Free Press* statewide poll in May 2010, Governor Granholm had a 71 percent negative job rating (AP 2010). The state has a strategy and has made hard political choices. But its leadership has not convinced a majority of the electorate that the actions are right or best for the state. Governor Granholm left office in January 2011.

From "Shaking the Sofa Cushions" to "Breaking the Furniture"

The initial state response to declining revenues was use of rainy day funds and fee and tax adjustments. *Time* reported that "leery of broad tax hikes in a bad economy, governments have instead chosen to shake the sofa cushions and punish the naughty, closing loopholes, cracking down on tax evaders and raising levies on tobacco, alcohol, gambling, soda pop and candy" (Van Drehle 2010, p. 26). Such strategies can address downturns; they cannot address economic freefalls. More difficult steps need to be taken to reach a new equilibrium in the current economic and political environment.

Some states have run up against structural barriers to reform, created when there was concern that taxes were getting too high or state government was getting too expensive. Whatever their value at the time, these rules now inhibit changes that would improve budgets and economic performance. California's economic challenges have been compounded by its structural tax challenges. The combination of economic challenges with these structural controls makes resolving problems impossible. California requires that all budgets and tax increases pass by a two-thirds majority; ballot measures have constrained both revenue and spending options for the state. In a similar vein, the state of Oregon has enacted a "kicker" law into the state constitution (2000) that requires rebates to taxpayers "whenever state revenue exceeds projected revenue by 2 percent or more" (Pew Center on the States 2009b, p. 40).

States may need to move beyond "shaking the sofa cushions" and begin "breaking the furniture" if they are going to handle the historic challenges they face. This could take a number of forms.

First, states will need to consider whether state constitutions and/or initiative programs have backfired in this time of crisis. State constitutions may need to be amended to allow the difficult and unpopular deals needed for fiscal stability.

Second, states need to work with the federal government to redefine their boundaries and responsibilities. The stimulus program and the debate that followed its enactment created considerable federal-state conflict, with some states proposing to refuse funding to avoid oversight in areas like unemployment insurance policy. Similarly with the passage of the health care reform package, a number of states challenged increased federal involvement in Medicare and new mandates to the states. Many of these responses are political in nature. But there is an underlying concern about lines of demarcation and the impact of federal mandates that highlight an ongoing tension. Working out these challenges could better define state missions and authorities and establish reasonable shared funding schemes to meet delivery programs.

Third, states and their local governments—counties and cities—need to better define relationships and roles. In some cases, states have eliminated funding for programs and have told counties and cities to take over responsibilities. Making these decisions ad hoc based only on revenue availability reflects poor judgment and weak leadership. However, it is not unreasonable to expect that both states and local governments should improve program administration and work together to lower costs.

A Strategy of Increased Collaboration

Integration of governance units (cities and towns) is one approach to government efficiency. *Time* reported in its June 28, 2010, issue (Van Drehle 2010) that New Jersey Governor Chris Christie is "backing a constitutional cap on property taxes in hopes of pushing the state's myriad villages and townships to merge into more efficient units."

The governors of Minnesota and Wisconsin have ordered an agency-by-agency review (Greenblatt 2009) to determine how they might save money. Gains are modest thus far. The hopes of saving each state $10 million are a long way from being realized. But active discussions are under way between a Republican governor (MN) and a Democratic governor (WI) across a broad range of areas including tourism promotion corrections and environmental initiatives.

In other states, governors have proposed that local governments share the cost of administration and consolidate administrative functions like information technology (IT) support. There is potential for states to work together to reduce procurement costs (the Western States Alliance is an example), to buy in bulk, and to gain the benefit of that cooperation. The state of Georgia consolidated buying across state agencies and incorporated its Board of Regents for state university management into statewide planning. This is expected to double the savings in procurement. Whether it's IT, or food service contracts, or any number of other goods or services, buying together can mean buying more cheaply and spending less on overhead. This may require a breakdown in tradition. But that may be preferable to a breakdown in performance because of inadequate funding. "Breaking the furniture" may be the best option for a difficult future.

What Lies Ahead?

Will the historic financial challenges of the last few years lead to drastic change in states or new models of governance? It depends on whether or not the financial and political pressures deepen and are prolonged. It also depends on whether state officials respond in constructive, creative ways and gain consensus behind their leadership. We see three possible approaches: (1) ping-ponged problem pushing, (2) incremental dissolution, or (3) phased reforms.

Ping-Ponged Problem Pushing

The party in power has to submit balanced budgets and execute the decisions made. The party out of power can kibitz, second-guess, and criticize the decisions that are made. The party out of power will likely not have a leader with the public profile of a governor. It will not be held accountable when programs are cut back and services to citizens are reduced. In the current environment, when decline in service and tax increases are unwelcome, being out of power has its attractions. Politicians who try to solve problems will be at risk; the solutions are painful and unattractive. Unless they demonstrate exceptional leadership and gain support for their reforms, they are likely to be replaced in elections. Doing "the right thing" is not always the best way to win elections. This is particularly true if the leader is not able to convince the electorate of the need for change, the imperative for difficult remedies. In partisan environments, the reward for trying to solve problems will be the loss of public support, the loss of elections. The winners will not be motivated to take the actions that got their predecessors defeated. This sets the table for elections that swing from one party to the other like a ping-pong match, with neither party having the time, energy, encouragement, or political support necessary to restructure the state. One should expect incremental change and little leadership.

Incremental Dissolution

As noted earlier in the case of Michigan, strategic leadership can backfire in a time of tight budgets and budget cuts. Programmatically, it is usually better to cancel programs than to keep them running with decreasing resources. Administrative costs increase relative to service delivered; less is achieved per dollar spent. Nevertheless, dramatic change can threaten the balance among interested parties and skew what the state can accomplish. This threatens the economic, social, and political stability of the state and yields unpredictable results. Most politicians, faced with such challenges, will move to incremental reductions in across-the-board spending. They will choose balance and political harmony over program efficiency and effectiveness. They will look for new ways to achieve social goals. There will be increased friction as they look for resources from the federal government to offset reductions. They will look to not-for-profits that deliver service to improve their efficiency and stretch their resources. Some nongovernment organizations (NGOs) will fail and there will be consolidation of resources. In this scenario, states won't run away from their missions and established structures and programs. They will gradually reduce funding for these programs, while putting increased pressure on program delivery arms to operate. In the near term, this is achievable with effective leadership. In the long term—if the economic pressures prove to be profound and sustained—this will result in gradual dissolution of government programs. Less will be achieved per dollar and fewer dollars will be available over time. States will be less effective in meeting the citizens' needs.

Phased Reforms

There is some value in gradualism. We don't know for sure how prolonged our current economic downturn will be. Some states may recover sooner than expected.

Federal programs could become more securely funded and more predictable. Thus, a third road—which moves states gradually toward new governance models—might be the best road. It will require political consensus across a range of programs. But this consensus could be developed over time. Government reform commissions, suggested by the NGA, could help build the consensus for change that any leader will need.

Most states should probably consider some tax reform. States that do not diversify their tax collection strategies (e.g., states that have low income taxes and rely on property taxes) have the most difficult downturns and problems meeting the needs of citizens. States need to look at their tax systems as part of their overall strategy to attract and retain citizens and businesses; they need to have sustainable assessments. Businesses and people can move—both within the United States and abroad—when burdens become too great or uneven. Reform to provide balance is more important than differentiation between states. States need to view themselves and their tax programs not just historically and parochially, but as part of a world marketplace. They need to deliver infrastructure for a high quality of life without undue burden; they need to be able to do this in good, and bad, economic times.

Spending reforms also need review; new models should be piloted and implemented. Although citizens typically prefer local decision making and control, leaders need to demonstrate how this can be achieved while still consolidating operations where it makes sense financially. Pragmatic centralization or cooperative agreements can promote local control on things that are important (e.g., where to build highways and route sewer lines) while achieving cost savings through multistate compacts to purchase in a standardized, competitive way. New models of cross-jurisdiction and cross-state cooperation hold great promise for lowering costs while delivering services.

Conclusion

The worldwide financial crisis has hit states hard. Adjustment will take time; more bad news could be coming. The budget pressures and the difficulty delivering services threaten the ability of state governments to respond. Some states are undertaking a drastic rethinking of their fundamental mission and purpose. But most states are taking gradual and measured steps to meet increasing demands for services while revenues are decreasing. This cannot go on indefinitely. States will need to either restructure key programs or restructure their relationship with each other and with the federal government to stay solvent and retain political support. Technology, collaborative multistate and multijurisdiction strategies, and broad political reform are all potential contributors to a new vision of government over the next decade. Whether states embrace these strategies or resist them is dependent on the persistence and severity of the current economic crisis. If it ends soon, strategies of "ping-ponged problem pushing" or incremental dissolution may be enough. A prolonged crisis will only be addressed by long-term reforms that introduce new ways of managing revenues, programs, and administration and balancing local control against the needs for improved efficiency and effectiveness in governance. This approach has the virtue of addressing the current economic crisis, while also reducing the cost of government and increasing its effectiveness when robust growth returns.

References

Associated Press (AP). 2010. "Michigan Voters' Opinion Better of Obama Than Granholm, New Poll Shows." Michigan Live, June 3. http://www.mlive.com/politics/index. ssf/2010/06/michigan_voters_opinion_better.html (accessed September 1, 2010).

Economist. 2010. "Can Pay, Won't Pay." June 19, p. 31.

Granholm, Jennifer. 2010. "Address to the Lansing Rotary Club," January 29. http://www. michigan.gov/gov/0,1607,7–168–55273–230618—,00.html (accessed September 1, 2010).

Greenblatt, Alan. 2009. "The Search for Interstate Cooperation." Governing, October 31.

The Pew Center on the States. 2009a. One in 31: The Long Reach of American Corrections. March, p. 31. Washington, DC: Pew Research Center.

———. 2009b. Beyond California: States in Fiscal Peril. November, p. 2. Washington, DC: Pew Research Center.

———. 2010a. The Trillion Dollar Gap: Underfunded State Retirement Systems and the Roads to Reform. February. Washington, DC: Pew Research Center.

———. 2010b. State of the States 2010: How the Recession Might Change States. February, p. 16. Washington, DC: Pew Research Center.

Thomasian, John. 2010. The Big Reset: State Government After the Great Recession. February 23, p. 1. Washington, DC: National Governors Association Center for Best Practices.

Van Drehle, David. 2010. "The Other Financial Crisis." Time, June 28, p. 26.

10

Turning Citizen "Enragement" into Citizen Engagement

Managing Expectations with Web 2.0 and Social Media

Alan R. Shark

The Rage

A citizen opens fire on a congresswoman in Tucson, Arizona, seriously wounding her and killing six others. Another opens fire at the Holocaust Museum. Still another intentionally flies a small airplane into an office building used by the Internal Revenue Service (IRS) in Austin, Texas. A military chaplain starts shooting at his fellow troops at Ft. Hood, Texas. They all had one thing in common: they posted their rage within cybercommunity groups that shared their anger. Of course, these are extreme cases—especially when we consider the entire U.S. population is well over 300 million. But even among those who would never turn to violence, looking at the local news there appears to be a growing sense of fear, frustration, and isolation that exists between citizens and their government institutions. Rage is growing in America—an ever-widening fissure in American life spurred on by chronic unemployment, alarming budget deficits, rising taxes, and increased government spending. While some attempt to rationalize current events or to place things in perspective, citizen perception trumps all.

Much of the rage stems from a growing segment of the population that feels frustrated and alienated as they see change all around them. This rage manifests itself in many forms, both digital and in town hall meetings. Nationwide protests at town meetings held by Congress in the fall of 2010 to promote President Obama's health care initiative are a poignant example. The message of despair and anger becomes further amplified as it permeates the electronic news and social media. Indeed, many of these angry people turn to 24/7 cable news, blogs, and other digital media to seek like-minded people who share their views, not to seek new ideas but to reinforce long-held beliefs (*Editor & Publisher* 2010). The problem is that many of these 24/7 cable news networks, websites, and blogs seem to have melded

155

together both in appearance and purpose. And so has news reporting and opinion broadcasting, once largely separate and clearly marked domains. "Citizen enragement" has become a contemporary norm; negativity and sarcasm have replaced optimism and hope. And, equally significant, sound bites have replaced objective thinking. The bottom line, however, is that it has become increasingly difficult to maintain and foster trust in government (2010).

Polls ratings for the president, the Congress, and governors and state legislatures are at record lows. This is no more apparent than in the reversal of Democratic Party fortunes in the 2010 midterm congressional and state elections. Local governments can take some comfort in that they have fared relatively better, with a 43 percent approval rating (Rasmussen Reports 2009).

Today's city or town hall may look the same from the outside, but the ways we connect with government and one another have forever changed. The Internet and its emerging social media sites and tools have helped change the landscape and focus to a new and unchartered cyber landscape where boundaries and interests are no longer bound by physical structures. They say all politics are local. This chapter focuses largely on local government; most citizens identify with local governments that are closer to home—even if they are surfing their "home" city website 3,000 miles away.

The Web 2.0 and Beyond

The very savvy Web 2.0 tools that allow citizens to seek information, search databases, complete applications and forms, and pay for services or fines using a credit card are quickly evolving into a new social media for greater interaction. No longer satisfied as a time-saving, efficient, one-way conduit of broadcasted information, the monolithic website has morphed into a new construct, where the home page becomes a launch pad—not a lone destination page. Today, we hear public leaders and citizens calling for compelling power terms such as *transparency, citizen empowerment,* and *citizen engagement.* This will enlarge the potential of government Web 2.0 and emerging social media applications.

Getting the News

Traditionally most citizens have received news about government largely from the print media. But there is a diminishing role for newspapers, as we have known them. Overall print media circulation is down 35 percent and declining an average 7 percent a year (Davy 2009). We also know that, depending on locality, citizens are turning to their local government websites to find out about something, fill out a form, or pay by credit card for a particular service. Local governments, after all, are usually the first place where a citizen turns. Moreover, local government websites are in a constant state of improvement: providing information, becoming easier to navigate, and providing greater opportunities to complete certain transactions online as opposed to standing in line. In a few short years, we have moved from merely posting information to transacting information, to allowing citizens to react to events and measures, to seeking two-way citizen engagement.

Until recently, citizens learned about what was going on in their community and local government through newspapers and television. Now there is a major shift from printed newspapers, as circulation continues to decline. Traditional newspapers are thinner, printed less often, and with less staff. According to the "Annual Report on American Journalism," one out of four Americans now get their news delivered to their smart phones instead of to their front door (Pew Project for Excellence in Journalism 2010). No doubt, that number will certainly continue to rise. Perhaps not surprisingly, the study also finds that the Internet has become the third most popular news source.

Local television has certainly become more regional and less local, with even less time devoted to local government—except for scandals, budget cost overruns, and crime.

During this steady decline in print journalism, some have expressed fear in what they see as a decline in literacy and critical thinking. There is also a growing concentration of media ownership. That can have the effect of taking a small news story in one locality and highlighting it in such a way that the significance is distorted, blown out of proportion, based on dramatic elements and available video. Just as bad, some stories that used to receive coverage have disappeared. Finally, daily *news* has transformed itself into daily *views.*

Citizens are not just reading news online, they are actually contributing to it. One study shows 37 percent of Internet users have contributed to the creation of news, commented about it, or disseminated it via postings on social media sites like Facebook or Twitter (Nielsen Wire 2010). Local governments realize they can no longer rely on traditional media to reach the public. Today they are developing new channels for broadcasting their messages through various new media. And this is where they have done an exceptional job. Many jurisdictions now offer citizens the choice of having specific news and information feeds sent directly to a laptop, home computer, or smart phone. Citizens can choose to receive public safety alerts, weather and traffic bulletins, or meeting notices. Local government news and information are updated with greater frequency and detail.

The Growth of Web 2.0 and Social Media

The growth in use of Web 2.0 applications and social media has been staggering in terms of not only the number of users but also the speed in which it has been adopted. For example, there were 1,000 Internet devices in 1984, 1,000,000 in 1992, and 1,000,000,000 in 2008. The number of text messages sent and received every day exceeds the population of the planet. Ninety-three percent of all adults own a cell phone. Cell phone manufacturer Nokia alone manufactures 13 cell phones per second. ABC, NBC, and CBS, around for a combined 200 years, collectively get 10 million unique visitors each month. MySpace, YouTube, and Facebook get 250 million unique visitors each month where none existed six years ago. In 2008, MySpace had 200 million users. If it were a country, it would be the fifth largest in the world (Fisch and McLeod 2009).

Newspaper circulation is down 7 million over the last 25 years. Nevertheless, in the last five years, unique readers of online newspapers are up 30 million. There are over 31 billion searches on Google per month. In addition, more video is uploaded to YouTube in just two months than if ABC, NBC, and CBS had been airing content 24/7/365 since 1948. Wikipedia was launched in 2001 and now features 13 million articles in more than 200 languages. Perhaps most remarkable is that all the statistics noted here are being eclipsed by newer and more dramatic examples; these data will be obsolete by the time you read this. The numbers are simply staggering in terms of the speed of acceptance and the growth of the new social media. Social media sites were built with individuals in mind and it was only a matter of time before business saw numerous applications they could develop. Following the lead of others, local governments also saw opportunities to reach out to their citizens. Now governments who are on Facebook have "fans." Those who are on Twitter have "followers." A different segment of the population finds creative ways to "tweet" in 140 characters or less (Fisch and McLeod 2009).

Toward Transparency

The notion of e-government, where the focus initially was on increasing efficiencies and reducing costs through online offerings, has moved toward Web 2.0 and social media applications. The concept of transparency has been the next phase in the evolution of government outreach (see Figure 10.1). Indeed, local government transparency has been hailed as a means of letting citizens see the workings of government: factual and raw data regarding budgets, operational metrics, indexed video clips of official meetings, and policy initiatives before they are acted on (Sunlight Foundation 2010). One local politician remarked that he was now getting better and more detailed information as a citizen than he did in his role as an elected leader from his own county website.

When transparency is deployed, citizens can enjoy data that can be presented graphically. In some instances, they can see special informational maps that can help them plan (e.g., school and voting districts, business districts, historic sites, police and fire stations, evacuation routes, hospital and libraries, parks and recreation). Many maps are becoming interactive; enter a zip code or a name or perhaps simply point to a map with a mouse click. This same geographic information system (GIS) technology is also available on smart phones. Many local government websites address information in multiple languages and in special fonts, and some even provide Braille readers for citizens with special needs.

Going back to the beginning of this chapter, one must also recognize the "uncivil" side of Web 2.0 and social media. The World Wide Web is filled with sites

Figure 10.1   **From Transparency to Engagement**

and attractive places for interactivity and engagement with all sorts of credibility and agendas. Websites, by design, are unregulated. And, as such, some can instill hate against another, spread misleading and false information, and undermine legitimate business and political institutions. People are able to post things and use pseudonames or aliases or simply remain anonymous and therefore unaccountable. Entirely new online communities have formed that bring people together by cause or purpose, thus filling an inner need for community perhaps not as easily found in traditional organizations. And the very functionality that makes e-government so compelling—being geographically neutral, always open, interactive, with ease of acceptance—is also available to just about anyone, regardless of motivations and political leanings. Some sites, intentionally or not, have certainly contributed to citizen rage.

From Transparency to Engagement

As local governments have worked hard to address the need to share and post greater information and detail, there's a new frontier where transparency is extended and enhanced through citizen engagement. Local governments have been rather eager to experiment with the likes of blogs, YouTube, Facebook, Twitter, and remote switching system (RSS) feeds, to name a few. While never intended for organizations such as local governments, Web 2.0/Social Media applications have been adopted as a means of better connecting or engaging with citizens. As a matter of course, the main local government Web portal usually provides and highlights the various information options for the public to search for information as never before—as well as conduct basic transactions—often by language of choice, using a credit card. In 2009, the Public Technology Institute (PTI) surveyed a national sample of cities and counties and reported that nearly 70 percent either had offered or were planning to offer some form of social media Web 2.0 application.

Unlike Web 2.0 functionality, social media sites can provide a high degree of interactivity and user generated content (USG). This is still an area where more work needs to be done. First, not everyone agrees with what citizen engagement means. To some it means providing citizens with the opportunity to comment on a specific issue. Others see it quite differently; interactivity and content development is both encouraged and processed. For example, a police chief from a small jurisdiction in the Midwest was complaining that some younger residents, wishing to be helpful, were sending in pictures from auto accidents and fires and were upset that the police and fire dispatch departments had no way to capture and process the photographs and that therefore it was not helpful at all. This is an example of a growing disconnect regarding how technology is being used and will increasingly be used by our citizens. If we want to engage citizens, engagement will certainly require a knowledge of the state of technology as well as the devices citizens are most comfortable using.

When it comes to devices, the cell phone has emerged as a very smart device that is now considered a pocket computer with a phone as an application. The Apple 3Gs and Motorola Droid are just two such examples, which will soon be replaced by even smarter and more functional devices. There is no such thing as a dumb wireless phone; it is just that some are getting much smarter than others. New tablet hybrid devices such as iPads with their rich user interface simply make it easier to get and respond to information with larger, high-definition screens and no external pointing device or cumbersome keyboard. New pocket cameras are on the market that not only take great pictures but record time and date and latitude and longitude, taking the concept of "neighborhood watch" to an entirely new level. Phone manufacturers are tripping over each other to bring new devices to the market that seamlessly integrate a number of leading social media tools into one unit. Engagement, then, is more interactive, as compared to transparency, with citizens having the ability to actually produce content. Social media are better geared toward social engagement and we are now seeing the start of an emerging civic engagement ecosystem in cyberspace. The "mobile device," be it a smart phone, tablet, laptop, or other medium, has become the central means of communicating two-way information—facts as well as opinions, text as well as photos and videos.

In Figure 10.2, we see a diagram of a citizen who might come to the traditional city hall and meet with someone to either gather information, ask questions, or mange a transaction. The same would be true for someone telephoning a local government facility. In either case, the citizen is confronted with having to wait in lines, schedule appointments, and/or travel to a physical structure. Should one prefer to call, finding the correct telephone number is quite challenging, if not impossible. By today's standards, the personal touch, person-to-person visit, or phone interaction is regarded as inefficient, however personal the experience might be. Many government agencies acknowledged these inefficiencies and began to place more information on the Web as a timesaver for citizens as well as government workers. Both time and money are saved and it is usually faster. It was, and still is, a win-win situation for most. However, placing things on the Web, although efficient, is impersonal.

With the new social media, there are many new possibilities to explore that maintain efficiencies while adding a sense of personalization. For example, most new computer devices, including smart phones, have built-in cameras with mi-

Figure 10.2 **Moving to the Future of Engagement**

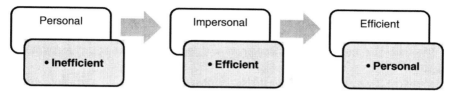

crophones. This technology trend will continue to expand exponentially where people can text, write, talk, and see one another—all on one device. They can communicate with someone in city hall from great distances as if they were across the street. With video and audio added, a sense of personalization and efficiency can be experienced. While all this might sound wonderful to most citizens, there are a number of key questions that need to be answered. *First,* can local governments truly handle the emerging media interactivity, especially citizen engagement, and move beyond simply posting stuff? *Second,* as people continue to purchase smarter and smarter devices, what happens to a significant portion of the population who either cannot afford such a device or fail to see the benefit of opting in. The bottom line is that they may be excluded from the new media platforms either by choice or by happenstance—hence widening the digital divide. Connecting with all citizens requires many strategies, including broadband affordability, availability, and accessibility. *Third,* who is the face of government? What does personalization really look like? What is the role of our government leaders when so much information and activity appear to be monolithic and web-centric, bringing everything back to a central Web portal? How do the emerging social media tools affect our concept of representative government? How can citizens be made to feel that they are truly being "listened" to? Hardly an evening goes by when a group, in front of a television camera, doesn't shout out that "their voices are not being heard." Regardless of the merits, it would appear at times we have lost our sense of just what a pluralistic society means and how it is supposed to function.

How Can Governments Process Citizen Engagement?

Perhaps the most daunting challenge is to develop realistic plans that take into account citizen expectations. One large county formed a series of focus groups of its citizens to help evaluate a new county website. To the chagrin of the staff, their original design was voted down a number of times in favor of a final design which was rather plain and simple looking. The staff was proud of the first designs, but the citizens were more interested in basics and functionality as opposed to beauty and functionality.

Developing interactive sites requires consistency, quality and accuracy of information, and constant monitoring and action—in fact, a completely new way of processing outbound as well as inbound information it receives in return. Citizens can be expected to post information, photos, and videos. Citizen engagement is about various forms of interactions, so citizens can share their comments and concerns both in print and by video commentary. Citizens themselves can design programs where charts and graphs are used to make their points, and can do so using video-authored software that costs next to nothing when compared with the hundreds of thousands of dollars professionals used to pay. They will expect some form of confirmation or attribution for their postings. For example, they might want to see how their vote on an issue stacks up with that of others in the community who might have weighed in on a particular issue. A more challenging task is to find ways to authenticate postings and seek ways to guard against or expose cybermob-like activities where only the most active, vocal residents, and the wealthy have their opinions heard as if their thoughts represented the majority. Just as important, governments must also seek out strategies to gather input from those who are less connected and represented. Moreover, as good as online citizen engagement can be, it cannot replace face-to-face, personal, citizen engagement.

There are some daunting issues associated with a government's ability to success-fully engage citizens in real time. In developing systems, one must be aware of the rules and regulations of the Federal Freedom of Information Act (FOIA) that need to be adhered to; as well, records need to be saved and archived (especially when they pertain to official business). Governments will need to plan for a dramatic increase in data storage, and for the costs of storing new media such as photos and video files which take up about 1000 percent more storage space than mere text files do.

Armed with video devices, government administrators will need to contemplate how public managers can respond to video requests and video postings. Some pub-lic managers who have enjoyed years of obscurity may not be at all comfortable chatting with someone via two-way video engagement. Yet this is exactly where technology is taking us; we cannot ignore citizen expectations and their new and enhanced communication devices.

Those who follow the emerging new media and Web 2.0 applications realize that no matter how simple or sophisticated, these services cannot work without broadband being available, accessible, and affordable. Toward this end, Congress charged the Federal Communications Commission (FCC) with developing a Na-tional Broadband Plan for America (FCC 2010). After much work, the plan was released to the public in March 2010. The report was divided into seven broad categories. One of the seven major categories is Broadband and Civic Engagement. Here, the FCC highlighted four key areas:

1. Release more government data online in open and accessible formats to enable the public to more actively participate in the civic life of their com-munities and their democracy and hold their government accountable.
2. Expand public media's use of digital online platforms and create a 21st-century digital national archive to empower people with information on broadband-enabled platforms.

3. Increase opportunities for citizens to participate in the civic life of their local communities and to engage their government through social media and broadband-enabled tools, like smart phones, as well as open platforms and innovative partnerships.
4. Leverage broadband-based technologies to modernize delivery of government services, enhance democratic processes, and ensure that they are accessible to all Americans.

While most applaud this report as a significant first step, much (if not all) of the recommendations are focused on the federal government and what its agencies should and must do to better engage the public through broadband technology. There is nothing to prevent local governments, as the level of government closest to the citizens, from adopting many of the key principles.

1. Engaging the Unengaged

Often referred to as the digital divide, there is a growing disparity between the digital haves and have-nots. The notion of the digital divide takes into account two major categories. The first is broadband access, affordability, and accessibility. The second major category is the need for access to content and essential services. As of this writing, the Commonwealth of Virginia's Department of Motor Vehicles charges people $5.00 for showing up in person as opposed to simply going online to renew their vehicle registration. Few people enjoy having to drive or be driven to a DMV office and then having to wait while standing in a long line. But to then have to pay a surcharge for the *service*. . . . Policies like this negatively impact seniors as well as those on the lower levels of the economic strata. Airlines charge for paper tickets. In some cities the only place to seek job opportunities is online postings. The disadvantaged are penalized, required to pay a fee simply for not conducting business online, whether they are able to do so or not.

Local governments have reached out to underserved populations by providing Internet connectivity and computers in public libraries and senior and public housing facilities. Visit a public library today and you will see more citizens on computer terminals (they are often fully utilized) than looking for a book to read. There is an equal need for training on how to maximize the computer as a tool as well as a bridge to vital services and information. People without computer-savvy children, or hands-on access to the evolving Web experience, are increasingly being left out of the civic and social dialogue. As more news and information is provided online, as more forms and transactions can be handled remotely, the more people of certain demographics will be excluded. Broadband connectivity and access can no longer be considered a luxury; it certainly cannot be left to the wealthy either.

According to the Pew Internet and American Life Project, people who participate in civic life online tend to be richer and better educated (Purcell et al. 2010;

Rainie 2010) The notion of "haves" and "have-nots" has taken on a new meaning to include access to information, knowledge, and participatory democracy.

2. Facing Government vs. The Face of Government

Tradition has it that when someone wanted to meet with their elected city council person or county commissioner they would call and make an office appointment. Many people were accustomed to special access because of their standing in a political party or as a campaign contributor. Now, however, with the majority of voting citizens claiming they are "independent," party affiliations have waned. With citizen engagement applications blossoming in the political arena, many citizens believe themselves entitled to connect directly with not only like-minded individuals and groups but politicians and public managers. This raises new challenges for those who are in charge of civic engagement policies and programs. Who is, or what is, the face of government? In recent years, citizens for the most part have been pleased with e-government online services. People did not care who processed their request, application, or form as long as it was completed in a timely fashion. Citizen engagement suggests a new dynamic where citizens may expect to hold certain individuals accountable—online!

The first attempts at engaging citizens began with blogs. Blogs, after all, are nothing more than a single-focus interactive website. A mayor's or city manager's blog may be helpful; it offers the opportunity to engage citizens. The problem is that most blogs posted by elected leaders contain boilerplate information and the information is not updated or changed. The emerging social media technology is taking citizens beyond blogs. It has the potential to raise expectations; people may expect or demand actual, live face-time via peer-to-peer video conferencing with elected leaders and public managers. Are our government structures equipped to present themselves in such a highly visible and perhaps vulnerable fashion? If governments move in such a direction, will they be subjected to "cyber mob think" by groups who claim they want to be heard when what they mean is they want their views to be accepted and acted upon. On a more positive note, video interactivity holds the potential to provide forums for civil discussions, an opportunity to regain much of the trust that has been lost. As broadband connectivity improves, so too will the quality of video conferencing. A case in point is Cisco's Telepresence Systems, which takes regular video conferencing to completely new heights. Imagine a small conference room where a few folks are 2,500 miles away yet you are seeing them up close on a large screen in high-definition video and voice. Being in such an environment is as close as you can get to someone without physically being in the same location—hence the term *telepresence.*

Currently, almost by default, the face of government has become nothing more than a city or county logo. Perhaps people know their mayor or county executive or administrative officer; most probably they do not. The new emerging social media offers opportunities for citizens to better engage their public leaders and managers.

There is, however, more to adding a face to government. Most social media systems used by local governments (e.g., Facebook, Twitter, YouTube, RSS feeds) are designed to bring people back to a central Web presence, usually the Web portal. Whereas this makes sense for obtaining different levels of information, it does not take civic engagement beyond basic information sharing. Do we expect citizens to be satisfied with engaging with a single website?

Given the advent of social media tools, it may be a perfect time to rethink how elected leaders communicate with their citizens. Many are doing this now with their own Web presence, their own blogs and postings, and communication with Fans, Tweets, and simple e-mails. The face of government might be better served by personalizing communications; citizens can view government as a human organization dedicated to carrying out essential services and other forms of government activities on their behalf. This provides the opportunity to plan for multichannel communication pathways where there are many forums and ports of digital entry.

3. Civic Engagement: Beyond the Rage

Even with the best of technology and innovation, civic engagement can only work with a willing and educated population. The current rage in contemporary American life is not necessarily new from a historical perspective. In the civic engagement sphere, technology and innovation are nothing more than a sophisticated set of tools. Their inherent and implied intelligence are determined by the wisdom and knowledge (or lack thereof) of our citizens who utilize them. Technology can be utilized to better gather and share information. We not only have tools that can measure whether someone is for or against something, but newer tools that can measure the intensity (or rage) factor, too.

The traditional notion that our primary civic responsibility is to merely cast votes for or against elected leaders is quickly being supplanted by new social media technologies where we can learn about issues and the views and rationales of others. One troubling finding suggests that citizens who use the Internet are often more interested in seeking out those with similar views than in learning more about how other citizens think and why. In other words, they have already made up their minds and are intolerant of other views. This suggests that if thoughts and beliefs are held in a static state, then only through external stimuli and communications can we hope to reach a point of civil respect. At this juncture, with all the technological tools in the universe, we simply cannot expect positive outcomes without positive political leadership.

From the technology point of view much more can be done. A survey taken from among 875 technology experts and other stakeholders conducted by the Pew Research Center's Internet and Family Life Project and Elon University found that innovative forms of online collaboration could result in more efficient and responsive institutions (and that includes government agencies) by the year 2020. While the findings are upbeat, those closest to technology developments among government agencies might find that future date rather surprising. So much innovation is occurring now on a constant basis. When people are enraged, it is a challenge to appeal to the rational mind and turn raw emotions into a more positive engagement process. Public managers, despite all the day-to-day pressures, have the ability and the need to navigate away from the political arena and steer toward informational services that provide transparency, engagement, and empowerment. This is exactly where innovation is happening. It has begun at the local level and has spread to the federal and state levels. Federal websites such as USA.gov, Data.gov, and White-House.gov are examples of extraordinary access to information. One cannot help but notice a change in tone, attitude, and substance directed to the public.

Local governments also have been actively sharing information on the Web. The District of Columbia launched its Apps For Democracy contest; citizens were encouraged to submit ideas and actually develop software applications. By all accounts, it was an amazing success, and many other jurisdictions across the nation are trying similar competitions. The government of the District of Columbia has even launched its very own mobile apps store. The state of Maryland offers a clever, highly interactive "Maryland Budget Map Game" that provides citizens an opportunity to weigh in on budget choices and policy consequences. The site—developed by the Maryland Budget and Tax Policy Institute and the University of Baltimore—is aimed at helping people see how difficult it can be to balance the State budget and also weigh in on policy choices that drive savings and expenditures (Batson and Hughes 2010).

The City of Boston developed the Citizens Connect suite of online services that enables residents and visitors to gather information about the physical state of the city and send that information directly to the appropriate city operation department through their iPhone. Key features include the ability to attach a photo, capture system-generated GIS coordinates, edit GIS coordinates to improve accuracy, and follow the service request with end-to-end tracking.

The City of Mesa, Arizona, developed a Citizen Dashboard for Bond and Capital Improvement Projects. Mesa provides various methods of keeping citizens apprised of the results of their bond votes—to enhance public confidence by providing project and financial data and visually engaging interactive updates.

Many cities and counties have developed applications that encourage citizens to submit pictures of potholes in need of repair, garbage that needs to be picked up, or graffiti that needs to be erased. These are just a few examples of local governments adapting to citizen engagement applications. Government agencies are moving from merely sharing information to actually seeking methods to generate new information and citizen feedback. Interactive maps are helping citizens understand their communities and service offerings in ways that are as helpful as they are visual. More mobile applications are being developed and there are growing numbers of "fans" of Facebook, as well as "followers" of Twitter feeds. Governments have turned to YouTube and provide health and safety information.

Others have indexed and made city and county council meetings available online so people can view a particular segment instead of having to wade through hours of items that they have no interest in.

Studies show that the younger segments of our population are most apt to take advantage of social media offerings as well as the political arena (Smith et al. 2010). This presents both an opportunity and a major social requirement moving forward. Our schools at every level must rethink how civic responsibility and engagement is taught in this new world of emerging social media and Web 2.0 applications. The traditional media environment is outdated and rapidly moving into new forms and platforms. How we learn, teach, and utilize the emerging social media tools as well as Web 2.0 applications are critical factors in maintaining a well-educated citizenry so vital to a successful democracy.

It is hard to imagine that just a few years ago voter apathy was a huge issue. Political experts were pleased that 56.8 percent of eligible-age voters voted in the 2008 presidential elections. This also means that 43.2 percent did not cast a ballot. And as the U.S. population grows, so too will the number of eligible voters who decide whether to vote or not. For the most part, the public gets involved in government during elections, counting on their elected leaders to represent their views. Now, however, many citizens feel that this basic principle has not worked and want to become more active.

As our technological tools of today quickly evolve to fill tomorrow's needs, we must always remember that civic engagement has always been a necessary component of a democracy. We must be principle driven in our approach and realize that government is stronger and more successful when there is transparency and engagement. With a growing population of 300 million-plus citizens, we have no choice but to turn to technology for new solutions that can help governments, at all levels, improve and restore trust with their citizens. These new Web 2.0 and emerging social media tools are being created to improve communications, better connect with citizens, and embrace transparency and civic engagement. There is no turning back. The digital town hall never closes.

References

Batson, Dan, and Kitty Hughes. 2010. *Maryland Budget Map Game.* University of Baltimore and Maryland Budget and Tax Institute. http://iat.ubalt.edu/MDBudgetGame/ (accessed November 30, 2010).

Davy, Steven. 2009. "How the Shift to an Online, On-Demand World of Content Could Impact Political Discourse." PBS, MediaShift, September 3. http://www.pbs.org/mediashift/2009/09/how-the-shift-to-an-online-on-demand-world-of-content-could-impact-political-discourse246.html (accessed November 30, 2010).

Editor & Publisher. 2010. "Pew Study: One in Four Now Read News on Cell Phones." March 1. http://www.editorandpublisher.com/eandp/news/article_display.jsp?vnu_content_id=1004071749 (accessed November 30, 2010).

Federal Communications Commission. 2010, March. *National Broadband Plan: Connecting America.* http://www.broadband.gov/ (accessed November 30, 2010).

Fisch, Karl, and Scott McLeod. 2009. "Did You Know? Shift Happens, version 4." September 14. http://shifthappens.wikispaces.com (accessed November 30, 2010).

Infoplease.com. 2008. "National Voter Turnout in Federal Elections: 1960–2008." http://www.infoplease.com/ipa/A0781453.html (accessed November 30, 2010).

NielsenWire. 2010. "Led by Facebook, Twitter, Global Time Spent on Social Media Sites up 82% Year over Year." January 22. http://blog.nielsen.com/nielsenwire/global/led-by-facebook-twitter-global-time-spent-on-social-media-sites-up-82-year-over-year/ (accessed November 30, 2010).

Pew Project for Excellence in Journalism. 2010. *The State of the News Media: An Annual Report on American Journalism.* March 1. Washington, DC: Pew Research Center. http://www.stateofthemedia.org/2010/overview_major_trends.php (accessed November 30, 2010).

Purcell, Kirsten, Lee Rainie, Amy Mitchell, Tom Rosenstiel, and Kenny Olmstead. 2010. *Understanding the Participatory News Consumer.* Pew Internet and American Life Project, March 1. Washington, DC: Pew Research Center. http://www.pewinternet.org/Reports/2010/Online-News.aspx (accessed November 30, 2010).

Rainie, Lee. 2010. *Lee Rainie Talks with Media Life About the Economics of Online News.* Pew Internet and American Life Project, March 15. Washington, DC: Pew Research Center. http://www.pewinternet.org/Commentary/2010/March/Media-Life.aspx (accessed November 30, 2010).

Rasmussen Reports. 2009. "43% Say Local Government Better Than Feds, States." February 16. http://www.rasmussenreports.com/public_content/politics/general_politics/february_2010/43_say_local_government_better_than_feds_states (accessed November 30, 2010).

Smith, Aaron, Kay Lehman Schlozman, Sidney Verba, and Henry Brady. 2009. "The Current State of Civic Engagement in America." In *The Internet and Civic Engagement.* The Pew Internet and American Life Project, September 1. Washington, DC: Pew Research Center. http://www.pewinternet.org/Reports/2009/15—The-Internet-and-Civic-Engagement/2—The-Current-State-of-Civic-Engagement-in-America.aspx?r=1 (accessed November 30, 2010).

Sunlight Foundation. 2010. "The Open Government Directive." http://sunlightfoundation.com/opengovernmentdirective/ (accessed November 30, 2010).

11

A New Kind of Public Square for Urban America

NORMAN JACKNIS

Especially for cities and other subnational governments, 19th- and 20th-century history enshrined the idea of a physical public square where citizens discuss and, often, protest the issues of the day. We see this in locations like New York's City Hall Plaza or in the town halls across America, or, more famously, in London's Speakers' Corner in Hyde Park.

It is a wonderful notion, but one that will not realistically survive the changes this century will bring—the combined effect of the ubiquitous communications revolution and the ever-growing proportion of economic activity devoted to the creation of knowledge and service delivery. These fundamental economic changes pose an existential challenge to the prevailing model and idea of the American city.

As a consequence of changes in the way that people will live, work, and play, the public square will change its nature and, in a sense, even its place. Beyond the public square, the nature of citizenship, and residence and participation in a city or local region, will be modified in ways that will require public leaders and government agencies to adapt.

This chapter elaborates on these changes (many of which are only dimly perceived by policymakers) and explores how subnational government might respond.

How We Got Here: The Urban Economy, from Manufacturing to Knowledge

It is important to start with economic growth because the modern city made possible the modern economy and the modern economy made possible the modern city. Economics is not the only important aspect of urban life, but it is the essential starting point.

How is wealth created and why would that have occurred in cities? In America, two factors are among the fundamental bases of the growth of wealth and income:

- Differentiation of skills of people, who subsequently exchange the services/goods that they are better able to provide;
- The creation of new knowledge and innovation in technology, which make possible new products and services, as well as increases in productivity.

If people cannot communicate, then neither differentiation nor innovation can occur between them. If people do communicate, they can collaborate to achieve differentiation; they can also communicate new ideas and collaborate to create new products and services. There is an important underlying principle here. What expands communications expands markets and wealth.

As the world economy globalizes, it is important to realize that this is not just an American phenomenon. Francisco Rodriguez, Director of Research at the Human Development Report Office of the United Nations and author of a recent study on the role of infrastructure investment on economic growth has noted (Uchitelle 2009): "The public works projects that have the largest effect on economic growth are those that integrate markets in different areas of the country."

A hundred years ago, a majority of Americans lived in rural areas. As our story unfolds with the migration of Americans from farms to cities for manufacturing jobs, we do not stop to think: what happened to food production when Americans went to cities? Food production went up. Even farm income went up in general. The United States did not get out of the business of producing food. It just did it with fewer and fewer people. This pattern has repeated more recently.

When manufacturing became the heart of the American economy, cities were central to economic growth because they increased physical proximity between people, which made communications easier than in a rural society. Cities had the mass of workers that were needed by the factories. The close proximity of so many people also made it easier to exchange goods, services, and the innovations that further increased wealth in the area. This, in turn, increased specialized skills and innovations that created more wealth. And that motivated more people to move to cities, which continued the cycle.

Getting a manufacturing plant built in a city gave jobs to many people and accelerated the economic growth cycle. So cities pursued an economic development strategy that is still widely used—get companies to move to a city, bringing jobs and employees with them, or get existing companies to create more jobs that will attract people. To get companies to do this, city governments provided tax and other incentives. They still do.

Cities also made possible what we now call the clustering of businesses related to a particular industry. There was finance in New York, autos in Detroit, rubber in Akron, steel in Pittsburgh, and film studies in Hollywood (even in the 1920s in the days of silent movies).

This worked well during the industrial age and, in due course, defined the modern American idea of the core city as the center of power at the subnational level. The role of urban political parties and the nature of local government functions were all developed in their modern manifestations during this period of industrial focus.

Although it was manufacturing that energized urban growth, over the last 40 years, manufacturing has employed fewer and fewer people. Services, office work, and the rest of the knowledge economy have taken the place of agriculture and manufacturing as the source of a majority of jobs. A hundred years ago, 71 percent of the labor force made goods or food (U.S. Census Bureau 1975). Now, only 21 percent do that and the other 79 percent provide services.[1]

Like food production, the value of manufacturing had gone up until the recent recession years. In 2010, again, production increased in value and can be expected to increase further in the future. Although this country will continue to make goods—and even has a national security requirement to manufacture certain kinds of goods—manufacturing, like agriculture, will no longer promise to be a source of an expanding number of jobs.

Most American city leaders understand this change in employment patterns, but old ways of thinking die hard. So, as services grew, the economic development strategy of offering incentives to manufacturers shifted to encourage the relocation of white-collar companies and the construction of office buildings in cities.

The shiny office towers in most American cities of more than 100,000 people have been expressions of this shift in employment and incentives policies to the service sector. The idea behind these policies was that offices would concentrate employment opportunities as factories did in the past.

Suburbanization: The First Shot Across the Bow

Central cities discovered, however, that office work could often be located as easily in suburban areas as in the downtown. Even when the work was downtown, the development of modern highways and regional mass transit systems enabled middle class people to live outside the city boundaries. In many important metropolitan regions—even New York and Los Angeles—the borders of the city contain less than a majority of the people living in the total region.

This shift in population led to a shift in political power and provided an early warning about future challenges for central cities. We have seen the development of many fragmented kinds of governance in urban areas in the surrounding region. Whether villages, towns, or suburban cities, these newer suburban governments have provided only a faint echo of the kind of public debate and concerns that had historically been associated with the big cities of America.

With declining crime rates and policies to gentrify previously poor and working class neighborhoods of many cities, the large city has sought to reclaim its role. And the American city has had its promoters who suggest that a cleaner version of the industrial golden age is just around the corner.

One example can be found in the work of Richard Florida, well-known champion of the "creative class" and its essential role in urban economic development. In his books, he elaborates on, as he puts it, "why place matters."

Not to overgeneralize, his main points are:

- Central cities have become more important and popular.
- Creative people are the foundation of urban economic growth in a knowledge-based economy.
- Creative people want to be around other creative, talented people and will concentrate in hospitable urban environments. That means that not all geographic areas will be equal in their economic development because they are not all equally welcoming of the lifestyles some creative people pursue.
- People, in general, have the option to live almost anywhere they want. Their wants will differ, so people will cluster in communities of like-minded neighbors. Thus different regions are becoming more differentiated from each other.

Of course, one can quibble with some aspects of his arguments—especially if one limits the definition of urban area to the central city. For example, there are clear counterexamples to the argument that creativity comes from the central core of urban areas. Arguably, the two greatest concentrations of American technological innovations—Silicon Valley and Route 128 in Massachusetts—are not located in the urban core of their regions, San Francisco and Boston, respectively. Rather, these suburban areas became hotbeds of creativity.

Similarly, part of the argument about the importance of the urban core is that it provides opportunities for the young and unattached to meet each other. But even that pattern may be moderated. The growth of Web services such as eHarmony, Match.com, and Chemistry.com, indicates that there are threats even to this function of the urban core. Even four years ago, according to a Pew survey, "15% of American adults—about 30 million people—say they know someone who has been in a long-term relationship or married someone he or she met online" (Madden and Lenhart 2006).

Others, such as Alan Ehrenhalt,[2] have intensified Florida's theme. Ehrenhalt explicitly criticized those who have made various pronouncements that the Internet and broadband networks have led to the "death of distance"—or at least that physical distance is diminishing as a factor in human relationships.

Is Distance Diminishing?

Or is this view of the increased importance of geography accurate? The patterns Florida documents no doubt exist today, but we should be careful about projecting them too far into the future because the challenges to the importance of physical proximity are only beginning. Some inklings of that future challenge to our traditional emphasis on physical geography are already appearing.

For example, getting a company to move to a city does not mean as much as it used to, at least in terms of jobs. There are frequent stories about how government incentives have not produced the expected private sector jobs. Missouri and St. Louis County have asked for a $7 million tax abatement back from Pfizer because the facility it broke ground on in 2008, and opened up in early 2009, was closed by December 2009 (Manufacturing.net 2009; Shapiro 2009). North Carolina asked for $6 million back in tax credits given a couple of years ago to Dell Computer for a plant that also closed in 2009 (Owens 2009). Years before the current recession, auditors in New York State concluded that a large portion of the incentives provided to companies have resulted in no job growth (Office of the New York State Comptroller 2006).

Then there was a news story in the *Wall Street Journal* in 2009 (Drucker 2009) about the large, ostensibly American, consulting company, Accenture, which officially moved its headquarters to Ireland. The *Journal* reported: "Despite the move, the company said it had no plans for its executives to move to Ireland. The company's chief executive is based in Boston. Its chief operating office is based in Austin, Texas. 'None of our top executives are moving to Ireland' said the company spokesman." Because of modern telecommunications, they could all work together, though separated by many miles.

Perhaps the problem is that companies cannot or just do not concentrate employment in a single location the way they used to. Historically, companies were strong economic units because of the relatively high cost of individuals working together. As noted in Coase's Theory of the Firm (1937), the company supplied the communications "glue" that enabled these individuals to work as a team less expensively than they could have separately.

However, the Internet dramatically reduces the costs of organization and will provide the means for people to collaborate and work together, inside or outside of companies. This is one of the themes that justifies the subtitle of Clay Shirky's popular book, *Here Comes Everybody: The Power of Organizing without Organizations* (2008).

Increasingly, the big company will itself no longer look like a single monolithic structure. This can be observed in the global supply chains, the outsourcing phenomenon, the increased use of freelancers, and the general dispersion of big company employees around the globe.

As noted, during the industrial era manufacturing companies in similar product domains would cluster. Among urban economic development specialists, there is still much talk about clusters. This talk is important because a cluster is, by definition, built on physical proximity and thus preserves the old model of cities.

Probably the most famous business cluster is Wall Street. Even within New York City, however, financial firms are not near Wall Street anymore. Moreover, there are financial services far from New York City or any other traditional center of finance.

The BATS Exchange in Lenexa, Kansas, only five years old, now accounts for

10 percent of securities trades. The New York Stock Exchange lost more than half of its market share from just four years ago (Bowley 2009) because that market share can now be serviced in places like Lenexa.

In a globally connected world, it is not just Lenexa, Kansas, that offers an alternative location for business. Support services—the marketing, financial, legal, and other services, even public services—that are critical to the success of other businesses are changing and becoming within reach of people in more locations than in the past. The typical help desk service from a foreign country is an early indicator of what is ahead.

Another early warning sign that central city geography might matter less can be found in office space. The recession has caused a noticeable increase in office vacancies. But there is a longer-term trend at work, too. Many companies are discovering that they need less space per employee. They are not generally publicizing this situation, but here is an example from Cisco. In its latest building upgrade, it achieved a 40 percent reduction in the amount of space required per employee, while increasing employee comfort, satisfaction, and productivity (Cisco Systems 2007). By the way, this dramatically reduced greenhouse gases and energy costs, too.

The Communications Revolution Is Just Beginning

Part of the reason for this reduction in space per employee is telecommuting. Even in 2006, a Gallup poll found that a third of adults telecommuted to work, at least part time (Jones 2006). Naturally, the figure was higher—60 percent—for those with graduate degrees, who are representative of the growing knowledge sector of the economy. This trend is likely to continue.

The dramatic increase in the penetration of the global communications network into home offices has provided the foundation for this telework trend. We see this in Internet growth; it is projected to increase by a factor of four from 2010 to 2014 (Duffy 2010).

We see it in higher-speed connections to the Internet, referred to as broadband. Overall broadband penetration across all U.S. homes grew to 63 percent in March 2009, according to a survey by Pew Internet researchers. In May 2009, they reported that broadband penetration among active Internet users in U.S. homes was 95 percent (Horrigan 2009). The average American clearly understands these patterns. When Pew asked about the value of broadband, a strong majority believed that broadband contributes to economic growth in their communities.

However, we are just at the beginning of the development of broadband networks, and this country has yet to see the ultrabroadband networks of the near future. In most parts of the United States today, the speed of typical Internet connections is barely sufficient for satisfactory compressed video streaming of YouTube.

While there has been a sharp increase in the use of video over the Internet, the speed needed for high-definition video-conferencing virtually equal to face-to-face conversation is still years away. So the long-term impact of the network has yet to be felt because for most people their Internet interactions with others are still missing a necessary component—high-quality visual communications.

Perhaps 10 or 20 years from now, ultrabroadband will be widely deployed and telework will be widely accepted as a standard. In this near future, we will live in a world of ubiquitous, high-quality visual communication and easy collaboration, enabling anyone anywhere to virtually meet anyone else, anywhere else.

Of course, we need to understand that the basic laws of economics will not change. The factors leading to economic growth, with which this chapter began, will not change. What *will* change is that physical proximity will no longer be the only way to connect people, and this will accelerate economic growth even more.

With easier access to business support services and the lower cost of organizing and coordinating people, we will see smaller and more fluid forms of organizations, not just the traditional large company. The network will be the glue that coordinates individuals more than the company organization. In a sense, then, the network enables individuals (or very small groups of individuals) to become the primary units of economic activity.

With this new communications capability, and an economy in which most workers will no longer be stuck on a farm or in a factory or office building, it will no longer be necessary that work be done in a building dedicated for work. Nor must work be near the rest of a cluster supporting a business. Many people will no longer go to work; work will go to them. More individuals will have more choices in where they live because they can take their economic activity with them wherever they go.

The key economic questions facing subnational government in 2030 will be: When most people can live and work anywhere, where will they choose to live and work? And where will they participate in "civic affairs"?

Communities in a Hybrid Physical-Virtual World

Asking questions would seem to support Florida's view that, more than ever in history, people have choices as to where to live and with whom to associate. Indeed, he is right, except for one critical detail. When the world becomes one virtual community, it will be virtual, not geographic, proximity that will rule. It will occur in the ways he claims that geographic stratification exists, but that stratification will take place globally in the virtual world.

So we can slightly modify his vision for a future virtual world: creative people will continue to be the foundation of economic growth in a knowledge-based economy; creative people will still want to be connected with other creative, talented people; and people, in general, will want to be connected with like-minded people—thus differentiating virtual regions in cyberspace.

The social and policy consequences of these trends are as significant as they would be in the physical world. Without urban plans and public policy focus on these trends, we can well imagine a variety of socially undesirable and unintended consequences—for example, "digital slums" (with inadequate broadband for residents to participate in the rest of the digital world) and the resulting segregation of have-nots from the opportunities they might have to escape poverty.

Ever since the Internet became widely adopted it has been clear that almost everything that humans might do in the "real" physical world they will try to do in the virtual world. The best lesson to be learned about what Florida has found in the physical world is not that the threat/promise of the virtual world is nonexistent. Instead, the best lesson is that we will have to address many of the same issues in the virtual as the physical world and, perhaps worse, the interaction between those two worlds.

The Changing Nature of the Local Government Debate

The substance of the local civic debate will likely be changed by the relative freedom of movement of citizens and the two necessary parts of a local government response: (1) create a good quality of life in the city so people will want to live there; (2) improve the ability of residents to provide ever more valuable goods and services, so they will have higher incomes.

Quality of Life

In the age of industrialization, the quality of urban life was often considered to be a luxury or even a detriment to economic growth. A recent example is China's willingness to accept a large amount of air and water pollution as a necessary cost of its economic development.

In the networked world, every city will have to fight harder to retain population. Rather than being a luxury that takes money from economic growth, quality of life—including a green environment, and cultural and social resources—will be a major differentiator in attracting people.

But every city need not emphasize the same amenities and qualities. People, after all, have different tastes and desires. Because not all people desire the same things, it will be up to the local leaders to determine what qualities they wish to emphasize. Each economically successful city, then, will maximize quality of life in different ways. But whatever qualities those are, the city had better assure they are at a high level.

Within larger cities, there will be more options and ways of differentiating. The decentralization of economic activity will enable the creation of multiple downtowns—areas that provide local shopping, learning, and other physical community activities closer to where people live. Each of these could develop in a way that would take on a distinctive feel and culture, thus allowing the city as a whole to retain people who would otherwise not be interested in the same things. But this will require a willingness to encourage neighborhood focus and pride, rather than solely focusing on the traditional center of the city.

In a sense, governments will have to treat every person—officially resident or not—like a tourist. A memorable "customer experience" and all the amenities that a tourist expects in deciding whether to visit will become the same factors that an individual may use to decide whether to live in a particular city. This shift in mindset will force local leaders to think of their urban areas less as centers of economic production and more as centers of economic consumption.

Despite Florida's thesis, people may or may not also find it necessary to live physically near like-minded people, for all or even part of a year. Where they are physically at any point in time will depend on how urban leaders design their areas to appeal to a particular "market segment" of citizens.

Learning Instead of Educational Institutions

If individuals, instead of companies, are increasingly the key to economic production, then government will need to make investments in its individual residents. If governments do not do this, it would be just another reason for those people to move elsewhere.

The U.S. Department of Labor has indicated that the average younger baby boomer has had nearly 11 jobs (U.S. Department of Labor, Bureau of Labor Statistics 2010). As changes in knowledge accelerate in the future, many of these job changes will require new skills. If the residents of a city are to increase their wealth, they must increase their knowledge over time. However, local governments cannot afford to extend the K–16 educational structure to cover the whole life of every adult. Indeed, the most important learning will occur after people are no longer in classrooms.

Partly in response to this coming demand, the networked world already provides many virtual places to learn. MIT put its courses online. Carnegie-Mellon is leading an open learning project. The University for the Third Age has seniors teaching other seniors. The state of Florida has a virtual reference librarian available 24 hours a day. There are training videos and tutorials in almost every subject imaginable to be found somewhere on the Internet.

Urban leaders in the 19th century recognized the economic importance of ensuring that all citizens could read; they created the public schools and libraries necessary to achieve that goal. In this century, urban leaders will need to ensure that all city residents are helped to identify where they can get 21st-century learning. This style is more facilitation than delivery of services. But it is an important skill that will have to be learned by government agencies.

Connecting People to a Growth Ecosystem

In the face of an economy ever more dependent upon knowledge and innovation, many local leaders have begun to try to imitate Silicon Valley's past success. They have tried to subsidize engineers or local research labs in universities. But

Silicon Valley's success is about more than a lot of smart engineers, supported by high-quality local universities. The "secret sauce" has been the financiers, lawyers, marketers, and others in business support functions who understood and were not averse to the risks of the innovative business of technology.

In a networked world, these services will become widely available. The best university research will be available through the network; capital will flow more freely. Whereas it is good for a city to have institutions, like universities, that create new ideas and new knowledge, connecting its residents with the creation of ideas and knowledge all over the world will be even more important.

New Areas for Oversight and Regulation

Considering the importance of the network, the governmental oversight and regulatory role will also have to address new issues. These issues will include presiding over an expected struggle over the meaning and protection of "intellectual property," finding the right balance between the need for strong electronic identities and security, and the preservation of privacy and individual liberties. How these issues are handled will also contribute either to economic growth or to the stagnation of people affected by each governing agency's jurisdiction.

In a networked world, the public's need for oversight, monitoring, and regulation of business will more easily be met through the rapid dissemination of information and the enablement of both paid civil servants and the general public to observe business behavior. To the degree that the rule of law plays a role in creating an environment in which buyers and sellers can establish a sufficient level of trust to deal with each other, this enhanced public oversight will be beneficial for economic growth.

Convergence of Physical Spaces and a Hybrid Physical/ Virtual Environment

We will be living in a hybrid world. The physical world, of course, will not disappear. Even in 2030, people will still physically be somewhere day and night.

Some parts of the economy will not be available through the communications network. For those nonvirtual economic activities, physical proximity will still be most important. However, even those who produce physical goods will be dependent upon the communications network to learn new innovations/technologies and to find optimal suppliers, willing customers, and the most cost effective shipping. While that part of the economy will have shrunk as a percentage of overall GDP, as the historic center of power it will linger in the public debate.

Even the physical world will become enmeshed with the virtual world, as can be seen in the complex urban environment of Times Square with its complement of computer-driven "walls" (i.e., screens). This combined physical/virtual environment will require new ways of thinking about urban planning, zoning, building codes, and infrastructure investments.

The impact of broadband communications networks will also be felt in the physical world. These trends should inform our understanding of urban planning and policy. For too long, urban planning has focused on sustaining—perhaps reviving—the ideal of the central urban core with clearly zoned and separated areas for working, living, and shopping.

Such an approach will fail to address the oncoming reality. The industrial era of separate places for working, living, and shopping will be replaced by blurred lines between these activities. The home will increasingly be the workplace and the shopping place. The traditional urban planners' use of zoning as a major instrument of policy will have to accommodate this change.

During the past hundred years, the place for work, the place for living, and the place for shopping have been separate. Vast transportation networks were built to move people from one place to another. That transportation model will need to be replaced. In the future, local leaders may hear less about traffic congestion and more about network congestion or perhaps network-based intrusion into privacy.

If such changes are not made, city leaders will find that most of their residents live in violation of most of their rules. The threat to their leadership will be as obvious as it was during the prohibition era, when drinking was not stopped, but respect for the law was undermined.

Much of this narrative assumes that metropolitan regions will have broadband and even ultrabroadband. Because of its centrality in the new economy and its ability to service other elements of infrastructure, the telecommunications network will jump to paramount importance in debates about public investments. The arguments of recent decades about where to build highways or other transportation will pale in comparison.

Changing Subnational Governance: The New Public Square

As with all significant socioeconomic transitions, the transition to this new world will also require enormous political and leadership skills. The need to play by the old rules in the short run and the public's limited understanding of the implications of the changes that are occurring will draw funds away from investments that are necessary to maintain a viable urban future.

Just as the ubiquitous communications network and socioeconomic trends will impact the machinery of economic growth, so too will it impact governance itself.

Global Metroplexes

The Obama administration is working hard to get state and local governments to take a regional approach to economic development and metropolitan governance, even threatening/promising to use funding to make sure such cooperation occurs. As the kind of impacts described above become clearer to local leaders, it might be reasonable to expect their first instinct to be to work more closely in their region. This may well happen, although it will take changes in attitudes. The central city will have to adjust to a world where it is no longer so central and the surrounding urban areas will have to adjust to a world where the expense of "home rule" can no longer be justified.

Just as the global communications network makes possible connections even among local areas that are not geographically near, there is also the potential for networks of local governments or regions to develop without regard to even national boundaries—virtual metroplexes. For example, it may be that two cities separated by thousands of miles—for example, New York and London—have more connections and more in common than nearby cities like New York and Syracuse. The global communications network makes it possible for these two distant metropolises to coalesce as one. We are already seeing several global networks of cities working together over the Internet for various purposes, such as education and trade.

The ability of distant urban areas to work closely together raises questions of governance, even governance issues that cross national borders. However, much of this activity is occurring "below the radar" of nation-states; they are unaware and cannot keep track of all such interactions. Interestingly, this point was made by Anne-Marie Slaughter (2004), when she was dean of the Woodrow Wilson School of Princeton University. Now she is the director of the Policy Planning Staff of the U.S. State Department—arguably one of the arch defenders of the concept of the nation-state. It will be interesting to see if and how the State Department adjusts as these global connections at the local level intensify.

Globally Shared Services

In the current recession, there have been many suggestions to save taxpayer money by sharing services, especially at the subnational level. The states of Minnesota and Wisconsin even began an effort to share services across state lines.

As the network starts to make available so-called cloud services, the concept of sharing services will be stretched beyond what is currently considered. In the network age, services could be delivered anywhere on the globe from anywhere on the globe. So why should local government only consider sharing services with a neighboring local government? To use the example of New York and London again, it may be that these two distant cities have more public services in common to share than New York has with its neighboring city of Yonkers. With the global communications network, New York City and London can work as well as New York City and Yonkers.

Given the disparity in the professional and technological capabilities of local governments, it would not be surprising to see leading local governments selling back end services to other governments. Nor would it be surprising to see leading local governments compete with each other to sell to the less technologically sophisticated governments.

What happens when citizens of a city realize they are really getting services from some other city's bureaucracy and systems is an interesting question. But it will certainly lead to some vigorous debates and some degree of confused accountability.

Typically, when officials discuss sharing of services, they think of back-office services, including IT operations, printing, personnel systems, and the like. But citizens too can decide that they will share services. Even before there was a global network citizens could decide, for example, that they liked to use a certain park outside of their own city.

Similarly, on the Internet, some government services cannot be limited to the residents, particularly those services that primarily involve the distribution of information like public health. That resident may decide that some other jurisdiction is a better source of information than his/her own local government. This situation also confuses accountability and creates interesting questions concerning where exactly that resident "lives."

Citizen-Delivered Services

In addition to turning to other governments for service delivery, local leaders can also now turn to their individual citizens for service delivery—what is sometimes called "coproduction." Just as the corporate organization was built in the industrial age because it made collaboration easier, so too did the government bureaucracy develop in the same time period. As the Internet makes it easier for people to collaborate without the benefit of formal organizational structures, this will not only impact the business world. It will also impact government. The nascent movement for coproduction is the beginning. In coproduction, in addition to or instead of paid civil service staff, local leaders ensure the delivery of public goods and services by facilitating the collaboration of citizens. For example, a mother whose child went through a summer camp program last year can provide guidance and assist in the application by a mother of a younger child who is first considering summer camp this year.

(While there is nothing that prevents national governments from using coproduction, as a practical matter, local government services lend themselves more naturally to this new approach to service delivery.)

Going back to the importance of quality of life and a positive "citizen experience," it is worth noting that peer-to-peer services usually result in more satisfaction on both sides of the service delivery equation than the usual anonymous organizational staff person delivering the service. As individual citizens will be able to participate more in the public sector, this may well contribute to the quality of life that will motivate them to live in one location rather than another.

Ambiguous Loyalties and Civic Participation

Ever since the earliest walled cities and then the development of the nation-state, governments have shared one characteristic: they were all about the control of a piece of geography. When people spend much of their time in virtual, not physical, communities, their sense of belonging and their allegiance to their local government will be challenged. This is a fundamental, almost existential, challenge to local government and its leaders.

The ability of the Internet to make government and its proceedings more transparent—and the demands of citizens around the world that the governments fulfill this potential—has both led to and been reinforced by a decreasing sense of deference to public leaders. In the virtual world familiarity may not breed contempt, but it most certainly obviates any belief in the godlike mystical talents of rulers—a belief that distance and closed geography once made possible.

While national leaders may face the same problem, local leaders—without armies, currency controls, and other sovereign tools of the nation-state, will discover that their hold on power is much more tenuous. In a sense, mayors and other subnational leaders will have to compete with each other for "mind share" and authority. Even today, as noted earlier, some citizens go to websites of other local governments—not their own—for some of the softer public services. Citizens no longer operate in a monopoly market for public services, and as the communications network develops the monopoly will break even more.

This raises the fundamental question: Where will a person be a citizen/resident? If a person spends part of the year in one area and a part in another, does he/she have to choose which one to be a participant in? Why not both?

This ambiguity can be stretched further. With many people able to earn an income from any location, some will choose to spend part of the year in one place and another part in a different place. (This has already happened on a smaller scale with retirees, the "snow birds" who go south during winter.) In which location are these people really residents? Do they have to be in one place for a certain percentage of the year to have the right to speak up in "local" debates?

If a person is away from his/her "home town," but can still participate in local policy debates from thousands of miles away, then the local public square becomes extended across the globe into one of many virtual public squares. If a person becomes interested in one of these public squares, but has not lived in the physical community, can they still participate? What if the person were willing to pay taxes for the privilege of getting services from that community's government?

In these early stages of the future ubiquitous communications world, we can at best ask questions in the hope that policymakers will start to think about what the answers might be. Whatever those answers, we are clearly at the beginning of some dramatic changes in the nature of subnational civic life.

Epilogue: The Arc of the Future Depends Upon the Actions of the Present

In the day-to-day acts of governing an urban area, it is easy to push off consideration of the implications of the trends in communications, economic activity, and society which have been described here. It is worth remembering, though, that this situation—this kind of fork in the road—is not without precedent.

At one of the seminars conducted by the FCC in preparation for its National Broadband Plan, a leading venture capitalist retold this bit of history:

> At the beginning of the 19th century St. Louis was the great city of the west, the Gateway City. Chicago was an upstart afterthought. St. Louis, however, was situated on the west bank of the Mississippi, the wrong side from the railroads that connected to the markets in the east. In part because of the shortsightedness of the boatmen who ferried cargo across the river, the town fathers refused to build a railroad bridge across the Big Muddy to connect with the rail lines heading east.
>
> Chicago's leaders, on the other hand, aggressively pushed for rail connections. By 1861 Chicago had 15 rail lines with hundreds of trains coming and going on a daily basis, and St. Louis was still arguing about the bridge. The Second City was born; St. Louis could no longer claim to be the Gateway to the West. (Wheeler 2009)

And by 1870, Chicago's economy and population started to surge past St. Louis. To this day, it is the dominant city of the interior of America. Local leaders choose to ignore developing trends at their own risk and at risk to the future of their citizens.

Notes

1. See U.S. Bureau of Labor Statistics and U.S. Census Bureau for data on the 2000 structure of employment.
2. Alan Ehrenhalt, "The Rediscovery of Place," *Governing Magazine,* June 2008.

References

Bowley, Graham. 2009. "Rivals Pose Threat to New York Stock Exchange." *New York Times,* October 15. http://www.nytimes.com/2009/10/15/business/15exchange.html.
Cisco Systems. 2007. "How Cisco Achieved Environmental Sustainability in the Connected Workplace" (Case study). http://www.cisco.com/web/about/ciscoitatwork/downloads/ciscoitatwork/pdf/Cisco_IT_Case_Study_Green_Office_Design.pdf.
Coase, Ronald. 1937. "The Theory of the Firm." *Economica* 4(16): 386–340.
Drucker, Jesse. 2009. "Accenture Is Seeking to Change Tax Locales." *Wall Street Journal,* May 27. http://online.wsj.com/article/SB124338175183056465.html.
Duffy, Jim. 2010. "IP Traffic Quadrupling by 2014: Cisco Study." The Cisco Connection, Network World, June 2. http://www.networkworld.com/community/blog/ip-traffic-quadrupling-2014-cisco-study.
Florida, Richard. 2005. *The Flight of the Creative Class: The New Global Competition for Talent.* New York: HarperCollins.
Horrigan, John. 2009. *Home Broadband Adoption 2009.* Pew Internet and American Life Project, June. http://pewinternet.org/~/media//Files/Reports/2009/Home-Broadband-Adoption-2009.pdf.
Jones, Jeffrey M. 2006. "One in Three U.S. Workers Have 'Telecommuted' to Work." Gallup, August 16. http://www.gallup.com/poll/24181/One-Three-US-Workers-Telecommuted-Work.aspx.

Madden, Mary, and Amanda Lenhart. 2006. *Online Dating.* Pew Internet and American Life Project, March 5. http://www.pewinternet.org/Reports/2006/Online-Dating.aspx.

Manufacturing.net. 2009. "Layoffs Could Cost Pfizer Tax Breaks." November 11. http://www.manufacturing.net/News-Layoffs-Could-Cost-Pfizer-Tax-Breaks-111109.aspx.

Office of the New York State Comptroller. 2006. *Industrial Development Agencies in New York State: Background, Issues and Recommendations.* Division of Local Government Services and Economic Development, May. http://www.osc.state.ny.us/localgov/pubs/research/idabackground.pdf.

Owens, Adam. 2009. "Dell to Close N.C. Plant, Eliminate 905 Jobs." WRAL News, October 8. http://www.wral.com/business/story/6156112/.

Shapiro, Mary. 2009. "Pfizer Opens New Research Facility in Chesterfield." *Suburban Journals,* April 14. http://www.stltoday.com/suburban-journals/metro/news/article_b9e6c40a-a3d8-5d7c-9790-63dbc020cc31.html.

Shirky, Clay. 2008. *Here Comes Everybody: The Power of Organizing without Organizations.* New York: Penguin Press.

Slaughter, Anne-Marie. 2004. *A New World Order.* Princeton, NJ: Princeton University Press.

Uchitelle, Louis. 2009. "Entering the Superproject Void." *New York Times,* November 29. http://www.nytimes.com/2009/11/29/weekinreview/29uchitelle.html?pagewanted=all.

U.S. Census Bureau. 1975. *Historical Statistics of the United States: Colonial Times to 1970.* Part 1 (includes 1900 data). Washington, DC: Government Printing Office. http://www2.census.gov/prod2/statcomp/documents/CT1970p1–01.pdf.

U.S. Department of Labor, Bureau of Labor Statistics. 2010. "Number of Jobs Held, Labor Market Activity, and Earnings Growth among the Youngest Baby Boomers: Results from a Longitudinal Survey." Press release, September 10, USDL-10–1243. http://www.bls.gov/news.release/pdf/nlsoy.pdf.

Wheeler, Tom. 2009. "FCC National Broadband Plan Workshop." September 26. http://www.broadband.gov/docs/ws_economy/ws_economy_wheeler_statement.doc.

Part III

How Will Government Respond?

12

The Horizon Problem in Public Administration

Shifting from *Crisis du Jour* to Deliberate Management

JOHN CALLAHAN AND ALAN LYLES

American public administration lurches from crisis to crisis, managing more often by response than by deliberate public administration for the long term. In the life of nations, planning and management horizons may be shortened temporarily. However, if this becomes the dominant governing practice, it compromises performance and the achievement of longer-term aims. Electoral cycles and the pulls across the political spectrum for control of bureaucracy almost ensure that the drama of the moment displaces rational and enduring solutions for a longer horizon. A Gresham's law of governing cautions that short-term considerations displace long-term aims unless there are structures and processes to resist the tug. It was not always so.

American government has witnessed significant and long-lasting policy and administrative changes, such as the Pendleton Civil Service Reform Act of 1883, the imposition of a federal income tax by the 16th Amendment to the Constitution, direct election of United States senators under the 17th Amendment, passage of the Social Security Act of 1935 and Administrative Procedure Act of 1946, and the Marshall Plan. These few examples provide evidence that it has been possible to accomplish large, meaningful, and enduring changes.

In this chapter, a selected set of public administration decision-making horizon issues are examined to ascertain how they are currently being handled in public administration and the political system. Then, recommendations by which more constructive attention and implementation could occur on these horizon issues are suggested. However, it is useful to remember that "no action taken or contemplated by the government of a democracy is immune to public debate, scrutiny, or investigation" (Appleby 1953, p. 63).

Decision Horizons

What are the requirements for deliberate public administration for longer-term objectives? The rational decision maker seeks to make objective decisions over an appropriate time horizon. We begin with the consideration of what are the appropriate time horizons for those decisions.

Horizons differ. There is the day-to-day horizon specified by the ever-present "to do" list. There is the 75-year actuarial time horizon embodied in the Annual Trustees Report of the Social Security Administration (2010). There is the annual one- or two-year budget cycle followed by state governments throughout the country. And there are the 5- and 10-year economic and fiscal forecasts included in Congressional Budget Office (CBO) budget estimates. (These estimates, however, can be abridged when fiscal decisions are made "on an emergency basis" as declared by the Congress, passed in legislation, and sent to the president.) The techniques, reliability, and relevant factors in each of these time horizons differ; however, the essential rational decision processes should be durable across them.

The horizon's time dimension is critical; it sets the boundary for relevant considerations and decision criteria. The decision maker wants the decisions that are made to work well within that time frame. In short, the decision maker does not expect his or her decision to fail. It may fail, but not by design.

Then why is the perception that public decision makers are doing poorly so persistent? What is required of the decision maker in that context? Good information, first and foremost, will help lead to a "good" decision, but does not assure it. Adequate resources to analyze the relevant alternatives under consideration are, of course, a must. Clear means and procedures for decision implementation are essential as well. Sometimes, however, lack of data or analysis of alternative plans is not the biggest problem. That may be the tyranny of the urgent, without countermeasures that balance decisions with goals or that consider their enduring significance. In 1968, Robet S. Herman, New York State's director of budget planning and development, observed: "Planning is not making future decisions. It is evaluating the future so that more intelligent current decisions might be made" (Alesch 1968, p. 265).

The current deficit "crisis," for example, has spawned a number of books on how such a crisis could be addressed (Walker 2009). Such books are only guides to action; they must be implemented by the actual decision makers.

There are reasons to be optimistic for improvements in the time factor for public administration decision processes, especially with the evolution of e-government through generations 1.0 and 2.0 (see Table 12.1).

E-government was defined in the E-Government Act of 2002 as

> the use . . . of web-based Internet applications and other information technologies, combined with processes that implement these technologies, to (A) enhance the access to and delivery of Government information and services to the public, other agencies, and other Government entities; or (B) bring about improvements in Government operations that may include effectiveness, efficiency, service quality, or transformation. (U.S. Congress 2002)

"Transforming American Governance" in the title of this book suggests that technological and social evolutions influence differences in governance. The three main

Table 12.1

Technology, Government Decisions, and Decision Horizons

Technology	Essential feature(s)	Decision horizon implications
Paper documents	Cumbersome	Slow → less immediate and ↑ bureaucratic resistance
	Incomplete	
	Low(er) transparency	
E-Government Web 1.0	Accessibility	↑ Operational speed Information overload for tactical and strategic actions
Web 2.0*	↑ Sharing and interactions	↑ Stakeholder awareness and participation ↑ Complexity for decisions affecting divergent interests

Source: Tim O'Reilly (2005), "What Is Web 2.0," O'Reilly.com, September 30, http://oreilly.com/web2/archive/what-is-web-20.html (accessed May 2, 2010).

sectors for e-government are Government-to-Government (G2G), Government-to-Business (G2B), and Government-to-Citizen (G2C). The impetus for each, their priorities, and their developmental stages differ, but the implications are similar for the availability of information and the expectation for reaction.

Where Web 1.0 referred to the appearance of the World Wide Web and its ability to present information, different media, and page views, it also identifies a relatively static and linear information flow. Web 2.0, however, is marked by a shift to networks—computer networks, of course, but more importantly user and social networks (O'Reilly 2005). With these networks, e-government evolved to capture the newer efficiencies made possible under Web 1.0; and enhanced information technology (IT) for management of business processes primarily concerned with the needs of G2G and G2B. G2C needs quickly led into Web 2.0, which is being used to connect citizens, elected officials, and civil servants. Under the Obama administration, for example, the White House has a presence and interacts on Twitter, Facebook, and MySpace, as well as blogs (Gaudin 2009). Web 3.0 refers to the as yet unrealized evolution to intelligent Web-based functionalities that identify interests and proactively present information, elicit responses, and perform with as yet unidentified capabilities. Achieving this goal will require overcoming the limitations of structure and culture in governmental bureaucracies. The three critical limitations have been identified as (1) an outdated, 20th-century technology approach, (2) an inability to relate data to information and information to decision making, and (3) a culture that inhibits collaboration (Digiammarino et al. 2009). We would add a fourth barrier, the personal time period over which key decision makers consider their potential gains versus costs of decisions.

The rate of change from Web 1.0 to Web 2.0 and then to the next stage(s) is increasing. This tempo provides more information and greater connectedness, but also an expected faster pace of decision making. However, will this "twitch speed" (Prensky 2001) for receipt and acting on information create a situation where the appropriate time horizons for decisions are not fully (or adequately) recognized? Will the flood of data, information, and contacts with stakeholders work against resolving horizon problems?

Public Administration Decisions

In 1947 Herbert Simon redirected the work of understanding how decisions are made from guidance based on the study of actions to the decision process itself. He launched a scientific approach to public administration, shifting from making observations that he labeled "Proverbs" (Simon 1947). However, Simon's publication drew immediate and intense opposition from Dwight Waldo, who argued in 1948 that values could not be dismissed and were central to understanding the actual decision-making process (Waldo 1948).

Decision theory is multidisciplinary, has efficiency as its goal and rationality as the means for achieving it, and is intended to explain how things actually work. There are two main approaches used by decision theorists: *consequences* (assessed by formal mathematical analyses), and *appropriateness* (in which assessments are more variable, and are influenced by the particularities of each organization, situation, and set of actors (Frederickson and Smith 2003). Under decision theory, goal-oriented actions are systematically quantified, analyzed, and ranked by their relative likelihood or probability of success (Frederickson and Smith 2003).

Rational choice theory "is not just . . . an explanation of how the world does work, but . . . an explanation of how the world *should* work" (Frederickson and Smith 2003). It builds from the three main features of neoclassical economics: a self-interested actor, competition, and free markets. Under this framework, minor adjustments are made to accommodate the differences between the public sector and the private marketplace. But the essential features remain. For example, where profit maximization is the goal of the private sector firm, budget maximization would be the public sector agency's goal. Frederickson and Smith (2003) identify a critical shortcoming of this approach: the bureaucrat's pursuit of self-interest is constrained in ways that do not apply to the private sector businessperson. For the purposes of this chapter, these theories do not force a decision process that explicitly weighs longer-term consequences. They provide a framework to do so, but actual applications too easily permit discounting on this critical dimension.

Prominent public administration theorists have long contended that rational decision making has some limitations (see Table 12.2). To wit, there is no "perfect" decision making, because often we are muddling through due to imperfect informa-

Table 12.2

Selected Approaches to Understanding Public Administration Decision Making

1947	Herbert Simon	Satisficing
1959	Charles E. Lindblom	Muddling Through
1970	Allen Schick	Incrementalism
2002	Lester M. Salamon	Tools of Government
2007	Nassim Taleb	Black Swan Events

tion, and we are selecting a decision that does not maximize our goals, but rather only "satisfices," achieving some but not all of them. That is, we may make good decisions for some subset of criteria, but not great decisions.

There are additional concerns to take into account. One is the "Black Swan" effect (see Taleb 2007). We simply do not always take into account the risk that something wildly unpredictable could happen in our decision making. Who had the foresight to caution specifically about changes to lower the risk of offshore oil drilling platforms in the Gulf Coast? Another consideration is that we shy away from transformational/revolutionary decisions and only make incremental or marginal decisions. Schick (2007) states it succinctly: "The main behavioral rule is that appropriations should vary only incrementally from the previous year's level. Ongoing programs should be continued, cuts in existing programs should be avoided or minimized, and increases should be modest and broadly distributed among an array of programs" (p. 240).

The weight of past decisions may prevent us from making truly "correct" decisions on into the future. Another consideration, of course, is that decisions rarely work out as we intended. The law of unintended consequences is almost always acknowledged posthumously but never welcome.

Moreover, according to Lindblom (1959), "theory is sometimes of extremely limited helpfulness in policy making for at least two rather different reasons. It is greedy for facts; it can be constructed only through a great collection of observations and it is typically insufficiently precise for application to a policy process that moves through small changes." But it is not just theory that catches up the poor decision maker. There are numerous practical constraints and impediments that bedevil, especially in the 21st-century American political system.

These conceptual impediments to selecting the appropriate time horizon are accompanied by practical constraints that must be addressed concurrently. We now examine the real world of decision makers.

First, in our current political system, usually no one person makes a decision that is not itself conditioned by, in response to, or thwarted by another's decision. Checks and balances between the executive, legislative, and judicial branches immediately come to mind. A second consideration derives from our intergovernmental system. Often financial decisions are made at one level and administrative decisions at another level—with the public left wondering as to who really made the decision. This polycentric decision-making system can frustrate and impede all but the most skillful decision maker. Two other cultural considerations apply. First, there is the human condition. Many people will wish to have public sector decision making that maximizes their services but minimizes their taxes. This might occur in a small jurisdiction, where the benefits of services received are commensurate with taxes paid. But it is unlikely in a larger one where there is inevitable cross-subsidization. The second issue is the basic nature of public goods that our public administrators are supposed to be responsible for providing. How do you implement a national defense policy when there is no real pricing policy that helps you determine an optimal value for public investments? At the state level, how do you determine an optimal educational policy when your state constitution requires you to provide equal educational opportunity to all your citizens? At a practical level, responsive government implies being responsive to those who make their preferences and rationales known to elected officials and government officials.

Representative government is determined by elections, but, once elected, legislators and chief executives may be more responsive to numerical minorities. Finances, other resources, and time are limited; even a responsive government must be selective in the issues and the groups to whom it responds. Public choice models provide a rationale as to why elected representatives may be more responsive to the immediate interests of a small portion of the electorate ("special interests") than to the larger mass of constituents. While the numerically superior individual constituents could organize to influence legislators and government administrators, there are rational explanations for why they generally do not do so, forfeiting the opportunity to bend government to its interests on particular issues. For an individual, the costs of staying informed and then for taking political action to influence legislators is high given the uncertain timing and small number of issues that may actually impinge on their interests. Advocates, or "special interest" groups, are organized around specific interests and positions that are durable across time, elections, and political parties. For special interest groups and their lobbyists, it is rational to invest time and resources into remaining politically informed and active. Because they are less numerous, their organizing costs are less than those for individuals. And matters affecting their interests generally occur with greater frequency than they do for individuals. Interest groups' consistent activity is also rewarded with a high likelihood that their campaigns will be successful, reinforcing the cycle. On the other hand, individual electors are generally episodically engaged at best, and unfamiliar with the legislative and regulatory processes and the context of deliberations. As a result, they are less successful in having their interests prevail, and their expected gains are on average exceeded by their expected costs of political participation (Jensen and Morrisey 1999).

There are some recent examples of limited mechanisms that move decisions out of the short-term political arena to longer-term strategic decisions. Military base closures are inherently partisan and locally influenced. The Defense Base Closure and Realignment Act of 1990 established an independent commission to "provide an objective, non-partisan, and independent review and analysis of the list of military installation recommendations issued by the Department of Defense (DoD)" (Defense Base Closure and Realignment Commission 2005). Similarly, health care reform established an independent commission, the Independent Payment Advisory Board (IPAB), to bend the cost curve of long-term trends in national health expenditures. The IPAB will monitor Medicare payments and, when increases exceed targets, recommend cost cuts to the Congress. Congress must then pass legislation that achieves savings at least as great as those recommended by the commission, or the IPAB's recommendations take effect (Patient Protection and Affordable Care Act 2010). Both of these aim for evidence-based, long-term decision horizons by circumventing the politics of Congress.

Rational decision making, customarily desirable to public administrators—especially using appropriate quantitative techniques—is hampered by the gap between theory and practice. In contrast to the behavioral and normative approaches to understanding the work of public administrators, a more recent push to rational management is adopting the evidence-based practice approach dominant in medicine, education, and the other professions. In public administration, however, when the evidence is assembled there is surprisingly little that supports the precepts of public administration (Meier and O'Toole 2009). It is also uncertain that the knowledge, skills, and abilities required to practice evidence-based public management are common among practicing public administrators (Lyles 2011). Consequently, statistical models can produce an unwarranted complacency by managing risks of enormous magnitude but low probability (a.k.a. "Black Swan" events).

"In actual fact, no one can practice the rational comprehensive method for really complex problems, and every administrator faced with a sufficiently complex problem must find ways drastically to simplify" (Lindblom 1959). More recently, Professor Lester Salamon has approached the challenges of public-private sector and intergovernmental interactions from a tools framework—which offers a broader range of options than the more comprehensive theory-based models that preceded it (Salamon 2002).

Conclusion

So whether it is theory or practice, we must pity the public administrator who is charged with making good, rational decisions that will stand the test of time, no matter what the time horizon should be. Is it possible to have such decisions in government? We are cautiously optimistic.

Take, for example, the Marshall Plan of Economic Recovery adopted right after World War II. We had just fought a world war, spending blood and treasure to defeat a totalitarian regime. Then the Truman administration, under the guidance of General George Marshall (Behrman 2007; Eggers and O'Leary 2009) and many other public-spirited individuals, spearheaded an economic recovery plan that helped our allies and enemies in Europe recover their economic strength and become a democratic bulwark against the USSR.

Why did this happen? First, there was the acknowledgment that we had to act quickly; inaction was inadvisable. Second, there was a calculation that good consequences could occur. European economies could grow and markets for our goods could expand as well. Third, there was a longer-term consequence as well, the containment of the territorial and political ambitions of a political system that was in conflict with our own. Finally, there was sufficient national support—as opposed to narrowly partisan support—to shift from tactical to strategic time horizons and decisions. So we bought political and economic advantages that some would argue have helped through today, nearly 60 years after the Marshall plan was adopted.

The "horizon issue" is influenced, but not solely determined by, partisan skirmishes, and must be addressed under any renewed model of governance. Specifically, American Governance 3.0 must promote a shift from crisis policy making to the deliberate adoption of policies with substantial and positive net benefits over an appropriate time horizon.

This chapter identified a gap between theory and practice that perpetuates narrowly focused, short-term practices. Current ad hoc policy and management approaches have notable shortcomings. They

- produce fewer positive results for the resources expended,
- breach the social contract,
- inhibit the development of reliable structures for managing crises,
- increase the severity of long-term problems.

So if, in the case of the Marshall plan, we could do it then why can't we do it today? There are some very pointed reasons. First, there is a declining public trust in decision makers. Second, there is even a growing distrust, almost hatred, of private decision makers as well.

> Sensible people believe rumors whether or not they are true. On the Internet, self-interested and altruistic propagators find it increasingly easy to expand rumors about prominent people and institutions. Such rumors cast doubt on the subjects' honesty, decency, fairness, patriotism and sometimes even sanity; often they portray public figures as fundamentally confused or corrupt. (Sunstein 2009, p. 10)

The "average" person sees the worst of both worlds. The private sector's turbo capitalism takes undue risk, reaps the reward, and leaves the pain to society at large (Lowenstein 2010). The public decision maker may only be interested in maintaining power and control, leading to the time-honored observation that power corrupts and increased power can lead to staggering if not absolute corruption.

So the basic questions recur. Can public decision makers make good decisions that will stand the test of time? And will Governance 3.0 allow decision makers the tools to have better decision horizons. We believe that the answer to these two questions is yes—under the following conditions.

First, adopt the approach that evidence-based decisions should be the principle by which decisions are made. This means, of course, collecting data assiduously and sticking to the facts no matter what the time horizon for the decision may be.

Second, accept responsible public debate about public policies. Responsible and spirited public debate is a way of continuing to unearth the policy preferences of the polity. This is essential to informed decision making and Governance 3.0 should be an essential tool in understanding the metes and bounds of policy debate.

Third, use acceptable decision models and clearly stated contingency plans. No decision, however well made, is perfect. Future events have to be taken into account and decisions should be suitably adjusted and revised. Decisions should be made to stand the test of time, but, at the same time, decision making does not stop once an initial decision is made.

Fourth, the key to durable, horizon-correct, decision making requires the continual use of audits and after-action reports. We cannot know whether our decisions are correct unless we continually examine them without fear or favor. Again Governance 3.0 is well designed to accomplish this task.

Fifth, accept the fact that good decisions require appropriate resources and competent people. While some say, it is "better to be lucky than good," that is not the appropriate approach to making durable decisions. Good information is needed, and competent people with the utmost integrity are needed to execute a decision.

Finally, and this is the most difficult issue of all, we must focus on governing for the long term and turn away from simply electioneering for the short term. Our democratic system does not need to focus always on the short term. Our basic Constitution sets out governing principles that are to stand for the very existence of the nation; it notes that our government is to promote "the general welfare," not just for tomorrow or the next year, but for as long as the Constitution is in effect. Thus, we have an obligation to govern for the long term, no matter when or how often elections are held.

Governance 3.0 will be an essential element in aiding better decision making over a longer time horizon. It may be at best a facilitator; more likely a source of stressors as well as solutions but at least a source of structures and processes that help decision makers assess the consequences of their decisions.

References

Alesch, D. J. 1968. "Government in Evolution: A Real World Focus for State Planning." *Public Administration Review* 28(3): 264–267.

Appleby, P. H. 1953. "Government Is Different." In *Ideas and Issues in Public Administration,* ed. D. Waldo, p. 63. New York: McGraw Hill.

Behrman, G. 2007. *The Most Noble Adventure: The Marshall Plan and the Time When America Helped Save Europe.* New York: Free Press.

Defense Base Closure and Realignment of 1990. P.L. 101–510.

Defense Base Closure and Realignment Commission. 2005. *Final Report to the President.* http://www.brac.gov/finalreport.html (accessed May 6, 2010).

Digiammarino, F., L. E. Trudeau, F. Forman, J. Kamensky, and D. A. Munz. 2009. Enabling collaboration: Three priorities for the new administration. Paper prepared by the Collaboration Project Advisory Panel of the National Academy of Public Administration, January. http://www.scribd.com/doc/11644716/Enabling-Collaboration-Three-Priorities-for-New-Administration (accessed April 3, 2010).

Eggers, W. D., and J. O'Leary. 2009. *If We Can Put a Man on the Moon: Getting Big Things Done in Government.* Boston: Harvard Business Press.

Frederickson, H. G., and K. B. Smith. 2003. *The Public Administration Theory Primer.* Boulder, CO: Westview Press.

Gaudin, S. 2009. "Web 2.0 White House Takes to Facebook, Twitter." http://www.computerworld.com/s/article/9132530/Web_2.0_White_House_takes_to_Facebook_Twitter (accessed April 3, 2010).

Jensen, G. A., and M. A. Morrisey. 1999. "Employer-Sponsored Health Insurance and Mandated Benefit Laws." *Milbank Quarterly* 77(4): 425–459.

Lindblom, C. E. 1959. "The Science of Muddling Through." *Public Administration Review* 19: 79–88.

Lowenstein, R. 2010. *The End of Wall Street.* New York: Penguin Press.

Lyles, A. 2011. "Analytic Reasoning for Evidence-Based Public Management: Adapting Education to Practice." In *Evidence-Based Public Management: Practices, Issues, and Prospects,* ed. A. Shillabeer, T. F. Buss, and D. M. Rousseau. Armonk, NY: M.E. Sharpe.

Meier, K. J., and L. J. O'Toole Jr. 2009. "The Proverbs of New Public Management: Lessons from an Evidence-Based Research Agenda." *American Review of Public Administration* 39(1): 4–22.

O'Reilly, Tim. 2005. "What Is Web 2.0? Design Patterns and Business Models for the Next Generation of Software." Oreilly.com, September 30. http://vision4work.org/~What%20Is%20Web%202.0.pdf (accessed April 3, 2010).

Patient Protection and Affordable Care Act. 2010. P.L. 111–148. 124 Stat. 119.

Prensky, Marc. 2001. "Digital Natives, Digital Immigrants." *On the Horizon* 9(5): 1–10. http://www.hfmboces.org/HFMDistrictServices/TechYES/PrenskyDigitalNatives.pdf.

Salamon, L. M. (ed.). 2002. *The Tools of Government: A Guide to the New Governance.* New York: Oxford University Press.

Schick, A. 1970. "Toward Systematic Incrementalism in Intergovernmental Relations." Symposium on Political Aspects of Intergovernmental Research Allocation, University of Maryland.

———. 2007. *The Federal Budget: Politics, Policy, and Process,* 3d ed. Washington, DC: Brookings Institution Press.

Simon, H. 1947. *Administrative Behavior: A Study of Decision-Making Processes in Administrative Organizations* (4th ed. published in 1997). New York: Free Press.

Social Security Administration. 2010. "Actuarial Publications. Reports from the Board of Trustees." http://www.ssa.gov/OACT/TR/ (accessed May 3, 2010).

Sunstein, C. 2009. *On Rumors.* New York: Farrar, Straus and Giroux.

Taleb, N. 2007. *The Black Swan: The Impact of the Highly Improbable.* London: Random House.

U.S. Congress. House. Committee on Government Reform. 2002. *E-Government Act of 2002.* 107th Cong., 2d sess. Rep. 107–787. http://frwebgate.access.gpo.gov/cgi-bin/getdoc.cgi?dbname=107_cong_reports&docid=f:hr787p1.107.

Waldo, D. 1948. *The Administrative State: A Study of the Political Theory of American Public Administration.* New York: Ronald Press.

Walker, D. M. 2009. *Comeback America: Turning the Country Around and Restoring Fiscal Responsibility.* New York: Random House.

13

Design Lessons for Smart Governance Infrastructure

Erik W. Johnston and Derek L. Hansen

> *It was the first Republican President, Abraham Lincoln, who said the role of government is to do for the people what they cannot do better for themselves.*
> —Barack Obama, Commencement address, 2010

Every day people are able to do more for themselves. Dramatic changes in individuals' ability to connect, mobilize, and collaborate provide unimagined opportunities to do more for themselves, although certainly not by themselves. Spontaneous citizen-led efforts have helped victims of natural disasters find housing and loved ones, neighborhood e-mail lists raise awareness of local public health concerns, grassroots mapping is used in the cleanup efforts of the Louisiana oil spill, and freecycle.com shares unused home goods with those in need. Online patient support groups like PatientsLikeMe.com help those with life-threatening illnesses band together to raise awareness, collect research funds, share best practices, identify competent professionals, and provide social support. Citizen groups like the Sunlight Foundation promote government transparency and accountability, while watchdog groups like Citizens Against Government Waste and Citizens for Responsibility and Ethics hunt down government waste and corruption. Social networks like LinkedIn help improve the efficiency of the employment market, while open education initiatives provide free access to content from leading educational institutions.

Each of these examples underlie larger societal shifts from government to governance and from citizen participation to citizen production. Instead of paying taxes to government institutions and waiting for them to solve our problems, individuals are directly engaging in community challenges. To foster participatory government through adulthood, a rethinking of government itself is necessary. The goal of this chapter is to advance that rethinking. To do so requires that we see collective action as more than "collective complaint" (O'Reilly 2010) and its accompanying expectation that "they the government" provide the solutions rather than "we the people." It suggests that we move beyond questions of how to best manage government institutions to questions of how to design smart governance systems with the appropriate incentives and rules to harness and coordinate the enthusiasm and capabilities of those governed.

For us, like others (Kooiman 1993; Lessig 2009; Rhodes 1996), governance is broader than government. We define governance as the interaction of processes, information, rules, structures, and norms that guide behavior toward stated objectives that impact collections of people. These objectives often involve the allocation of scarce resources including public goods, the coordination of diverse participants and stakeholders, the establishment of clear processes for decision making, and the resolution of conflict. Participants in these efforts can be both paid and voluntary, citizen and noncitizen, professional and amateur, and private and public.

Although we are well into the age of participation (Grossman 2006), the transformative effects of technology-mediated social participation, particularly on national priorities, are only in their infancy (Shneiderman 2009). Examples of technology-enabled coproduction in the private sector abound: the media is shifting from paid professionals to a vast collection of amateur bloggers; eBay and Craigslist host the transactions of an extraordinarily varied marketplace; Wikipedia distills the collective wisdom of thousands into the most comprehensive tome the planet has ever seen. In each of these examples, the information and communication technologies work with people's own interests across a governance infrastructure that coordinates constituent participation and contributions. President Obama's chief information officer, Vivek Kundra, already aims to leverage technology to create opportunities to cultivate citizen production in the services of traditional government: "Think about Apple and the iPhone. Apple didn't go out and build 150,000 applications. It built a platform, and the innovation happened. . . . What we need to start doing as the federal government is to tap into the energy and spirit and innovation of the American people" (originally cited in Gohring 2010).

As communities struggle with reduced resources, they need to cultivate efforts from new sources. The most untapped potential is in the enormous capabilities of individuals. However, like the potential of solar power, we need to develop pathways to convert the energy into useful applications. Previous efforts of e-government, like e-voting, are making services more accessible online; they have focused on making government more efficient at what it already does (Lathrop and Ruma 2010). As we think about the potential of Governance 3.0, rebooting the public square is about more than just paving over existing cow paths; it is about redesigning governance infrastructures to be smarter, more responsive, and more efficient.

Smart Governance Infrastructures

> *From antiquity to modern times, the nation has always been a product of information management.*
> —*The Economist* 2010, p. 11

Information technology, or IT, especially communication and computational technologies, continues to augment society's ability to organize, interact, and govern. To realize the potential of our collective abilities, smart governance infrastructures need to be mindfully designed to facilitate, coordinate, and reward collective action that leads to desired social outcomes. We are familiar with the concept of infrastructure through our everyday use of the state highway system, electrical grid, postal service, and satellites providing GPS. The postal service highlights the fact that infrastructure can include more than just technology; it includes employees, policies for appropriate use, standard practices, and expectations of performance.

These examples of government-mediated infrastructures differ from governance infrastructures in the activities they support. Instead of supporting the efficient exchange of power, transportation, or mail, governance infrastructures support governing activities such as the allocation of scarce resources, collective decision making, public debate, public mobilization, and the resolution of conflict. Thus, a *governance infrastructure* is the collection of technologies, people, policies, practices, resources, social norms, and information that interact to support governing activities. We agree with, and expand upon, the notion of "smart" that was used by Kanter and Litow as they discuss the potential of smarter cities (2009, p. 2):

> A smarter city infuses information into its physical infrastructure to improve conveniences, facilitate mobility, add efficiencies, conserve energy, improve the quality of air and water, identify problems and fix them quickly, recover rapidly from disasters, collect data to make better decisions and deploy resources effectively, and share data to enable collaboration across entities and domains. Its operations are instrumented and guided by performance metrics, with interconnections across sectors and silos.

A smart governance infrastructure provides transparency of public efforts, promotes cultural flourishing, and increases accountability. To be accountable is to be held responsible. Ideally, those who are governing will be continually held directly accountable (Kjaer 2006). As power is returned to people, the responsibility for our actions should be as well. In the past few decades there has been a growing disconnect in the United States between a government of the people and a government to serve the people. Partly this is due to an increase in the size and scale of government, where accountability chains "may simply disappear in such a web of institutions because defining who did what is no longer straightforward" (Rhodes 2000, 76–77 as cited in Kjaer 2006). The current governance infrastructure is not a scale-free network. As the nation grows, voices become proportionally diminished; additional layers are added to the hierarchies of representation so that individuals increasingly believe they have no influence on government decisions. As the social identity of government continues to be separated from individuals, the responsibility for solving inherently social problems continues to be separated from society (Catlaw 2007).

This chapter anticipates how the interaction of technology and society can be leveraged to design problem-defined, participation-based governance infrastructures to return power to the people while increasing accountability and efficiency. We echo Herbert Simon's claim that "everyone designs who devises courses of action aimed at changing existing situations into preferred ones." And that fields as diverse as engineering, medicine, business, architecture, and government are "concerned not with the necessary but with the contingent—not with how things are but with how they might be—in short, with design" (Simon 1996, p. iix). Of course, designing for social systems is always wrought with unpredictability and imprecision, suggesting that we can (and should) "cultivate" certain behaviors, rather than force them (Wenger, McDermott, and Snyder 2002). This is particularly true when dealing with a complex system of self-organizing individuals and institutions. Knowing which "design levers" to pull, whether they involve the market, laws, social norms, or architecture (Lessig 2006), is a considerable challenge, but one with great promise.

In this chapter we outline design levers and lessons learned from successful examples of novel governance infrastructures that are currently used in online communities, innovative businesses, nonprofits, and governments. We discuss the challenges and possibilities of new governance infrastructures that retrofit and complement existing government initiatives or address unmet community needs and national priorities. In addition, existing concepts in public administration, such as citizen coproduction, become more relevant and viable with advances in technology. This chapter explores the possibilities of how smart participation-based governance infrastructures can be designed to empower, or more appropriately return power to, the people while increasing accountability to an active, diverse, and continually changing populace.

Lesson 1: Organize Around Specific Problems Rather Than Institutions or Geography

One of the greatest powers of the Internet is that it has allowed people with similar interests to band together, independent of geography. This makes it possible for those with similar interests, preferences, and problems to find one another (Anderson 2006). Patients with rare diseases are brought together via the Internet to share resources, provide social support, and advocate for funding or research. Likewise, citizens with unique political or social views find like-minded people to discuss issues, promote agendas, and advocate for causes. Of course, this may not always be good for society, as niche groups can become echo chambers that create and reinforce their own distorted view of reality (Sunstein 2007).

So, how can we benefit from the Internet's ability to span geographic limitations without creating a more polarized populace? One promising strategy is to use online governance infrastructures that help people with common problems (as opposed to common ideologies) work together to develop solutions (as opposed to commentaries). Communities are sometimes defined by geography. But many government approaches are implemented through a fixed jurisdiction for a fixed period of time. People's daily interface with government, business, markets, and communities regularly span traditional jurisdictions. Within the course of an hour, an individual can use local government services while also purchasing tax-free gifts from across the country for international colleagues before gambling real money in cyberspace. Although geography is still important and highly correlated with citizen interactions, constituents now organize according to the most appropriate form for the community served. Specialized governance infrastructures can now support particular challenges or communities and do not need to be wrapped into existing, jurisdictionally bound organizations because of convenience.

A central organizing quality of powerful new scale-free collaborations, like open source software development, is the coordination of individuals working together to advance specific problems (Malone 2004). As Clay Shirky, author of *Here Comes Everybody* (2008), says in a Technology, Entertainment, Design (TED) talk (2005):

> When you build coordination into the infrastructure, which is the [collaboration] answer, you can leave the people where they are and you take the problem to the individuals rather than moving the individuals to the problem. You arrange the coordination in the group and by doing that you get the same outcome without the institution difficulties . . . and you shed the institutional costs which gives you greater flexibility.

This organizational shift is happening in businesses, nonprofits, and universities. One government use of problem-focused organization is the Obama administration's appointment of czars (and czarinas) to oversee problems such as AIDS, Auto Recovery, Domestic Violence, WMD Policy, and over 20 other problem areas. Although the term "czar" is not one that conjures up images of collaborative problem solving, the idea of organizing activity around problems rather than existing government agencies is a promising one. Another approach is to facilitate citizen self-organization through initiatives like serve.gov, a platform similar to meetup. org that allows for private and public organizations to post volunteer opportunities and enables individuals to search for local opportunities of interest. Each represents another step toward organizing around problems and enabling the coordination of geographically independent public, private, and governmental efforts to address national priorities.

Lesson 2: Crowdsource: The Identification of Clear, Approachable Problems and Promising Solutions

In our complex, highly interconnected world, it is rare that a single person has all of the information, skills, and insight needed to identify and characterize a problem accurately or generate the most promising solutions. The first step in solving a problem is to clearly articulate the problem and recognize it as a priority. Those who develop complex software have learned that "given enough eyeballs, all bugs are shallow" (Raymond 2001). In addition, a group of diverse individuals regularly outperform small collections of expert individuals (Page 2007). If there is a large enough crowd identifying problems and recommending solutions, almost every problem can be characterized quickly and a solution will be obvious to someone. While fixing software bugs may be easier than fixing their societal counterparts, the principle is the same. Identifying problems and potential solutions is best done by gathering input from the crowd, with its collection of uniquely skilled and experienced members.

Smart governance infrastructures are needed to effectively harness the unique skills and knowledge that too often lie dormant in the crowd. Outsourcing tasks traditionally performed by an employee, contractor, or government agency to a large group of people or community is known as *crowdsourcing* (Howe 2006). A range of tools has been adopted in recent years to do just that. Issue tracking systems and related "bug trackers" are used by computer programming companies to help assure high-quality service through the systematic collection, aggregation, and follow-up of problems. These systems provide a bottom-up approach to problem identification and prioritization, as well as a means for following up on potential solutions. Issue tracking systems that collect, aggregate, and follow up on citizen-identified problems are increasingly possible. Initiatives like FixMyStreet.com have run with this idea by encouraging citizens to document graffiti, broken paving slabs, and burned out streetlights, while tracking their resolution by government. The site has shown strong potential as a proof of concept, although it has been criticized for its lack of connection to government and for missing a sense of community among contributors (King and Brown 2007). Hopefully, similar government issue tracking systems will continue to improve through closer partnerships with relevant government, corporate, and nonprofit organizations.

While crowdsourcing the identification of problems can be fruitful, crowdsourcing is particularly well equipped to identify optimal solutions to known problems. There are many cases where the problem is clear: encouraging exercise, reducing a public health outbreak, cleaning up flood or oil damage, caring for the elderly, and identifying fraud and abuse. In such cases, smart governance infrastructures can tap the crowd for innovative solutions, as well as feedback on others' ideas. A new cottage industry of "innovation solutions" and "crowdsourcing products" such as Innocentive and IdeaScale has emerged in recent years. Whereas used primarily in corporate settings, they are beginning to be applied to social and government contexts. For example, community open source problem solving publicly posts challenges and the public is invited to help solve the problem (Goldsmith 2010; Schweik, Evans, and Grove 2005). Similarly, online social collectives like amazee.com act as platforms to connect people with shared interests and enable them to coordinate people, organizations, and resources in a variety of collaborative forms. The Open Government Dialog, sponsored by the National Academy of Public Administration (NAPA), welcomes the public's ideas on specific challenges, providing a forum to refine and vote on the best ones. The most recent challenge was, "How can we strengthen our democracy and promote efficiency and effectiveness by making government more transparent, participatory, and collaborative?" (NAPA 2009). While new insights may be gained from broad questions such as this one, devising specific questions on approachable problems is more likely to lead to actionable solutions. New governance infrastructures could use decision-making structures like prediction markets or intraorganizational auctions to harness the wisdom of crowds to predict future needs and challenges, as well as the likelihood of successes and failures (Arrow et al. 2008; Malone 2004; Surowiecki 2004).

Lesson 3: Provide Clear and Meaningful Pathways to Contribute

In many cases, people have a desire to contribute, but are not sure how. This is often manifest after natural disasters when empathy can overtake logic, leading to the provision of unnecessary supplies that clog scarce transportation channels. The advent of the Internet has allowed for a more coordinated effort, where volunteers find meaningful ways to directly contribute, such as offering their home to those affected by Hurricane Katrina or helping reunite families that were separated. More generally, smart governance infrastructures support clear and meaningful individual contributions that can be aggregated in useful ways.

The challenge is to architect an infrastructure that provides clear options for making meaningful contributions, while allowing individuals enough choice to want to stay engaged. An excellent example of this approach is Kiva, a nonprofit organization that helps reduce poverty by helping individuals make microloans to people in developing countries. Making a contribution to Kiva is painless and simple. Donors register, provide money to Kiva through an online transaction, choose loan recipients based on their profile information and photos, and click on a button to lend them up to $25. Contributing to the alleviation of poverty has never been so simple, or perhaps, more important, so personal. Like all functioning infrastructures, Kiva's international banking arrangements, legal requirements, technical and personnel support all fade into the background, leaving the contributor one simple, but profound choice: who should I lend to? The clear tie between lender and recipient makes giving infinitely more meaningful than sending money to an agency or nonprofit to administer. There is also a feedback loop for a donor to track both how their specific contribution was used and, in the case of a loan, how quickly it is being paid back. The availability of this information engages donors and reduces another participation barrier.

Whereas microloans illustrate the power of providing clear and meaningful contributions, there are many other examples of meaningful microcontributions. For example, public volunteers known as "clickworkers" helped NASA identify craters on Mars by clicking on relevant sections of high-resolution images from the comfort of their own home. Genealogists at FamilySearch Indexing help transcribe 19th-century U.S. Census records into searchable databases of genealogical information. Volunteers at Project Gutenberg create free ebooks of public domain works by fixing one "scano" at a time as they read the books themselves. More recently, sites like Grassroots Mapping help citizens resolve disputed flood plain categorizations of individual's homes or use balloons and kites to produce public domain aerial imagery of the April, 2010, oil spill in the Gulf of Mexico that can be used for environmental study, for coordinating volunteer efforts, and for legal cases in the future (Sutter 2010). In all of these examples and many more (such as FixMyStreet, already mentioned), the infrastructure makes contributing simple and clear and also meaningful. In other cases, where the work may not be as socially rewarding, companies and researchers are turning to a diverse and decentralized workforce—like Amazon's MechanicalTurk—to have a cadre of human volunteers perform microcontributions for micropayments.

Although not all tasks are easily decomposed into clear, distinct, chunks that can be aggregated together into a meaningful whole, there are likely many more that we have not yet considered. Increasingly popular, smart mobile devices are creating more opportunities to collect and annotate data, as well as provide opportunities for meaningful microcontributions while in line at the store or at home watching TV.

Lesson 4: Encourage Continuous, Increasing Engagement

Most endeavors cannot be maintained by periodic microcontributions alone. They require leaders willing to expend significant amounts of time and effort working on solutions to problems. Studies of collaborative systems such as e-mail lists, wikis, and photo sharing sites support the idea that the majority of contributions are made by a relatively small group of contributors, while a large group of contributors only participate periodically. In cases where participation cannot be mandated, there is a constant need to help some individuals develop from peripheral and passive roles into more central and active roles.

The ease with which we can now collect information on participation increases the feasibility of new metrics and design strategies that can be used to encourage continual, increasing participation within a community. For example, members of the online community Slashdot can earn increasing levels of responsibilities and rights based on their involvement in the site. Slashdot administrators created a Karma system to reward people who constructively contribute to the advancement of the community. If a user posts a comment that others find and rate as valuable, their Karma increases. If a user reads a large number of stories, their Karma increases. Once the Karma increases to a level set by the site administrators, the user earns additional mechanisms for participating within the community. A secondary consequence of such legitimate peripheral participation (Lave and Wenger 1991) is that participants understand the norms of the community and, consequently, they learn to make more socially valuable contributions (Lampe and Johnston 2005). A range of related usability and sociability suggestions intended to move people from "readers" to "contributors" to "collaborators" to "leaders" are provided by Shneiderman and Preece (2009). These include ideas like making user contributions visible to other members, providing low-threshold interfaces for easily making microcontributions, providing high-ceiling interfaces that allow large and frequent contributions, giving awards, matching people with mentors or other experts, and providing conditional privileges.

We see considerable potential in applying some of these approaches to develop governance structures that support a more civically active population. Repeated calls to return power to the people have echoed from American presidents, from Lincoln's "A government of the people, by the people, and for the people," to Kennedy's "Ask not what your country can do for you but what you can do for your country" and now Obama's "We are the ones we have been waiting for." What is unique now is the potential to heed their call. The information age has decreased communication costs, increased information availability, and increased computational power, enabling individuals to analyze that information and convert it into actionable knowledge (Malone 2004). The potential avenues to organize and participate are more abundant than ever. New governance infrastructures include advances in informatics that create new opportunities for citizen engagement, collective action, and representation, as discussed throughout this chapter.

New avenues for participation will also help to reconceptualize volunteerism and its relation to government. Initiatives such as Serve.Gov give notifications of volunteer opportunities, but provide relatively few opportunities for people to become more central members of the service community. Perhaps it is time for a service reputation system that would enable friendly service-based competitions between neighborhoods and towns, provide evidence to future employers of social responsibility, and help identify experts who can share best practices? There is now precedent for forgiving student loan repayments for individuals who have been employed full-time for 10 years in public service. This may be helpful in attracting individuals to work as full-time public servants, but it falls short of encouraging all citizens to perform public service. A smarter governance infrastructure for citizen engagement might provide the mechanisms and metrics that would provide strong incentives for encouraging continual, increasing public service by all citizens. The existing tracking of community service hours by high school students in many states suggests this approach may be viable. An earned participation approach would reframe our relationships in the social contract, returning to the notion that the social contract requires mutually enforceable responsibilities.

Lesson 5: Coordinate Decentralized Effort, But Not Diverse Value Judgments

An individual's incentive to participate in a community is closely aligned with their experiences (Lampe, Johnston, and Resnick 2007). As organizations and communities become more diverse and active, the nature of leadership must also shift from centralized planning to coordinating (Shirky 2005). In a new governance infrastructure, instead of controlling the behavior of individuals by predetermining their service options, leaders release power back to the community through the use of an incentive-centered design that creates conditions for people to customize how they want to participate in their communities. This is a shift from a command and control to a coordinate and cultivate style of management (Malone 2004).

Online communities like Slashdot.org and digg.com provide a proof of concept for how to enable member participation and coproduction to serve key governance functions. From the microparticipation of many, the massive task of allocating and matching resources to appropriate communities and evaluating the performance of public services can emerge. Within Slashdot, hundreds of thousands of unique, daily users provide hundreds of comments on technology stories that are posted every half hour. How to accurately differentiate high-quality comments from low-quality comments is essential to the survival of online communities that face massive competition for the attention of their users. The administration of Slashdot quickly realized that the site would grow beyond what they could centrally manage. Instead of hiring additional administrators or adding layers to a bureaucratic hierarchy, they decided to allocate the tasks of finding, categorizing, and moderating new content to the community at large. To address this challenge, Slashdot deployed a *distributed moderation system.* Unlike a centralized moderation system, where site administrators evaluate the quality of comments based on established criteria, the system allows a diverse population of experienced participants to rate the quality of the posts they read, pushing each one higher or lower in the queue. The system administrator creates and facilitates the activity of the community but does not pass value judgments on the content within the space.

Recently, the United Kingdom invested in personalized websites for every citizen (*The Telegraph* 2010), enabling a new suite of interaction options with government and each other. These sites may eventually allow individuals to provide feedback on specific government employees or branches, engage in new forms of organization, opt into or out of public services and have their tax obligations modified accordingly, or hold regular online votes for issues more important than *American Idol*. The sites can also be used to share information about community participation and to share best or common practices. For instance, if you want high-use energy consumers to become more energy efficient, reveal what they are spending on the bill, along with what their average neighbor is spending and the use of an energy-conscious neighbor, because awareness of social information influences individual behavior (Cameron 2010). The possibility for innovative group-level policies with predictable outcomes also becomes more viable. The most famous example of this approach is the Nobel Prize–winning design of microloans, championed by Muhammad Yunis, where the responsibility to pay back a loan is shared among community members. This shared responsibility leads to higher than normal payback rates and is similar to Kiva, which boasts a payback rate above 98 percent (Kiva.org 2010). A false paradox of releasing control to the community is that government officials will have less control over desirable community outcomes.

An example in a government context is the use of human-centered policies, putting the resources in the hands of the individuals to allow their decisions to emerge as the mechanism for change. One example of such a policy is open-enrollment education, where education funding is tied to the student and each student is allowed their choice of which school to attend, including private schools. The families then invest time to find schools that match their values, assess quality, gather information on performance, evaluate which options are feasible, and ultimately make a choice according to their preferences and options. Sites like GreatSchools.org, which integrate government-reported data on individual schools with comments from parents, students, and teachers, suggest the value of smart governance infrastructures in helping families find the best schools. An important consequence of this self-organization is that it also enables diverse values to coexist without the need for a central administrator or authority to determine what is the proper set of values. With such facilitative leadership, much of the efforts should be on understanding the situation, protecting the participation process, presenting the choices available to parents, and providing mechanisms that encourage collaboration.

The added value of tailoring participation opportunities to those most concerned and affected by the issue at hand is that it avoids top-down value judgments and unnecessary citizen conflict. By giving up administrator control over the specific content of a website or the existence of particular schools, individuals are able to choose according to their own values and preferences. The emerging school system then, for example, is accountable to directly reflect the values, preferences, and norms of its participants.

Lesson 6: Provide Open Access to Useful Data and Tools in Usable Formats

One of the greatest lessons of the Internet age is that data is power. O'Reilly points out that "virtually all of the greatest Internet success stories, from eBay, Craigslist, and Amazon through Google, Facebook, and Twitter, are data-driven companies" (2010, p. 31). Data are more valuable than ever, because data can be shared more easily, mashed up with other data more readily, and mined and visualized more thoughtfully. Companies are learning how to extract as much value as possible from their data. For example, in addition to making money through ad revenues, Google uses its ocean of data to provide better search results, learn how to translate languages more effectively, and train speech recognition software. Amazon uses its data to provide personalized recommendations to individuals based on the aggregate purchasing patterns of the masses.

On his first day in office, Obama issued a presidential memorandum ordering the heads of all agencies to make as much information publicly available as possible and, when in conflict, give the benefit of the doubt to openness (*The Economist* 2010). Unfortunately, in far too many cases, our government has not allowed the public to reap the benefits of the data they paid to have collected. Often government faces legitimate, unresolved privacy or security concerns. But it may also simply leave the data in inaccessible or unusable formats. Opening and sharing information is key to unlocking the power of smart governance infrastructures that are transparent. Recent initiatives to make government information available to the public, including data.gov, will enable a new level of transparency and innovation by citizens who can build upon that data. In recovery.gov, the administration has started an initiative to increase transparency in stimulus money spending. O'Reilly (2009) describes his vision of "government as platform" in this way:

> Government maintains information on a variety of issues, and that information should rightly be considered a national asset. Citizens are connected like never before and have the skill sets and passion to solve problems affecting them locally as well as nationally. Government information and services can be provided to citizens where and when they need it. Citizens are empowered to spark the innovation that will result in an improved approach to governance.

Several researchers have already strongly argued that a usable data format is at least as important as the fact that it is available in the first place (Lathrop and Ruma 2010). To be useful, data must be machine-readable and provided via Application Programming Interfaces (APIs) that other programs can call upon to serve up data in a useful manner. The federal government's chief information officer is working to create a culture of accountability through policy and redesigning how national data are stored and made available. He proposed the largest data consolidation in history to reduce government IT operations (currently distributed over 1,100 data centers), and develop an information infrastructure that is more efficient, accessible, and secure (Miller 2010).

Citizens have shown that they will develop tools and resources to analyze and make sense of government data. Some of the most innovative uses of technology to increase transparency through public data are happening at the local level. Integration of data, social media, and visualizations are enabling novel approaches to neighborhood watches, illness tracking, city maintenance, and policing (Catone 2009). Policy informatics approaches use real-time analytics and data visualization to provide a systems perspective for decision makers that vastly improves the use of micro and macro data for early interventions and policy deliberations (Kanter and Litow 2009). Dynamic websites like Nation of Neighbors overlay law enforcement information with maps to empower citizen involvement in keeping neighborhoods safe. The Missouri Accountability Portal (mapyourtaxes.mo.gov) provides the information and the data processing tools to spatially and programmatically visualize where every tax dollar is spent in the state.

Layers of bureaucracy increase the size of government, separate people from their government, create long accountability chains between action and responsibility, obfuscate mistakes, inhibit scrutiny, and create more avenues for political influence (Kjaer 2006). Thus, transparency, the accurate availability of information about performance, is needed more than ever. Theoretically, if an elected representative is responsible for representing all the people in her district, it should not matter what political party she is affiliated with; the people in her district and their interests are the same either way. Yet few deny the influence of lobbyists. And now corporations enjoy the same degree of influence as individuals with the 2010 Supreme Court decision in *Citizens United v. Federal Election Commission* (2010) to overrule two precedents that limited corporate spending on elections. Another challenge of a representation system is the split accountabilities of representatives. Elected officials should be accountable to their constituents, but are now strategically accountable to their party and are incentivized to be accountable to those that subsidize their elections (Lessig 2009). Although movements like changecongress. org are attempting to create fair election standards, another approach is to increase transparency through an increase of publicly available data. Competitions such as Apps for Democracy showcase other examples, as do the tools provided by the Sunlight Foundation to increase transparency in government.

While providing raw data via appropriate means will enable the creation of thousands of novel mashups, mobile apps, and visualizations, there are other valuable government resources that should be kept open. Most notably, access to scholarly publications funded by the U.S. government should be made available to all. Historically, this has not been the case; many publishers retained copyright and included contracts that did not allow authors to repost articles. A healthy "open access movement" has emerged in recent years, led by The Scholarly Publishing & Academic Resources Coalition (SPARC). Some open-access victories were achieved when recent legislation mandated that all National Institutes of Health (NIH) funded research publications be uploaded to PubMed Central within 12 months of appearing in peer-reviewed journals. Current legislation is now being considered that would extend this mandate to other federally funded research papers. These are promising steps in turning our national assets into a valuable resource for citizens.

Conclusion

As government budgets are tightened, a central question is how we make things better without spending more money (Cameron 2010). The ongoing economic crisis, coupled with a political ethos to open government and the widespread use of information and communication technologies, have created an environment of accelerated change (*The Economist* 2010). As our capacity for useful, flexible information management increases, so does the potential of our nation. If governance is the institutional capacity of a public organization (Kjaer 2006), the capacity of that system can be increased by the thoughtful application of information technology to increase the role of the public in governing. Smart, participation-based governance infrastructures will organize around specific problems, identify clear problems and pathways to contribute, coordinate participation while avoiding value judgments, encourage long-term community involvement, and provide open access to useful resources.

Every day, technology advances and enables people to do more for themselves. This chapter only scratches the surface of how we will continue to discover new forms of organizing, to innovate and use new knowledge creatively, and to push assumptions of what governance infrastructures are and how they can be used. As new technologies like cloud computing, augmented reality, ubiquitous computing, data mining, and whatever follows develop, so will possibilities for smart governance infrastructures. Investing in smart governance infrastructures returns power back to the people; greater participation comes with higher expectations, accountability, and responsibility. Evolution of governance is inevitable, but the time frame and path are unknown. Instead of stumbling forward and reacting with ad hoc governance fixes as problems emerge or exacerbate, we can engage these challenges by designing systems to act proactively.

Note

This research is funded by NSF grants 0838206 and 0838295 and is an extension of the article: Johnston, E. (2010). "Governance Infrastructures in 2020." *Public Administration Review,* 70(1) s122–s128.

References

Anderson, Chris. 2006. *The Long Tail: Why the Future of Business Is Selling Less of More.* New York: Hyperion.

Arrow, Kenneth J., Robert Forsythe, Michael Gorham, Robert Hahn, Robin Hanson, John O. Ledyard, Saul Levmore et al. 2008. "The Promise of Prediction Markets." *Science* 320 (5878): 877–878. http://www.sciencemag.org/cgi/content/short/320/5878/877 (accessed March 15, 2010).

Cameron, David. 2010. The Next Age of Government. Technology, Entertainment, Design, February. Video. http://www.ted.com/talks/lang/eng/david_cameron.html (accessed March 15, 2010).

Catlaw, Thomas J. 2007. *Fabricating the People.* Tuscaloosa: University of Alabama Press.

Catone, Josh. 2009. Virtual Neighborhood Watch: "How Social Media Is Making Cities Safer." Mashable, October 1. http://mashable.com/2009/10/01/social-media-public-safety/ (accessed October 1, 2009).

Citizens United v. Federal Election Commission. 2010. 130 S. Ct. 876.

The Economist. 2010. "Data, Data, Everywhere." February 27. http://www.economist.com/node/15557443 (accessed October 1, 2009).

Gohring, Nancy. 2010. "Federal CIO Describes Problems, Changes in IT." *PC World,* March 4. http://www.pcworld.com/article/190864/federal_cio_describes_problems_changes_in_it.html (accessed May 13, 2010).

Goldsmith, Stephen. 2010. "Open Sourcing Innovation: Citizens, Community Problem Solving, and Digital Media." The Case Foundation, March 30. http://www.casefoundation.org/blog/open-sourcing-innovation-citizens-community-problem-solving-and-digital-media (accessed May 13, 2010).

Grossman, Lev. 2006. "Person of the Year: You." *Time,* December 25. http://www.time.com/time/magazine/article/0,9171,1569514,00.html (accessed May 13, 2010).

Howe, Jeff. 2006. "The Rise of Crowdsourcing." *Wired,* June. http://www.wired.com/wired/archive/14.06/crowds.html (accessed March 17, 2007).

Kanter, Rosabeth Moss, and Stanley S. Litow. 2009. "Informed and Interconnected: A Manifesto for Smarter Cities." Working Paper 09–141, Harvard Business School.

King, Stephen F., and Paul Brown. 2007. "Fix My Street or Else: Using the Internet to Voice Local Public Service Concerns." In *Proceedings of the 1st International Conference on Theory and Practice of Electronic Governance*, pp. 72–80. Macao, China: Association for Computing Machinery (ACM).

Kiva.org. 2010. "Facts and History." http://www.kiva.org/about/facts (accessed May 13, 2010).

Kjaer, Ann Mette. 2006. "Making Sense of Governance." *Politica* 38(1): 116–118.

Kooiman, Jan. 1993. *Modern Governance: New Government-Society Interactions.* Newbury Park, CA: Sage.

Lampe, Cliff, and Erik Johnston. 2005. "Follow the (Slash) Dot: Effects of Feedback on New Users in a Virtual Public Sphere." In *Proceedings of the International SIGGROUP Conference on Supporting Group Work*, pp. 11–20. Sanibel Island, FL: Association for Computing Machinery (ACM).

Lampe, Cliff, Erik Johnston, and Paul Resnick. 2007. "Follow the Reader: Filtering Comments on Slashdot." In *Proceedings of the SIGCHI Conference on Human Factors in Computing Systems CHI-2007*, pp. 1253–1262. San Jose, CA: Association for Computing Machinery (ACM).

Lathrop, Daniel, and Laurel Ruma (Eds). 2010. *Open Government.* Sebastopol, CA: O'Reilly Media.

Lave, Jean, and Etienne Wenger. 1991. *Situated Learning: Legitimate Peripheral Participation.* New York: Cambridge University Press.

Lessig, Lawrence. 2006. *Code Version 2.0.* New York: Basic Books.

———. 2009. "Institutional Corruption." blip.tv, October 8 [Video]. http://blip.tv/file/2711623 (accessed October 10, 2009).

Malone, Thomas. 2004. *The Future of Work: How the New Order of Business Will Shape Your Organization, Your Management Style and Your Life.* Boston: Harvard Business School Press.

Miller, Rich. 2010. "Feds Commence Huge Data Center Consolidation." Data Center Knowledge, March 1. http://www.datacenterknowledge.com/archives/2010/03/01/feds-commence-huge-data-center-consolidation/ (accessed March 15, 2010).

National Academy of Public Administration (NAPA). 2009. *Open Government Dialogue.* Washington, DC: NAPA. http://opengov.ideascale.com/akira/panel.do?id=4049 (accessed June 1, 2009).

Obama, Barack. 2010. Commencement address, May 1. Ann Arbor: University of Michigan.

O'Reilly, Tim. 2009. "Gov 2.0: The Promise of Innovation." *Forbes*, August 10. http://www.forbes.com/2009/08/10/government-internet-software-technology-breakthroughs-oreilly.html (accessed March 15, 2010).

———. 2010. "Government as a Platform." In *Open Government*, ed. D. Lathrop and L. Ruma, pp. 11–39. Sebastopol, CA: O'Reilly Media.

Page, Scott E. 2007. *The Difference: How the Power of Diversity Creates Better Groups, Firms, Schools, and Societies.* Princeton, NJ: Princeton University Press.

Raymond, Eric. S. 2001. *The Cathedral and the Bazaar: Musings on Linux and Open Source by an Accidental Revolutionary.* Sebastopol, CA: O'Reilly Media.

Rhodes, R. A. W.1996. "The New Governance: Governing Without Government." *Political Studies* 44(4): 652–667.

———. 2000. "Governance and Public Administration." In *Debating Governance*, ed. J. Pierre, pp. 54–90. Oxford: Oxford University Press.

Schweik, Charles, Tom Evans, and J. Morgan Grove. 2005. "Open Source and Open Content: A Framework for Global Collaboration in Social-Ecological Research." *Ecology and Society* 10(1): 33. http://www.ecologyandsociety.org/vol10/iss1/art33/ (accessed October 11, 2009).

Shirky, Clay. 2005. "Clay Shirky on Institutions vs. Collaboration." Technology, Entertainment, Design, July [Video]. http://www.ted.com/talks/clay_shirky_on_institutions_versus_collaboration.html (accessed October 11, 2009).

Shneiderman, Ben. 2009. "A National Initiative for Social Participation." *Science* 323 (5920): 1426–1427.

Shneiderman, Ben, and J. Preece. 2009. "The Reader-to-Leader Framework: Motivating Technology-Mediated Social Participation." AIS Transactions on Human-Computer Interaction 1(1): 13–32.

Simon, Herbert A. 1996. *The Sciences of the Artificial*, 3d ed. Cambridge, MA: MIT Press.

Sunstein, Cass. 2007. *Republic.com 2.0*. Princeton, NJ: Princeton University Press.

Surowiecki, J. 2004. *The Wisdom of Crowds: Why the Many Are Smarter Than the Few and How Collective Wisdom Shapes Business, Economies, Societies and Nations*. New York: First Anchor Books.

Sutter, John D. 2010. "Citizens Monitor Gulf Coast after Oil Spill." CNN.com, May 6. http://www.cnn.com/2010/TECH/05/06/crowdsource.gulf.oil/index.html?hpt=Sbin (accessed May 13, 2010).

The Telegraph. 2010. "Every Citizen to Have Personal Webpage." March 20. http://www.telegraph.co.uk/technology/news/7484600/Every-citizen-to-have-personal-webpage.html (accessed May 13, 2010).

Wenger, E., R. McDermott, and W. M. Snyder. 2002. *Cultivating Communities of Practice*. Boston: Harvard Business School Press.

14

Creating and Sustaining Change

GARY A. CHRISTOPHERSON

As we look around us in America and in the world, much of what is important to us is already broken, or is endangered, much of it unnecessarily so. If we are to achieve a better future, we need to use "next generation" strategy for solving large problems and creating and sustaining positive, large-scale change. The "via" strategy set is one proposed "next generation" strategy.

Why "Next Generation" Strategy?

First, let me strongly suggest that our "mission" should be to build a better future and our "vision" should be to achieve a positive, sustainable future.

But how do we do it? Based on 30 years of work at the national and local levels, most current policy and strategy models are too limited in scope to address today's problems and wholly inadequate for succeeding with a much more challenging future. Generally, current policy and strategy models fail to learn from past failures and fall far short of being "next generation." "Next generation" policy and strategy models must succeed with a future world that is at high risk with threats to its sustainability, is large and broad of scope, is complex, is highly interactive and interdependent, will depend heavily on what people do, and will change with or without us.

Many people, with good intentions, are trying to fix large problems and build a better future. That is good news, to some extent. Unfortunately, it includes much bad news unless we change our approach. Most people are focused on single-issue areas, for example, housing, health, income, transportation, education, plant/animal habitat, climate, and natural resources. And most are focused on only a part of a single-issue area. Most treat other people as parts rather than as whole persons. If successful, most people make some progress in the near term and relatively little for the longer term. Most waste valuable resources and reach less than optimal near- and long-term solutions because they do not coordinate their work with that being done in related issue areas.

All this can be helpful, but solving a community's, a nation's, or a broader area's (e.g., a region or larger) problems takes more than this. We need "next generation" strategy. But what does it mean to be "next generation"?

- First, "next generation" strategy must focus on individual whole "persons"—individuals with unique abilities, motivation, and behaviors uniquely affected by and affecting their "environment." After all, it is people who create most problems and it is people who can and should fix the problems, create and sustain positive, large-scale change, and build a better future.
- Second, "next generation" strategies need to be much more effective at addressing the important issue areas, especially large, complex ones.
- Third, "next generation" strategies need to effectively handle the cross-cutting issues of a highly interactive and interdependent world.
- Fourth, "next generation" strategy and policy must tackle issues as a system (e.g., a health system, a resource system, a community) interacting with other systems and within larger systems (e.g., communities, nations, the world).
- Fifth, "next generation" strategies need to effectively handle whole systems, including whole persons, whole communities, whole nations, and whole broader areas.
- Sixth, "next generation" strategies need to effectively handle the future in terms of both sustaining whatever progress we make and adjusting to a changing future.

No single strategy, model, or tool by itself will help us do all this. But a core set of "next generation" strategies, models, and tools together can help if the core set (1) is effective for individual and cross-cutting issues; (2) can incorporate and work well with other effective strategies, models, and tools; (3) is effective as a coordinated approach for addressing the "systems" and "wholes" requirement; and (4) can not only effectively address the future but also adjust to and sustain the future. One such core set exists and is labeled "via," a term whose definition is "by way of, through the medium or agency of, or by means of."

Why the "via" Strategy?

As suggested, potential "next generation" models do exist for strategy at system (issue area, community, nation, broader area) and person levels. The "via" strategy—a core set and system of supportive models addressing persons, systems, motivation, ability, behavior, performance and its improvement, process measures, and, most important, positive outcomes and improved status—is one proposed approach.

Why the "via" strategy? Going back to what it means to be "next generation," here is how "via" matches up.

- First, the "via" strategy focuses on individual "persons"—individuals with singular abilities, motivations, and behaviors uniquely affected by and affecting their "environment." "Person" aspects are addressed by the Behavioral Effectiveness Model (BEM) and the "Person Model."

- Second, the "via" strategy is designed to be more effective at addressing issue areas, especially large, complex ones. Large, complex issue areas (e.g., health) have been addressed with the full "via" strategy core set.
- Third, the "via" strategy is designed to effectively handle the cross-cutting issues of a highly interactive and interdependent world. Cross-cutting issue areas ("e.g., vulnerability) have been explored with the full "via" strategy core set.
- Fourth, the "via" strategy is designed to tackle issues as a system (e.g., a health system) interacting with other systems and within larger systems (e.g., communities, nations, broader areas). Systems (personal health, health care delivery systems, and public health) have been addressed with the full "via" strategy core set, including the System Models.
- Fifth, the "via" strategy is designed to effectively handle whole systems, including whole communities, whole nations, and whole broader areas. Systems have been addressed (e.g., population-based health, large health care delivery systems) or explored (e.g., vulnerability, community, nation) with the full "via" strategy core set.
- Sixth, the "via" strategy is designed to effectively handle the future in terms of sustaining whatever progress we make and adjusting to a changing future. Sustainable, future-adaptive systems have been addressed (e.g., personal health, large health care delivery systems) or explored (e.g., vulnerability, community, nation) with the full "via" strategy core set, including the predictive aspects of the core set's models.

What Is the "via" Strategy Core Set and *How Does It Work?*

The "via" overall strategy core set is explored here along with three areas of potential application:

- Health, a large, complex, individual issue area, where it has already been applied
- Vulnerability, a large complex cross-cutting issue area, where it is being explored to develop coordinated strategy and policy
- Whole communities, whole nations, and whole broader areas where it is being explored to develop coordinated strategy and policy

What does the "via" strategy core set consist of? As shown in Table 14.1, the core set includes the overall "via" strategy, the Performance Improvement Model, the "via" Model, the Behavioral Effectiveness Model, the Person Model, the Population Model, the System(s) Model, the Strategy Model, and the Status Model. The overall core set and the supportive components can be applied to a single-issue area, cross-cutting issue areas, and whole communities, nations, and broader areas. Although in this chapter I focus on the models as a set, each can be used independently as well. All of these models are described and discussed in more detail in the rest of the chapter.

Table 14.1

"via" Strategy Core Set and Applicable Issue Levels and Scope

"via" strategy core set	Issue level and scope		
	Single issue area (e.g., health)	Cross-cutting issue areas (e.g., vulnerability)	Whole community, nation, broader areas
Overall "via" strategy	X	X	X
System(s) Model, including "ideal" systems	X	X	X
Performance Improvement Model	X	X	X
"via" Model	X	X	X
Behavioral Effectiveness Model (BEM)	X	X	X
Person Model (applying BEM over individual person's lifetime and life stages)	X	X	X
Population Model (applying BEM over multiple persons' lifetime and life stages)	X	X	X
Strategy Model (strategies and interventions)	X	X	X
Status Model	X	X	X

Overall "via" Strategy

What Is It?

As displayed in Figure 14.1 and detailed in Table 14.2, the overall "via" strategy is to effectively use the "via" strategy core set as a set of integrated, coordinated components to produce the necessary knowledge and an effective overall strategy with supportive strategies. By using the full core set, we can better identify and understand the targeted system (e.g., community, nation), decide what we want to achieve on a sustained basis, understand and select the target behaviors, design and select what interventions we need, and develop the overall strategy and supportive strategies to achieve the desired state.

How Does It Work?

The overall "via" strategy works through the systematic application of the core set by people who have both the motivation and the ability to help create and sustain positive, large-scale change.

Although the steps laid out in Figure 14.1 and Table 14.2 imply their sequential

Figure 14.1 **Overall "*via*" Strategy Model**

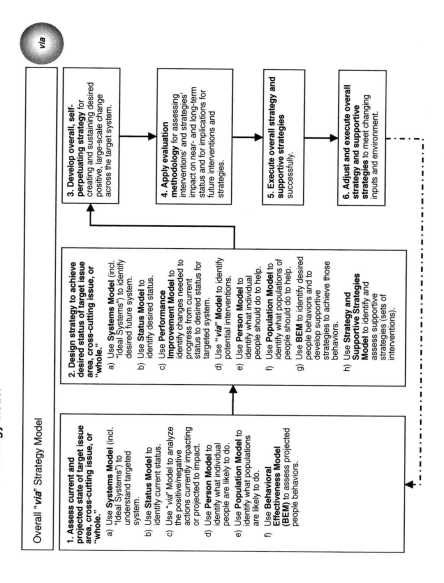

Table 14.2

Overall "via" Strategy: Creating and Sustaining Positive, Large-Scale Change

The overall strategy for creating and sustaining positive, large-scale change is as follows:

1. Assess current and projected state of target issue area, cross-cutting issue, or "whole."
   a. Use Systems Model (including "Ideal Systems") to understand targeted system (e.g., health system, community, nation, broader area) today.
   b. Use Status Model to identify current status for "whole" (e.g., community, nation, broader areas), issue areas (e.g., health, education), or cross-cutting issue area (e.g., vulnerability, climate, habitat) targeted for positive, large-scale change.
   c. Use "via" Model to analyze the positive/negative actions currently impacting or projected to impact issue area, cross-cutting issue, or "whole."
   d. Use Person Model to identify what individual people are likely to do in the future.
   e. Use Population Model to identify what populations are likely to do in the future.
   f. Use Behavioral Effectiveness Model (BEM) to assess projected people behaviors.
2. Design strategy to achieve desired status for target issue area, cross-cutting issue, or "whole."
   a. Use Systems Model (including "Ideal Systems") to identify desired future system state.
   b. Use Status Model to identify desired status for targeted system.
   c. Use Performance Improvement Model to identify changes, including behavior, needed to progress from current status and achieve desired status for targeted system.
   d. Use "via" Model to identify potential interventions for creating and sustaining desired positive, large-scale change.
   e. Use Person Model to identify what individual people should do to help achieve the desired positive, large-scale change.
   f. Use Population Model to identify what populations of people should do to help achieve the desired positive, large-scale change.
   g. Use BEM to identify ability, motivation, and desired behaviors that help achieve desired change and to develop supportive strategies to achieve desired behaviors.
   h. Use Strategy Model and supportive strategies to identify and assess and organize supportive strategies (sets of interventions) for creating/sustaining desired change.
3. With above inputs, develop overall, self-perpetuating strategy for creating and sustaining desired positive, large-scale change across target system.
4. Apply evaluation methodology for assessing strategies' and interventions' impact on near- and long-term status and for implications for future interventions and strategies.
5. Execute overall strategy and supportive strategies successfully.
6. Adjust and execute overall strategy and supportive strategies to meet changing inputs and environment.

application, that is not always the case. Step 1 is important in our understanding of what the current system is, its status, its projected actions, and its projected people and population behaviors. Step 1c helps us organize that thinking of how we might get from the current situation to the desired status for the targeted system. Step 2 helps us work through what needs to be changed and how we might make that change. Step 3 pulls all this together to help us create and execute the overall strategy and supportive strategies. Step 4 is to make sure we evaluate how we are doing and provide input for changes in strategy. Step 5 focuses on the successful execution of the overall strategy and supportive strategies. Step 6 makes sure we understand that strategy is not static and needs to adjust to unanticipated input and environmental changes, and the strategy needs to be executed successfully on an ongoing basis.

How Has It Been Used and How Has It Helped?

The "via" strategy has been used for several large-scale changes, including systems such as the $15+ billion Military Health System (Department of Defense), the $1+ billion HealtheVet VistA health information system (Veterans Health Administration), the draft Strategic and Operational Plan for the $500+ billion Center for Medicare and Medicaid Services (CMS), a potential strategy for reducing vulnerability for communities and nations, and a potential strategy for "building a healthy America" (over one-sixth of the U.S. economy).

The "via" strategy was used in 2006 for one single-issue area, to draft a strategic and operational plan for the CMS in 2007–2012. Essentially, the whole strategy was used, working with the CMS staff, to develop a strategy covering six years for the $500+ billion agency and its programs. The desired health status and outcome measures were identified. The "ideal" system was identified. The performance improvement model was developed as the framework. Evaluation measures were developed. The strategy addressed "person," "population," and behavioral issues and how to do so. The end result was a comprehensive draft strategic and operational plan that was developed with the staff and presented to but not signed by the CMS administrator. The plan remains available for future CMS use.

In a single-issue area within health, it was used in the early 2000s to create and sustain positive change to the Veterans Health Administration (VHA) health information system, a nationwide system covering over 1,000 sites of care and with an annual budget of over $1 billion. The desired change was to build upon and expand the capability of VHA's existing VistA health information system by creating a sustainable "next generation" system named HealtheVet VistA. The new system was approved by the VHA, the Department of Veterans Affairs, and the Office of Management and Budget, and received increased funding of about $125 million annually. Much of the new system is already in place and operating successfully.

The strategy is being explored on the cross-cutting issue of vulnerability. Here it is being used to create a potential strategy for minimizing vulnerability and maximizing thriving for a whole population (e.g., community, nation). The resulting strategy addresses the system of a community or a nation. It sets the desired status as minimized vulnerability and maximized thriving and includes a set of measures for that status. It uses the full core set to lay out the performance improvement framework, to analyze and design interventions, to determine how best to address both an individual person and whole populations over time, to develop the behavioral interventions, and to design the overall strategy and supportive strategies. While the strategy has not been used to date, it is ready for application.

The strategy's application to whole communities, nations, and broader areas is also being explored as a total system interacting with other systems outside. In this case, the focus is on the whole population and its individual whole persons. It also addresses animals, plants, and natural resources in the context of the community, nation, or broader area. The full range of significant issue areas within the target community, nation, or broader area is explored, including their interaction and interdependency. Status indicators to assess current and desired future state are being developed. The intended result is an overall, sustainable, executable strategy for improving the status of a community, a nation, or a broader area.

Performance Improvement Model

What Is It?

The Performance Improvement Model (see Figure 14.2, Table 14.3) lays out the process by which a desired performance or status (e.g., minimized vulnerability and maximized thriving, high health status, sustainable and good animal habitat, sustainable energy) is set and compared with the current status. Based on that, a strategy is developed that makes the necessary changes to achieve the desired performance or status.

How Does It Work?

Based on an understanding of the system that is to be improved and its current status or performance level, a desired level of status or performance is chosen. The model is designed to help determine what it will take to achieve that performance or status level.

How Has It Been Used and How Has It Helped?

The Performance Improvement Model's primary use to date has been to improve health care quality, outcomes, and status. Potential applications are being explored in creating an overall strategy for reducing vulnerability and improving the status of a community, nation, or broader area.

Figure 14.2 **Performance Improvement Model**

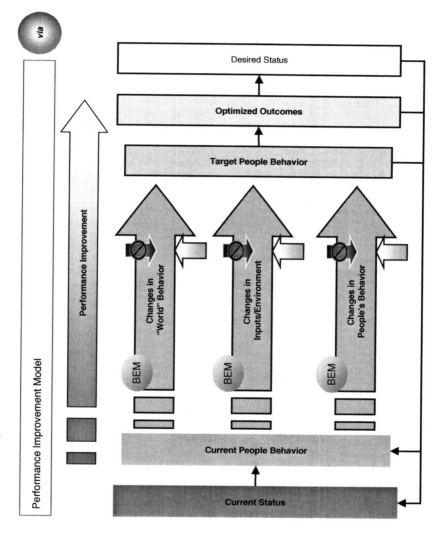

Table 14.3

Performance Improvement Model: Strategies for Improving Performance to Achieve Desired Status

The overall strategy for improving performance is as follows:
1. Based on an understanding of the system that is to be improved, assess its current status or performance level.
2. Determine what should be the desired level of status or performance.
3. Assess what is the delta (difference) between those two levels.
4. Determine what outcomes need to be produced in order to achieve the desired level of status or performance.
5. Determine what people's current behaviors are.
6. Determine what people's target behaviors should be.
7. Assess what is the delta between those two sets of behavior and what behavior changes are desired.
8. Determine how "world," input/environment, and people behavior already occurring or projected to occur affect people behaviors. "World" behaviors are changes in people behaviors that are outside the system being changed. "Inputs/Environment" changes are non-people behaviors such as climate change, and plant and animal change.
9. Determine the set of strategies and interventions needed to change people behaviors by using other models, including the Behavioral Effectiveness Model (BEM), the "via" Model, and the Person and Population Models. These strategies and interventions may be applied to any or all of "world," input/ environment, and people behavior already occurring or projected to occur.
10. Measure the effect that these strategies and interventions are having on changing people's behavior, the outcomes, and the status.
11. Feed the strategies and interventions into the Overall Strategy and Supporting Strategies.
12. Determine how changes in status, outcomes, and behavior create a new level of "current" status, outcomes, and behavior and rerun the Performance Improvement Model on an ongoing basis.

At the CMS, the Performance Improvement Model was used in 2006 to design an overall strategy for national quality improvement for health care, including but not limited to care funded by Medicare and Medicaid. The desired status was health status based on the best knowledge on how much health status can be improved through health care. The current status was based on the best available information on current health status. The model helped identify what outcomes, properly optimized, could best produce the desired health status. Furthermore, it helped identify what target people's (persons, health care personnel) behaviors could best produce those optimized outcomes. The Person Model was used to understand how individual persons do and should behave over time. The Population Model was used to understand how populations do and should behave over time. The BEM Model was used to determine what interventions would likely produce the desired behavior change. The "via" Model was used to determine how to apply those interventions as a coordinated, ongoing strategy. These strategies and interventions were meant to enhance the overall quality improvement program for CMS.

"via" Model

What Is It?

The "via" Model (see Figure 14.3) serves as a basic framework for interventions that improve the status of an issue area (e.g., health, vulnerability, climate, animal habitat) or a "whole" (e.g., community, nation, or broader area).

How Does It Work?

As detailed in Table 14.4, the "via" Model includes what it is we want to achieve and avoid, how to work through interventions and actions that affect that achievement, and how to measure progress.

How Has It Been Used and How Has It Helped?

The "via" Model's primary application to date has been to improve health care. Its potential use is being explored in creating an overall strategy for reducing vulnerability and improving the status of a community, nation, or broader area.

In 2006, the model was applied to designing the draft CMS Strategic and Operational Plan for 2007–2012. It assessed current and projected actions by CMS and others affecting health status. It identified new interventions to stop actions that lower health status and to support actions that increase high and low status. New interventions were also identified that directly help to achieve high and highest health status, to prevent lowering of health status, and to move up from low health status. These "via" Model interventions were then used to develop the overall draft Strategic and Operational Plan for CMS.

The model is being used on the cross-cutting issue of vulnerability, to help create a proposed strategy for minimizing vulnerability and maximizing thriving for a whole population (e.g., community, nation). In this case, high status was "high thriving" and low status was "high vulnerability." An assessment is being done on what actions are already occurring or projected to occur that will affect vulnerability. The model helps determine what interventions could be used to reduce vulnerability and maximize thriving. As indicated earlier, the overall strategy has not been used to date, but is ready for application.

Preliminary work has also been done for communities, nations, and broader areas. That work incorporates the work done on health and vulnerability into an expanded application to whole communities, nations, or broader areas. The focus is on a whole population and its whole persons, along with the respective animals, plants, and natural resources. It addresses the target area as a system with subsystems (e.g., issue areas like health, income, habitat, climate) and with interactions and interdependencies with other systems (i.e., other communities, nations, and broader areas).

224

Figure 14.3   **"via" Model: Interventions Improving Status**

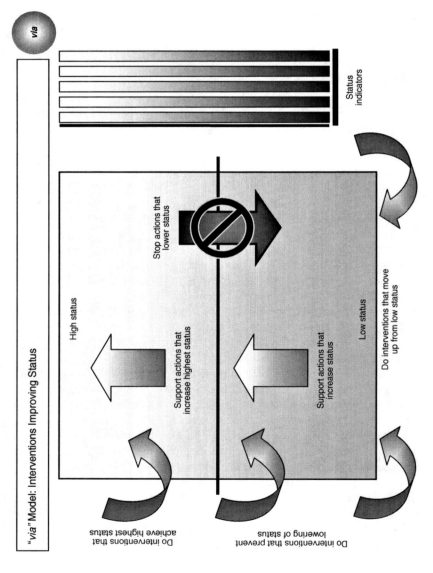

"*via*" Model: Interventions Improving Status

Table 14.4

"via" Model: Interventions Improving Status

The "via" Model use for interventions improving status is as follows:

1. Decide what issue area or "whole" needs status improvement.
2. Decide what status indicators will be used to measure current and desired status.
3. Identify current and projected actions that affect status in one of the following ways:
   a. Actions that lower status
   b. Actions that increase status for that portion above the mean or median
   c. Actions that increase status for that portion below the mean or median
4. Identify new interventions that positively affect status in one of the following ways:
   a. Interventions that help achieve highest status, including supporting actions that further increase high or highest status
   b. Interventions that help prevent lowering of status, including stopping actions that lower status
   c. Interventions that help move up from low status, including supporting actions that increase status
5. Measure the effect that the interventions are having on the current and projected actions and on the status indicators.
6. Feed the interventions into the Overall Strategy and Supporting Strategies.

Behavioral Effectiveness Model

What Is It?

The Behavioral Effectiveness Model, or BEM, is built upon several related models (see Figure 14.4). These run the gamut from expectancy theory, instrumentality theory, and theory of reasoned action to contingency theory, system theory, social cognitive theory, behavioral theory, and so on, whose applications have been refined for over 30 to 40 years. The "via" approach is built upon the premise that a person's or a population's behavior is key to what creates and sustains change.

BEM's value lies in (1) being relatively parsimonious, (2) incorporating key aspects of other behavioral models, (3) being "computable"—that is, the model can employ databases (personal characteristics, desired behaviors, tailored interventions), (4) tailoring applicability to more than one person simultaneously by using individual characteristics and desired behavior(s), and (5) using evidence-based interventions that can be tailored to those characteristics and the desired behavior.

How Does It Work?

As shown in Table 14.5, the BEM Model is designed to apply interventions that help achieve the desired target behavior, and to increase knowledge about the

Figure 14.4 **Behavioral Effectiveness Model (BEM)**

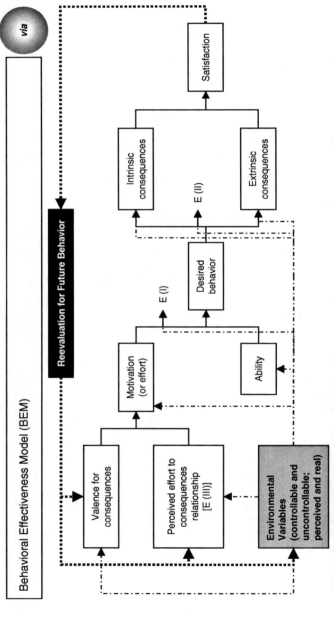

E (I): Perceived motivation (effort) to behavior relationship

E (II): Perceived behavior to intrinsic and extrinsic consequences relationship

E (III): Perceived effort to consequences relationship

Source: Based on Behavioral Effectiveness Model (BEM) in Gary A. Christopherson, "People Planning: Increasing Planning Effectiveness by Working with User and Implementer Behavior" (master's thesis, University of Wisconsin, Madison, 1974).

Table 14.5

Behavioral Effectiveness Model (BEM): Improving Personal Human Behavior/Performance

The BEM Model use for achieving desired behavior is as follows:

1. Identify the person or population whose behavior is targeted.
2. Decide what the desired behavior or behaviors are. Note that some behavior is one-time and some is recurring.
3. Assess motivation in terms of its current and future characteristics.
4. Assess ability in terms of its current and future characteristics.
5. Assess environmental variables, both controllable and uncontrollable and both perceived and real.
6. Assess how motivation, ability, and environmental variables are likely to affect future behavior without further intervention.
7. Assess what are likely to be the intrinsic (internal to the person or population) and extrinsic (external to the person or population) consequences of projected behavior and what is likely to be the person's or population's satisfaction.
8. Assess how consequences and satisfaction are likely to affect future behavior.
9. Assess how projected behavior, without further intervention, matches to desired behavior.
10. Assess what interventions will best move projected behavior to desired behavior for the near and long term.
11. Apply the interventions and assess their effect.
12. Adjust the interventions as needed over time and based on result.
13. Feed the interventions into the Overall Strategy and Supporting Strategies.

person or population involved, the interventions themselves, and the "system" in which interventions are applied. It can also be used for prediction, analysis, and program development. The model can be applied to (1) an individual person, (2) populations whose characteristics are sufficiently the same, and/or (3) populations of individuals in which each individual gets a personalized and tailored intervention. The model can be linked to a database so that it can both make use of and produce information as well as support personalized and tailored interventions

- for any number of individuals and over any period of time
- for one-time behaviors and behavior over time
- for change in a single behavior and multiple behaviors

How Has It Been Used and How Has It Helped?

The Behavioral Effectiveness Model's primary application to date has been to improve health. Its potential use is being explored in creating an overall strategy for reducing vulnerability and improving the status of a community, nation, or broader area.

The model's earliest use was in the mid-1970s to help develop a high blood pressure control program in Milwaukee, Wisconsin. The desired behavior was adherence to methods for controlling high blood pressure. These methods could be medication use and/or lifestyle change (e.g., diet, exercise, stress reduction). With the BEM, the program had greater success in convincing people to get their blood pressure checked and in determining the likely success of particular methods with a specific person or with persons with similar characteristics. The blood pressure control program was seen as a national model for community blood pressure control.

At the CMS, the model was used in 2005 to design an overall strategy for national quality improvement for health care, including but not limited to care funded by Medicare and Medicaid. The desired behavior was that health care providers provide high-quality care. The model helped identify which target people's (persons, health care personnel) behaviors could best produce those optimized outcomes. An assessment was done of the motivation and ability factors driving current and future behavior. Based on that assessment, an approach was laid out using current and new interventions to move health care provider behavior toward the target behavior to produce the improved outcomes and health status. These interventions were to enhance the overall quality improvement program for CMS.

BEM is also being used on the cross-cutting issue of vulnerability, to find out what behaviors are associated with vulnerability and thriving. The model helps identify the ability and motivational factors that are and would be determinants of vulnerability and thriving behavior. The model determines what interventions could be used to improve the motivation and ability factors and, as a result, reduce vulnerability and maximize thriving. Based on these, a potential strategy has been created for minimizing vulnerability and maximizing thriving for a whole population, in this case the United States as a whole. As indicated earlier, the overall strategy has not been used to date, but is ready for application.

With respect to communities, nations, or broader areas, BEM helps in addressing the full breadth of issue areas and of people, animals/plants, and natural resources. Here it helps identify behaviors associated with the relevant status indicators, and what ability and motivational factors are and would be determinants of improving status. The model helps in determining what interventions could be used to improve the motivation and ability factors and, as a result, improve status. Based on these, a strategy is being created for improving status for a whole population, in this case the United States as a whole.

Person Model

What Is It?

The Person Model (see Figure 14.5) helps us to understand that each person goes through several life stages depending on how long they live. If status (e.g., health, income, performance) is to be improved, it is seldom a one-time intervention and

Figure 14.5   **Person Model: Applying BEM Over an Individual Person's Time and Life Stages**

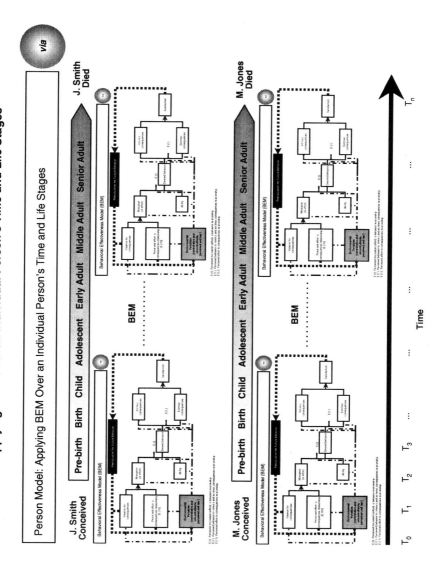

generally should be done across the life span. As a result, the Person Model works by applying the Behavioral Effectiveness Model over an individual person's lifetime and life stages.

How Does It Work?

The Person Model, with BEM as the underlying model, recognizes that each individual is different at the beginning of life, throughout his or her life stages, and near the end. For status to be improved, the strategy needs to be both specific to each person across the life span and effective across all persons' life spans (see Table 14.6).

How Has It Been Used and How Has It Helped?

The Person Model's primary use to date has been for improving health. Its potential use is being explored in creating an overall strategy for reducing vulnerability and improving the status of a community, nation, or broader area.

The earliest application of the Person Model was, like the BEM Model, to develop a high blood pressure control program in Milwaukee, Wisconsin, in the mid-1970s. The desired behavior was ongoing adherence to a method for controlling high blood pressure. With the Person Model, understanding how to match the intervention to time and different life stages increased. With respect to time, the interventions needed during the initial treatment were different from the ones needed during the maintenance phase of treatment. With respect to life stages, interventions had to be refined to match the behavioral determinants for a younger person versus a middle-aged person versus an older person. The blood pressure control program was seen as a model of community blood pressure control programs.

At the CMS, in 2005, the Person Model was used to enhance the overall strategy for national quality improvement for health care. The desired behavior was of health care providers over time and their careers. The model helped with the identification of which target health care personnel behaviors could produce the best ongoing outcomes. Based on that, an approach was laid out using current and new interventions to improve health care provider behavior in a way that would produce improved outcomes and health status for the foreseeable future and over the health care providers' careers (life stages). These interventions were used to improve the overall quality improvement program for CMS.

The model was also used in the early 2000s to create a new model called "person-centered health." The Person-Centered Health Model has helped to refine the programs of the Veterans Health Administration, including overall care, care in the community, and the VHA health information system (electronic health record and personal health record systems). It was also used at the CMS to help with the quality improvement program and the draft strategic and operational plan.

The Person Model also comes into play regarding the cross-cutting issue of

Table14.6

Person Model: Applying BEM over Each Person's Time and Life Stages

The Person Model use for achieving desired behavior is as follows:

1. Identify the person or population whose behavior is targeted.
2. Decide what time frame or life stage(s) are to be addressed.
3. Decide what is the desired behavior or behaviors over time and through life stages.
4. Apply the BEM Model as a recurring model (running the model as many times as necessary), adjusting to changes in motivation, ability, and environmental variables.
5. Assess what interventions will best move projected behavior to desired behavior for the covered time and life stage(s).
6. Apply the interventions and assess their effect on an ongoing basis.
7. Adjust the interventions as needed over time and based on result.
8. Feed the interventions into the Overall Strategy and Supporting Strategies.

vulnerability. Because vulnerability is relevant over a person's life and changes throughout the life stages, the model helps identify which ability and motivational factors, over time and across life stages, would be determinants of vulnerability and thriving behavior. It recognizes that reducing vulnerability prior to birth is very different from doing so for an adolescent or for a senior adult. Some factors (e.g., financial and cognitive ability) carry across a person's life span and can help lower vulnerability throughout a person's lifetime. Other factors (e.g., ability reduced by Alzheimer's disease or low birth weight) always or most likely occur at a specific life stage. As a result, the strategy for minimizing vulnerability and maximizing thriving is a living strategy that adjusts for time and life stages. The overall strategy has not been used to date, but is ready for application.

Population Model

What Is It?

The Population Model (see Figure 14.6) addresses status from the perspective of what is happening at any point in time and the effect on a diverse population. Again, BEM is the underlying model for adjusting strategy to address points in time across persons and their life stages. This model also applies to other differences (e.g., racial, ethnic, income, vulnerability) in the target population.

How Does It Work?

The Population Model, with BEM as the underlying model, recognizes that strategy, at any point in time, needs to be both specific to each person across the life

Figure 14.6   Population Model: Applying BEM at a Point in Time Across Persons and Their Life Stages

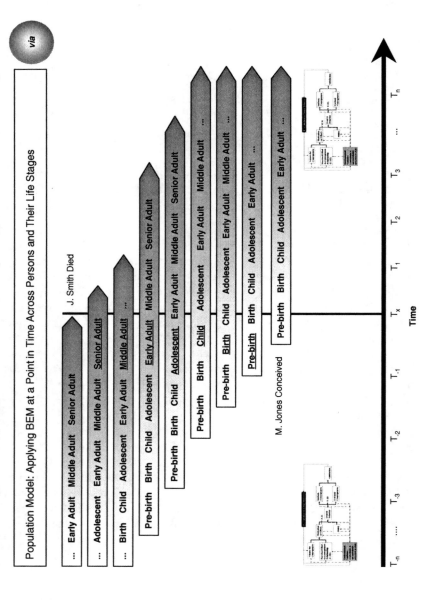

span and effective across all persons across their life spans. Taking a time slice, the model recognizes that at any moment in time, the target population will likely include persons from all different stages of life (pre-birth, birth, child, adolescent, early adult, middle adult, and senior adult). At that moment in time, each person has different status levels, different factors affecting status, and different responses to efforts at improving status. This can be seen in how major disasters (e.g., tsunamis, earthquakes, disease outbreaks, crop failures, drought) affect people differently. This can also be seen in how program interventions (e.g., education, housing programs, financial assistance, health insurance programs, heating assistance, taxes) affect people differently (see Table 14.7).

How Has It Been Used and How Has It Helped?

The Population Model is primarily concerned with health improvement. Its potential use is being explored in the creation of an overall strategy for reducing vulnerability, and for improving the status of a community, nation. or broader area.

The model was used in 2006 to design the draft CMS Strategic and Operational Plan for 2007–2012. It addressed CMS's disparate beneficiary population and the timing and design of program interventions. Interventions then helped with the development of the overall plan. The plan was designed to address as well the needs of both younger and older Medicaid beneficiaries, beneficiaries with disabilities, and healthier and severely ill Medicare beneficiaries. It also addressed the populations that are pre-Medicaid and pre-Medicare. The plan recognized that over time, these populations change as new age cohorts move into the program.

For the Department of Defense Military Health System (MHS), the model was used in the 1990s to work with pre-military, active service, Guard and Reserve, veterans, and retirees and their families. All are the responsibility of the MHS. Key points in time greatly affect how the health programs work and their effect. Earlier wars (and their effects), such as the two world wars and the Korean War, were very different from the Vietnam War, which was different from the first Iraq War, which was different from the second Iraq War. They are all likely to be different from future wars and other military actions. All of this was built into the overall strategy for the future Military Health System, which was reengineered to improve performance, and which adopted a force health protection program and was made more flexible to adjust to different futures.

The Population Model is also being used on the cross-cutting issue of vulnerability. Vulnerability is relevant at different points in time and across persons and life stages, and the model helps identify what ability and motivational factors at different points in time across persons and life stages would be determinants of vulnerability and thriving behavior. For example, applying new policies on financial assistance or taxes over the next 12 months will have very different effects across the population of persons. If the intent is to reduce financial vulnerability across the U.S. population, then the new policy(ies) should be modeled, at a minimum, against each subpopulation and,

Table 14.7

Population Model: Applying BEM at a Point in Time Across Persons and Their Life Stages

The Population Model use for achieving desired behavior is as follows:

1. Identify the population whose behavior is targeted.
2. Decide what point(s) in time and life stage(s) are to be addressed.
3. Decide what is the desired behavior or behaviors at different points in time across persons and their life stages.
4. Apply the BEM Model across time and across persons and their life stages, taking into account their different motivation, ability, and environmental variables.
5. Assess what interventions will best move projected behavior to desired behavior across time and across persons and their life stages.
6. Apply the interventions and assess their effect on a population on an ongoing basis.
7. Adjust the interventions as needed over time and based on result.
8. Feed the interventions into the Overall Strategy and Supporting Strategies.

preferably, against each "person." The more desirable policies would be the ones that both reduce vulnerability most for the most vulnerable and reduce vulnerability substantially for all persons. The most desirable policies are the ones that do this and continue the positive effect as the population moves through time (i.e., sustainable, reduced vulnerability for all people). As indicated earlier, the overall strategy has not been used to date, but is ready for application.

System(s) Model (Including "Ideal" Systems)

What Is It?

The System(s) Model views the world as a system of systems. When a strategy is being designed, it is important to determine what the target system is, what system it is part of, what its subsystems are, and what other systems it relates to. A system can be a community, a nation, or a broader area. It can be an issue area system such as a health system, an education system, or an ecological system. The Ideal Systems Model, developed by people such as industrial engineers (e.g., Gerald Nadler) decades ago, is another key model for looking at how well a system could perform and how to achieve the highest performance for that system (Figures 14.7 and 14.8).

How Does It Work?

For efforts to improve status to be successful and sustainable, the strategy and its execution needs to be systematic and must positively change a system (a whole community, a whole nation, or a whole broader area) of systems (e.g., health, education, employment/income, housing, habitat, climate) on a sustained basis (see Table 14.8).

Figure 14.7 **Ideal Systems Model**

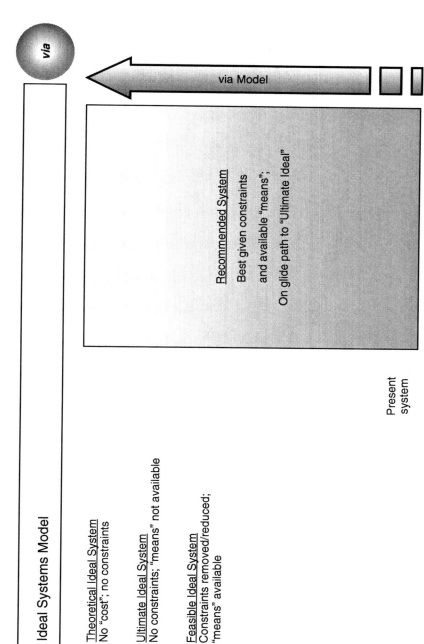

236

Figure 14.8 "System(s)" Model: Systems Impacting Status

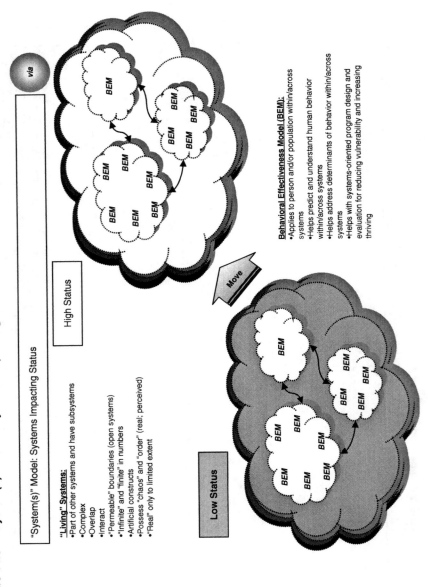

"System(s)" Model: Systems Impacting Status

High Status

"Living" Systems:
- Part of other systems and have subsystems
- Complex
- Overlap
- Interact
- "Permeable" boundaries (open systems)
- "Infinite" and "finite" in numbers
- Artificial constructs
- Possess "chaos" and "order" (real; perceived)
- "Real" only to limited extent

Low Status

Move

via

Behavioral Effectiveness Model (BEM):
- Applies to person and/or population within/across systems
- Helps predict and understand human behavior within/across systems
- Helps address determinants of behavior within/across systems
- Helps with systems-oriented program design and evaluation for reducing vulnerability and increasing thriving

Table 14.8

Systems Model: Systems Impacting Status

The Systems Model use for achieving desired status is as follows:

1. Identify the target system within which status is to be improved.
2. Identify other systems that are related and might either be impacted or have an impact.
3. Identify the status (lower than desired) for the current system and key characteristics of the current system.
4. Identify the desired status and characteristics for the future system using the Ideal Systems Model.
5. Identify the key behaviors in the current system and what they need to be in the future system.
6. Determine what changes need to be made to the current system to move it to the desired system.
7. Assess what interventions will best change the current system into the desired future system.
8. Apply the interventions and assess their effect on behavior change and on status.
9. Adjust the interventions as needed over time and based on result.
10. Feed the interventions into the Overall Strategy and Supporting Strategies.

In a Systems Model, there is recognition that systems are "living." They change internally, impact other systems, and are impacted by other systems. Systems are part of other systems and they have subsystems themselves. They are usually complex. They often overlap with other systems. They interact with other systems, sometimes fairly predictably and sometimes not. They often have permeable borders that are not always understood or constant. They may be nearly infinite in number. Often we apply an artificial construct to them to help us understand and work with them. Some systems are formal constructs (e.g., the British National Health Service system, the Kaiser Permanente system) and some are informal constructs (e.g., the American "health system"). They may be or appear to be "chaotic" or "ordered." They may be or appear to be "real."

To positively change a system (e.g., the American "health system") on a sustained basis, we need to understand the impact that existing and future systems will have on each person's or a population's status. We need to understand the impact that systems we create, change, or delete will have on other systems and, ultimately, on each person's status.

Within "human" systems are real people (individual persons, populations of persons) and organizations (made up of persons) whose behaviors collectively help determine the behavior of the system. The Behavioral Effectiveness Model helps us understand the behaviors and their determinants (ability, motivation, environmental factors) on an individual level and on the level of a population of individuals. In the Systems Model used here, there is recognition that moving from low status to high status requires moving individual behavior on a massive scale if it is a large system like the American "health system." This movement includes the persons we want to move to higher status and the persons who help or hinder that movement.

As shown in Figure 14.7, the Ideal Systems Model helps determine what the desired system should be. It starts out by assessing the current system. It then sets a theoretical ideal system, assuming there are no costs or constraints preventing us from reaching that system. The theoretical ideal is a guide but is not reachable in the real world for the foreseeable future. Then the model helps us think through the options between the current system and the theoretical ideal system. The ultimate ideal system is one that imposes no constraints but is not yet feasible because the "means" are not yet available. The feasible ideal system is one where the constraints are removed or reduced and the "means" are available. Finally, the recommended system is the best given the constraints and available means and is on the glide path to the ultimate ideal. The "via" Model helps in designing and assessing these different systems.

How Has It Been Used and How Has It Helped?

The Systems Model's (this adapted version) primary use to date has been for improving health. Its potential use is being explored in creating an overall strategy for reducing vulnerability and improving the status of a community, nation, or broader area.

One of its earliest uses was in the late 1970s, to design and execute an inner-city health system for Milwaukee, Wisconsin. The result was a new public/private multiclinic system providing preventive services, primary care, maternal and infant care, mental health care, dental care, and social services for the community's poorest and highest-risk people. The total system also included hospital services from public and private hospitals. The system operated successfully for over 30 years and has been viewed as a successful model for improving inner-city health care.

At the CMS, the Systems Model was used in 2006 to design the draft CMS Strategic and Operational Plan for 2007–2012. Rather than approaching the plan as a program-by-program plan or a CMS-only plan, the American "health system" was used as the framework. The plan was designed using the Ideal Systems Model to improve health across the total American population and to use the entire American "health system" to accomplish that. The strategies with the CMS plan were built on how best to move to high health status by using both CMS programs focused on Medicare and Medicaid beneficiaries and programs with broader scope. For example, CMS's quality improvement program has impact far beyond care for CMS beneficiaries. Similarly, CMS's payment programs serve as the driver for non-CMS payment programs (e.g., health insurers). The plan was designed to address the needs of both younger and older Medicaid beneficiaries, beneficiaries with disabilities, and healthier and severely ill Medicare beneficiaries. It also addressed the populations that are pre-Medicaid and pre-Medicare. These Systems

Model interventions were then used to develop the overall draft Strategic and Operational Plan for CMS.

For the Department of Defense (DoD) Military Health System, the model was used in the middle 1990s to work with a full set of DoD health-related programs. The Military Health System was handled as a system that encompassed health care for service members when not engaged in military action, for service members (including the Guard and Reserve) when engaged in military action, family members, retirees, Guard and Reserve in nonactive status, veterans served by other providers (e.g., VHA and private providers), preventive services for service members, and force health protection (including protective tools when deployed). The overall strategy for the MHS was built using the Ideal Systems Model coupled with other "futures" models. It included the health of all of these people, and all of the services needed to protect and improve their health. It included working with other entities, including the VHA and the Centers for Disease Control (CDC). All of this was built into the overall strategy for the future Military Health System, which was reengineered, adopted a force health protection program, and was made more effective and efficient, and more flexible to adjust to different futures.

The Systems Model is also being used on the cross-cutting issue of vulnerability. Because vulnerability is both personal and heavily affected by the "system" in which people live, the model is the best way to address both. Similar to what is shown in Figure 14.8, the idea is to move from low status (high vulnerability and low thriving) to high status (low vulnerability and high thriving). The Systems Model is the best way to accomplish that because it addresses the whole system (e.g., the United States) and yet has its impact on the person level. The Ideal Systems Model is used to determine what overall strategy would not only minimize vulnerability and maximize thriving at a point in time but also do it on a sustainable basis. The strategy identifies what status measures would be relevant at the systemwide level and at the individual-person level. It identifies the interventions and actions that would both reduce vulnerability the most for the most vulnerable and reduce vulnerability substantially for all persons. The Ideal Systems Model ensures that the strategy is one that does this in both the near and long term. As indicated earlier, to date, the overall strategy has not been used, but is ready for application.

The model's application to whole communities, nations, and broader areas is also being explored as a total system interacting with other systems outside. Building the set of status indicators, that is, assessing current and desired future status, is a critical step, given the breadth of such systems. The focus is on the whole population (and its individual whole persons), animals, plants, and natural resources within the targeted community, nation, or broader area. The full range of significant issue areas within the target community, nation, or broader area is explored, including their interaction and interdependency. The Ideal Systems Model is used to both set the vision and design the recommended systems for now and for the future. The intended result is an overall, sustainable, executable strategy for improving the status of a community, a nation, or a broader area.

Strategy Model

What Is It?

The Strategy Model builds on the groundwork discussed earlier, bringing it all together to develop and execute sustainable, effective strategies for improving status. It includes the model for building the strategies as well as the framework into which the strategies fit. The model includes both the overall strategy and supportive strategies and the actual interventions supporting the strategies (see Figure 14.9).

How Does It Work?

The model brings together all the previous information into an overall strategy and supportive strategies to improve status such as health, income, vulnerability, habitat, and climate (see Table 14.9).

How Has It Been Used and How Has It Helped?

The Strategy Model's primary application to date has been in the area of improving health. Its potential use is being explored to creating an overall strategy for reducing vulnerability and improving the status of a community, nation, or broader area.

At the CMS, the Strategy Model was used in 2006 to design the draft CMS Strategic and Operational Plan for 2007–2012. For each of the supportive strategies, a set of specific interventions were developed to make the plan fully operational. With respect to quality improvement for CMS, a more in-depth strategy was developed using the Strategy Model and in parallel with the overall CMS plan.

The model is being applied to the overall American health system, to try to answer how we would "achieve a healthy America" using the whole and enhanced health system. With similarities to the CMS plan, it helps create a strategy but with the larger scope of all Americans and all health providers.

The Strategy Model is also being used on the cross-cutting issue of vulnerability. As indicated earlier, to date the overall strategy has not been used but is ready for application. Similarly, the model is being used to build an overall strategic approach to addressing whole communities, nations, and broader areas.

Status Model

What Is It?

The Status Model identifies the desired and current status for the "whole" (e.g., community, nation, broader area), the issue areas (e.g., health, education), and cross-cutting issue areas (e.g., vulnerability, climate, habitat) targeted for posi-

Figure 14.9 **Strategy Model: Improve Status**

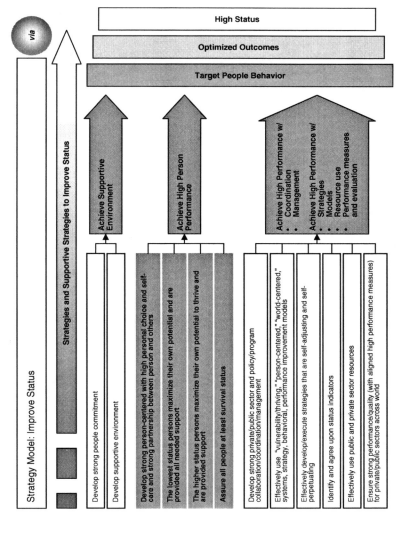

Source: Gary Christopherson, 2009; Adapted from Gerald Nadler, *Work Design: A Systems Concept* (Homewood, IL: R.D. Irwin, 1970).

Table 14.9

Strategy Model: Improve Status

The Strategy Model use for achieving desired status incorporates previous work from the other models and input and is as follows:

1. Load the desired status and the associated indicators.
2. Load the optimized outcomes that will best produce high status.
3. Load the target behaviors that will best produce the optimized outcomes.
4. Use the "channels" to connect how the Supportive strategies will best produce the target behavior. The "channels" are customized to the issue area or "whole."
5. Identify the specific supportive strategies that, working through the "channels," will best produce the target behaviors.
6. Execute the strategy and its supportive strategies effectively.
7. Assess the progress on improving status. Assess the effectiveness of the strategy and its supportive strategies.
8. Revise strategy and supportive strategies as needed to be effective and sustained over time.

tive, large-scale change. It also includes the status indicators and their supportive measures (see Figure 14.10).

How Does It Work?

For efforts to successfully create and sustain positive systems we need to determine how we are doing today, as we progress to the desired system, and when we achieve and sustain the desired system. The Status Model helps do that, as shown in Table 14.10.

How Has It Been Used and How Has It Helped?

The Status Model's primary use to date has been for improving health. Its potential use is being explored in creating an overall strategy for reducing vulnerability and improving the status of a community, nation, or broader area.

In both the draft CMS Strategic and Operational Plan (2006) and the work being done on how to "achieve a healthy America," the applications of the model are similar. Both include status indicators that apply across the United States. Both depend on more detailed measures to support and add depth to the indicators. The CMS approach focused a bit more on CMS beneficiaries but did include all Americans. The "healthy America" approach uses status indicators that would cover all Americans. The health status indicators address the person's ability and motivation to achieve high health status. The same is true for health care providers. These are more process indicators. The status indicators include outcomes of various treatments and other health interventions. They include what most consider as "health status" indicators such as low morbidity and mortality, high quality of

Figure 14.10 **Status Model**

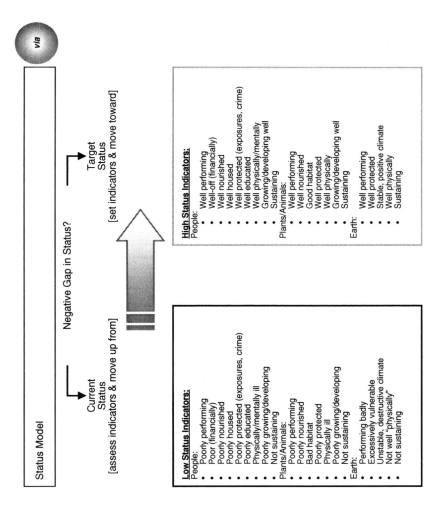

Table 14.10

Status Model

The Status Model is as follows:

1. Determine the issue area, cross-cutting area, or "whole" for which the strategy is targeted and status indicators are needed.
2. Decide how high, in general, the desired status is. Is it optimal? If not, how close can we get to optimal?
3. Identify all of the indicators that, as a set, indicate the desired high status. These are the "Target Status" set of indicators.
4. Decide what each indicator's level should be to match the desired high status.
5. Decide what each indicator's level is to describe low status.
6. To the extent needed, identify more detailed measures for each indicator.
7. Assess the "Current Status," that is, the current level of indicators for the target population.
8. Assess the "Negative Gap" between the current status and the desired target status. This is the gap to be closed with the overall strategy.
9. Execute the status model effectively and measure progress.
10. Assess the effectiveness of the status indicators.
11. Revise status indicators, individually and as a set, as needed to be effective.

life, high satisfaction, and low future risk for adverse events. Current status is assessed as well as the negative gap between future high health status and current lower health status.

In the cross-cutting work on human vulnerability, the primary status indicators being used are the ones in the overall model that apply to people. However, there are several others that are important in working on human vulnerability, including some of the "earth" and "plant/animal" indicators.

For the broader work on communities, nations, and broader areas, the full set of status indicators is very large but can be grouped into high-level categories with supportive measures. They should encompass all the significant indicators covering the full breadth of the target area. On the highest level, they must be meaningful enough to provide guidance on improving the whole target area as a whole system. They must be supported by measures that are clearly defined by data available into the future. Furthermore, the status indicators must be flexible enough to adjust to changing future conditions. With these status indicators, a strategy can be developed and its progress assessed.

The Path Ahead

As suggested, potential "next generation" models do exist for strategy at system (issue area, community, nation, broader area) and person levels. As proposed here, one such approach is the "via" strategy—a core set and system of supportive models addressing persons, systems, motivation, ability, behavior, performance and its improvement, process measures, and, most important, positive outcomes and improved status. Parts of the strategy can be used independently, but potentially they have more power, and are more likely to produce the best results, when used as a full set.

The path ahead offers many opportunities, as outlined in this chapter, to tackle large, complex issue areas, cross-cutting issues, and whole communities and nations. Already late, now is the time to aggressively apply "next generation" strategies for solving large problems and creating and sustaining positive, large-scale change.

Why? It is because our "mission" should be to build a better future, and our "vision" should be to achieve a future that is positive and sustainable.

Part IV

Is the Force Already with Us?

15

Reforms Needed to Meet Future Challenges

DWIGHT INK

Polls continue to show a dismal opinion of our federal government; some approval ratings are not far from single digits. True, the media contributes to these poll results by giving so much space to real and imagined shortcomings of government and so little to its achievements. Nevertheless, there are valid reasons for public concern as we lurch from one crisis to another, with war and an out-of-control national debt clouding our nation. Our difficulties in responding to Katrina and our failure to prevent the Gulf oil spill have further undermined public confidence. It is no wonder so many question our ability to meet the big challenges of this new century, many of which require rapid, well-coordinated action by a large number of organizations inside and outside the government. Yet, as one looks at the problems that have undermined recent responses, their solutions seem more possible than one might think. Understandably, the media is preoccupied with controversial policy issues, generally overshadowing the critical role of effective policy implementation. In their recent book, *If We Can Put a Man on the Moon . . .* , William Eggers and John O'Leary (2009) suggest that past successes in "getting the big things done in government" have shown how important renewed attention to effective policy execution will be to meeting future challenges. This chapter adds several suggestions on this theme.

Public administration observers are recognizing that any hope of success in meeting national challenges of the future will require a more comprehensive attack than we have employed in handling recent government crises—one that more successfully integrates many facets of federal government management. It will generally require attention to both vertical and horizontal dimensions of its structure and processes. Boldness will need to characterize the actions to be taken. Our government is too massive to change through timid, piecemeal approaches.

The following section reviews reasons so many earlier government efforts to reform have fallen short. It is followed by suggestions intended to move us toward a federal government better able to cope with the more critical challenges of the 21st century.

Operational Problems in Coping with Recent Crises

Policy questions about government shortcomings in handling recent crises have been well publicized. Less well known operational deficiencies have also contributed directly to the government's failures, including the inability to avoid crises in the first place. Several examples follow.

A more effective White House national security operation should have probed the reliability of intelligence reports concerning possible weapons of mass destruction (WMDs) in Iraq. The National Security Council seems to have been largely dysfunctional at the time. This operational problem at the highest level was then exacerbated by the tragic misuse of a czar role in the early days of rebuilding Iraq after its military defeat (Comarow and Ink 2009). The Katrina recovery debacle remains a textbook case in how to mismanage recovery from a disaster. More effective regulatory monitoring likely would have sensed the obvious danger of the growing volume of risky subprime loans that contributed to the costly banking crisis.

Contributing to the apparent failure of the Minerals Management Service (MMS) to carefully review the BP application for the deep water oil well that created the horrendous Gulf Oil spill was its weak staffing and the conflict of interest inherent in its badly designed organization. The Bush administration began to question the effectiveness of the agency; and the Obama administration became even more concerned. But there was little government capacity to rapidly analyze the extent of the MMS problems and better equip the agency to prevent disasters.

The more one looks at these recent crises, the more one realizes that it would not have been difficult to avoid several, or to have recovered more quickly and at lesser cost from those that were unavoidable. In none of these cases would these better outcomes have required expensive or highly sophisticated measures. Admittedly, stronger political leadership would have made a big difference. But the failure to organize the federal government properly and to provide experienced management leadership contributed heavily either to the unfolding of each crisis, or to the unsatisfactory recovery effort, or, at times, both.

We read about exciting new management developments in various agencies, some of them impressive. But these encouraging advances in specific activities obscure the more negative picture of getting the various parts of government to work together. Presidents inherit an executive branch that lacks a managerial capacity commensurate with the magnitude of its broader program responsibilities which cross over jurisdictional lines of agencies. As new challenges emerge, and additional programs are enacted to meet these challenges, government becomes more and more complex. Globalization adds to the complicated environment in which our government must function. In my opinion, the gap between demands on our government from ambitious national policies and our ability to meet them effectively is growing. These trends will likely continue. It is of the utmost importance that we find ways to address program needs that are more streamlined than the ways our current practices provide. We must develop a government that can move more quickly to prevent crises, and recover more rapidly from those that cannot be prevented.

The urgency for doing so seems especially clear as one considers the impact of potential attacks from a sophisticated terrorist group of the future. It is equally evident when one watches our current march toward a national fiscal crisis of unprecedented proportions. Although this formidable challenge is gaining a modicum of public awareness, we are ill prepared to take the required actions even when sound policies begin to take shape.

Advancing the federal government's capacity to handle major challenges of the future will require broad reform. Two are key: strengthen the political will to work across political lines and streamline government operations. This chapter deals with the latter.

Mobilizing Interagency Resources for Large Undertakings

Most large government undertakings require rapid mobilization of resources from many agencies, as well as from state and local governments and the private sector. These resources must be organized in a cohesive, coordinated effort, counter to the normal centrifugal forces of a sprawling bureaucratic system. Major crises require this to be done with great speed, no matter how complex the problem. Outcomes are measured in the short term. The larger challenges of the future will need the capacity to address a number of specialized management fields in an integrated fashion. Today, our government is ill equipped to meet those challenges.

In the case of natural disasters, the emergency response machinery must be in place within several hours, and the basic structure for the more complex and expensive recovery phase must be established within several days and operational in about two weeks. The Federal Emergency Management Agency (FEMA), when permitted to operate as intended, is reasonably well equipped to handle its immediate response role quite well in helping state and local governments. But the federal government is poorly equipped to handle the recovery from a catastrophic natural disaster or terrorist attack that is likely to be well beyond the capacity of state and local governments. Even in the case of a more slowly developing crisis, such as the fiscal crisis now looming, we tend to stumble our way slowly forward. Our inability to move quickly increases the cost of recovery substantially. Here are several suggestions for improving our capacity to handle large undertakings, especially recovering from crises.

Networking

Networking among federal agencies received little attention until the Lyndon Johnson administration brought the Assistant Secretaries for Administration Group into a more active collaborative role, and established the Federal Executive Boards in the field. Networking was the backbone of Johnson's Alaskan earthquake recovery program (see The White House 1964) described later in this chapter, involving nearly every federal, state, and local government organization, the private and nonprofit sectors, and the beleaguered citizens. All were woven together in community reconstruction recovery projects within several weeks of the earthquake. But the experience was not extrapolated to other large government endeavors.

President Richard Nixon did build on this Alaskan experience, and took a leap forward in applying several of the lessons learned throughout the domestic portion of government. The Undersecretaries Group was established, co-chaired by Patrick Moynihan, assistant to the president, and Phillip "Sam" Hughes, deputy director, Bureau of the Budget (BOB). With support from the Office of Executive Management (OEM) in BOB, the Assistant Secretaries Group also increased in stature during the first two Nixon years; their work spawned special interagency groups such as administrative services and financial management. Nixon established 10 interagency regional councils in the field that covered the whole nation. They provided federal-local linkage in hundreds of federally assisted programs.

This strong intergovernmental dimension included Bureau of the Budget circular A-95, which greatly enhanced state and local government collaborative planning and led to a large number of local councils of government being established across the nation. Institutionalized federal government networking reached its peak during the early 1970s, then lost ground.

However, a quarter-century later, we saw the impressive networking led by John Koskinen, deputy director for management at the Office of Management and Budget (OMB), in leading the Y2K program for President Clinton. His mission involved the identification, repair, and testing of millions of systems and data exchange points involving every government agency and major private company. Koskinen chaired the President's Council and established 25 working groups covering every critical sector of the country's infrastructure, with both public and private members. Koskinen and the council, working through the United Nations, developed an international network for sharing information and produced public status reports each quarter. The second international conference organized by the council included 170 countries, the largest single-issue meeting ever held at the United Nations.

Employing a very small staff and few special procedures, Koskinen was able to quickly put in place possibly the most comprehensive networking operation in history. Had he elected to follow conventional wisdom by setting up the typical large organization and endowing it with extensive operating procedures, it is likely that he would have spent most of his time planning the structure and systems and making them operational, resulting in chaotic information failure here and abroad.

There has been a revival of interest in networking, including some impressive examples at the regional and local levels. At the federal level, there have also been significant networking advances by some departments. In his Chapter 2, "From Conflict to Collaboration," William Eggers (see Eggers and O'Leary 2009) describes one such case, at the Department of Interior, called "cooperative conservatism" and strengthened by the issuance of Executive Order 13,352 in 2004 by President George W. Bush.

We need an OMB-led effort to establish a broad, institutionalized arrangement of networking that ties together federal agencies at different levels both in Washington and in the field. It needs to have an intergovernmental dimension, as well as a capacity to recognize the role of the private and nonprofit sectors. The future will present increasing circumstances in which a comprehensive networking capacity will be needed to bring about quick action in complex undertakings, as was demonstrated by the Alaskan and Y2K cases. However, developing the full networking capability of the government requires central leadership. Central guidance is also needed to ensure that institutionalized networking reduces red tape, rather than adds to it. Also, the advantages networking has to offer in fostering creativity and innovation should not be permitted to diffuse accountability. Today, OMB lacks the organization expertise to fulfill that leadership role, a deficiency that needs to be remedied.

Interdependence of Actions

Management leadership in the Executive Office of the President (EOP) and the departments has become fragmented. As a result of this stovepiping, we have lost the synergistic value of interdependence and lowered the influence management leaders exercise within the OMB and the departments. The strength of the director of the former OEM came about in part because of his active participation in the daily 7:30 A.M. West Wing meetings of the top White House staff. He was constantly called upon for consultation by White House staff and cabinet members on broad management issues of direct interest to the president's role, an occurrence not likely with the stovepiped management staff at OMB today.

The director of Johnson's Alaskan Disaster Recovery Commission was given tacit approval by the president and key congressional committees to streamline, or even suspend, any agency process that jeopardized the tight construction schedules required to save the state. This unprecedented flexibility has not been given since. It was possible only because the recovery operation (a) was conducted exclusively by highly experienced career leaders (under policies of able political leadership), (b) enjoyed unusually close linkage with Congress, (c) had in-depth General Accounting Office (GAO) oversight from the first days, and (d) operated with an unprecedented level of openness. For example, most formal hearings were suspended, as plans and decisions were all developed in public sessions where anyone could ask questions or voice opinions.

Quickly weaving together a series of bold, interdependent initiatives into a single comprehensive management reform saved the state of Alaska from ruin. A number of those operational tools are not available to crisis managers today.

Legislation should be passed that provides temporary grants of authority to take special actions during crises such as a catastrophic natural disaster or terrorist attack. This law would provide safeguards against abuse of those flexibilities: oversight provisions should be included. Congressional approval would be required in each instance. The president would be required to state at the beginning the conditions for the authority to expire. Should Congress not find that the conditions in a specific case warranted granting the authority, or regarded the proposed expiration conditions as too vague, the authority would not be granted.

White House Role

Brad Patterson's chapter in this volume (Chapter 16) describes the evolution of the role of White House staff. As he notes, top staff now play a very different role than the one recommended to Franklin D. Roosevelt by the Brownlow Commission. President Nixon initially sought to roll back the growing influence of the staff by proposing his ambitious reorganization to reduce the cases in which a single function sprawled across the organizational lines of many agencies. He nearly succeeded. But he became impatient with the deliberate pace of Congress and tried to accomplish his objectives by presidential action. Bypassing Congress proved an ill-advised move that quickly failed. No president has since proposed similar consolidation of federal agencies. It is unlikely that future consolidations will alter the trend toward strengthening the White House staff role. Therefore, it is important to consider how the White House staff can play a positive role in equipping the government to handle big undertakings.

The White House staff should include a presidential assistant with a background in managing large enterprises, as well as prior government experience. The assistant's role should not deal with specific structures and systems; that is the role of OMB. Rather, the assistant could utilize his or her White House influence to help OMB in bringing the executive branch together in support of important presidential initiatives or in response to major crises. The assistant would also be in a position to counsel other White House personnel on management implications of proposals before the president becomes committed. With access to the president, she or he could be of continuing help to the OMB deputy director for management in sharing the president's thinking on issues affecting the operation of government. This person would also be helpful to any other official (or so-called presidential czar) having a presidential assignment that cut across agency lines. Admittedly, there is some danger that the occupant would misuse his position and undermine, rather than reinforce, the work of a czar or OMB's deputy director. For that reason, this presidential assistant must have other assignments of significance, making her/him less tempted to do so. In directing presidential initiatives, I found such an ally in the White House to be of great help. These assistants served as liaisons to the White House, but not as channels through which the OEM had to go for access to others in the White House.

Role of Czars

President Obama uses a number of so-called czars, although the concept certainly did not originate with him. Persons appointed by the president to carry out an important task that cuts across agency lines are often labeled czars by the press, even though there is no such title. They have no legal authority; their influence depends on their relationship with the president.

If highly qualified, these appointees can be quite effective in helping a president handle an undertaking that cuts across departmental lines. They are especially useful in temporary assignments designed to help a president coordinate the work of several departments in accomplishing a specific task, after which they depart. Continuing assignments, especially when their mission is vague, are more likely to develop tensions with the affected departments, undermine accountability, and create distracting controversies for the president.

Much depends on how the role of a czar is defined and what relationships the czars develop with the affected agencies. Key to success is their ability to help department heads in carrying out their own responsibilities, rather than becoming competitors. In considering future presidential appointments of this type, the OMB should provide the president with suggestions on the role of the appointment, and the appointee's relationship with affected departments and the Congress.

Simplicity an Underlying Theme

We have fallen into a pattern of solving complex problems with complex solutions, when the opposite is often needed. We need to recall the KISS (keep it simple, stupid) approach to managing complex undertakings, even though some operations within a large undertaking may be anything but simple. Unnecessary complexity handicaps any operation, but the larger the number of government agencies and programs involved in an undertaking, the greater the penalty it exacts.

For a number of years the Atomic Energy Commission (AEC) and the National Aeronautics and Space Administration (NASA) were regarded as having top-flight management that could perform at a high level. This reputation came about because both agencies gave priority to (a) highly competent program and administrative managers, and (b) a decentralized operation, with a minimum amount of formal procedures. The AEC was helped by organic legislation that exempted the agency from federal procurement procedures and the Title V federal personnel regulations. The simplified management approaches encouraged innovation and facilitated fast-moving operations.

The need for arrangements that enable the government to handle disaster recoveries effectively is illustrated by the contrast between President Johnson's employment of an approach to the Alaskan earthquake disaster recovery and the cumbersome machinery used by President Bush in the slow Katrina recovery.

The only organization formally established for the Alaskan recovery was a commission created by executive order and composed of cabinet members. It was chaired by a powerful Senate ally. No new agency was established. Through the chairman, an unusually close relationship with Congress was established without adding a liaison office. No additional government positions were added to staff the commission. The executive director was on a six-months detail from the Atomic Energy Commission. The small, full-time professional staff of five were also detailees, as were the additional 11 part-time staff who continued to perform their usual agency responsibilities.

The executive director established nine interagency task forces to help in developing reconstruction and economic development plans, as well as a field committee of federal officials in Alaska to coordinate the rebuilding activities. None of these special organizations was given any legal authority, depending instead on the legal authority of the agencies they represented. These groups functioned as expediters, rather than another layer of government.

Most Alaskan field committee members were given authority to commit their agency to assignments of responsibility, reconstruction timetables, and funding. These field officials were of modest rank. There was no time to refer proposed actions back to Washington for review and approval. They had to come to meetings prepared to commit their agencies to actions and the necessary funding. Because the Alaskan recovery involved virtually every agency in the federal, state, and local governments, this simplified approach saved a huge amount of time and money.

Another measure that expedited recovery was the one described earlier, whereby the executive director was authorized to modify, or even suspend, any agency procedure that jeopardized reconstruction timetables.

These lessons were ignored by those designing President Johnson's Great Society programs in the 1960s. They believed that because the areas with which they were dealing were complicated, the assistance programs required detailed plans for Washington's approval, detailed operating procedures, and voluminous reporting, plus extensive auditing to assure compliance with the voluminous federal regulations. Many small communities simply did not have the staff to do everything required. As a result, some of the communities most in need of the assistance failed to receive funds. Studies showed that the percentage of funds going into overhead was often 40 to 60 percent, causing people to suspect foul play. Accountability was lost, buried in a sea of committees, and required concurrences.

The Nixon reengineering of these Great Society programs, called the "New Federalism," simplified the detailed plans requiring Washington approval. This reduced the steps involved in applications for federal assistance. One striking example involved a group of small health research programs where the steps required to approve applications, and the administrative costs involved, were both cut nearly 90 percent. A review by the GAO one year later concluded that there had been no deterioration in the quality of the programs and that the applicants were much better served.

The red tape slashing program of Nixon's New Federalism emphasized decentralization—the single most important element of his initiative to streamline federal domestic programs. Later decentralizations often faltered because of failure to understand the importance of (a) providing guidelines for the units receiving delegations of authority, (b) providing the training needed for the recipients to administer the delegated authorities effectively, (c) ensuring the capacity of the delegating organization to monitor the performance of the recipients, and (d) retaining the capacity to take quick corrective action when problems develop. Otherwise, decentralization of authority turns into abandonment of authority and accountability, leading to recentralization and new operating complexities.

Although there is no institutional capability to measure the value of government-wide programs to simplify government structures and systems, our experience has shown impressive results when programs are designed and managed properly. There is constant talk about the need to simplify. And there have been numerous limited projects. But our capacity to undertake a bold and determined drive across government under experienced leadership is missing. The penalty for this failure is most severe when the government is faced with crises requiring close interagency collaboration. The cumulative burden of excessive processes borne by the participating agencies rises exponentially when agencies are called upon to join forces in a common endeavor.

Under OMB leadership, a renewed program to streamline administrative and program processes needs to be launched throughout the federal government. It should include a strong decentralization component for discretionary programs.

As was done with Nixon's New Federalism, and with Carter's 1978 Civil Service Reform, described later in this chapter, each process should be rigorously reviewed in its entirety, not piecemeal. Flowcharting should record all steps that actually occurred in a sample of cases for each significant process, rather than the more typical recording of only those steps required by formal procedures.

When state and local governments are involved, their processes should be included. The resulting streamlined processes should then be audited to determine how well the recommendations have been implemented, and what impact the changes have had on the effectiveness of the activity.

Executive Office of the President

The most important single step to equipping the federal government to handle large undertakings better would be the restoration of a management arm in the Executive Office of the President. It should be more broadly based than the current, fragmented OMB organization, and linked less with the budget process. Such an office should have the expertise to help presidents with government organization, and provide leadership in establishing interagency and intergovernmental arrangements. It should lead a continuing government-wide drive to simplify structures and systems. Program management should be an important part of its agenda. It should foster interdependence of management areas of specialization.

Over many years, presidents had such help from the BOB and OMB. Don Stone and his small BOB management staff helped FDR organize the wartime agencies, and then close them after the war. He helped Truman and Paul Hoffman organize and staff the landmark Marshall Plan. Later, less than 48 hours after the 1964 Alaskan earthquake, the BOB director of the organization staff, Harold Seidman, presented President Johnson with the innovative organization concept for its recovery that proved so useful. This management staff then designed and led Nixon's

New Federalism (except for Revenue Sharing), his government-wide productivity enhancement program, as well as handling reorganization proposals such as OMB and the Environmental Protection Agency (EPA). At its peak, this staff played an important role in tracking and expediting implementation of presidential initiatives and in helping agencies streamline their operations.

Today, OMB has several statutory offices devoted to important specialized areas of financial management, acquisition, and regulatory review. Important as these are, they leave huge management gaps.

There is no longer any professional expertise in organizing or eliminating departments and agencies. This skill was sorely missed when a group of inexperienced people designed the huge Department of Homeland Security that has failed in dealing with disaster recoveries. OMB was not in a position to advise the White House on the controversial elimination of the United States Information Agency or the ill-advised burying of the United States Agency for International Development in the Department of State. Neither was professional advice available in the reorganization of intelligence agencies.

The OEM organization staff provided the leadership for developing the coordinating machinery for domestic programs built on institutionalized networking at the levels of undersecretaries, assistant secretaries, and regional field offices. The streamlining of discretionary domestic programs was a key objective of this earlier coordination activity. It was an essential tool in the program streamlining that characterized the New Federalism. This capability will be needed even more in handling large federal undertakings in the future requiring rapid planning and implementation.

Need for Intergovernmental Management

OEM also developed an active intergovernmental management capability in the executive branch that earned respect and support from the "Big Seven" public interest groups. These interagency and intergovernmental roles complemented each other in many governmental actions. The termination of the Advisory Commission on Intergovernmental Relations (ACIR) was a grievous mistake and should be reversed. However, intergovernmental management was performed through the leadership of OEM, not ACIR. Although both institutions should be restored, it is the executive branch capability that is an especially critical resource in dealing with catastrophic disasters.

A modernized version of the OEM leadership capacity for government organization and systems, especially those required to meet large, complex challenges, could be established very easily. OMB already has the authority to perform these functions. It simply does not carry out this role. OMB does perform specialized management functions. Therefore, it is reasonable to expect that cross-cutting management functions could be restored with a simple amendment that required OMB to establish such a staff. No turf issues need be involved.

An alternative would be to establish a separate independent Office of Federal Management within the EOP. Headed by a director experienced in managing large organizations, with access to the president when necessary, it would not be dominated by the budget process, a problem perceived as weakening the management part of OMB. On the other hand, if the appointment became a payoff to an inexperienced political donor, or the director lacked access to the president, the agency would not be productive.

Much of this reform agenda can be accomplished without legislation. But elements require congressional action. Securing support in Congress would be more likely if packaged as changes to enable government to respond to future crises, rather than a "good government measure."

Is Government Reform a Pipe Dream?

Significant reform, especially the capacity to handle crises, is wishful thinking if we continue to make the mistakes that have characterized recent reform efforts. Why would this agenda for change have any chance of success? In answering this question, it is useful to examine several problems that have weakened past efforts.

Failure to Base Reforms on the Facts

It is surprising how we have launched important reforms without understanding the problem we are trying to solve. An example was the ill-designed slashing of the federal workforce near the end of the last century. Loosely linked to the Reinventing Government movement, the major cuts in federal staff bore no relationship to effective government. Instead, they were based on political objectives. No studies were made that might have led to reductions that would have been warranted. There was a strained rationale based on a superficial comparison with private sector spans of control. This misleading analysis was then used to conclude that middle management in federal agencies consisted of superfluous bureaucrats. One unfortunate result was the elimination of many contract administrators, without whom the government could not manage its thousands of contracts effectively. The impact of this unwise action was greatly compounded by the strong surge in outsourcing government services, increasing the need for qualified contract managers at the very time they were being sharply reduced in number. The resulting costs in delays, money, and program outcomes have been enormous over the years.

The value of establishing the facts before designing reforms can be illustrated by two successful reforms: President Nixon's New Federalism and President Carter's Civil Service Reform.

Nixon's New Federalism provided the framework for arguably the most comprehensive reform in the management of our domestic programs, beginning with those that provided assistance to states and communities. The need for action had become clear. But what those actions should be had generated widely diverse ideas, most of which were conceptual rather than specific. Nixon moved forward with a bold and comprehensive set of reforms that were initially derided as typical of a new president. However, by basing his actions on hard data, rather than conventional opinions that were often misleading, he was able to move forward quickly and confidently with a wide range of interrelated initiatives.

Under the leadership of the Office of Executive Management in the Bureau of the Budget, the country was divided into 10 regions for delivery of domestic programs, each with a regional city and a regional council that consisted of the top field officials in that region. Task forces in each agency were established to recommend specific steps to streamline the assistance programs. Data flowed in from these regional councils and from the "Big Seven" public interest groups (PIGS). Extensive flowcharting was done, often including the combined steps of federal, state, and local governments. They reflected the actual steps taken in a sample of typical cases, not the much simpler steps prescribed by formal procedures. Despite unprecedented deadlines for streamlining hundreds of programs, a massive amount of information was assembled for use by the task forces before they settled on actions to be taken. Similar reviews were then extended to other government activities. There was widespread skepticism about the feasibility of attempting the sweeping changes envisaged by this reform that initially alarmed scores of special interest groups. However, because they were so thoroughly grounded in a factual base, the president was able to make dramatic changes that affected every state and community in the nation.

Similarly, staff recommendations for President Carter's Civil Service Reform were forwarded to the president and Congress only after nine task forces had examined a wide range of issues in depth and solicited the views of hundreds of organizations and thousands of federal employees. An additional task force flowcharted the processing of each major personnel function before recommending reforms. These data turned on their head several widely held notions of why poor-performing employees could not be removed. Rather than union-instigated special legal protections, which most thought to be the cause, poor management of employees was shown to be the overwhelming reason for failure to act. For example, in surprisingly few instances were management's performance expectations made clear to the employee. Rarely was poor performance addressed at an early stage and the employee given an opportunity to improve. Training was rarely adequate. In the absence of good management to improve performance, frustrated managers often took adverse actions precipitously, resulting in lengthy appellate processes that denied the actions that conventional wisdom chalked up to restrictive laws.

The broad scope of Carter's civil service review was regarded as highly unrealistic. Unions failed to pay attention to it until the recommendations were well along in development. Because the recommendations were bolstered by an in-depth set of facts, Congress exhibited confidence in them. It enacted most of the president's proposals as the most comprehensive reform of the federal personnel system since its inception in 1883.

Of course, crises severely limit the time available for fact-finding. But this is a problem that is overstated. In times of crisis, fact-finding can be expedited dramatically. Experience has also shown the importance of making sure the White House is drawing upon experienced leaders who thoroughly understand the federal organizations and processes involved. They should not be political appointees learning the territory while trying to cope with a catastrophic disaster. The disaster recovery team will frequently need to include engineering and scientific expertise from around the nation and even overseas.

OMB has provided strong leadership in improving the linkage between the budget and credible performance indicators. With respect to presidential initiatives directed toward management reforms, however, OMB has lost much of its capacity to ensure thoroughly researched fact gathering before initiatives are launched. This capacity needs to be strengthened.

Slow to Gear Up

Incoming administrations are slow to launch government reforms; this often establishes a pattern that handicaps the government in mobilizing the resources to meet later crises. The first years of Reinventing Government and the Bush Management Agenda were occupied with deciding what to do. The second years were spent developing specific plans to implement concepts produced the first year. The best opportunities for launching major initiatives occur during the first months in office.

One reason management initiatives are late is a view that the new president's team must first use all its resources translating campaign rhetoric into specific policy initiatives, especially those that have to be sold to Congress. After those are developed, inauguration has taken place. New cabinet members have been confirmed and are comfortably in charge of their departments and agencies. Only then can the president's team turn to consideration of how the new initiatives are to be managed. This unfortunate de-linkage of policy and policy implementation at the outset leads to implementation difficulties and disappointing outcomes throughout a presidency. There are always some department heads with sufficient experience and initiative to overcome this, but most do not. Transition teams do not realize how vulnerable the country is to sudden crises because they fail to address the management dimension of the new administration.

Parliamentary countries do better in preparing new leadership for both policy and policy execution. Our system makes the task of marrying the two essential elements of action more difficult. We can do much better.

The quickest start for presidential management reform was under President Nixon. The day after inauguration he sent a proposal to the Hill to provide him with authority to send reorganization plans to Congress for an up or down vote, authority quickly granted. On March 17, 1969, less than two months after taking office, Nixon ordered 10 departments and agencies to decentralize, to streamline assistance to states and communities, and to strengthen interagency coordination in working with states and communities. The same day, he ordered departments with the most grant-in-aid programs to install 10 standard regions with standard regional cities so that "all agencies involved in social or economic programs requiring interagency or intergovernmental coordination" could have common administrative boundaries and regional field office locations. These were specific actions to carry out the most comprehensive changes of federal field operations ever proposed, not simply announcing an intent to develop plans. One week later, Robert Mayo, director of the Bureau of the Budget, requested a progress report by May 1, 1969, of actions taken.

This fast beginning was due to extensive management planning during Nixon's transition period, rather than putting management on the back burner until after inauguration. This made possible bold Nixon management reforms while he had the political capital to succeed. It elevated management to an integral part of accomplishing presidential program initiatives where it remained throughout his first term. This management focus declined sharply during the 1972 presidential campaign and the Watergate disaster that destroyed his presidency.

President-elect Carter's transition team gave serious consideration to civil service reform, enabling that effort to begin early. President-elect Reagan established a small management office as part of his transition team, a move that helped develop plans for the first months of his presidency. But, for the most part, incoming administrations have given little attention during the transition to actions to be taken after taking office that relate to government operations. Thousands of pages of transition material covering detailed administrative processes are written. But little is developed for the broad strategies to mobilize the resources of the government to recover from major crises or for large undertakings to carry out key campaign promises. It is not difficult or expensive to give attention to the government's capacity to execute the policies advanced by the president-elect once he or she takes office, thereby enhancing the chances of success.

Poor Congressional Relations

The current level of partisanship has made the functioning of government so difficult that few believe it possible to restore the cooperation with Congress required to support management reforms. I believe we have departed so far from earlier successful approaches to Congress that we no longer realize what may be possible.

As point man on presidential initiatives, I found a bipartisan approach with Congress usually possible on management issues even when the general political climate was volatile. With presidential approval for an initiative requiring congressional action, I met jointly with key committee chairs and ranking minority members to outline what the president wished to accomplish and why the president believed that the proposal would improve government operations. At times, this was quite difficult to do. But the fact that I was speaking for the president usually gave me the entrée I needed. Also, in nearly every case, it was possible to align the president's objectives with one previously espoused by the committee, even though there might be acrimonious debate over other issues. To the extent possible, we isolated the proposed management-focused legislation from partisan issues that might then be raging, including those related to the budget. As we fleshed out the details of the bill, we worked with committee staff, jointly with majority and minority to the extent possible. This continuing dialogue produced ideas that both improved the bill and enhanced the likelihood of its passage. It also developed a measure of congressional ownership in the bill, providing an incentive to work with the president in ensuring passage.

We found it advantageous to practice a high level of transparency in our work. That appealed to our committees. For example, we invited congressional staff to staff meetings while designing President Carter's Civil Service Reform. They seldom attended, but the opportunity to do so instilled congressional confidence in the integrity of our work. When directing the 1964 Alaskan earthquake recovery, I detailed several highly qualified congressional staff members to my staff. They not only performed superbly for me, but kept two key congressional committees informed of our progress and our setbacks, establishing a level of confidence in our work no level of my reporting could provide. Combined with the fact that the chair was a senator, it contributed to our ability to break through a bitter 57-day civil rights filibuster, enabling us to pass urgently needed disaster legislation when no other legislation moved. I invited key congressional staff to several of our staff meetings while closing the antipoverty agency; GAO staff members were always welcome.

There were times when we agreed to disagree with congressional leaders. But the end result of our collaborative efforts was that the president had a high success record on government operations issues, without rejection of any major initiatives. Cooperation increased presidential strength, rather than weakened it, as some would assert. Presidential objections to adverse congressional suggestions were taken seriously on the Hill, and contributed to success in killing most of them. When encountering the occasional member who took advantage of this openness by releasing draft documents or misrepresenting informal comments made during consultations, our broad congressional support enabled us to take countermeasures with that member without undermining other relationships.

Admittedly, the political acrimony in Washington makes a return to collaboration on management reform difficult. But I believe we would be surprised at the result of adapting earlier successful approaches with Congress together with new ideas attuned to the current environment. Success would require skill and patience. Especially important would be taking time to develop a high level of trust and mutual respect that can surmount disagreements. It is worth recalling that many of the delegates to our Constitutional Convention, including George Washington, thought it unlikely that they could produce much of value. Yet they managed to emerge with a comprehensive organizational plan despite a series of highly emotional, fundamental conflicts that underlay the initial pessimism; large colonies vs. small ones, northern colonies vs. southern, and slave vs. nonslave.

The OMB management and budget staff relationship has a significant bearing on congressional relations. Whereas the management staff members benefit from exchanging information with those concerned primarily with the budget, involving management initiatives in the issue-laden budget process is a different matter. By removing the OMB management staff from the budget process and the controversial political issues inevitably involved in the budget, there would be a greater chance of being able to advance management initiatives on the Hill. The type of congressional relations that were successful in the past could be more easily adapted to persuading Congress to partner in new management reforms. Conversely, at times there are bold management proposals with controversial provisions that should not encumber the selling of the president's budget.

Poor Utilization of Career Service

Many presidential candidates campaign against Washington and promise that, if elected, they will take government from the bureaucrats and "give it back to the people." Career leaders are not those who incoming political appointees intend to turn for help to bring about reform. Yet the success of the new president in bringing about change will be limited to mere rhetoric without the full engagement of the career service. Few recognize this fact; the involvement of careerists in developing new initiatives is rarely done well these days. Seldom is a broad cross-section of employees, including those in the field, actively engaged in planning how initiatives can be implemented.

Will future White House and departmental political leaders better appreciate the career service resources they inherited? Or will they proceed under the illusion that they can reform government without the career service playing a major role? Several examples of earlier reform efforts are relevant.

President Reagan's Grace Commission task forces sharply limited the involvement of careerists. They were interviewed, but played little role in developing recommendations. Nevertheless, several task forces did develop useful recommendations for change, only to be overruled by Grace and his close associates. Those task forces were thought by Grace to "have been co-opted by the natives." Greater trust in career leaders, and better utilization of their knowledge, would have resulted in the Commission accomplishing much more.

Reinventing Government's National Performance Review produced a number of constructive recommendations. But implementation was handicapped by a flawed concept of how to utilize the career service. Locating reform leadership for implementation in a political office, rather than in an institutionalized organization such as OMB, made it difficult to engage the career service effectively. Few of those in lower-level headquarters positions or in the field were engaged in a meaningful way. They never developed a good grasp of what was expected and certainly had no sense of ownership. Few gave more than lip service to the well-intentioned program, contributing to disappointing results. Reinventing Government did engage a small number of career people in steering groups near the heads of departments and agencies, giving the vice president and White House staff the impression of broader government engagement and support than existed.

The Bush Management Agenda was led by OMB, with a stronger institutional capacity to reach the various levels of the federal government. But it did not do particularly well in engaging career people throughout government in the development of the agenda or in planning its implementation. Some departments made little effort to involve the field, and OMB had lost its capacity to engage the field years earlier. The New Federalism and the Civil Service Reform, with which I am familiar, suggest the value of relying heavily on career leaders for true government reform.

The New Federalism, which played such a prominent role in the Nixon administration, was designed and implemented exclusively by career men and women, and quickly gained the support of Nixon and the White House staff. The leadership was provided by the Office of Executive Management in the BOB (later the OMB). Much of Nixon's departmental reorganization program, the most ambitious ever advanced, was suggested by the president's Ash Council. But design of the various legislative proposals, and the selling of the proposals to Congress, were all led by career people. The proposal to create the EPA was conceived by career staff, although it would not have been adopted by Nixon without the support of the Ash Council. OEM led the successful drive for congressional support of the agency, as it also did for establishing OMB and other reorganization proposals.

Significant concepts of President Carter's Civil Service Reform first gained impetus in discussions within the National Academy of Public Administration (NAPA), composed primarily of current and former career leaders in government. An October 1976 NAPA symposium, "The President and the Executive," composed of its most illustrious leaders, urged that the president-elect (Carter) support a thorough comprehensive study of the federal civil service system, a recommendation well received by Carter's transition team. Combined with strong support from Scotty Campbell, dean of the Maxwell School at Syracuse University, it was instrumental in Carter's decision to proceed. All nine task forces established to design the proposed reform were staffed by current or former career men and women. All but one was chaired by current or former career personnel. The executive director in charge of the task forces was a careerist. The recommendations of the director were forwarded to President Carter and the Congress without change; most were enacted into the Civil Service Reform Act (CSRA).

There continue to be political appointees who believe the first step upon taking office is to "establish control of the bureaucrats." That includes freezing career service out of the design of reforms and minimizing their role in implementation. These appointees regard career service members as lacking initiative, incapable of innovation, and unreliable holdovers, too strongly tied to a prior administration to be trusted with helping the new president. This view was shown to be wrong by the critical role the career service played in President Reagan's elimination of the antipoverty independent agency, the Community Services Administration (CSA). This was the acid test of whether the career service would implement presidential policies with which they totally disagreed.

Reagan's announced intention to eliminate the agency was expected to provide a focal point for opposition to his administration. This was perceived as the action that would most clearly personify his big business view, which ignored the plight of minorities and the poor. Protest marches and huge rallies across the nation were predicted, with Congress expected to easily block the closure. Fueling much of this opposition would be the activist CSA employees who would bend every effort to undermine the president. Any right-wing conservative director chosen to lead the closure would soon find himself under siege in his office, ensconced with a handful of despised political aides.

None of this happened. Instead of a political campaign donor, Reagan appointed an experienced career person to head the agency. Although this new administrator agreed that the time had come to eliminate the agency, he trusted the career service and believed that successful closure depended on them. Against the advice of right-wing leaders, he refused to replace the career regional administrators with political appointees. Moving in the opposite direction, career people replaced former political appointees in recommending all grants and contracts. Previously, careerists had not been permitted to recommend these awards; actions were left to political appointees who seldom understood the programs well enough to make the best program judgments, but were in a position to include political considerations in the dispensing of federal funds. With front office encouragement, career employees initiated innovative approaches to closure. Although none of the employees agreed with the closure that would end their employment and the programs they supported, they responded to the president's policy decision with hard work rather than the activist undermining so widely predicted. Because of their knowledge of how government worked, and their dedicated effort, the agency was closed only seven weeks after Congress agreed—a remarkable accomplishment.

A few years ago, a Department of Energy career leader, Jessie Roberson, directed a remarkable reform of the controversial approach that had been followed in the cleanup and closure of the Rocky Flats facilities, near Denver, Colorado, containing radioactive structures and high-level nuclear wastes. Closure was expected to take decades. As a new manager of Rocky Flats, Ms. Roberson changed all that. Through technical and managerial innovation by the small federal workforce and its contractors (in combination with a fundamental change in contracting), decades of time and billions of dollars were saved. The political leadership of the department established ambitious goals and provided the support essential for her to proceed with changes. But the design and implementation were done by career personnel.

These cases illustrate the importance of reliance on career leaders—and full engagement of the career service at all levels—in meeting the difficult challenge of reform. Management reforms under Nixon were arguably the most comprehensive advanced by any president. Based on recommendations from career task forces, the CSRA was the most comprehensive reform of the federal personnel system since the 1883 Pendleton Act. President Johnson enabled careerists to change disaster recovery operations. The elimination of an independent federal agency, the CSA, was done through management innovations developed and led by a career leader. A career manager directed the Rocky Flats closure, one of the success stories of recent times.

There have been few comparable examples of political leaders having designed and implemented government reforms as successful as these handled by experienced career personnel. To meet future challenges, we need to restore confidence in the ability of career personnel to design and implement change and reform.

Utilizing career leaders in leadership operational roles requires investing in their training and development, always a hard sell under tight budgets. Diversified senior management experience is an essential part of developing high performers. This was one of the reasons for establishing the Senior Executive Service (SES). Yet the mobility component of the SES has been ignored or mismanaged, at times abused in ways that made the SES more vulnerable to politicization. During the George H. W. Bush administration, Office of Personnel Management (OPM) began to develop a more comprehensive career-long development program for employees from entry through the SES. But it was not pursued after Bush left office. The current OPM director is trying again to move in this direction; his initiative deserves strong support. It should phase in a new framework for mobility. For example, experience in more than one major organization should be a requirement for advancing to the SES, with more mobility opportunities after entering the service. Field experience should earn credit for advancement. Mobility assignments should be an integral part of career development, carefully considering both the development of the employee and the needs of the receiving organization. OMB needs to provide continuing support to OPM in the mobility feature of the SES.

Mobility should not be mandatory for those following a technical career. However, a modified form of mobility for technical careerists is often useful, such as experience in different components of the same program or even among closely related technical programs in other agencies.

To strengthen the leadership role of OPM, and ensure continuity of an active mobility program from one administration to another, the CSRA should be amended to formalize the mobility feature of the SES. The legislation should be enabling rather than prescriptive; mobility programs need to be flexible and adaptable to changing circumstances.

Role of Political Appointees Undervalued

Having stressed the importance of relying on the career service to design and implement major government undertakings, it is important to enhance the equally essential, but different, role played by political appointees.

It is the president and the president's team of top political appointees who develop the broad policies within which the career service works. These policies can be shaped in ways that facilitate effective implementation, or they can make implementation unduly costly and ineffective. It is the job of the political leadership to provide an environment conducive to career service innovation and initiative. Some do. Others provide a negative environment that discourages innovation and productivity. It is also the responsibility of political leaders to track performance and ensure that career service leaders are effective. But their backgrounds do not often equip them well for this role.

Greater attention needs to be given to how the political appointees can be most effective in increasing the capability of the federal government to handle large operations, especially in times of crisis.

Congress can help. Policy issues require much of the attention during confirmation hearings. But more time is needed to examine the qualifications of department officials to help the president carry out his constitutional role as chief executive. One way would be to illuminate this role and its importance in successful outcomes in programs authorized and funded by Congress.

A presidential commission should be established to review the role of political appointees insofar as it can impact the operation of an agency, both positively and negatively. It would not address their political role or their policymaking. Jim Webb of NASA fame had a tremendously positive impact on how successful his agency was. So did John McCone in turning around the performance of the controversial Atomic Energy Commission in only four months. In the area of national security, high marks for operational success are generally given the former secretary of defense, Frank Carlucci, and the former deputy secretary of defense, David Packard. Former FEMA director James Witt is widely credited with rescuing a troubled agency and making it a success story.

It is not difficult to think of other appointees whose impact on operations has been negative. The increase in political appointees over the years has drawn considerable criticism. Paul Light has described how this trend has contributed to the "thickening of government" (Light 1995). New layers of departmental structure are believed to have increased the complexity of departmental operations and diffused accountability. Lower-level appointees often have vague, shadowy roles that complicate the work of career leaders. Especially troublesome is the extent to which these appointments have limited opportunities for career leaders to fill leadership positions.

This commission should examine those political leaders who were especially successful in energizing the career service and effective in fostering innovation. How were they characterized? What were the positive sides? What were the negative ones? How can political leaders exercise their departmental oversight role effectively? What types of background seem to best equip political appointees to provide an environment that maximizes career service performance? Has the increase in lower-level appointees had the negative consequences described earlier?

Should their role be similar to that found in other countries where they more clearly confine their work to policy?

The commission should be composed of former heads of departments and agencies that were regarded as high performers. Two members should have high-level career service in several agencies. A former governor might be included. The chair must have a proven record in leading at least one government department or independent agency.

Political-Career Partnership

In carrying out the roles in which political appointees are accountable for policy, and career employees are accountable for policy execution, each must appreciate the role of the other and the interdependence of these two basic components of public service. In the successful examples cited earlier, political and career leaders functioned as partners, with the political leader the senior partner. A partnership requires communication and trust we seldom see, especially during the first months of a presidency. It must exist from day one when dealing with a catastrophic disaster or terrorist attack. This partnership concept needs to become a part of the orientation of new employees and political appointees. It is a concept that should be more actively encouraged and nurtured by OPM and OMB.

Recommended Actions

Without a broadened central management leadership capacity, the changes proposed in this chapter cannot make a difference. The organic OMB legislation should be amended to require the establishment of an office to provide leadership for government organization and systems not prescribed for other statutory offices. It would be comparable to the existing statutory organizations for financial management, procurement, and review of regulations. No additional OMB authority is needed; the recommended functions were previously performed in the BOB and OMB under existing authority. Since OMB leadership has declined to assign staff to carry out these functions, statutory direction to renew their performance is needed.

This office should be headed by a person with substantial government operating experience. Private sector experience could also be useful, but not at the expense of assuring current or prior government service.

Areas to be addressed by this new OMB management capacity should include:

- Integration of program management and administrative management into one overarching design of program delivery systems.
- Simplification of actions throughout government, reversing the current trend toward greater structural and systems complexity. Streamlining measures should be accompanied by greater transparency and careful monitoring to guard against abuse of the flexibility provided by these actions.

- Involvement in new program initiatives to ensure that the workability dimensions are included in their design.
- Design of new departments and agencies, and reorganizing or eliminating existing ones.
- Development of guidance on the role of so-called presidential czars and their relationship with affected departments. This would be advisory.
- Establishment of institutionalized interagency and intergovernmental networking arrangements. These need central monitoring to ensure that they expedite governance, rather than evolving as additional layers of bureaucracy.

The increased OMB capacity would be used primarily to (a) help departments and agencies strengthen their own capacity to manage, and (b) serve as a presidential arm in mobilizing the resources of agencies into an integrated team for handling crises and other large undertakings. Any OMB effort to manage departments and agencies would be counterproductive and must be avoided.

After establishing policies and goals, department heads and the White House should rely more on career leaders for design and implementation of large reforms and in recoveries from catastrophic disasters or terrorist attacks that overwhelm state and local governments. Because of their detailed knowledge of government and how it works, experience has shown they are in the best position to assess what needs to get done and to act.

This heavier reliance on career personnel requires action by the Office of Personnel Management to establish a broader program of career development. A new, broader OPM program would strengthen the mobility feature of the CSRA, as well as amend the CSRA to ensure the establishment of a government-wide mobility program and its continuity from one administration to another.

A presidential commission should be established to review ways in which political appointees can provide effective leadership for career personnel in the operation of their agencies. This commission would examine approaches used by political appointees who have been especially successful in utilizing career personnel and encouraging innovation. What approaches have characterized appointees who have failed? What backgrounds have helped to equip appointees for their government leadership roles? The commission agenda would not include their policy or political roles except as they affect agency operations.

OMB and OPM should help political appointees and career leaders develop the partnership type of relationship that has characterized so many large, successful undertakings of government in the past.

Legislation is needed to provide temporary grants of authority to modify or suspend agency procedures that jeopardize timely recovery from natural disasters or terrorist attacks. None of these actions could, by themselves, restore public confidence in government's ability to meet its obligations. But as a package, they would make a huge difference in the capacity of the federal government to carry out major reforms and meet future challenges and crises.

References

Comarow, Murray B., and Dwight Ink. 2009. American Czars. National Academy of Public Administration (NAPA). Unpublished manuscript.

Eggers, William D., and J. O'Leary. 2009. *If We Can Put a Man on the Moon . . . Getting Big Things Done in Government.* Boston: Harvard Business School Press.

Ink, Dwight. 2001. "The President's Managerial Leadership Responsibilities." In *Triumphs and Tragedies of the Modern Presidency,* ed. David Abshire, pp. 244–267. Westport, CT: Praeger.

Light, P. C. 1995. *Thickening Government: Federal Hierarchy and the Diffusion of Accountability.* Washington, DC: Brookings Institution Press.

The White House. 1964. "Establishing the Federal Reconstruction and Development Planning Commission for Alaska." Executive Order no. 11,150. *Code of Federal Regulations.*

16

American Governance

The Role of the White House Staff

Brad Patterson

Governance from the White House: A Bit of History

On November 20, 1969, the news ticker spat out the headlines:
"Indians seize Alcatraz!"

In Richard M. Nixon's White House, Leonard Garment was special counsel to the president; I was Garment's executive assistant. "Which agency has jurisdiction over Alcatraz?" Garment demanded. I checked: it was the General Services Administration (GSA)—which handled surplus federal real property; the abandoned island was surplus (with only a GSA custodian on duty). The GSA was headed by Robert Kunzig, a senate-confirmed presidential appointee. Garment telephoned Kunzig: "What are you planning to do with the Indians on Alcatraz?" "Simple," the administrator responded, "We are calling in the federal marshals and we will have the Indians out of there by noon tomorrow." Garment, from the White House, instantly countermanded Kunzig: "You will do nothing of the sort! Such an action would likely involve violence and violence is no longer our method of dealing with Native Americans. Call off your cops!" Kunzig was unapologetic. "I am a presidentially appointed agency head and that piece of federal property is my responsibility." With his White House voice Garment told Kunzig to do exactly what he had instructed. Kunzig, infuriated, snarled "I'll never talk to you again!" and slammed down the phone.

Garment's office reached out and contacted GSA's regional administrator in San Francisco, who, taking a boat out to the island, brought candy and cigarettes to the Indian invaders and talked with them, thereby providing the White House with on-the-spot information about what was happening on the island.

Garment convened, and chaired, an interagency group to discuss what the next steps might be to be helpful to the San Francisco urban Indians, from which the Alcatraz occupiers came. A special White House emissary (a gent from the vice president's staff) was picked and he in turn made several trips to Alcatraz trying to negotiate with the Indians.

The media carried the Alcatraz story heavily. Entertainment stars (Merv Griffin and Jane Fonda) visited the island; Republican senator George Murphy called for Alcatraz to be made into an "Indian National Park." Politics was never far from the picture: Ethel Kennedy went out to the island, and later in a lengthy phone conversation needled Garment to be more forthcoming as to the Indians' point of view. Indians destroyed the controls for the Alcatraz lighthouse; maritime merchants complained about dangers to bay boating. The *San Francisco Chronicle* loaned the Indians generators, illustrating how the press not only covers a newsy story, but helps keep it alive. Sixteen months of palaver went nowhere; Indian numbers and media interest declined.

In June 1971, 35 marshals peacefully escorted the 15 remaining Indians off the island. The *San Francisco Examiner* commented: "The federal government wisely let the Indians play out their string."

During the remaining three and a half years of the Nixon administration the same group of activists from the American Indian Movement (AIM) perpetrated two more crises, both of them more threatening than the Alcatraz escapade: the occupation of the Bureau of Indian Affairs building in Washington, and the seizure of the village of Wounded Knee, in South Dakota. In both of these instances, the White House (Garment and I) took the lead in setting the policies that were employed (of firmness but restraint) and, in person, handled the negotiations with the Indian organizers—who themselves were consummate experts in guerrilla theater (Patterson 1988, pp. 72–81).

Did Garment break the rules about how White House staff should operate? Presidential scholars still remember Franklin D. Roosevelt's instructions when he established the White House staff by his Executive Order 8248 in September 1939: "In no event shall the Administrative Assistants be interposed between the President and the head of any department or agency, or between the President and any one of the divisions in the Executive Office of the President." Garment was perfectly aware of this, but he was equally aware of President Richard Nixon's own personal interest in and compassion for Native Americans. He correctly interpreted what he knew would be Nixon's own determination—and Kunzig never tried to appeal the order Garment gave him.

Senior White House staffers constantly transmit presidential decisions to cabinet and agency heads and officers. Those transmissions are often relayed with both urgency and vigor—and may even seem authoritarian. Every cabinet officer of course has the right of appeal. Woe is unto the junior White House officer who, out of bounds, gets caught trying to play president.

Strategic and Frequent Tactical Management of National Security Affairs: These Are White House Functions

There are doubters about that proposition. Twenty-five hundred years ago, Chinese adviser Sun Tzu wrote: "He will win who has military capacity and is not interfered with by the sovereign." Some officers in the Pentagon are still imbued with that sentiment. In 1855,

> After a whole series of pedantic suggestions from the Emperor Napoleon III had poured into French Headquarters [in the Crimea] Marshal Jean Baptiste Vaillant curtly wired back "It is impossible to discuss strategy by telegraph." Whereupon the Emperor replied: "I do not discuss; I give orders." To this, Vaillant's terse report was: "You cannot command an army from the Tuilleries." (Patterson 1988, p. 65)

It would take a whole book—in fact there are scores of books already extant—to describe how the White House, especially in the past 70 years of American governance, has more and more centered to itself the controlling role in crisis management—in each case not just in setting the policy which will govern, but also in conducting the tactics to be used. For example:

I interviewed former president Dwight Eisenhower at his Gettysburg office in October 1965. The question put: Did Ike, as commander in World War II, ever get tactical instructions from Roosevelt? "If I had gotten anything more than a birthday card from FDR," Eisenhower responded, "I would have thought the world was coming to an end." But then he recalled an instance at the Casablanca conference where Roosevelt did make a tactical suggestion: send a regiment of Allied troops to capture Dakar. Eisenhower flatly told Roosevelt, the former remembered, that if the president wanted serious attention given to such a suggestion, he should make it to the combined Chiefs of Staff; they were the ones from whom Eisenhower took his orders. Ike added, "I never heard anything more about Dakar." I then asked: as president, did Eisenhower ever issue tactical instructions in a national security situation? "Yes":

> When the CIA needed just two more P-51 fighter-bombers during the U.S. action in Guatemala in 1954, the request was brought to Eisenhower, who authorized them. . . . Ike acknowledged that whenever military operations are bound up with diplomatic, economic and psychological initiatives, a president must be a close and detailed manager. (Patterson 1988, p. 68)

Eisenhower could have added another instance of detailed presidential operational control: when the U-2 spy-plane was secretly operating over Russia. In his book *Mayday*, Michael Beschloss tells how every U-2 flight was subject to personal presidential approval:

> [National Security Assistant] Goodpaster ordinarily stood over the President's shoulder as [the CIA's Richard] Bissell laid out his maps on the desk, lecturing on the expected risks and rewards. Eisenhower sometimes said, "I want you to leave out that leg and go straight *that* way. I want you to go from B to D, because it looks to me like you might be getting a little exposed over here." (Beschloss 1986, p. 140)

Kennedy's supervision of operations during the Cuban missile crisis was "unparalleled in modern relations between American political leaders and military organizations," commented Graham Allison in his book *Essence of Decision.* A group of presidential advisers recalled 20 years later: "[Kennedy kept] continuously attentive control of our options and actions."

So did Lyndon Johnson during the Vietnam conflict:

> The Joint Chiefs of Staff argued stoutly that both [ground and air] elements of the war should be left to the field commanders, but they gave way to presidential insistence on detailed White House control of the bombing. And tight control was prudent, for the "Rolling Thunder" campaign, as it steadily expanded, carried an ever-present risk of military confrontation with Russia or China. (Hoopes 1969, p. 62)

In his book *White House Years,* former National Security Adviser Henry Kissinger reported that while President Nixon did not want to engage in "nervous meddling with tactical details or formative deliberations . . . he left the shaping of those to the governmental machinery under my supervision."

The visitor to the Gerald Ford Museum at Grand Rapids will see an entire exhibit wall recounting the *Mayaguez* crisis of 1975, when Cambodian armed forces captured the crew of a U.S. merchant ship in the Gulf of Siam. The exhibit states: "President Ford personally took command of the military operation, directing and supervising the diplomatic, political and military phases of the effort to free the crew and ship."

President Carter and his national security adviser, Zbigniew Brzezinski, were completely in charge of managing the crisis in November 1979 when the Islamic radicals took over the U.S. Embassy in Tehran. For at least the first six months, a "Special Coordination Committee" (SCC) of cabinet-level national security advisers (including the vice president) literally met daily. Brzezinski himself chaired all of these sessions, wrote up brief summaries of the issues which required presidential decision, and then relayed Carter's determinations to the SCC members. Former White House aide Gary Sick relates this whole affair in his 1985 book, adding that all meetings were held in the White House and that summaries were "held tightly within the White House" (Sick 1985, pp. 247–248).

A dozen more similar examples could be cited from the presidencies of Reagan, Bush 41, Clinton, Bush 42, and Obama. Such is the contemporary meaning of the hierarchy which is implied in Article II of the Constitution. Where does this hierarchical mode leave the cabinet departments? Ted Sorenson reflected:

> [Kennedy] could not afford to accept, without seeking an independent judgment, the products and proposals of departmental advisers whose responsibilities did not require them to look, as he and his staff looked, at the government and its programs as a whole. He required a personal staff, therefore—one that represented his personal ways, means and purposes—to summarize and analyze those products and proposals for him, to refine the conflicting views of various agencies, to

define the issues which he had to decide, to help place his personal imprint upon them, to make certain that practical political facts were never overlooked, and to enable him to make his decisions on the full range of *his* considerations and constituencies, which no Cabinet member shared. (Sorenson 1965, p. 258)

As Lloyd Cutler put it: "The whole government has grown to the point where the Cabinet departments, important as they are, have become what you might call outer-moons, and the president's need for an intimate personal staff, who used to be the Cabinet, today requires that he create his own" (Patterson 2001, p. 419). What is this "intimate personal staff"? How does it support Article II's hierarchical "executive power"?

A Candid Look at the White House Staff

The White House staff family is composed of nearly 6,600 men and women. A preliminary review shows that the Obama White House has some 139 separately identifiable offices: 77 of them are policy advisory associates with approximately 470 staffers, 22 are policy-supporting units with some 220 persons, and 40 are professional and technical offices in which probably more than 5,910 men and women serve. (The staffs in this third category—for example, the Military Office, the protective units of the Secret Service—are neither "intimate" nor "personal" but are nonetheless indispensable parts of the White House staff family [Patterson 2008, pp. 31–32].)

Of the 6,600, more than 150 are "commissioned" staff seniors, that is, they have the word "president" in their titles. Some 30 of these are assistants to the president; they head up the principal offices which handle substantive policy matters.

Hierarchy rules. None of the 6,600 has *tenure in* the White House. Every one serves at the pleasure of the president. (Many lower-ranking aides are on detail from cabinet departments; they have career status only in their home agencies.) Topmost among the White House staff is a single demanding superior: the chief of staff, who, with the firm support of the president, is prescribing—as several of his predecessors have prescribed—a very tight set of hierarchical disciplinary commandments:

- Every policy issue which is of presidential concern has one home
- In the White House
- In the hands of just one of the assistants to the president—who of course reaches out to his/her White House colleagues and to cabinet members for facts and advice—
- Who prepares the resulting policy document for the president in a balanced fashion, displaying all sides of any controversial matter, including his/her own—
- Who presents it to the president at the call of the deputy chief of staff for policy

who, along with the chief of staff, determines its readiness for presidential decision.

- No paper moves into the Oval Office without going through the gamut of coordination within the White House run by the staff secretary—who enforces merciless deadlines.
- No person except a very few (such as the National Security adviser, the secretaries of state and defense, the CIA director) gets an appointment with the president or attends a meeting there without the concurrence of the chief of staff. He is gatekeeper.
- Jurisdictions of White House officers are specific, specialized, and firm. No White House staffer invades the territory of another assistant to the president without consent, that is, no staffer conducts negotiations with members or committees of Congress without the concurrence of the assistant for legislative affairs; no staffer gets into legal affairs without the OK of the counsel to the president; no White House officer promises any senior federal appointments to an office-seeker without clearance from the Presidential Personnel Office, and so on.

Governance at the White House is also interdepartmental. The assistants to the president are not only helpers to the chief executive; each is also the center—and the leader—of an advisory circle throughout the cabinet. The White House press secretary calls the signals among the departmental press secretaries; if a newsworthy issue arises, a conference call will determine which of them is to say what. The counsel to the president is in constant touch with the counsels in the several departments—in fact helps pick them—so they respond to him with hierarchical alacrity. Likewise with the assistant for communications, who tightly manages the hub of communications chiefs in the cabinet agencies; the same with the assistants for legislative affairs, and for presidential personnel.

A White House staff is on the one hand diverse: ethnically and culturally, consisting of men and women, civilians and soldiers, elders with vast government experience and 30-year-olds brimming with energy; it also includes advocates from different wings of the party. On the other hand all of them are in one fashion identical: they are loyal to the president.

Whatever are the assistants' jurisdictional specialties, however, these egotistical separations melt into the necessity of coordinating with and collectively contributing to a cross-cutting presidential initiative. And amid all of the disciplined hierarchies there is usually personal congeniality.

Every White House staff officer works in an environment of privilege. The higher his or her rank, the more elevated are the prerogatives. His office may be near the president's; its furnishings may be impressive; he is sheltered from public access or attention—no visitors can get to him without an appointment; he can call up official (radio-equipped) limousine service for his trips around town; his telephone calls are answered; his meals can be brought to his desk; his parking space is close by. The most senior assistants have Secret Service protection.

There is a risk: the staffer may come to think that these privileges are extended because of who he or she is. Not true; the prerogatives that surround White House aides are there only to maximize their effectiveness in helping the president. Explained Clinton aide Dick Morris: "My sense of reality was just altered. I started out being excited working for the president. Then I became arrogant, then I became grandiose" (Patterson 2008, p. 58). G. H. W. Bush Chief of Staff John Sununu suffered from this delusion, and was forced to resign.

Additional candor: how much does it cost to run the modern White House? Readers may be surprised to learn that there is no one place in the national compendium of expenditures where one, overall figure appears. Besides reviewing the "White House Office" listing, presidential scholars must dig into the budgets of 12 separate departments or agencies (e.g., Defense, State, Homeland Security, General Services Administration, Interior, and others) to find the appropriated sums those agencies contribute to the total for the White House staff family. I discovered that the FY2008 aggregation was $1,592,875,254—and this did not include unmentionable additions which were security-classified. (It also did not include $7,509,449 in gifts from the White House Historical Association for the renovation or restoration of the mansion's public rooms [Patterson 2008].)

The White House staff is much larger and more costly than is ever revealed by any president.

Hierarchy Personified: The President as Chief Diplomat

It is in the conduct of national security affairs that the American president has, more and more, taken up the role of personal negotiator with the chiefs of state of other nations. None has followed the example of Woodrow Wilson, who spent from December 13, 1918, to June 29, 1919 (interrupted by one visit home), in Paris, personally overseeing the negotiation of the Versailles Treaty and its establishment of the League of Nations. Looking at the past 70 years, however, in American governance, the presidency has become the operating center of profoundly increasing responsibilities.

In addition to his several face-to-face encounters with Prime Minister Churchill and his two summit sessions with Stalin (at Tehran and Yalta), Franklin Roosevelt exchanged dozens of private cabled communications with both those heads of state and others during the war years. This is evidenced by a September 17, 1942, FDR memorandum to White House Naval Aide Admiral Leahy: "I am anxious to get the cables to me from the Prime Minister and other heads of government in various countries, and my replies to them, coordinated through Harry [Hopkins] because so much of them refer to civil things" (Elsey 2005, pp. 84–85). George Elsey, a naval assistant in the White House Map Room, summarizes a May 1945 meeting which Leahy asked him to have, in Leahy's office, with James Byrnes, about to be nominated by President Truman as secretary of state:

In addition to the summaries of all agreements Roosevelt and the Chiefs of Staff had made at the various summit meetings that he [FDR] asked me to write, Byrnes also wanted to see the full texts of all messages exchanged by Roosevelt and Truman with Churchill and Stalin since Yalta. "How long will it take to get those?" Byrnes asked. "Ten minutes" was the answer that surprised him. "How long will it take me to read it all?" was the next question. "This afternoon, with hard work." (Elsey 2005, p. 18)

One piece of equipment which FDR's Map Room did not have was a secure telephone to Churchill; General Marshall had one and Truman was apparently the first president to use this communications method. (Elsey recounts that in April of 1945 Leahy had to escort the president over to Marshall's Pentagon office to reach Churchill in a secure voice conversation.)

By Eisenhower's time, the White House Communications Agency had several secure telephone connections in place. Stephen Ambrose, in his book *Eisenhower the President,* for example, recounts the several phone conversations Ike had with British Foreign Secretary Anthony Eden during the Suez crisis in November 1956, arguing against the use of British armed forces in Egypt (Ambrose 1984, p. 369).

President George H. W. Bush participated in hundreds of telephone conversations with other chiefs of state. When the U.S. sent troops into Panama in December 1989, Bush had personally called "Virtually every head of government in Latin America," comments Security Adviser Brent Scowcroft. In the Bush and Scowcroft book, *A World Transformed,* Scowcroft observes that in some nations, the foreign offices in those capitals would have prejudices or hold views different from those of the chief of state; it would take a presidential phone call to his opposite number to straighten out such policy blockages. Bush himself emphasizes:

For me, personal diplomacy and leadership went hand in hand. . . . If a foreign leader knows the character and heartbeat of the president (and vice versa), there is apt to be far less miscalculation on either side. . . . This knowledge helps a president formulate and adjust policies that can bring other leaders along to his own point of view. It can make the difference between suspicion and giving each other the benefit of the doubt—and room to maneuver on a difficult political issue. . . . If a president delegates too much high-level diplomacy to subordinates, he conveys the impression of indifference toward foreign leaders. (Bush and Scowcroft 1998, p. 60)

Every succeeding president has in effect adapted the G. H. W. Bush viewpoint—and uses the secure telephone very extensively to communicate with the chiefs of state in other countries.

A detailed examination of presidential records reveals that in his first seven years in office, President George W. Bush conducted at least 748 personal telephone conversations with other chiefs of state or world leaders, and participated in at least 674 face-to-face meetings with them singly or in groups (Patterson 2008). As described in two recent news stories, respectively:

> President Obama was angry. He was on the phone with President Dmitri A. Medvedev last month to finalize a new arms control treaty with Russia, only to be confronted with new demands for concessions. . . . "Dmitri, we agreed," with a tone of exasperation . . . "We can't do this. If it means we're going to walk away from this treaty and not get it done, so be it. But we're not going to go down this path. . . ." . . . Mr. Obama hung up the phone again with Mr. Medvedev on Friday, this time having finally translated aspiration into agreement. (Baker 2010)

> President Obama spoke by phone on Thursday night with President Hu Jintao of China for about an hour—so long that Air Force One had to be held for 10 minutes on the tarmac at Andrews Air Force Base after landing. (Jacobs 2010)

Over the past several years, White House national security advisers have aped these communications arrangements; they have set up direct telephone links with their opposite numbers—national security advisers in London, Paris, Bonn, and elsewhere: when they lift the phone from the hook they are connected.

One very recent example of the president's personal "chief diplomat" role came in April 2010 when President Obama hosted an international conference of 46 nations in a Nuclear Security Summit in Washington.

> In his role as host . . . Obama gave his fellow heads of state a taste of what has been familiar to many Americans who followed the domestic political debate over the past year: the president as seminar leader. For four hours Tuesday, Obama led a pair of planning sessions to iron out the final details of the communique that was the culmination of the summit. He sat at the center of the gathering, calling on leaders to speak, embellish, oppose and offer alternatives to the plan taking shape. Only heads of state, and, at times, two senior aides were allowed in the room. "He's never better when he's the teacher," said a European diplomat. (Wilson 2010)

The president is now, in person, chief diplomat—a responsibility implied in that famous first sentence of Article II, but in an operational style that would indeed surprise the members of the "Committee on Detail" who proposed those words to the Constitutional Convention in August 1789.

Beyond the Telephone: The Chief Diplomat's Situation Room

During the Civil War, the War Department established a telegraph office (on the site of the future Executive Office Building); President Lincoln frequently visited this facility to read incoming reports from the fighting front; Lincoln reportedly sent 1,000 telegraphed instructions directly to his generals. President McKinley set up a similar "war room" in the Executive Residence during the Spanish-American War in 1898, but it was closed when the war ended.

Immediately following the Pearl Harbor attack, Roosevelt Naval Aide Captain John Beardall used a windowless room (later the "Fish Room," now the

Roosevelt Room) opposite the Oval Office to post battle maps on easels. Here he installed safes for filing military messages and the cables being exchanged with Churchill and Stalin. A few military staff officers kept an around-the-clock watch.

When Prime Minister Churchill came to the White House for an extended visit in December 1941, he brought with him his own portable map room. He in effect took over the Queen's Bedroom and an additional room across the hall on the second floor of the mansion.

> Roosevelt was a daily visitor to the prime minister's sophisticated presentation of military fronts and vivid displays of allied and enemy naval fleets. Enchanted, Roosevelt told Beardall after Churchill's departure, "Fix up a room for me like Churchill's." (Elsey 2005, p. 18)

The Trophy Room on the ground floor was selected; it was directly across from the private family elevator, and was set up in early April 1941. The walls were covered in soft wallboard, so that maps could easily be posted and changed. These maps were covered with plastic and movements of both allied and enemy forces shown by grease-pencil markings; colored pins designated each allied and enemy ship. Desks and file cabinets were placed in the center of the room, leaving space for FDR, in a wheelchair, to closely examine the wall exhibits. Couriers delivered to the Map Room all the cables exchanged among Roosevelt, Churchill, Stalin, and Chiang. (Outgoing messages were coded and sent by the Navy Department, incoming messages were separately decoded and brought in by the War Department. Why the separation? Roosevelt did not want any place in Washington, except the Map Room, to have a complete file of these exchanges.)

George Elsey's book, *An Unplanned Life,* describes his four and a half war years in the Map Room. It was disestablished on December 22, 1945, when the White House chief usher persuaded the president to move all military facilities out of the executive residence. (Elsey saved one of the final war maps and later donated it to the White House where it hangs in what is still called the "Map Room" on the ground floor of the residence.) Stung by the failure of the Bay of Pigs invasion in April of 1961, President Kennedy and National Security Adviser McGeorge Bundy decided that

> they must have the same facts that the bureaucracies of State, CIA and Defense had used for their individual, institutional analysis and interpretation of national security matters. The White House staff's knowledge of the fundamental facts underlying issues could be used, in the words of [James] Schlesinger, to "make impolite inquiry and the rude comment," ask the right questions and evaluate the answers. The best way to get the facts was to get the cables that U.S. embassies abroad sent to the State Department, messages that U.S. military commands sent to the Pentagon, and the intelligence reports that collectors sent to CIA headquarters—in other words, set up a communications center at the White House. (Bohn 2003, pp. 23–24)

The chosen location was not to duplicate FDR's Map Room in the residence, but to tear out both the bowling alley and the duplicating room used by the White House messengers in the West Wing basement (the mimeograph machines there were used in the Eisenhower period to reproduce cabinet papers). Seabees from Camp David assisted with the construction. The name given to the new facility was "Situation Room"—to avoid the idea that this was a "War Room" which by itself possessed any command authority. It was in business in May 1961.

At first, pneumatic tubes replaced the old courier system; finally, "through a combination of shrewd manipulation and old-fashioned jaw-boning," National Security Council (NSC) Executive Secretary Bromley Smith obliged the initially reluctant national security agencies to relay their important cables and reports to the new Sit Room electronically. By the 1990s, the incoming flow was—and now is—numbered in the thousands; 1,500 may come from the State Department each day (4,000 in a crisis). The most significant of these cables (according to criteria which are raised or lowered to match whatever is the degree of interest or urgency) are relayed instantly to senior White House staff members or to NSC staff officers—who now have secure video screens on their own desks. The Sit Room computers can be programmed to relay, or to select out, communications that contain certain words, names, or phrases, or to create a personalized "profile" for a given recipient.

The Situation Room staff composes an early-morning summary for the president, the vice president, and the national security adviser. It also prepares and distributes to the national security agencies themselves a weekly checklist identifying the topics that will be of special interest to the White House in the forthcoming days.

By 2003, it became clear that over the years since 1961 the layout of the Situation Room had become too confined to handle its steadily increasing workload. A reelected President Bush (in 2004) made the approximately $20 million investment to rebuild the facility completely.

American Governance: The Chief Diplomat of the 21st Century

On May 18, 2007, the White House held a ribbon-cutting ceremony. The occasion was the opening of the newest and, in my belief, one of the most significant elements in American governance: the revamped White House Situation Room.

The White House Situation Room at present consists of 13 areas: a main conference room plus four others of varying smaller sizes, a watch room, a switch room with six consoles for the receipt and distribution of the incoming electronic messages, a communications area, staff offices, a reception room, and a mini-kitchen. At one end of the principal conference room is a 5-by-11-foot "knowledge wall" on which can be displayed up to 16 images, pictures, texts, photographs, maps, and reconnaissance or satellite photos. An electronic write-board permits lines to be drawn on any of the displays; the room's "whisper walls" of a special fabric absorb any ambient sounds. The full suite is staffed by some 32 men and women, many of whom are detailed from State, Defense, CIA, and the other national security agencies—which have operational Sit Rooms of their own.

The most significant new development is that the Situation Room is now the locus of a 21st-century capability which is transforming American governance: secure, international video teleconferencing. Toward the end of the George W. Bush administration, and from now on, the American president was—and will be—commander-in-chief and chief diplomat in a history-making fashion. He is able to converse, face to face, in top-secret mode with any of his principal military commanders worldwide, and with many of our U.S. ambassadors at their posts overseas (Patterson 2008). One recent news story recounted that at nearly every meeting in the White House Situation Room, General Stanley McChrystal has been joined on the video screens at the end of the table by Karl W. Eikenberry, the U.S. ambassador to Kabul, and Anne W. Patterson, his counterpart in Pakistan. There are regular "team meetings" with this group.

Most significantly, the president meets in this security video teleconference fashion with several of the chiefs of state of foreign nations (at present including the British prime minister, the president of France, and the German chancellor). The other National Security Council members can be with the president at the Sit Room table, or in effect with him while they sit in their respective departments. Those foreign chiefs of state who do not at present have this new equipment at their own headquarters can and do come to the U.S. embassy in their capitals to deal directly with the American president. President George W. Bush regularly engaged in such video teleconference calls with the leader of Pakistan and also with the prime minister of Iraq. In November of 2007, a groundbreaking example of the process of actually negotiating international agreements was consummated: President Bush and Iraqi prime minister al-Maliki signed, via secure video teleconference, a declaration of principles about a "more normalized, long-term relationship between the United States and Iraq" (Patterson 2008, pp. 367–372). In addition to their meetings in person, Afghanistan president Karzai has spoken several times by video with President Obama.

Other White House staff officers use the teleconference facilities: the advance teams planning presidential trips carry abroad with them a portable version of this equipment—which connects them with the chief of advance or the chief of staff enabling them to specify, visually, every last detail of an upcoming presidential visit.

The Situation Room and its breathtakingly impressive capabilities are not only changing the conduct of the American president, but are adding substantial new responsibilities to the White House staff. Every telephone call, every video teleconference, every document being visually/electronically exchanged with a U.S. ambassador or with a foreign chief of state means more in-advance briefing memoranda, more follow-up record keeping. The White House national security staff (jointly supporting both the National Security Council and the Homeland Security Council) currently numbers some 250.

As of this writing, additional White House improvements keep arriving, or are in the foreseeable future. The presidential press briefing room has been completely remade; new, more-capable presidential helicopters are on the drawing board; there is a new helicopter hanger at Camp David; and a much more capable Air Force One is being planned (the existing one is 19 years old).

Readers are reminded that in addition to the responsibilities, activities, and facilities described here as being possessed by President Obama, Vice President Joseph Biden, just like his predecessors Gore and Cheney, has been assigned as a leading representative of the United States in the conduct of national security affairs. Mr. Biden has been to Iraq several times, and also to Israel and Spain, negotiating on behalf of the president; he chairs monthly national security meetings in the Situation Room. All three of the most recent vice presidents have had staffs of more than 90 assistants, and as such, in addition to their constitutional role in the Congress, they have been principal policy and operating members of the White House team.

American governance: the executive power thereof has from the beginning been vested in a single hierarch, the president. As this chapter illustrates, however, the presidency—meaning the president, the vice president, and the 6,600-strong White House staff—has been changing. He—they—have more and more become the center of this executive power in an operational and tactical sense, beyond any previous White House and far beyond (but not inconsistent with) the dreams of the drafters of the Constitution itself.

References

Ambrose, Stephen. 1984. *Eisenhower the President.* New York: Simon and Schuster.
Baker, Peter. 2010. "Twists, Turns and Anger on Way to Arms Pact with Russia." *New York Times,* March 27, A-4.
Beschloss, Michael R. 1986. *Mayday: Eisenhower, Khrushchev and the U-2 Affair.* New York: Harper and Row.
Bohn, Michael K. 2003. *Nerve Center: Inside the White House Situation Room.* Washington, DC: Brassey's.
Bush, George H. W., and Brent Scowcroft. 1998. *A World Transformed.* New York: Knopf.
Elsey, George M. 2005. *An Unplanned Life: A Memoir.* Columbia: University of Missouri Press.
Hoopes, Townsend. 1969. *The Limits of Intervention.* New York: McKay.
Jacobs, Andrew. 2010. "Asia: A Long Chat for Obama and Hu." *New York Times,* April 10, A-7.
Patterson, Bradley H. 1988. *The Ring of Power: The White House Staff and Its Expanding Role in Government.* New York: Basic Books.
———. 2001. *The White House Staff: Inside the West Wing and Beyond.* Washington, DC: Brookings Institution Press.
———. 2008. *To Serve the President: Continuity and Innovation in the White House Staff.* Washington, DC: Brookings Institution Press.
Sick, Gary G. 1985. *All Fall Down.* New York: Penguin.
Sorenson, Theodore. 1965. *Kennedy.* New York: Harper and Row.
Wilson, Scott. 2010. "On World Stage, Obama at Ease as Seminar Leader." *Washington Post,* April 14, A-1.

17

Obama's Stealth Revolution

Quietly Reshaping the Way Government Works

Donald F. Kettl

Quiet grumbling has surfaced among the inside-the-beltway crowd—and not just over health care reform. People are asking, "Where is Obama's big-bang reform of government?"

Government reform has been a staple of presidential management for the past 50 years. President Kennedy brought in his whiz kids, led by Robert McNamara. President Johnson mandated a programming budgeting system (PPB) to link program goals and costs. President Nixon upped the ante with a management-by-objectives budget system, and President Carter trumped him with zero-based budgeting, which promised to force budgeters to explain the extra value that marginal dollars would bring.

Next, President Reagan privatized everything he could and created a special commission led by a private sector executive to review the entire government and its operations. During the Clinton administration, Vice President Al Gore identified hundreds of recommendations for reinventing government. By day 200 of his administration, President George W. Bush had launched a top-down performance system tied to the budget. Does Team Obama have something on the way?

First Postbureaucratic President

There has been no big-bang announcement, but a stealth revolution is in the works. President Obama is quietly shaping a strategy to become the first postbureaucratic president.

Presidents might be chief executives, but they don't really behave much like CEOs. Nevertheless, for more than half a century, presidents have felt obliged to demonstrate to voters—and especially to the permanent government—that they take the job of running the government seriously. Presidents seem to have worked out of the vending-machine model of government: insert cash (a lot of it), push the button, and wait for services to come out. The goal: Figure out how to make the vending machine work better.

Pressed by angry taxpayers, most presidents have tried to squeeze out more services for the same amount of money. Reagan tried to rewire the vending machine by giving the private sector more management over more of its parts. Clinton's reinvention of government was part good cop (trying to smooth government's machinery for federal employees caught in bad systems) and part bad cop (downsizing the machinery itself). Bush torqued down the machine by forcing managers to better explain what they were trying to accomplish and to measure how well they did.

Enter Hurricane Katrina. Team Bush recovered from a remarkable collection of crises, but the blow from which it could never bounce back was FEMA's fumble. October 2005 was the first time that the president's negative ratings exceeded his positive numbers. It was not just a public relations disaster; it was a profound failure of vending-machine government. The administration inserted the cash and pushed the buttons, but the mechanism jammed.

For Team Obama, ever-mindful of history, the lesson is clear. The top-down, process-driven, budget-based reforms of the past 50 years have run out of coins. The vending machine is broken, and more presidential tinkering cannot fix it.

In Search of a New Idea

It is time for a new idea. It will have to be outlandishly huge to get the attention of government workers, who have become used to the escalating promises that have come with the regular rising and setting of the reform sun. However, there isn't a consensus of what "big idea" ought to drive the next beam of government reform.

Top administration officials also know that they need a new plan. They need it in part to demonstrate their seriousness about government and in part to make sure their own—inevitable—Katrina doesn't torpedo them as it did Bush. So, they're hitching up their governance strategy wagon to transparency and working organically from the bottom up. They want to test their ideas before they latch themselves to a loser.

The stimulus is proving the perfect test vehicle. It's moving broadly (so it's affecting almost everything in government), and it's moving fast (so no one is looking too closely at what's coming). It's a stealth revolution quietly taking shape with very little notice.

But what does this stealth revolution look like?

Virtually Connect with Citizens

The Obama administration came to Washington as master of the new media. The White House was soon "tweeting" out its own exclusives. Damon Weaver, an 11-year-old ace reporter from Florida, got an interview with the president. Even though his broadcast news show reaches only 500 students at Canal Point Elementary School, his "tweeted" interview and YouTube video soon hit the broadcast networks and reached millions.

Obama has sometimes gotten clobbered in turn by the viral media, especially in the storm of opposition to his health care reform. But those in the administration are betting that the virtual networking force will be theirs—even if they've banned Twitter from the White House and the Oval Office.

Create Czars to Sidestep Bureaucratic Roadblocks

From Katrina, Obama learned that coordination failures can cripple a president, both administratively and politically. To break the bureaucratic boundaries, the administration appointed a gaggle of policy czars—three dozen by one count—loosely coordinated by then-chief-of-staff Rahm Emanuel.

There's a bank czar to oversee executives' pay and a car czar to reorganize the auto industry. There are special envoys for Afghanistan and the Middle East, and czars for energy and the environment, as well as for health care and the stimulus package. None of these officials are confirmed by the Senate or answer to Congress. This is part flattening-the-hierarchy, part move-fast/travel-light, part don't-let-Congress-meddle, and part don't-let-the-bureaucracy-slow-you-down. All presidents have used special representatives for particular issues, but this is a revolutionary-in-scale move to maneuver past the permanent bureaucracy.

Herd Cats When Dealing with Congress

From every corner, there has been criticism of Obama's strategy of setting broad principles on big issues—the stimulus, climate change, health care reform—and then tossing the debate to Congress to resolve. This strategy has led to a porkfest in the stimulus package, a giveaway of hundreds of billions of dollars of pollution credits in the climate change bill, and wobbly wheels on the health care reform wagon.

Although it hasn't been easy to watch, straightforward presidential proposals have become a skeet shoot on Capitol Hill, with specifics tossed up only to be shot down. Congress is good at short-term deals, building broad coalitions by horse trading, and stopping big ideas dead in their tracks.

Obama is willing to accept half a loaf rather than no loaf, because he believes there may be a chance in the future for another trip to the bakery. It appears, though, that Obama won't make that trip if he can't get some policy wins. Take what you can get, fix it later, but make sure you get something to sign now for the 2012 campaign later seems to be the administration's strategy. So far, it's gotten the stimulus bill and seen movement on climate change and health care reform enacted.

Redefine Accountability Through Transparency

Team Obama quickly concluded that it couldn't steer the government through the usual mechanisms. No one would pay attention to more rules, and traditional authority broke down. The budget is the usual presidential ace card, but with Washington printing money so fast that it risked brownouts, the budget was useless.

Instead, the administration has pushed out enormous quantities of information about federal programs and has relied on citizens (and interest groups) to digest the data and figure out what it means. The stimulus program is the point of the spear. Want to know where the money is going and how it's being used? Go to the Recovery.gov website for a dazzling—and staggering—collection of information. But that's just part of the enormous avalanche of data pouring out of the new administration.

Vivek Kundra, Obama's information czar, brought the strategy from his previous position as Washington, D.C.'s chief technology officer. The city's "Apps for Democracy" contest produced hundreds of new ways to "mash up" real-time data. The city received several new applications at relatively little cost, citizens received access to data on programs ranging from crime to construction to vacant property, and Harvard's Innovations Award named Kundra's effort a finalist for "democratizing data."

Building virtual links with citizens, sidestepping bureaucracy, herding Congress, and democratizing data; without having launched a big-bang initiative, a stealth revolution has come together in Obama's first nine months.

Whither Transparency?

This stealth revolution is an incredibly high-risk venture. It's a game changer. Two things seem clear. One is that transparency is the "next big thing" in governance—even though no one really knows what "transparency" means. Like so much of the rest of Obama's frenetic policy juggernaut, there's a shell without much content.

The other is that we're postbureaucratic, with players across many federal agencies, multiple levels of government, public-private-nonprofit sectors, and international boundaries.

Consider the 2008 dog food recall. Melamine was introduced into the canine food chain through a Chinese company, imported by a Canadian company, manufactured in plants in New Jersey and Kansas, and distributed through more than 100 dog food brands throughout the United States. Getting leverage on such complex policy networks which are proliferating throughout all of government, while at the same time operating through traditional bureaucracies, is a fundamental challenge of 21st-century government.

So Obama is conducting a postbureaucratic, stealth revolution—through transparency—to deal with networked policy problems. The administration has the problem defined just right. Nevertheless, not only is the strategy unproven, it's full of risks that could blow up.

The implosion of health care reform illustrates the risks of the congressional strategy. They might get some kind of signable bill, but in a policy world where everyone plays and no one leads, the rudder is sitting there for anyone to grab. And whereas the administration has mastered virtual networking, opponents have flipped the game back on it. The electronic campaigns of the "death boards" show how easy it is to die by the sword as to live by it. No one owns or steers the new media.

The policy czars give the administration "point persons" for its policymaking. But making the policies work will require bringing in the permanent government, which has been dealt out of the policy flurry. Except when it comes to problems. The National Highway Traffic Safety Administration, the regulatory agency charged with overseeing child safety seats and auto recalls and drunk-driving rules, was attacked for not moving the Cash for Clunkers money fast enough, a program about as far from its mission as one can get. Feds everywhere are nervously eyeing the transparency rules embedded in the emerging stimulus reports.

Experienced feds know that eagle-eyed critics will mine the data for horror stories. Glenn Beck has already hijacked Recovery.gov to attack the stimulus for "just peeing your money away (Media Matters 2009)."

Results-Oriented Problem Solving and Leadership

If the Obama administration has defined the problem correctly, it's going to have a serious problem solving it. If the federal government is postbureaucratic—and no agency can control any problem it's given to manage—solutions can't come through spontaneous combustion produced by dumping information into the Internet.

Hurricane Katrina showed how postbureaucratic government ought to work. When retired Coast Guard Admiral Thad Allen replaced Michael Brown as coordinator-in-chief, things started to move—through two lessons. First, government works when problem solving rather than boundary protecting defines who does what. Second, this requires a leader with the instinct—and salty language, if necessary—to drive relentlessly toward results.

So far Obama's stealth revolution has the postbureaucratic vision. Nevertheless, it needs to learn the Katrina lessons—fast—if President Obama is going to avoid having the tough realities of 21st-century government eat him up as they did his predecessor.

Editors' Note

This article was originally published as "The Obama Administration's Management Agenda," *The Public Manager,* 38 (4) (Winter 2009–2010). Used by permission.

Reference

Media Matters. 2009. "Note to Beck: Doors Repaired with Stimulus Funds Were Hangar Doors and Did Not Cost $1.4 Million." July 21. http://mediamatters.org/research/200907210005.

Part V

What Does the Future Hold?

18

Government at the Edge

PAUL JOHNSTON AND MARTIN STEWART-WEEKS

Good government and governance have never been more difficult to define and deliver. There is a mismatch between the challenges governments and communities face and the tools and institutions on which they rely to make decisions, invest resources, and commission results. Indeed, it is often difficult even to define what the results should be.

While traditional functions of compliance and business-as-usual operational performance remain important, the governance agenda is crowded with complex ("wicked") risks and opportunities demanding new and better responses. Some governments have concluded that an effective response has to involve lifting the quality and mix of skills, resources, and expertise on which they can call. And if they haven't worked that out for themselves, there are plenty of people outside government urging a more rapid and robust embrace of a new governance that relies on collaboration, coproduction, and a rising instinct for reform and innovation.

White House Deputy Chief Technology Officer (CTO) for Open and Transparent Government Beth Noveck, the author of *Wiki Government,* captured the dilemma when she noted recently (2010, p. 10):

> The problems we're trying to grapple with—or at least many of them—are long-term, complex and wicked, but the decision-making systems we can draw on are largely hostage to short-term political cycles. We have grown used to the center taking more and more of the decisions, despite the fact that in almost all cases the knowledge, expertise and experience required to inform those decisions are at the edge. [And] the problems we're trying to fix, or at least some of them— borderless, diffuse and systemic—are looking less and less like the institutions and practices we tend to rely on to fix them—sovereign, territorially-defined and symptomatic.

A New Operating Model for the Public Sector

Those unsettling conclusions imply the need for a new operating model for government and the public sector. The emergence of a more connected world has changed the way all organizations operate, enabling distributed operating models that are less dependent on hierarchy and command and control. The public sector needs to embrace and master this new operating model. It is akin to the distributed networking design that provides the foundation of the Internet.

Part of the new operating model implies a new role for citizens, too. In a connected world, citizens are not prepared to be passive recipients of what the state delivers either in relation to public services or in relation to public decision making. The public sector needs to understand better, and engage more effectively with citizens who are much more empowered than they have been in the past.

In the age of mass production, government relied on bureaucracy as the appropriate form of public sector organization. The focus was on producing public value at scale and with integrity. The state would ensure that everyone received a basic level of goods and services and the state machine would do all this noncorruptly and within a framework of law and democratic accountability.

This approach is no longer appropriate in a connected world because:

- It is not good at dealing with change.
- It is not good at tackling complex problems.
- It delivers standard rather than personalized solutions.
- It treats the citizen as a stand-in-line recipient of public services.
- It is based on an "expert/leader knows best" philosophy.

Nevertheless, there are enduring attributes we need to retain. We still want public services that act with integrity and within a framework of law and democratic accountability that aim to treat everyone fairly and equally, and that seek to be inclusive (i.e., recognize that some groups in society will find it harder to get a fair deal than others).

So, if the new governance is set to explore the possibilities of the "postbureaucratic" age, its institutions and practices must be different.

- It must be better able to predict and preempt change (anticipation).
- It must be better able to deal with failure (resilience).
- It must be better able to generate and implement change.
- It must give more power to the public sector edge (frontline).
- It must give more power to citizens.
- It must enable citizens to do more for themselves.
- It must do more to support public value creation beyond the public sector.

Driving everything is a rising innovation agenda, including a new focus on social innovation, fueling a quest for bolder policy ideas, better public services, and new ways to engage citizens and communities in the decisions and trade-offs of governance.

The search for better models of governance has to accommodate the human instinct to connect to others to form real communities wherein people manifest an instinct for freedom, autonomy, and control, and a capacity to have some influence over their lives.

At the same time, invigorated by the potential of social technologies, opportunities are emerging to position the citizen at the heart of democratic action. Already governments are moving to allow beneficiaries to tailor and self-direct personal budgets. The recipients of public programs have the opportunity to become active coproducers of the services they access. Mutual responsibility, founded on collaboration, has the potential to become a vehicle for real social change. Britain's new coalition government has signaled its intention to pursue this agenda with some vigor, bringing a number of distinct themes and policy commitments together under the "Big Society" umbrella. Announcing "a new era of people power at the centre of the new Government," Prime Minister David Cameron and Deputy Prime Minister Nick Clegg explained that they wanted to "give citizens, communities and local government the power and information they need to come together, solve the problems they face and build the Britain they want. We want society—the families, networks, neighborhoods and communities that form the fabric of so much of our everyday lives—to be bigger and stronger than ever before" (British Cabinet Office 2010, p. 1).

Governing with and at the Edge

There is an underlying theme that links these emerging trends and the search for an effective governance model in a more complex and connected age. We describe that theme as "governing with and at the edge."

Networks pose particularly interesting questions about the relationship between the center and the edge, between what controls the network and how its nodes connect. In a centralized network, the relationships are fairly straightforward, with a strong center essentially controlling the interaction of the nodes which have to work through the center to connect to others. Decentralized networks offer a variation on the theme, creating a milder version of the same instinct for hub-and-spoke models of authority and control.

Distributed networks, on the other hand, generate new possibilities in the relationship between the nodes. Interaction is less dependent on a strong, controlling center (which does not exist anymore) and more reliant on shifting patterns of communication across and between the nodes. The Internet, of course, is a distributed network. Its guiding principle is to enable the nodes in the network to flourish, and often to accelerate the ways in which they do so, ways that are emergent and responsive to shifting priorities, context, and conditions.

It's a little simplistic to suggest that government has to become more like the Internet. But it's not a bad heuristic to guide the emergence of new models of governing in a world that increasingly looks like, and often adopts many of the new rhythms and attributes of the Internet.

Governing with and at the edge is the natural consequence of evolving away from traditional centralized and decentralized networks and moving toward more distributed network models. Remember Beth Noveck's diagnosis at the start of this chapter? "We have grown used to the center making more and more of the decisions," she explained, despite the fact that "in almost all cases the knowledge, expertise and experience required to inform those decisions are at the edge." We are being challenged to find new ways to resolve the perennial contest between center and edge. Our instinct should be to privilege the edge but not to underestimate the role and significance of the center. Finding this new accommodation is fundamental to the discovery of new methods and models of governing that make sense in a more complex, connected world.

For example, the problems with which governments are confronted are growing more complex and varied. They require solutions that need to draw on the insights and energy of a much more diffuse, dispersed, and diverse mix of people and organizations. They seek new ideas, new energy, and commitment and an appetite for risk and sometimes profound change. To the extent that such innovation, both incremental and disruptive, is the order of the day, the search for those inputs needs to be wide, inclusive, and sometimes unexpected. In particular, it needs to find and nurture the often small experiments with new services, new models, and new approaches that invariably start and thrive on the edge, and not at the heart of large organizations or systems.

Governing with and at the edge will manifest some important principles, including:

1. Ideas, authority, and some measure of control will move toward the edge and away from the center.
2. For the most part, the job of the center will be to create the right frameworks for interaction rather than use command and control to deliver specific outputs.
3. Individuals and communities will have a much greater capacity to determine public sector priorities and actions.
4. There will be a new premium on communication and connectedness as empowered individuals seek coherence between their actions and the larger context on which they have an impact.
5. There will be an increased capacity to innovate and respond to new challenges, since this invariably happens best at the edge of larger systems where the signs of change and renewal are often most urgent and obvious.
6. There will be more variation in how things are done and what is achieved. If at least part of the success with which we tackle some of the big risks and opportunities of public policy is increasingly dependent on the behavior of people and their willingness to act and to embrace change, almost by definition the results will be uneven. Different people and different communities will have a different capacity and willingness to respond and not everyone will respond in the same way.

Confronting the resulting variability will be a key policy issue in its own right.

The instincts and opportunities of governing with and at the edge make sense and have an intuitive appeal. They speak to a natural desire to give people more room to make decisions and influence the context in which they live and to rescue and protect a sense of personal agency and autonomy. They reflect growing evidence that giving people room to move and the freedom to choose the best way to respond to change is a powerful way to nurture resilience and innovation.

Empowering the edge will be a challenge to traditional, more centralized approaches. Indeed, in some cases technological change, as well as supporting the edge, can also offer new forms of control to the center. Inevitably, there will be a struggle between two apparently contradictory forces—one that seeks to privilege the edge because that's where new ideas and energy usually come from and one that seeks to centralize and command because that makes government feel safer and more in control. Finding a resolution between these two persistent and apparently competing instincts will not, we think, be a function of one of them winning and the other losing. Mutual accommodation is the answer, with each—center and edge—doing what they do best but understanding how they impact one another.

Innovation and promising new ways to work or solve problems often start with a vibrant "edge" community and culture which, often in the face of considerable opposition from the "center," has the freedom and courage to try something new. From those experiments and often unorthodox first ideas, the call for change gathers energy and momentum.

There are a number of reasons the edge is often so good at the business of innovation. Edge communities are usually relatively small and coherent with considerable stocks of social capital and trust. Both cooperation and collaboration, the hallmarks of innovation, are much easier to demand and sustain.

Edge communities are often the "canary in the mine," the first to sense shifts in the wider political, social, economic, and cultural environments which offer early signals that change is either happening or required. And because edge communities are relatively autonomous and self-contained, the permission to experiment is easier to come by and often not needed at all.

In government, the center remains important. There are policy, regulatory, and performance monitoring and reporting roles that need to be done well. But the new governance is making demands for innovation and rapid change, which suggests that, notwithstanding the imperative for some level of central control, it is the edge that needs to be nurtured. And nurturing the edge, as part of a new model of inventive, responsive governing, now becomes a new capability for government.

Some Examples

The shift toward an "edgecentric" model of governing is already evident. Innovations like FixMyStreet.com and TheyWorkforYou.com from serial innovators at MySociety; the work of the Sunlight Foundation in the United States working to make the processes and decision making of government more transparent and intelligible; the use of a wiki by the city of Melbourne, Australia, to increase the range and mix of people able not just to give an opinion about the new city plan but to help draft some of its key provisions; and the use of community budgeting techniques in Porto Alegre, Brazil, and other cities and towns are all straws in the wind.

In Australia, the federal government recently released a major report into key policy options for the National Broadband Network. The report was released on a wiki site (Department of Broadband Communication and Digital Economy 2011) that broke the recommendations down into their individual components and invited people to respond directly to each recommendation, as well as to the overall report.

Citizens and consumers will not wait for an invitation to engage and connect for shared purposes and to create a sense of power and solidarity. It's likely, for example, that there will be more examples of groups of public service users collaborating around their experiences to generate powerful insights into the performance of existing services and, more important, the aspirations and values that should inform new services and responses into the future. HealthChapter (http://www.healthchapter.com/) "is a health based social network of people sharing their disease experiences, treatment options, knowledge and giving support to other people suffering from similar health problems."

PatientsLikeMe (http://www.patientslikeme.com/) is committed to "providing a better, more effective way to capture valuable results and share them with patients, healthcare professionals, and industry organizations that are trying to treat the disease." It is designed as "a new system of medicine by patients for patients. We're here to give patients the power to control their disease and to share what they learn with others."

Or maybe it will be something as simple as The Weight Tracker iPhone application which allows you to easily track your weight on a daily basis. It can also synchronize your personal weight entries with ThisCityIsGoingOnADiet.com.

The Patent Office in the United States was established by Thomas Jefferson, an example of Government 1.0 if there ever was one. The Peer-to-Patent initiative in the United States, pioneered with early contributions from Beth Noveck, effectively institutionalized a social networking platform at the heart of this core public function to lift efficiency and, at the same time, engage a wider, more dispersed community of expertise. The Patent Office recognized that they often are not the best placed to assess whether a patent application is actually worthy of the patent protection—is it new, has it been done before, how significant is the new idea seeking a patent? It is one example of the way in which Noveck argues that new tools and technologies are creating the opportunity to make government both more expert and more democratic at the same time. The ability to square the circle between the enduring instincts of self-government and collaborative expertise and the unforgiving demands of scale, speed, and complexity is one of the tricks that governing with and at the edge will become increasingly adept at pulling off.

Technology and the new platforms of social networking make it possible to engage in new ways of achieving policy outcomes. A good example is the Urban

EcoMap program which Cisco pioneered with the city of San Francisco (www. urbanecomap.org).

This is a Web-based tool that makes it easier for people to see how their community is performing on sustainability measures, especially in relation to energy, transport, and waste.

People track their community's comparative performance and can use the site to learn more about practical things they can do, often with others in their community, to improve their own performance in these key domains.

The solution is data driven, which implies openness and transparency from public and private sector organizations. It is user centered. It engages people's capacity to change their own behavior and to influence others. It creates new platforms for engagement, visualization, and decision making. It is, in effect, public policy delivered by a networked, platform-based solution whose success is largely dependent on the actions and decisions of people, companies, and communities, not on government officials, regulations, and directives. It is an example of the center engaging and empowering what will become a growing edge community of citizens and business connecting for sustainable change.

In the realm of politics, the instinct to connect for shared purpose and solidarity is reflected in initiatives like the Democracy Club (n.d.) in the UK (http://www. democracyclub.org.uk/). The Club is a nonparty political group of volunteers keen to hold candidates to account, and stimulate public engagement. The key is to connect people to "small, easily achievable tasks." These small tasks then add up to useful resources that others can use, too.

These are the questions our volunteers are helping each other answer:

- Who are the candidates in my constituency for the next election? What are they saying in the media, and what are other people saying about them? (in collaboration with YourNextMP).
- What do they think about issues that matter to me? (in collaboration with TheyWorkForYou).
- What are they saying on leaflets they post through the door? How is what they're saying on leaflets different from what they're saying elsewhere? (in collaboration with The Straight Choice).

The website explains that "we're not part of any organization and have no agenda other than increasing transparency and civic participation. We don't even know exactly how this is going to work out. But along the way, we hope to build up a picture of what people care about across the country; connect with other people who care about the state of politics in the UK; and have some fun." Starting something with an admission that "we don't even know exactly how this is going to work out" might not sound comfortable to traditional public sector ears, but it's likely to be a more common operating principle in many of the practical applications of an instinct to govern with and at the edge.

Taking a rather different angle is the work of UK public services design firm Participle and other partners in the development of Southwark Circle in London (http://www.southwarkcircle.org.uk/). It is a project that looks at different ways to respond to the needs of older people. Rather than take a service-centric approach, assuming that the challenge was to improve current services or even think up new ones, the project started from a deep understanding of the way older people actually live or, more important, want to live. And the insight that emerged was about the need for engagement and participation, not necessarily more services.

The website explains that Southwark Circle (n.d.) is a membership organization that "provides on-demand help with life's practical tasks through local, reliable Neighborhood Helpers, and a social network for teaching, learning and sharing." Members are introduced to one another as well as to Neighborhood Helpers.

Southwark Circle was codesigned with people over 50 years old and is a social enterprise registered in the UK as a Community Interest Company (CIC). The work of an organization like Hope Street (http://www.hopestreetgroup.org/index.jspa) is another indication of the new kinds of public purpose organizations that are starting to emerge. Hope Street explicitly focuses on "policy 2.0," "a different way of thinking and acting in the policy arena, bringing new talent and tools to traditionally partisan debates." The group convenes leaders from business, government, and civil society "to develop actionable proposals that expand economic opportunity." They also provide young professionals and practitioners an online platform where they can collaborate on policy ideas that are then shared with decision makers. The model follows three simple steps:

- Recruit engaged citizens from outside of government—most important, the people directly impacted by the policy.
- Provide them with the tools to learn about, collaborate, and refine real-world policy recommendations.
- Give them a microphone and access to government leaders to advocate for and implement these recommendations.

What these examples all have in common is an instinct for collaboration and coproduction, the idea that better policy and public services outcomes and better decision making will emerge from a process in which accessible, attractive, and simple tools make it easier for citizens with requisite experience and expertise to make their contribution.

These are examples that go well beyond consulting and seeking input and opinions. They give effect in one way or another to the radical notion that, in the process of determining which priorities and problems to deal with and then looking for solutions and testing those most likely to work, citizens and businesses and social entrepreneurs should be at the heart of the process.

The growing evidence suggests that collaboration and coproduction are going to be increasingly indispensable to the new governance. They imply a set of values and beliefs about the nature of the tasks of governing in a complex, networked age. They demand a way of behaving and a set of individual and organizational cultural habits and practices that are distinctive and, in some situations, quite different from those that pervade much of the business of government today.

The North Atlantic Treaty Organization (NATO) recently undertook what they called a "policy jam," which, according to one report, was an " unusual online effort by NATO, the European Union, governments and research groups to ask a broader public for ideas on the future of Western security policy." It produced a series of recommendations that called for NATO to develop a civilian arm and the European Union to create its own intelligence agency. The discussion brought together some 3,800 people from 124 countries with expertise or interest in transatlantic security issues. They logged in over five days in February for thematic conversations led by many senior officials and scholars in Europe, Russia, China, and the United States. There were 10 streams of work, 26 "hosts" of the various conversations, and 75 trained and skilled facilitators working with the participants.

We can expect to see more of these kinds of "jams," more or less structured and with varying degrees of openness and reach. But the instinct is the same—to throw the net much more widely to capture a more varied set of insights and experience which in turn will start to redefine what constitutes "expertise" in the first place and where it might be found.

All of these examples hint at a new operating style which harnesses an instinct for sharing, openness, and diffusing control and authority, but without jeopardizing direction, purpose, and execution. And they reflect a set of tools, processes, and capabilities that anyone would need if they are involved in the new work of public-purpose problem solving, whether they work in the formal structures of government and public service or in formally structured organizations outside of government or as individual entrepreneurs or innovators.

New Theory of the Business

All of this implies that we're entering into some new territory insofar as the way we understand how to approach the business of governing well in the networked age. It is territory we cannot afford to ignore. It implies a liberating and sometimes confronting instinct for openness, inclusion, and collaboration. Exploring that new territory suggests something more profound is going on.

Although incremental change and evolution play a large part in the search for new tools and practices of governance and government, there are some serious implications for the art and practice of public administration. What seems to be at stake is something akin to the "theory of the business" changes which, as author Peter Drucker has explained, face organizations; and when organizational capability and culture become dangerously misaligned with market shifts and customer sentiment.

Rethinking the theory of the business for the public sector is the purpose of the

New Synthesis for Public Administration project (http://www.ns6newsynthesis.com/). The project is being coordinated by former senior Canadian bureaucrat and leading public administration thinker and writer Dr. Jocelyne Bourgon.

Dr. Bourgon argues that for over 30 years or more of public sector reform we have failed to offer public sector workers and leaders a set of tools and a set of values and mandates that would allow them to deal with the "wicked" (complex) problems we now face. She believes that improving the anticipative capacity of government is a function of its willingness to enter into explorative conversations. "The greater the openness," she suggests, "the higher the density of connections between government and other actors, the better the chance of detecting emerging trends and emergent phenomena."

Furthermore, she explained that resilient societies have at least three significant characteristics. "They have an active citizenry with the skills and confidence to take action. They have solid networks and community groups with the capability to mobilize resources in support of common solutions. And they have the ability to learn and innovate." She goes on to reinforce the importance of a participatory approach to public policy and of experimentation and pilot projects to "accelerate collective learning." She argues:

> Resilience and adaptive capacity cannot be bought or wished for when it is most needed. It grows out of the bonds built over time among people, organizations, communities and governments that have learned they can work together and count on each other. It is based on a stock of trust and mutual understanding that allows people to act, learn and adapt collectively. It is acquired and expanded by doing. Practice is the only guarantee that it will be there in abundant supply when it is most needed. (Bourgon 2009, p. 1)

Glimpses of a Future

The conclusion that working with and at the edge offers a better way to govern in a connected and complex world begs the question what might that look like? If combining an open and transparent culture with new tools and platforms of collaboration and coproduction is at the heart of this steady, if sometimes uneven progress, what might we expect to see as it starts to work?

Policy innovation is more likely to spring from a process of systematic serendipity, a conscious attempt to find good ideas and potential solutions to the policy challenges from a much wider mix of people and places. Perhaps we'll see more examples or variations of the NATO "policy jam," that is, crowdsourcing, in which as a matter of course policy discussions take place on platforms that make it easier to integrate the views and ideas of larger, dispersed networks of expertise. New ways to visualize the outcome from those kinds of discussions, along the lines of the U.S. State Department's Opinion 2.0 or the UK attempt to make budget information more accessible and interactive, will become more widespread.

Policy and program design will likely move away from detailed prescription and complex definitions of targets and outcomes toward a more "values and principles" approach. Much greater latitude will be given to those closer to the action in order to determine the best way to respond to specific issues and challenges. Especially in social policy domains, the emphasis will increasingly be on relationships and connections between people—people who use services, families and friends, professional advisers and support resources, public servants and people working in nonprofit organizations, perhaps—rather than on rules and regulations. As Charlie Leadbeater suggests, governments will be less inclined to do things to and for people and more inclined to do things with and by people.

Perhaps early experiments with tools like the Urban EcoMap will lay the groundwork for similar platforms that assume a policy outcome is a function of changing behavior and social networking among citizens and communities. Information and performance monitoring remain key. Large amounts of data, including more qualitative and experiential data, often in the form of shared video, will have to be created, shared, stored, and accessed in flexible and rapidly changing formats and spaces.

Much of the work involved in achieving policy outcomes and aspirations will be the responsibility of a more diffuse, complex, and shifting mix of organizations, some of them in the formal structures of the public service and others in the corporate or social sectors. The impetus for policy change and reform, or for the rapid evolution of program and service design, is as likely to emerge from outside government and the public service as it is from inside.

The locus of authority for change, renewal, and innovation will shift, less tied to status and formal authority and more contingent on contribution, insight, and experience. People will achieve both prominence and influence more as a function of the quality of their ideas and insights than of the position they hold in formal organizational structures. In that sense, governing with and at the edge will pioneer a "reputational democracy" in which people get to lead and be listened to because they earn a reputation based on the value and relevance of their contributions.

A "public purpose" sector that systematically spills over inherited and, to some extent, still necessary boundaries and distinctions will develop shared systems and processes with which to do their common work. As the flow of knowledge, experience, and expertise becomes more critical to good policy outcomes and better decision making and service design, the tools and platforms for sharing also become more critical. More and more, these tools and platforms have to be designed so that people can both get the information they need quickly and contribute the knowledge they have to share. So, for example, information systems about "chaotic" families involved in intensive programs of support and engagement have to avoid the duplication that sometimes occurs when people are required to tell different agencies the same information multiple times. Resolving issues of privacy, security, and the maintenance of the physical infrastructure and networks on which the new communities of practice and action rely will be at a premium.

Resources of all sorts—money, physical assets, and especially information—

will diffuse to the edges of large public systems, driving new levels of autonomy, choice, and control. Accountability mechanisms must evolve in order to meet two critical demands: *First,* manage the information and knowledge that will be created and shared as the basis for monitoring performance and understanding real outcomes. The more dispersed the networks of activity and the more diffuse the location of real action becomes, the more important will be the enduring instincts for coherence and proper accountability for performance. But accountability will be as much outward and downward to partners, communities, and service users as it will be upward to the formal structures of vertical accountability. That task will fall especially to the "center" which will be less engaged in the detailed work of designing and implementing services and engaging with users and more focused on building the shared systems of knowledge and communication that keep the larger community connected. The center becomes responsible for giving the larger system a sense of coherence and meaning, without resorting to traditional tools of centralized control and command.

By governing with and at the edge we are also going to discover new ways to achieve mass and scale in the delivery of services and support, but the resulting engagement with people will feel small and local. Experiments will emerge into what NESTA calls "mass localism" (Bunt and Harris 2010), that is, solutions that work on a larger canvas not by creating monolithic and cumbersome organizations but by connecting smaller pieces into networks that achieve the same impact without jeopardizing the ability to respond quickly.

Finally, the public service itself as an institution will evolve to reflect, and to some extent lead, the emergence of an "edge" model of government and governance. That will be obvious in some very practical ways. An underlying commitment to the enduring values—fairness, transparency, accountability, integrity—will be reinforced not just for the public service but for anyone involved in doing public work.

The formal public service will start to manifest its own version of the "contribution, not status" model of reputational influence in which individual public servants will be encouraged to think and share new ideas and solutions, often harnessing the more widespread and accessible tools and platforms of social networking. These will cease to be seen as exotic distractions and will simply become indispensable tools of the trade for anyone who wants to be effective in their public service work.

The processes of systematic serendipity will become increasingly common in engaging people outside government in policy, services, and public innovation. In much the same way will their easy and safe availability become the hallmarks of a modern and effective public service. People will share and crowdsource project ideas and contributions on collaboration platforms within the public service. In some cases they will be created with levels of security that are required to ensure that, where it is appropriate, a safe environment for internal discussion and advice can flourish.

Organizational structures, boundaries, and status will start to matter less (although they will always matter) as public servants become more involved in cross-cutting and boundary-shifting teams clustered around policy issues or program design and delivery challenges. It will start to matter less which agency you are from and what level you are and more which projects you are engaged in and to which spreading networks of practice and influence you are connected and contributing. And underlying this new public service will be easy, ubiquitous, and secure access to devices and networks and other tools for the people that work in the agencies of government that give them the "anywhere, anytime" opportunities for flexible working.

The workplace becomes anywhere you want and need to be to connect with the people you need, real or virtual, rather than a single place you have to be.

Conclusion

Looking forward, we expect to see the center and the edge arrive at a new accommodation. This will be driven by the more insistent and well-resourced capacity of the edge to demand not just to be heard but to be more influential in the search for new ideas, new models, and more effective solutions. One of the center's most demanding jobs will be to make it easier for the edge to thrive. However, next-generation governing models can claim no respite from persistent demands for efficiency, equity, productivity, and the relentless demand to be more open and transparent. Perhaps the best available summary of this new model are the values from the "open and transparent" reform program launched by President Obama on his first day in the White House.

In his memorandum to senior officials, he reduced his aspiration for change in the conduct and impact of public administration to three powerful ideas—participation, transparency, and collaboration.

These three interlocking ideas, and the culture, practice, and systems on which they rely, should become manifest in the day-to-day business of public leaders and organizations. They remain the simplest summary of the DNA whose patterns and consequences should become increasingly evident to people who interact with government and, just as important, to people who work in and with government as part of an evolving "public purpose" sector.

Governing well has never been easy. Under new pressures for relevance and resilience, it is becoming more complex and demanding.

Collaboration and coproduction are likely to feature as increasingly prominent capabilities in the new governance, giving effect to a governing model that privileges the edge without undermining the legitimate, but different, role of the center.

We're still at the beginning of a process of exploration and innovation in the design and use of some of these new tools. Fuelling that process at the heart of a more robust embrace by the public sector of innovation and reform will itself become a hallmark of effective governance into an uncertain and unpredictable future.

References

Bourgon, Jocelyne. 2009. "Serving Beyond the Predictable." Keynote address, CISCO Public Services Summit, December 9, Stockholm, Sweden.

British Cabinet Office. 2010. *Building the Big Society.* London: Cabinet Office, UK Government. http://www.cabinetoffice.gov.uk/media/407789/building-big-society.pdf (accessed January 18, 2011).

Bunt, Laura, and Michael Harris. 2010. *Mass Localism: A Way to Help Small Communities Solve Big Challenges.* February. National Endowment for Science Technology and the Arts (NESTA). London: NESTA.

Democracy Club. n.d. "Want to Know What Your Parliamentary Candidates Think?" London: Democracy Club. http://www.democracyclub.org.uk (accessed January 18, 2011).

Department of Broadband and Digital Economy. 2011. "Blog Posts." Canberra: Department of Broadband and Digital Economy, Government of Australia. http://www.dbcde.gov.au/about_us (accessed January 18, 2011).

Noveck, Beth. 2010. *Wiki Government.* Washington, DC: Brookings Institution Press.

Southwark Circle. n.d. "About Us." London: Southwark Circle Community Interest Company. http://www.southwarkcircle.org.uk (accessed January 18, 2011).

19

The Millennial Generation

ROBERT D. CHILDS, PAULETTE ROBINSON, TERRY M. MCGOVERN, AND GERRY GINGRICH

DARPA's Great Red Balloon Hunt

The Defense Advanced Research Projects Agency (DARPA) created a Great Red Balloon Hunt Contest to study how information spread virally through the Internet. The contest was designed to "explore the roles the Internet and social networking play in the timely communication, wide-area team-building and urgent mobilization required to solve broad-scope, time-critical problems." Ten red balloons were launched from readily accessible locations visible from nearby roads. DARPA ensured that no one person could observe all of the balloons that were spread across the country.

Nine hours after the balloons were launched DARPA announced MIT had won the $40K contest by posting the latitudes and longitudes in DDD-MM0SS format on the DARPA website. How did MIT do it? The MIT team learned of the contest just a few days before it started. In true millennial fashion, within 48 hours the MIT team created a website and designed an information-sharing reward system that not only awarded $1K to those who located balloons, but also $500 to those who made the connections between the MIT team and the balloon finders. MIT's reward system also included a social consciousness incentive; they ensured a portion of the money paid to participants, both balloon finders and connectors, went to charity.

The technique MIT used to filter real data from fake data sent by competing teams is being analyzed by DARPA for possible Department of Defense implementation. This contest demonstrated how social media can be combined with collaborative networks and smart incentive systems and used for many things, including finding criminals and missing children and halting impending terrorist attacks (Hauger 2009).

Millennials and Work

Millennials as a group have not known an environment without computers and mobile technologies. They are the most connected generation. They are connected globally to people, information, and digital tools. Within an environment of technology immersion, Millennials are guided by eight norms: freedom, customization, scrutiny, integrity, collaboration, entertainment, speed, and innovation (Tapscott 2009). When they bring these norms into the workplace, they expect to be immersed in and connected through technology. They expect meaningful work and to solve problems through collaboration. How will the government attract, retain, and mentor this generation to lead our future? What do they expect from their workplace and colleagues?

To attract and retain Millennials requires an understanding of what they value. They don't value work as much as they value their families, friends, social networks, co-workers, and themselves. Because of their sheer numbers, organizations have no choice but to learn how to accommodate them as the boomers retire. Organizations can expect Millennials to quit if they disagree with the work culture. Money is important to Millennials. They research salary ranges in a given field for a specific area. They do not come to interviews if salaries are not competitive. If the salary is competitive, then salary becomes a nonissue. Other things, such as relaxed environment, family support, supportive culture, work-life balance, vibrant volunteer programs, and varied experiences will attract talented Millennials. It should not be surprising that Millennials will take a job just to work with friends. They are also far more likely to work in an organization that supports collaborative rather than dictatorial relationships with co-workers.

Understanding that Millennials are the most coddled generation in history helps explain why they expect a supportive work culture. Their loyalty to an organization is directly tied to their relationships throughout the organization. Their supervisor is the most important connection to the organization. To be kept in an organization, they require mentoring, consistent development, and rewards within a caring environment. Millennials value their time. Because of the pervasiveness of technology in their lives, Millennials see very little difference between work and personal activity. They require good reasons to work late. Millennials will work 60-hour weeks when required or if they see value in it. However, they don't want it to be a way of life. Flexible work schedules and reasonable hours are key factors for Millennials when making job decisions. They will not check their values at the office door. What they value in their personal life influences their work life.

Millennials expect the pace of work to be much faster and they also expect to be promoted quickly. Continuous feedback on their performance helps them understand how fast they are moving on their career track. They see no need to follow an industrial chain of command process when they know the quickest way to achieving a decision is to go directly to the decision maker. So they do. Speed also affects how they develop. The "chalk and talk" approach to corporate training will not work well with Millennials. Instead, they thrive in immersive programs, where, like in a video game, they can experiment, collaborate, and learn by doing. They see no need to go too deeply into a subject unless it applies to the task at hand, then they will Google the knowledge they need. Not only will the characteristics of Millennials shape the nature of work, but so too will their reasons for working and the rewards they expect to receive for work well done.

Millennials expect their workplaces to be places of strong values. They expect an organization to contribute to society and value an organization's environmental policies. Many companies are responding by allowing workers to take paid sabbaticals to volunteer with nonprofits or struggling small businesses. Volunteer programs assist in developing Millennials, while providing them with diverse experiences. A 2006 survey of 1,800 Millennials found that 79 percent want to work for a socially conscious company (Needleman 2008). Sixty-four percent of Millennials report being more loyal to socially and environmentally engaged organizations.

Generations Collide

Generations are shaped by a common set of historical and cultural experiences that form their values. Technology and tools often define the way in which a group interacts in the world and becomes a critical part of communication and work. The Millennial expectations for a work environment described earlier are colliding within organizations managed by the boomer generation. The boomers grew up in a competitive and hierarchical work environment. They followed the rules, worked extra hours, and earned their promotions over time. They find the Millennials presumptive in their expectations and scary in their lack of respect for procedures and seniority.

Technology Shapes Interactions

Whereas historical and cultural events shape our values, technology is the major driving force shaping how we interact with our environment. For boomers, television was the major technological advance. It is a passive technology demanding nothing from the viewer. Media is delivered at prescribed times and broadcast news is trusted as a reliable source. Programs are watched from beginning to end. There is no dialogue or interaction. Television organizes information about the outside world. The political process is dominated by this passive delivery of information and media. Many boomer voters watch the candidates on television, without dialogue, and then vote as their conclusive input into the democratic process. The government then governs until the next election, when the boomer votes again. Information is controlled and delivered in a one-way manner. Messages are prescribed. Boomers choose the flavor or channel for passive delivery, but often do not seek beyond this passive mode. While the Internet has flourished with boomers taking the early lead, they use it predominantly to receive and deliver controlled and carefully crafted information. No dialogue is expected. They are slow to adopt social media tools. It is additional information noise and overhead. Interaction is small talk and not valued.

It is interesting to observe a Millennial "watch" television. The television is a backdrop to their information gathering and multitasking. When interesting pieces of information are available on television, they look for more information on the topic, ask their friends about the program, and text about activities for the next day. They often multitask while watching. Television programs are often recorded on TIVO-like devices. They control what they watch and when they watch it. Commercials are irrelevant and are quickly dispatched. Programs are watched in pieces based on their interest. News is gathered off the Web on a regular basis during the day using RSS feeds. They do not rely on the television or newspapers which limit the news to a snapshot in time.

Millennials have always had computers and connection to the Internet, even as children. The body of research on Millennials contains a wide range of descriptions related to their use of technology. A normal 25-year-old in the workforce today has, on average, 5,000 hours of video game playing; exchanges of 250,000 e-mails, instant messages, and phone text messages; 10,000 hours of cell phone use; and 3,500 hours online before they enter the working world at 22 (Rainie 2006). Each has a cell phone customized with tools to enhance their connections with others and to provide them with information quickly. This generation took the passive Internet created by the boomers and reshaped it into a dynamic place through shared networks, collaboration, and media created, remixed, and delivered back to the community. The MIT solution to the DARPA contest demonstrates this dynamic use. Millennials manage the large influx of information with multitasking, search, and collaboration strategies. They use their collaboration to improve products, sound a warning on faulty products, and encourage friends to buy the best products. Customers can rate products on websites like Amazon and Walmart. They act as employees by providing product reviews, which help online retailers sell their merchandise. The blurring of lines between customer and employee, employee life and personal life, are part of a Millennials' integrity-based living paradigm.

Millennials expect to participate in the conversation, offer solutions to problems, and be heard. They refuse to passively listen. Through the technology, they can amass global resources to support a tragedy like the earthquake in Haiti or to organize against an injustice like the elections in Iran. Content is produced and shared with others through YouTube, Facebook, Twitter, Flickr, and so forth. They are a force for change at every level of our society. They will change how we do business in the government through the use of technology. As part of this change, traditional work boundaries are being reshaped.

Place Boundaries Redrawn

The most traditional work boundary being reshaped as a result of technology is the physical boundary of place. The requirements for a physical location to work are often tied to the nature of the work and the resources needed to produce a product or service. In the industrial age, workers were required to work as an organized group with machines to produce a product. Even services organized around a business unit with resources for the delivery of that service were based in a physical location. A physical location where work is organized with a group requires everyone to be at the place for particular time periods. The eight-hour day in the United States was the result of a 147-year struggle between management and labor which resulted in the Fair Labor Standards Act (29 U.S. Code, Chapter 8), creating the eight-hour workday (Foner 1986).

The need for a workplace is being transformed within the nature of work. Over the past 100 years, work has been changing from industrial production to service based. The types of workers needed have changed from highly skilled on a particular machine in a certain location to highly knowledgeable workers within a particular field. Modern workers have become the "machine." When the freedom of location is coupled with advances in transportation and technology, modern knowledge workers can apply their knowledge, skills, and abilities where and when needed (Toffler 1991). Today, knowledge workers outnumber all other workers in North America by at least a four-to-one margin (Haag et al. 2006). It is only with the advent of the Internet and access to digital tools, services, and information that physical space became less important for those workers whose primary activity is knowledge and information. Knowledge workers leverage social media tools such as Facebook, Twitter, YouTube, and Flickr to form collaborative networks of experts to assist in creating new products and services (Tapscott and Williams 2006). Millennials, by virtue of their being born and raised in the digital age, are destined to become exceptional knowledge workers.

Government services and activities are largely tied to resources that are location based. Information is located in physical agency silos and dominated by print. Historically, citizens are required to either come to a government office or use the mail to receive government services. More and more information is digital and available outside and inside government through internal and external networks. Working from any place at any time is now possible in the government with an Internet connection and access credentials. Citizens can receive information and services not only from physical locations, but also from websites, through e-mail, by telephone, or through real-time interactions over the Internet. The access to resources and collaboration from any place and any time changes the options where the government worker can do work and connect with the citizen. The "place" of work has shifted.

Boomers have been tethered to their work location for much of their careers. They nest in this physical space, adding pictures, mementos, and so on to make the space their own. Although they can appreciate the option to occasionally work from home, they are generally suspicious of those whom they manage who are working from home. Millennials have worked with digital tools for access and work since childhood. They are connected at all times. Their personal space is the electronics they carry with them. They are surprised that in government (1) there are often not the tools they typically use to collaborate and connect and (2) their managers require them to physically be at a specific location to do their work. This is particularly problematic when they have more productive tools at home than the computers, social media tools, and access they have in their agency.

In the industrial age, the machine was the foundation of work so in order to work it made sense for workers to be located where the machines were. In the information age, human capital is the foundation of the workplace, which now means the work goes with the expert. Millennials, who are virtually connecting using mobile devices, inherently understand that work isn't a place, it's a task, an applied expertise. Where or how a task is accomplished is not as important as its accomplishment; results are what count.

Millennials value and demand freedom in their jobs and their private lives. They are redrawing the physical boundaries of work by demanding programs such as teleworking, virtual teams, and "hot desking." If the programs are not present, Millennials are voting with their feet and freeing themselves to work elsewhere. Recruitment firm Robert Half International surveyed 1,400 chief financial officers; 50 percent said telework arrangements are the second-best recruiting inducement, after salary. One-third classified it as the best incentive (Abate 2008). Nearly 50 million U.S. workers (about 40 percent of the working population) could telework at least part of the time. But, in 2008, only 2.5 million employees did so (not including the self-employed). Most organizations consider teleworking as a benefit instead of the primary method of business.

Some government organizations, such as the U.S. Patent Office, understand the value of telework. The Patent Office started a teleworking program in 1997 with significant benefits (Gross 2007). Employees cite teleworking as a reason for staying with the Patent Office. Some left Fortune 500 companies to join the Patent Office because of the policy. Between 2006 and 2007, the Patent Office hired 1,200 new examiners without leasing any additional office space based on their teleworking option. The agency saved hundreds of thousands of dollars per year. The National Defense University iCollege's telework capabilities are another example. Their experience with telework enabled the Washington, D.C.–based faculty to teach their graduate courses during a series of debilitating snowstorms in February 2010.

Telework blurs boundaries between work and private life. Technology allows staff to work from anywhere. Does this mean workers are expected to work any time and all of the time? Are the eight hours only counted when they are worked in the office? When a staff person teleworks, are they expected to work the same prescribed hours as in the office or can it be any eight hours during that day? Even if staff are not permitted to telework, their smart phones and computer access into the agency provide a mechanism to respond to e-mail and work well beyond the eight-hour day. Private life and work no longer have hard boundaries. The communications that apply to private life occur during the workday and work communications occur during hours beyond the traditional eight hours. Boomers, by their sheer numbers, have competed for positions in the workplace for their entire careers. In order to have a job and a promotion, they pushed themselves above and beyond the requirements of the job to set themselves apart. Whereas access to technology has made work possible anytime and anyplace for all generations, boomers come into work for eight hours but also work beyond the eight hours away from the workplace. They demonstrate their willingness to get the job done no matter what the price personally. Millennials use the technology to give themselves freedom to choose when they do work, not to work all of the time. They use the technology to make themselves more efficient and effective; to give themselves time to pursue other interests in their lives. It is not a lack of dedication to their work, but a commitment to balance in life. They do not work for work's own sake. Boomers are puzzled by this approach and often comment that Millennials are lazy and will not step up when they are needed, as described in the iCollege student exchange that follows.

Collision in the Classroom

A recent iCollege classroom exchange between a Millennial and a boomer high-lights what is at play in government workspaces around the world. The millennial, a 32-year-old GS15 disagreed with a boomer, a 61-year-old GS15, about working harder versus working smarter. The boomer insisted that workers should remain at their desks until the boss leaves for the day in case an unexpected event should arise. The Millennial differed, suggesting the boomer could text, IM, e-mail, call, or tweet the boss if needed. There was no need to be present at work if there was no work to do. He could better spend his time with his family. The boomer commented that if the Millennial worked in *his* office, he wouldn't last long. To which the Millennial agreed, noting if the boomer were *his* boss, he would have quit in the first week. The boomer then suggested that this would not happen since the Millennial would have to find a new job to pay his mortgage. "What mortgage?" replied the Millennial. "Well, you'll need to pay rent," commented the boomer. "No I don't. I'll move back in with mom and dad," was the response. At this point, several boomers in the room nodded their heads in agreement with the Millennial. The professor asked why they agreed, and three boomer students commented that they had a 20-plus-year-old Millennial living at home with them. The professor asked if this was a sign of failure on behalf of their children for not establishing their independence. One boomer replied, "Not at all. My kids are always welcome back home regardless of their age. We can afford it and we love them."

Communication Patterns Reshaped

Technology has not only changed where and when we work, but also how we communicate. The world is being driven to connect on a global scale and messages are sent around the world through social media in a matter of minutes. Twitter takes on an organizing force for political action (e.g., Iranian elections) and disaster response is immediate during any global event with current communications technology. Everything is recorded on the digital highway where input devices are ubiquitous and mobile. Everyone can be connected to everyone else.

Privacy no longer exists and secrecy is a commodity impossible to guarantee. Transparency is more than just a buzzword. It is a real outcome of the information age. Just ask professional golfer Tiger Woods, presidential hopeful John Edwards, and any number of others who have been exposed, judged by the court of public opinion, confessed, apologized, and punished through loss of income, reputation, or both in our new transparent world. It's not just people who are feeling the effect of transparency: large organizations and governments are dealing with the consequences.

The major forms of communication for the boomers are text, telephone, and face-to-face meetings. While it is rare to see a boomer without their Blackberry, the conventions of e-mail within business are still bound by printed conventions (spelling, grammar, etc.). A work e-mail is often carefully crafted not only for written text conventions but for a formal tone and message. They often have the look and feel of written office memos. Interaction is not required. E-mails are often used to deliver information or instructions. E-mail provides a means to leapfrog hierarchical communication conventions, but boomers are less likely to make the jump. They respect and support hierarchical structures. They reinforce them in their communications. Boomers prefer face-to-face meetings to using digital tools as a replacement for those meetings. This is not surprising because their workplace has been dominated by work in a physical space. The spontaneity of response and the rich interpersonal cues of a face-to-face meeting give boomers the assurance of attention and reaction to meeting issues. Many boomers' communications in social media are static pronouncements or messages (at least when they first start). Messages are characteristically not personal and often market the person (as an expert), work products, or services. Websites designed by boomers, like the organization's marketing materials, are often dominated by information delivery and text-heavy messages. Interactions from the public are not controllable in terms of message and building social media into websites is met with the concern, "What if someone said something negative about my organization on the website?"

Whereas the boomers have relied on formal written text to communicate, the Millennials are inventing their own communication grid with social media and smart phones. They understand the global nature of today's communication while remaining somewhat naïve on the long-term implications of living their private lives out in public. If they have a problem, they often create communication tools to respond to the situation. Facebook was created by Mark Zukerberg in 2004 to help him study for an art history exam for a class he had not attended at Harvard. He posted all of the pictures from the course onto a website with some information hoping other students in the course would add more information. Within 24 hours, the comments were so complete that he not only passed the exam with flying colors but provided a study space for all the other students.

Millennials are so used to interacting with others they have created a new form of "socialism" in the 21st century. Social networking, social media, social rating, social bookmarking, social news, and so on are terms that have entered into our vernacular because of the ability to interact virtually. Millennials stay connected through social media (Facebook, Twitter, Flickr, and so on) with an ever-larger circle of "friends." This network is more loosely related at the edges, but can be called upon to solve problems, respond with information, or provide additional connections. The closer to the Millennial, the more trusted the source and the more they will rely on these connections for advice. A formal hierarchy does not exist, but communication is based on trust. Collaborative, team-based activity is the epicenter of the Millennials' life and shapes what the new workforce looks like. While the boomer generation often lets information come to them, the Millennials actively seek out information from a variety of sources. Communications are media rich and text is limited. Since text messaging is one of the dominant connections with friends and family, meaning is more important than grammar and spelling. Millennials rarely use e-mail unless required to do so at work. They find it too formal and restrictive. Millennials prefer to do projects together, to take advantage of everyone's strengths. Rather than passing documents through e-mail, they prefer collaborative tools like a wiki to write ideas and refine documents. For them, processes evolve with the use of the tools. Crowdsourcing problems are the norm as demonstrated in MIT's solution to the DARPA balloon challenge. For example, the development of Intellipedia in 2005 was the brainchild of Millennials Sean Dennehy and Don Burke, when they were tasked with increasing knowledge sharing across the intelligence community.

It's not surprising that there's a tension between generations over the use of communication models. In the government, whereas boomers are comfortable with hierarchies in their agencies, Millennials seek out information wherever they can find it. When they have access to everyone, they use it. Access to information is flattened and less privileged. Millennials are surprised when social media tools are not available at work, or when using them is viewed suspiciously as wasting time. Years ago organizations were reluctant to allow employees to use e-mail. Now e-mail is an integral part of communication in every organization. However, there are still few social media tools for communication within organizations, although this situation is improving. New communication processes within agencies are responding to the demand for these tools by workers and citizens. The use of external social media tools is increasingly taking cues from the Obama administration's use of these tools with the public. An agency's reluctance to use these tools is also surprising to a generation who values transparency and dialogue. Rather than maintain strict control of the message, Millennials want to have an honest dialogue with the citizen.

Information Technology Hurdles

IT network boundaries provide organizations with protection of their data behind their digital boundary or firewall from malware and intrusion. Government takes the protection of citizen information and information regarding the security of our country very seriously. In the government, policy mandates information security for software and for networks. Policies and guidelines are often slow to change. Social media have been met with suspicion because of their collaborative open design. Tools behind the firewall, where information can be contained, are not met with as much constraint as tools facing out. Public social media tools have often been blocked by agency IT security. As the tools have been scrutinized, some of this is changing.

IT security is only one of the constraints. There is also the process of traditional release of information by an agency. Information release is tightly controlled by processes and policy. Information released to the public is required—minimally—to be approved by the agency's public affairs officer and often the legal officer. With information deemed politically sensitive, it may require review by the agency leadership. Boomers have lived their entire careers within a hierarchy that reinforces the protection of agency information and the control of agency messages within a prescribed process. Millennials have grown up with open access to the Internet, tools, and information. They are adept at showing their managers how there is no privacy and that most information is available. Collaboration and dialogue is their expectation with any and all organizations. They are surprised at the government's reluctance to interact with the citizen beyond delivering and controlling information.

Workplace boundaries in work are not easily changed. The tensions between the generations provide a momentum for the change. How can government leverage these tensions and ensure changes that benefit not only government workers, but also the citizens?

Leveraging Millennials in Government

You can never solve a problem on the level on which it is created.

—Einstein

Boomers have created—along with previous generations—the forward leaps that characterize our country's social advancements. However, they have also created the complex problems that our government and society must solve. The Millennials offer us a new approach to problems that is collaborative, global, and innovative in approach. The Millennials can help the boomers think outside the box they've created.

Millennials automatically choose to collaborate and share information as part of the process. Social media tools become invaluable in solutions to problems. The winners of the DARPA contest leveraged individuals to get the information they needed to win the prize. The recent application of social media in the Haiti disaster demonstrates how Millennial responses to events and problems result from collaborations that erupt out of a need. And those responses are shaped and resourced on multiple fronts without an official authority guiding them or giving them permission to act. Large amounts of information from multiple sources and in multiple formats are collected, organized, and disseminated using social media tools created from around the world.

There are a number of ways government can leverage the talents of Millennials and their approach to information and problem solving. A couple of suggestions are offered in the following paragraphs.

Leaders can task Millennials in their organization to find social media solutions that can be used by the organization to facilitate collaboration, information sharing, and improved business processes. Once the environment is designed, the Millennials can be an important part of cross-generational teams to examine how business processes can be reengineered to make the agency more effective and efficient using these new tools. They can be part of the implementation and adoption process across the organization.

The Millennial generation is our future workforce. Leverage them to create recruiting and retention programs targeted for their generation. Involve them in shaping a workplace that is attractive to their generation. Work with them in teams to examine all organizational assumptions, processes, limitations, and leadership styles. Create a safe place for all generations to give input and suggestions.

The federal government is siloed into various agencies which in turn are siloed into various organizations. Congressional funding reinforces these silos. The government as enterprise is rarely evident on any level beyond the agency. Interagency projects are difficult to create and fund, yet the thorny and complex problems our government faces require interagency collaboration, information sharing, and innovative approaches. Millennials can offer us social media strategies to connect government workers across government. They can help us think outside of the box.

Citizens, in particular, have been separated from their government in helping to solve problems. They often have no input into government solutions beyond their vote or pressuring their representatives into particular actions. There is a feeling of disempowerment, particularly at the individual level. Millennials want to have a part in shaping their future. President Obama's election and the participation of Millennials show this promise and hope. They want to be a part of government, to be part of the solution. If the government ignores the Millennial citizens, they will organize outside of the government and demand change. Iran has had direct experience of the power of this type of organization.

The government could start by setting up a myGov website that allows citizens to shape a Web portlet customized to their individual needs and information interests in government. They will be able to select government blogs, RSS feeds, connections to services, and so forth. It would be a dramatic way for citizens to choose how they want to connect to government. They can determine what is relevant to them. But this will only be a start.

Agencies need to find ways that individuals can offer input connected to the agency mission. For example, in the State Department's Public Diplomacy office

Millennials created a contest for individuals across the world to create a video describing democracy. Winners were flown to Washington, D.C., and a trip to Hollywood was donated for the winners. The videos were uploaded onto YouTube and people from all over the world could view them and vote on their favorite. The mission of Public Diplomacy is to spread democracy and U.S. values to people in other countries. They met this mission with this project in a very different approach that appealed to Millennials through social media techniques. The Environmental Protection Agency has a blog that seeks input and solutions from the environmental community. The army has created a myArmy capability wherein individual citizens can shape their reception of information and participation with the army. Millennials can help design social media solutions that meet the needs of both the agency and the citizens.

Management Considerations

The Millennial influence and impact across the world is striking and ubiquitous. Through technology and the ability to gather data on a global scale quickly, they are influencing industry development, education, nongovernmental organizations and fund-raising, government, and so on. There is not a sector unaffected. As a government manager it is important to consider the following questions:

1. Who on your staff are Millennials and what are their pain points in the organization?
2. In what ways can Millennials be tasked within the organization to find the best solutions for identified pain points (e.g., social media use, both internally and externally)?
3. For what complex issues within your organization can you ask Millennials to consider outside-the-box innovative solution(s)?
4. How can you encourage citizen involvement in your organization's mission?
5. If you do not consider what the Millennials have to offer your organization (both as workers and as citizens), can your organization remain relevant?

Evolution or Revolution

Technology is the main driver shaping the way in which Millennials approach life and work. It shapes their expectations of government as a workplace and as a citizen service. Millennials are reinventing communications, methods for collaboration, and work processes and services. One only has to look at the slow demise of printed newspapers to understand the impact of ignoring this generation. Millennials are demanding change in government both as employees and as citizens. While change appears to be inevitable, the rate and means of change will determine whether the changes will be evolutionary or revolutionary.

Demographics are a prime determinant of the rate of change. Earlier labor statistics (2004) projected a mass exodus of boomers (40 percent) from the federal workforce. This number has been recently adjusted by the U.S. Department of Labor's Employment Projections Program for 2008–2018 (U.S. Department of Labor 2009). The boomers are expected to remain in the labor force longer than did previous generations. Thus, the problem will not be solved by expecting boomers to retire en masse.

> As the members of the large baby boom generation grow older and continue their trend of increased labor force participation, the number of persons aged 55 years and older in the labor force is expected to increase by 12.0 million, or 43.0 percent, during the 2008–18 period. Persons in the 55 years and older age group are projected to make up nearly one-quarter of the labor force in 2018. Young people (age 16–24) are expected to account for 12.7 percent of the labor force in 2018, and persons in the prime-age working group (age 25 to 54) to account for 63.5 percent of the 2018 labor force (U.S. Department of Labor 2009).

A second factor that will determine the rate of change depends on the boomer adoption and adaptation of new technologies to meet the current collaboration, communication, and business and information processing needs of the government. Boomers are currently adopting social media tools at a greater rate than any other generation. A "Boomer and Technology" study commissioned by AARP and Microsoft in October 2009 explored boomer use of technology (Rogers 2009). The report suggests that Millennials are "the technology pioneers, the first to explore new territory, the Boomers are the settlers, arriving a bit later to set up the schools, libraries, churches and hospitals, to sink deep roots and build permanent structures." Boomers are not afraid of the technology, but will weigh the uses of the technology and integrate these technologies and new ways of doing business into the system.

A third factor for change is leadership. President Obama's willingness to use social media in his election and then to communicate with the public after his inauguration has created a government environment where adoption of social media and tools commonly used by Millennials is possible. In addition, the Open Government initiative has provided a model for collaboration and communication that is being built on throughout government. Agencies and organizations within various agencies are providing innovative services to the citizen and providing tools for collaboration.

Conclusions

What will the future government look like? It's clear that both generations will be working in government in large numbers. Will the government be an appealing place to work where the technology needs of both boomers and Millennials will be met?

Change will happen. It is already begun. The time is right for both an evolution and a revolution of government. Technology is moving at a revolutionary pace, driving the environment to change and adapt at breakneck speeds. Millennials are the pioneers, testing and innovating the art of the possible as it breaks upon the government workplace, and boomers can take advantage of these pioneering efforts to create new government places, structures, and processes. Both generations can work together to co-evolve government to the next stage.

References

Abate, T. 2008. "Group Touts Telecommuting's Green Benefits." *San Francisco Chronicle,* April 22. http://articles.sfgate.com/2008–04–22/business/17146154_1_carbon-dioxide-telecommuting-advantage-telework (accessed March 2, 2010).
Foner, P. S. 1986. *May Day: A Short History of the International Workers' Holiday, 1886–1986.* New York: International Publishers.
Gross, G. 2007. "U.S. Patent Office Leverages Telecommuting." *Infoworld,* March 20. http://www.infoworld.com/t/communication-and-collaboration/us-patent-office-leverages-telecommuting-102 (accessed March 2, 2010).
Haag, S., M. Cummings, D. McCubbrey, A. Pinsonneault, and R. Donovan. 2006. *Management Information Systems for the Information Age,* 3d ed. Whitby, Ontario, Canada: McGraw-Hill Ryerson.
Hauger, D. 2009. "DARPA's Red Balloon Hunt 2009." Associated Content, December 14. http://www.associatedcontent.com/article/2479096/darpas_red_balloon_hunt_2009.html?cat=15.
Howe, J. 2008. *Crowdsourcing: Why the Power of the Crowd Is Driving the Future of Business.* New York: Random House.
Jarvis, J. 2009. *What Would Google Do?* New York: HarperCollins.
Lancaster, L., and D. Stillman. 2002. *When Generations Collide.* New York: HarperCollins.
Levine, R., C. Locke, D. Searls, D. Weinberger, and J. McKee. 2009. *The Cluetrain Manifesto,* 10th Anniversary Edition. New York: Basic Books.
Lister, K. 2009. *Undress for Success: The Naked Truth about Making Money at Home.* Hoboken, NJ: Wiley.
Needleman, S. E. 2008. "The Latest Office Perk: Getting Paid to Volunteer." *Wall Street Journal,* April 29, D1.
The Nielsen Company. 2007. "Word-of-mouth the Most Powerful Selling Tool." Nielsen Global Survey, October 2. http://asiapacific.acnielsen.com/news/20071002.shtml (accessed March 2, 2010).
Rainie, L. 2006. "New Workers, New Workplaces: Digital 'Natives' Invade the Workplace." Presentation, September 28. Pew Internet and American Life Project. http://www.pewinternet.org/Presentations/2006/New-Workers-New-Workplaces.aspx (accessed March 2, 2010).
Rogers, Michael. 2009. *Boomers and Technology: An Extended Conversation.* October. Washington, DC: AARP and Microsoft.
Schuman, H., and J. Scott. 1989. "Generations and Collective Memories." *American Sociological Review* 54: 359–381.
Tapscott, D. 2009. *Grown Up Digital: How the Net Generation Is Changing Your World.* New York: McGraw-Hill.
Tapscott, D., and A. D. Williams. 2006. *Wikinomics: How Mass Collaboration Changes Everything.* New York: Portfolio.

Toffler, A. 1991. *Future Shock.* New York: Bantam Books.

U.S. Department of Labor. Bureau of Labor Statistics. 2009. "Employment Projections: 2008–2018 Summary." Press release, December 10. http://www.bls.gov/news.release/ecopro.nr0.htm.

Volti, R. 2008. *An Introduction to the Sociology of Work and Occupations.* Los Angeles: Pine Forge Press.

Zemke, R., C. Raines, and B. Filipczak. 2000. *Generations at Work: Managing the Clash of Veterans, Boomers, Xers, and Nexters in Your Workplace.* New York: American Management Association.

20

Leadership-Purpose Chain in Governmental Organizations

Scott Blanchard, Drea Zigarmi, Dobie Houson, and Vicky Essary

The ancient Chinese curse, "May you live in a time of change," appears to be more relevant today. Pace of change seems more rapid than it was 10 years ago. President Obama was elected on the premise that he would change things. He has set in motion fundamental changes that challenge leaders in government to do things differently (Balutis 2009; Kettl 2009). The president's agenda involves initiatives such as replacing the existing performance appraisal process with a new improved framework, transforming the federal workforce, managing across sectors, and enhancing transparency, technology, and participatory activities (Balutis 2009). Leadership or management reform in government agencies needs to change not only because of presidential initiatives but also because of some fundamental, relevant, social, economic, technical, and global realities.

Factors outside the government have implications for leaders in governmental organizations. First, the global workforce is aging. In the United States there are 18.4 million workers who are 55 or older, a figure representing 13 percent of the workforce. By 2015 this number is projected to grow to 31.9 million or one in five employees. Forty-one percent of the Canadian workforce population is expected to be between the ages of 45 and 64 by 2021. In the UK, 30 percent of workers are over 50. Across the European Union, the proportion of workers over 50 is expected to rise nearly 25 percent in the next 15 years (Avery, McKay, and Wilson 2007). The graying of the workforce will change the way people expect their government to serve them. It will also increase workforce diversity as well as turnover that leaders face when engaging and involving the present and future workforce to do more with less.

Second, the economic realities need no further description than to recall a recent examination of the ups and downs of the Dow Jones, the current state of the banking industry, and an overview of the United States budget deficit, not to mention the balance-of-trade figures. The U.S. public debt has increased over $500 billion each year since 2003, with increases of $1 trillion in 2008 and $1.9 trillion in 2009. These facts have huge implications as to how much and how the American people will support their governmental services. The current economic picture also implies more scrutiny, more accountability, and more productivity from those who are leaders in governmental agencies. These budgetary trends will result in more limited resources for governmental agencies. The economic trend also implies the need for a more engaged workforce, with leaders who know how to support the development of employee engagement.

Third, technological advances have resulted in the accumulation of massive amounts of information, and an exponential growth is projected in the amount of data that organizations will collect, store, access, and exchange (Sindelar, Mintz, and Hughes 2009). Governmental agencies could be awash if they do not learn how to technically manage their informational environments and requirements. Couple this fact with the ease that the "Y" generation has with computers, and it's easy to see how their expectations for governmental agencies will change. Add to this the rising demand for transparent yet secure online services that ensure privacy, the global challenge of the war on terrorism, and competing markets that require information sharing and collaboration, and again it is easy to see why new and creative leadership is at a premium.

Last, the 2008 Federal Human Capital Survey showed only 42 percent of governmental employees were satisfied with the policies and practices of their senior leaders (U.S. Office of Personnel Management 2008, p. 14). Only 48 percent were satisfied with information from management on what's going on in their organizations. These and other factors suggest that present and future leadership in governmental organizations is going to be challenged to adapt and to understand what their role is and can be.

A Study of Leadership

In 2005 The Ken Blanchard Companies began to explore the fundamental question, "Why is it important to build leadership capacity in any organization?" We believed that if we were to effectively teach leadership theory, it was imperative to understand the long-term impact that leadership could have on organizational productivity, longevity, and vitality. Secondary questions were formulated such as, "What specifically can leaders do to increase organizational performance?" "What role does leadership play in driving organizational vitality?" "What is the connection between leadership, customer perceptions, and employee perceptions?" "How are customer loyalty and employee commitment linked to organizational performance?"

A year-long effort to understand what the research had to say about these questions included a literature review of hundreds of studies from 1980 through 2005. This review showed a proliferation of definitions, terms, metrics, and points of view. Yet we found that there were five common critical elements or reoccurring concepts in this research literature:

1. Welfare or the vitality of the organization
2. Employee engagement or work passion

3. Customer loyalty or devotion
4. Overall or strategic leadership
5. Operational or tactical leadership

More important, these elements are connected, resulting in some imperatives for leaders.

These researched connections were supported by hard measures using quantifiable numbers such as stock price, available venture capital, return on investment (ROI), gross revenue, net profit, absenteeism, employee turnover, and cost of employee sabotage, as well as soft measures such as surveyed subjective opinions or perceptions of customer satisfaction, employee morale, intention to leave, employee satisfaction with leadership, and community goodwill.

There were, of course, some differences of opinion and theoretical explanations in the research literature as to why various findings were supported; however, it seems those differences were based on the context and focus taken by various studies. Research showed that there could be various *logic chains* which described or explained service-profit outcomes, value-profit outcomes, or employee-customer-profit outcomes. Although most studies focused on the for-profit organization sector, there were some data on the nonprofit sector as well.

Our purpose here is to present an adapted version of our findings taking into consideration the contextual differences of a public governmental organization versus for-profits. This chapter outlines some differences and similarities between public and private sector organizations, defines the elements of a leadership-purpose chain, discusses five research findings, and outlines three implications for leadership behaviors. We will show the interrelated logical connection between the five elements found in the organizational, psychological, and theoretical leadership literature, which seemed to be connected to leader and public nonprofit organizational effectiveness.

Some Differences and Similarities

We are aware and respectful of the differences that exist between public and private sector organizations. We are also aware of the diversity of opinions as to whether or not researched organizational principles and theories can be used without regard for the type of organization in which the theories are applied. We are of the opinion, after a moderate review of the existing literature on public sector governmental organizations, that general theories of organizational function or normative theories of leadership will not work if not appropriately altered to take into consideration the nature of public organizations.

A recent example of the assumption that private and public organizations are similar enough that performance identified in one sector should be expected in another can be seen in the Clinton administration's initiative of the National Performance Review (NPR). The underlying assumption of this initiative is that governmental organizations should be as effective as business organizations (Parhizgari and Gilbert 2004). Initiatives such as the NPR and the total quality movement have resulted in a number of studies that assessed the possible application of these theories in a government setting (see, e.g., DeLeon and Denhardt 2000; Swiss 1992).

There are the authors who do not believe that the use of business principles and theories should be applied to governmental or public sector organizations (see, e.g., Bozzo 2000; Lindenberg 2001; Swiss 1992; Zimmerman et al. 2003). There are many more authors, however, who assert that generalized organizational theories and research can be used with both profit and nonprofit organizations if there is an intelligent consideration of the differences between public and private sector organizations through the careful modification of terms, intervention strategies, and measurement tools (see, e.g., Beck, Lengnick-Hall, and Lengnick-Hall 2008; A. C. Brooks 2002; Kushner and Poole 1996; Parhizgari and Gilbert 2004).

We postulate there are at least three main differences between private, profit, public, and nonprofit organizations: purpose, structure, and the concept of performance. These give rise to unique leadership challenges for leaders. The first difference between profit and nonprofit organizations lies in the vision and purpose of these two types of organizations.

Organizational Purpose

A strong effective vision of an organization relates to the underlying "cause" of the organization (Greenberger and Sexton 1988). The concept of cause is best understood by answering questions such as, "Why was the organization formed?" or "What reasons brought the organization into being?" The vision of an organization relates to the purpose of the organization. The vision of an organization is defined by the purpose and operational values the organization serves in the context in which it exists. A social mission is one distinction between profit and nonprofit organizations, and this results in unique characteristics, constraints, and challenges for the leaders and followers. Nonprofit governmental organizations seek to serve the public good by providing services or promoting social goals for the communities in which they serve. With governmental organizations, vision is not so much an extension of the leader or the entrepreneur who founded and shaped the organization's purpose as might occur in for-profit organizations.

The purpose of service to the general public good gives rise to a different client–customer interaction. In some cases the primary stakeholders are not the client or end user. The recipient of the service may or may not want the service offered by the governmental organization, as in the case of organizations such as federal correctional facilities, environmental protection agencies, immigration services, and—last but not least—the Internal Revenue Service. Some governmental institutions satisfy the interests of more distant stakeholders and, of course, are not the individuals the organization's employees deal with on a regular basis (Parhizgari and Gilbert 2004).

Nonetheless, the concept of vitality is similar in that both public nonprofit and private for-profit organizations have to be viably supported philosophically as well as economically by the constituents they serve and by the organizational employees who serve those constituencies. Measures of constituent support in governmental contexts would imply appropriate levels of funding, appropriate legislative support, a majority of strong constituent affirmations, and perceptions of the public's general goodwill (Herman and Renz 2008).

Organizational Structure

The second main difference between public and private institutions is organizational structure. With for-profit organizations, they are shaped by boards of directors and chief executive officers whose focus and prerogative is to make a profit and provide for stakeholder or shareholder wealth. Therefore, the internal structures and processes of for-profit sector organizations are to satisfy the consumers who provide the revenue that gives rise to a service-profit chain or an employee-customer-profit chain.

At the state and federal levels the public sector in most organizations is led by elected officials who are voted into office. They are accountable to their voting constituents or stakeholders, but these stakeholders may not be customers or end users of the agency's services. As a result of this structure, the internal organizational policies, processes, operating philosophies, and the elected (and their appointed representative) leaders become oriented toward satisfying the interest of a more distant group of people, sometimes at the disadvantage of the direct end user.

Concept of Performance

The third main difference has to do with the concept of performance. In the case of nonprofit public governmental institutions, the concept of effectiveness, using measured outcomes, has been hotly debated and still seems unsettled. Because public governmental organizations are established to fulfill social aims, the question of believable, quantifiable, uncontroversial, and agreed-upon measures and standards for organizational performance seems to be "under construction" (Herman and Renz 2008). While private for-profit organizations have the luxury of using financial data as "proof" of performance or vitality, the same cannot be said for nonprofit governmental organizations. Nonetheless, it still remains the fundamental challenge for leadership to establish appropriate measures for both the distant stakeholders and the end users of the organization's services (see Rainey and Steinbauer 1999).

These differences exist, but they do not prevent certain commonalities between private and public organizations. While we have acknowledged these differences, we must also acknowledge certain similarities. Both types of organizations have four common organizational needs to be sustained over time:

1. Resource acquisition
2. Selected goal accomplishment
3. Efficient and effective employee effort
4. Client satisfaction

Whether we are concerned with effectively leading a private for-profit organiza-tion or a public nonprofit organization, these needs must be dealt with in order for the leadership to be labeled effective and the organization to remain vital. As the reader will see, the four needs are correlated with the five elements.

Defining the Elements

Regardless of whether the organization was nonprofit or profit, several conceptual elements arose that need to be understood by a leader to grasp what could be done to make use of this research.

The five elements found in our research were: *Organizational Vitality, Employee Work Passion, Customer Devotion, Strategic Leadership,* and *Operational Leader-ship.* We changed these terms to create a broader set of constructs than the previ-ously used terms found in the literature such as organizational success, employee engagement, customer loyalty, and leadership. Language is crucial to the process of framing and visualizing what needs to be done to appreciate and use these terms to guide action. We have also changed these terms to fit the context of government nonprofit organizations.

Organizational Vitality

The concept of organizational vitality is defined as the *degree to which an orga-nization has continually been successful in meeting performance expectations in the eyes of its customers, employees, stakeholders, and relevant communities, which results in the organization remaining economically viable and stable over time.* "Hard" outcome measures found in the research literature for organizational vitality include contract retention, revenue retention, stock price, profits/funding, revenue/funding growth, venture capital, and the balancing of operating costs. "Soft" outcome measures, which usually meant the surveying of relevant percep-tions, include examples such as perceptions of public trust, employee commitment, and constituent satisfaction. In most studies researchers use multiple criteria often comprising many of these examples.

Employee Work Passion

Employee work passion is *an individual's persistent, emotionally positive, mean-ing-based state of well-being stemming from reoccurring cognitive or affective appraisals of various job and organizational situations that result in consistent, constructive work intentions and behaviors.* There were several different terms found in the literature for this concept such as employee commitment, employee job satisfaction, and employee engagement. Employee work passion stems from the employee's positive job experience and satisfaction with the organization—its vision, values, job meaning, job activities, policies, procedures, products, and management.

Hard outcome measures of employee work passion found in the research literature include retention, absenteeism, tenure, organizational citizenship behaviors, sabotage, and productivity. Some of these hard measures are more relevant, of course, for career governmental employees than for elected or appointed leaders. Soft measures include employee perceptions of trust in leadership, endorsement of management, positive affect, intent to turnover, and general morale. Again we found researchers using multiple criteria such as that listed earlier. In the case of employee work passion, we think this title is aptly named no matter what type of organization because it refers to the persistent, emotionally positive, meaning-based sense of well-being present in most individual employees of a given organization.

Customer Devotion

Customer devotion is defined as *a constituent's persistent, positive, emotional meaning-based sense of well-being stemming from reoccurring cognitive and affective appraisals of the quality of product/service offered by the organization which results in consistent, constructive intentions and behaviors that support the organization's purpose.* It should be noticed that both the employee and constituent make appraisals that are both cognitive and affective; meaning they make their appraisals with their head and their heart. These appraisals lead to intentions and, depending upon the sense of well-being derived from the appraisal, these intentions can result in positive or negative behaviors which may or may not be in concert with the organization's purpose or welfare.

Customer devotion occurs as a result of positive experiences with the organization's products, services, policies, procedures, and personnel. We suspect that the title "customer devotion" can be viewed as slightly naïve on our part when writing about nonprofit organizations. Perhaps more appropriate terms might be citizen appreciation, public affirmation, or constituent respect. In any case we are referring to client perceptions and their resultant behaviors. Steps must be taken to identify the perceptions of the distant stakeholders as well as the end users concerning the quality of the organization's product or service.

Hard outcome measures of customer or constituent respect found in the literature include customer retention, the repeated use of the product or service, length of customer relationships, number of transactions, size of transaction, referrals of new clients, continued levels of funding, and legislative support. Soft measures of customer constituent respect are, of course, more appropriate given the many different constituents that are served by governmental agencies. Soft measures include survey-based perceptions of satisfaction on themes related to perceived quality, value, customer service, product expectations, and overall constituent satisfaction. Using multiple criteria researchers seek to judge what a "quality" service experience or a "quality" product is.

It is our opinion that while a majority of those serving within governmental nonprofit organizations have alternative images of the citizen, the predominant image of the public is one based on an economic model in which the citizen is primarily motivated by the desire for material rewards by which maximum self-interest should be served (Tyler, Rasinski, and Griffin 1986). The assumption of self-interest leads to an image of the public as an egotistic utility-maximizer who interacts with or supports government for personal gain.

This model underestimates the fact that the public is capable of using their past experience to develop "reasonable" expectations concerning the future interactions they may have with their governmental agencies. If the image of the public were based on a psychological model of fairness, then public service employees might be able to view what the public wants from its governmental organizations differently, thereby changing and perhaps delivering a different constituent experience. This approach would require the exploration of what citizens view as fair in the arena of governmental decision making, allocation, and service delivery. It would require governmental agencies to recalibrate their services and reestablish, reconstruct, and rejuvenate their service models. As most public employees want to be seen as motivated by the desire to improve the public "good," it would be helpful to believe that a majority of the tax-paying public could be motivated the same way if the service warranted that perception (Bright 2009).

Strategic Leadership

Strategic leadership is marked by the concern for the performance and evolution of the organization as a whole, including its changing aims and capabilities. Strategic leadership defines the imperatives for everyone in the organization by creating and communicating a vision for the future; developing organizational structures, processes, and controls; managing multiple constituents; sustaining an effective organizational culture; and infusing ethical values systems within the organization's culture (Boal and Hooijberg 2001). Strategic leadership provides the directives that define the key relationships and metrics needed to ensure that all units follow the same strategy. Using the organization's purpose as a guide, strategic initiatives must be identified, and these strategic initiatives become criteria that are determinants of follower behavior.

Operational Leadership

Operational leadership provides the day-to-day interpretation of the strategic mandates or policies. Operational leadership enables departments and employees to understand how they specifically contribute to organizational success. Leaders at the operational level provide guidance, support, and feedback to direct reports as day-to-day problems and unanticipated circumstances arise in the course of implementing the organization's purpose and strategic initiatives. Leaders at the operational level must be concerned with how the special interests created by narrow fields of knowledge and expertise in "silo-ed" departments or units can be merged to contribute to the organization's purpose and outcomes through strategic initiatives.

Discussion of Five Key Research Findings

We have represented the five elements and significant connections in Figure 20.1. Our findings support several connections, and the overall framework of the model can be used to illustrate those connections. In general, employee-client relationships are dependent upon the strategic-operational leadership connection. The integrity of the leadership-purpose chain lies in the inner triangle. Effective interconnection of strategic leadership, operational leadership, employee work passion, and customer-constituent respect is *absolutely critical* to the organization's success. We found overwhelming empirical evidence for five conclusions:

1. Strategic leadership and operational leadership directly predict employee work passion.
2. Employee work passion directly predicts constituent respect and organizational vitality.
3. Customer-constituent respect directly predicts organizational vitality.
4. Operational leadership directly predicts constituent respect.
5. Strategic leadership can only indirectly influence organizational vitality.

Let us explain.

Leadership Predicts Employee Work Passion

There is a direct connection between employee work passion (no. 2 in Figure 20.1) and strategic (no. 4) and operational (no. 5) leader behaviors (see, e.g., Judge and Piccolo 2004; Lowe, Kroeck, and Sivasubramaniam 1996; Mathieu and Zajac 1990; Meyer et al. 2002). However, there is a caveat: communication of policies, procedures, and informal philosophies established by those at the strategic leadership level, while critical, must be supported and executed through operational leadership practices. For employees to understand how their work contributes to the organizational vision, to buy in to the culture and what the organization stands for, and to understand how to connect their work to the strategic imperatives, leaders at the operational level must be faithful to the organization's purpose, values, and strategic initiatives.

Figure 20.1   **The Leadership-Purpose Chain for Public Governmental Organizations**

The Leadership-Purpose Chain

Even in regulated organizations there is still employee latitude used to carry out organizational aims. Without operational leaders who are committed to the espoused purpose, values, and strategic initiatives, a gap occurs between strategic mandates and operational practices, thus breaking the chain between desired organizational performance and realized employee outcomes. When there is little or no agreement, communication, or common focus between the organization's strategic and operational leaders, strategic initiatives are either inconsistently executed or never executed at all (O'Reilly et al. 2010).

Leadership, in general—both strategic and operational—predicts employee commitment, employee engagement, or employee work passion. We found study after study substantiated that leaders greatly influence the affective and cognitive perceptions employees form about their job and about their organization's culture. Employees form opinions about job factors such as job autonomy, task variety, meaningful work, feedback, and workload balance. They also form opinions concerning organizational factors such as distributive fairness, procedural fairness, growth opportunities, a collaboration emphasis, and performance expectations. Last, but not least, employees form opinions about their connectedness with their colleagues as well as their connectedness with their strategic leaders and operational managers. Depending on those perceptions, employee engagement or work passion may or may not be the result. When strategic and operational leadership do not pay attention to those formulated opinions, they often get less employee commitment, discretionary effort, endorsement, and performance.

Employee Work Passion Predicts Constituent Respect and Organizational Vitality

Employee work passion (no. 2 in Figure 20.1) predicts customer or constituent respect (no. 3) (see, e.g., R. Brooks 2000; Chuang and Liao 2010; Haskett et al. 1994; Johnson 1996; Schmidt and Allscheid 1995; Tornow and Wiley 1991). This positive connection between employee work passion and customer devotion has been documented through hard and soft measures. The most powerful connection we found was the link between employee work passion and customer devotion (constituent respect). When employees are passionate about what they do, are clear about their roles and goals, and perceive the organization as fair and just in its treatment of co-workers and customers, then the impact on their desire to serve the customers can be tremendous.

Studies strongly link employee job and company satisfaction to customer satisfaction. There was some evidence that not only does employee satisfaction lead to customer satisfaction but also that the reverse is true. Customer satisfaction can shape employee satisfaction in their jobs (Ryan, Schmit, and Johnson 1996). However, a majority of the research suggests the causal relationship to be that employee work passion is more influential on customer satisfaction than the other way around. When we connect this fact with the fact that leadership establishes employee work passion, the way leadership is perceived as treating the employee is the way the employee will treat the constituents they are charged to serve.

A secondary correlation shows that employee work passion (no. 2) and customer or constituent respect (no. 3) predict organizational vitality (no. 1). Employee work passion (no. 2) predicts organizational vitality (no. 1) in part because enthusiastic committed employees do things for the organization, go the extra mile, and look after their colleagues' welfare and their constituents.

Constituent Respect Predicts Organizational Vitality

Constituent respect (no. 3) or customer devotion is a powerful driver of organizational vitality (no. 1) (see, e.g., Anderson, Fornell, and Mazvancheryel 1994; Chuang and Liao 2010; Fojtik 2002; Hallowell 1996; Schulte et al. 2009; Wiley 1991). In the private sector it costs six to seven times more to gain a new customer than to retain one. When a customer is lost because of poor service, they often do not tell the organization why. To make matters worse, that disenchanted constituent will often convey their displeasure to as many as 10 other people, which may result in poisoning what goodwill the organization has garnered up to that point with any neutral or positive constituents the organization may have created.

Customers care about the good service they receive from an organization and the positive experience they may have with the product, policy, or procedures of a given organization. While they may be concerned with price or cost, they are most observant of the quality of service or treatment they receive. Leaders of exemplary service companies emphasize the importance of each employee and customer, and they maintain a culture that is centered on service to both customers and employees. In the public governmental sector, if the organization is effective in the minds of the constituents who are served, there is data to suggest that supportive behaviors from external stakeholders such as political authorities, agency autonomy in refining and implementing its mission, and reasonably viable economic support could result (Rainey and Steinbauer 1999).

Operational Leadership Predicts Constituent Respect

Operational leadership (no. 5) develops constituent respect (no. 3). Constituents or customers seldom interact directly with strategic leadership personnel. "Let me talk to your supervisor" seldom results in talking to the president. Leadership translates strategic initiatives from everyday problems into workable solutions for employees and constituents. If the organization has a strategic initiative such as the delivery of quality products and/or services, it is leadership that must make it happen as they work with and through employees to serve the customer.

Operational leadership or management practices such as sharing information, providing training, and rewarding/recognizing excellence are positively related to constituent satisfaction with service quality. These dimensions are related in that the underlying component is information. Seeking information from other employees and/or end users as to how service can be improved, conveying information as it pertains to training, and sharing information with employees in the form of recognition and rewards are the responsibility of competent operational leaders (see, e.g., Chuang and Liao 2010; Hallowell 1996; Lundby, Fenlason, and Magnan 2001; Schmit and Alscheid 1995; Tornow and Wiley 1991; Wiley 1991).

The research findings support the relationship between training and customer satisfaction as it pertains to delivering service. Divisions of an organization that invest in service delivery training experience higher rates of customer satisfaction. It is up to the operational leadership to manage this training if they are to succeed in this strategic initiative to gain constituent respect.

Strategic Leadership Can Only Indirectly Influence Organizational Vitality

As the reader examines Figure 20.1, the arrows pointing from employee work passion and constituent respect point only one way. We found no studies that used organizational vitality as the dependent variable. In other words, researchers were looking at the effect employee work attitudes or constituent satisfaction perceptions had on the organization's vitality and not the other way around. There is little that upper-level executives can do to influence the bottom line (organizational vitality) except to conceptualize and advocate mergers and acquisitions. In the end, they're stuck with problems of managing employee and end-user satisfaction. The only way strategic leadership can directly take care of business is by taking care of their employees and their end users through their operational leaders.

Creating an organization that is successful and effective is an inside-out proposition. The quality of the organizational culture, the quality of the management practices, and the alignment of these practices to key strategic initiatives rest with strategic leadership. Strategic leaders who hold operational leaders and their employees accountable to ensure productive behaviors from all will be effective influencers and drivers of the organizational results. Equally important is the leader's ability to affect the mood, attitude, and engagement of employees, as well as the culture of the organization overall, through a specific chain of events that are implicitly linked.

The key to organizational vitality is creating a work environment that allows employees to succeed and to become passionate about what they do. By taking care of employees, leaders establish an environment in which employees can take care of the constituent at a level that causes the constituent to value the organization's purpose and positively support it through their actions.

The Leadership-Purpose Chain and Implications for Leader Behaviors

There are three fundamental leadership considerations based upon the leadership-purpose chain:

1. A concern for a strong strategic/operational leadership link
2. An emphasis by strategic leaders on strategically targeted initiatives of concern for employees and concern for quality constituent service
3. A reemphasis and commitment to servant/service-based organizational culture

A Mandatory Strategic/Operational Leadership Link

The implementation of organizational purpose cannot be accomplished without the cooperation and commitment of those who interact with the end user and constituents of the organization's service. Strategic initiatives such as exemplary service can only happen when the vision is clear, when outcomes and guidelines have been formulated and communicated that favor employee concerns and voice as well as constituent satisfaction and voice. Then operational managers can emphasize the strategic initiative to all who serve the constituent. All employees must move beyond a transactional approach with the client. All employees, managers, and line nonmanagers must increase their level of awareness for the desired organizational outcomes and move beyond self-interests as they serve the constituents.

Strategic leaders must understand, and hold an appropriate focus on, what they want to accomplish through other people. If strategic leaders want transformational change or if they want specific results related to an initiative, they must appreciate how their actions will influence operational leaders and their followers. Strategic leaders must realize that for a transformation to occur, standards and values inherent in the initiative must become the standards and values of those who carry out the initiative.

Strategically Targeted Initiatives on Employee Work Passion and Constituent Respect

Can present governmental leaders keep their eye on the ball rather than the scoreboard? In other words, can governmental leaders focus their activities and intentions on employees and the constituents the organization serves, rather than on scanning the business environment, political obstructions and pressures, competing entities, and personal ambitions?

The 2008 Federal Human Capital Survey showed several revealing doubts held by federal employees (U.S. Office of Personnel Management 2008). Items such as "I have a high level of respect for my organization's senior leaders" (item 37, p. 14) showed only 52 percent in agreement. Other questions such as "How satisfied are you with the information you receive from management on what's going on in your organization?" showed 48 percent of the population in agreement (item 56, p. 14); "How satisfied are you with the policies and practices of your senior leaders?" showed 42 percent in agreement (item 58, p. 14). And the item "In my organization leaders generate high levels of motivation and commitment in the workforce" showed only 40 percent in agreement (item 38, p. 14). While these questions showed some improvement of 1 or 2 percent over the 2006 survey, if these differences were not above the standard deviation, these changes may not have occurred by chance.

There is a challenge that must be met by present and future leaders within governmental organizations if they are to generate the type of work passion needed to meet the challenges of the present and future. The concept of employee work passion/engagement, as well as its formulation and development, must be understood, fostered, and monitored if human energy is to be liberated to help with the problems in the future (Zigarmi et al. 2009).

An example of a possible initiative on employee work passion might be for strategic governmental leaders to examine the presently held perceptions employees have in order to understand what leader behaviors may change those perceptions on the four items described earlier. This approach is especially important if elected and appointed officials, who come and go because of our democratic process, do not understand how to build environments that foster work passion and commitment within the majority of career government employees.

If the research on the leadership-purpose chain is to be taken seriously, strategic leaders must keep their focus on the development of employee work passion and cultivation of constituent respect. One cannot be achieved without the other.

Commitment to a Servant/Service-Based Organizational Culture

Strategic leaders must appreciate and use their abilities to influence their organization's culture toward some clear values-based vision. Since governmental agencies are in the business of serving the social welfare, the idea of service in general—both internal and external—ought to drive the fundamental vision of all employees. It has been said that "the noblest motive is the public good." Because the salary ranges for public governmental employees are considerably less than what might be made in for-profit organizations, "throwing money at performance" is not possible in most nonprofit organizations. Career governmental employees have been known to see purpose as a reason for service rather than money.

Are governmental strategic and operational leaders skillful enough to create organizational cultures that encourage and support an idealistic, altruistic, work environment? We are not talking about an environment that takes advantage of employees through mistreatment and deprivation of basic needs and still asks them to be idealistic. Rather it must be clearly spelled out upon entry into the organization that there are limitations to the resources of public service organizations, but there are also the psychic benefits that can be realized in the actions of creating better social conditions for all. Asking and allowing people to become excited about what they can "do for their country," while at the same time providing reasonably fair working conditions and wages, is a realistic and motivating work environment that can be achieved.

What the research shows regarding employees passionate about their work is the conditions and culture that foster that work passion stem from perceptions of meaningful work, procedural justice, autonomous job conditions, connectedness with colleagues and leaders, task variety, specific feedback, opportunities for professional growth, and work-life balance (Zigarmi et al. 2009). We echo Kettl's concern for management reform in government. Can leaders figure out the "strategies (and leader behaviors) necessary for doing hard things in a steady high-quality way?" (Kettl 2008). Can governmental leaders, including elected, appointed, and career leaders, find ways to influence the cultures of their organizations to foster work passion in their employees?

The empirical evidence clearly supports the fact that organizational culture, leadership style, and performance are directly connected (see, e.g., Denison and Mishra 1995; Ogbonna and Harris 2000; Schulte et al. 2009; Sorensen 2002). Strategic leaders must become adept and skillful at using and shaping their organizational cultures to support employee work passion and engagement. Leaders who see themselves as servants start by understanding what the environmental conditions are for people becoming engaged in their work.

References

Anderson, E. W., C. Fornell, and S. K. Mazvancheryel. 2004. "Customer Satisfaction and Shareholder Value." *Journal of Marketing* 68: 1–27.

Avery, D. R., P. F. McKay, and D. C. Wilson. 2007. "Engaging the Aging Workforce: The Relationship between Perceived Age Similarity, Satisfaction with Coworkers, and Employee Engagement." *Journal of Applied Psychology* 92: 1542–1556.

Balutis, A. P. 2009. "Introduction: What Is Happening, and Why and So What." *Public Manager* 38 (Winter): 11–12.

Beck, T. B., C. A. Lengnick-Hall, and M. L. Lengnick-Hall. 2008. "Solutions Out of Context: Examining the Transfer of Business Concepts in Nonprofit Organizations." *Nonprofit Management and Leadership* 19: 153–171.

Boal, K. B., and R. Hooijberg. 2001. "Strategic Leadership Research: Moving on." *Leadership Quarterly* 11: 515–549.

Bozzo, S. L. 2000. "Evaluation Resources for Nonprofit Organizations: Usefulness and Applicability." *Nonprofit Management and Leadership* 10: 463–472.

Bright, L. 2009. "Why Do Public Employees Desire Intrinsic Nonmonetary Opportunities?" *Public Personnel Management* 38: 15–37.

Brooks, A. C. 2002. "Can Nonprofit Management Help Answer Public Management's 'Big Question'?" *Public Administration Review* 62: 259–266.

Brooks, R. 2000. "Why Loyal Employees and Customers Improve the Bottom Line." *Journal for Quality and Participation* 23-(2): 40–44.

Chuang, C., and H. Liao. 2010. "Strategic Human Resource Management in Service Context: Taking Care of Business by Taking Care of Employees and Customers." *Personnel Psychology* 63: 153–196.

DeLeon, L., and R. B. Denhardt. 2000. "The Political Theory of Reinvention." *Public Administration Review* 60: 89–97.

Denison, D. R., and A. K. Mishra. 1995. "Toward a Theory of Organizational Culture and Effectiveness." *Organization Science* 6: 204–223.

Fojtik, C. 2002. "Calculating the Value of Customer Satisfaction." *Graziado Business Report* 4: 1–4.

Greenberger, D. B., and D. L. Sexton. 1988. "An Interactive Model of New Venture Initiation." *Journal of Small Business Management* 26: 1–7.

Hallowell, R. 1996. "The Relationship of Client Satisfaction, Client Loyalty, and Profitability: An Empirical Study." *International Journal of Service Industry Management* 7: 27–42.

Haskett, J. I., T. O. Jones, G. W. Loveman, W. E. Sasser, and L. A. Schlesinger. 1994. "Putting the Service Profit Chain to Work." *Harvard Business Review* 72(2): 164–174.

Herman, R. D., and D. O. Renz. 2008. "Advancing Nonprofit Organizational Effectiveness Research and Theory." *Nonprofit Management and Leadership* 18: 399–415.

Johnson, J. W. 1996. "Linking Employee Perceptions of Service Climate to Customer Satisfaction." *Personnel Psychology* 49: 831–851.

Judge, T. A., and R. F. Piccolo. 2004. "Transformational and Transactional Leadership: A Meta-analytic Test of Their Relative Validity." *Journal of Applied Psychology* 89: 755–768.

Kettl, D. F. 2008. "Paradoxes of Management Reform." *Public Manager* 36(4): 7–9.

———. 2009. "Obama's Stealth Revolution: Quietly Reshaping the Way Government Works." *Public Manager* 38: 39–42.

Kushner, R. J., and P. P. Poole. 1996. "Exploring Structure Effectiveness Relationships in Nonprofit Arts Organizations." *Nonprofit Management and Leadership* 6: 171–180.

Lindenberg, M. 2001. "Are We Cutting Edge or the Blunt Edge? Improving NGO Organizational Performance with Private and Public Sector Strategic Management Frameworks." *Nonprofit Management and Leadership* 11: 247–270.

Lowe, K. B., K. G. Kroeck, and N. Sivasubramaniam. 1996. "Effectiveness Correlates of Transformational and Transactional Leadership: A Meta-analytic Review of the MLQ Literature." *Leadership Quarterly* 7: 385–425.

Lundby, K., K. Fenlason, and S. Magnan. 2001. "Linking Employee and Customer Data to Business Performance: Difficult But Not Impossible." *Consulting Psychology Journal* 53: 22–34.

Mathieu, J. E., and D. M. Zajac. 1990. "A Review and Meta-analysis of the Antecedents, Correlates, and Consequences of Organizational Commitment." *Psychological Bulletin* 108: 171–194.

Meyer, J. P., J. D. Stanley, L. Hercovitch, and L. Topolnytsky. 2002. "Affective, Continuance, and Normative Commitment to the Organization: A Meta-analysis of Antecedents and Consequences." *Journal of Vocational Behavior* 61: 20–52.

Ogbonna, E., and L. C. Harris. 2000. "Leadership Style, Organizational Culture and Performance: Empirical Evidence from UK Companies." *International Journal of Human Resource Management* 11: 776–788.

O'Reilly, C. A., D. F. Caldwell, J. A. Chatman, M. Lapiz, and W. Self. 2010. "How Leadership Matters: The Effects of Leaders' Alignment on Strategy Implementation." *Leadership Quarterly* 21: 104–113.

Parhizgari, A. M., and R. G. Gilbert. 2004. "Measures of Organizational Effectiveness: Private and Public Sector Performance." *Omega* 32: 221–229.

Rainey, H. G., and P. Steinbauer. 1999. "Galloping Elephants: Developing Elements of the Theory of Affective Government Organizations." *Journal of Public Administration Research and Theory* 1: 1–32.

Ryan, A. M., M. J. Schmit, and R. Johnson. 1996. "Attitudes and Effectiveness: Examining Relations at the Organizational Level." *Personnel Psychology* 49: 853–882.

Schmit, M. J., and S. P. Allscheid. 1995. "Employee Attitudes and Customer Satisfaction: Making Theoretical and Empirical Connections." *Personnel Psychology* 48: 521–536.

Schulte, M., C. Ostroff, S. Shmulyian, and A. Kinicki. 2009. "Organizational Climate Configurations: Relationships to Collective Attitudes, Customer Satisfaction, and Financial Performance." *Journal of Applied Psychology* 94: 618–634.

Sindelar, J., D. Mintz, and T. Hughes. 2009. "The Past Is Prologue: The Obama Technology Agenda." *Public Manager* 38: 24–27.

Sorensen, J. B. 2002. "The Strength of Corporate Culture and the Reliability of Firm Performance." *Administration Science Quarterly* 47(1): 70–91.

Swiss, J. E. 1992. "Adapting Total Quality Management (TQM) to Government." *Public Administration Review* 54: 356–362.

Tornow, W. W., and J. W. Wiley. 1991. "Service Quality and Management Practices: A Look at Employee Attitudes, Customer Satisfaction and Bottom-line Consequences." *Human Resources Planning* 14: 105–115.

Tyler, T. R., K. A. Rasinki, and E. Griffin. 1986. "Alternative Images of the Citizen: Implications for Public Policy." *American Psychologist* 41(9): 970–978.

U.S. Office of Personnel Management. 2008. Federal Human Capital Survey 2008. http://www.fedview.opm.gov/2008/.

Wiley, J. W. 1991. "Customer Satisfaction: A Supportive Work Environment and Its Financial Cost." *Human Resources Planning* 14: 117–127.

Zigarmi, D., K. Nimon, D. Houson, D. Witt, and J. Diehl. 2009. "Beyond Engagement: Toward a Framework and Operational Definition of Employee Work Passion." *Human Resource Development Review* 8: 300–326.

Zimmerman, J. A., B. W. Stevens, B. J. Thames, C. R. Sieverdes, and G. M. Powell. 2003. "The DIRECTIONS Nonprofit Resource Assessment Model: A Tool for Small Nonprofit Organizations." *Nonprofit Management and Leadership* 14: 79–91.

21

The Evolution of Collaboration

LENA TRUDEAU

> *In the long history of humankind (and animal kind, too) those who learned to collaborate and improvise most effectively have prevailed.*
>
> —Charles Darwin

The Need to Evolve

Much has been written about the increasingly complex, interconnected, and severe challenges facing the nation today, and the structural barriers that prevent our public institutions from effectively addressing them. Consider just a few of these enormous problems: getting the economy back on track without compounding the bleak, long-term, fiscal outlook; making sustainable progress in two wars (three, if one is still counting the global war on terror) while facing the likelihood of cuts to the defense budget and continued pressure to draw down troop levels; developing new energy policy and fostering sustainable alternative fuel sources while still leveraging the economic benefits of the nation's legacy energy infrastructure. The list could easily also touch on health care implementation, education reform, and securing the homeland from myriad threats, both natural and man-made.

The extent to which these problems are interconnected is unprecedented. What's more, the risks associated with *mission failure* have never been higher. Yet, as public administrators, we've tended to do things in much the same way as we've always done, hoping that through hard work and sheer determination we will see a different result. It brings to mind the sage advice of W. C. Fields: "If at first you don't succeed, try, try again. Then quit. There's no use being a damn fool about it" (W. C. Fields, n.d.). But the unfortunate consequence of a bureaucratic system, which is *intended* to support stability and permanence, is that it's really very hard to quit doing things that aren't working. Sadly, government is not well positioned to effectively address the problems facing the nation.

Part of the difficulty stems from the industrial era model upon which our government functions. As Goldsmith and Eggers write in their seminal book, *Governing by Network:* "Rigid bureaucratic systems that operate with command-and-control procedures, narrow work restrictions, and inward-looking cultures and operational models are particularly ill-suited to addressing problems that often transcend organizational boundaries" (Goldsmith and Eggers 2004). Barack Obama struck at the heart of the issue is his speech accepting the nomination for the presidency when he said, "we cannot meet 21st-century challenges with a 20th-century bureaucracy" (Obama 2008). At the same time, public trust in government, and its capacity to solve these problems, has reached historic lows. According to a recent Pew Research Center study, "Rather than an activist government to deal with the nation's top problems, the public now wants government reformed and growing numbers want its power curtailed" (Pew Research Center for the People and the Press 2010).

Fortunately, a growing number realize that the answer lies not in government solving these problems for people, but rather in tapping the capacity of the people themselves to innovate and problem-solve. In her remarks to the National Conference of the American Society of Public Administrators, former National Academy of Public Administration (NAPA) Board Chair Valerie Lemmie chided public administrators—herself among them—for having "unwittingly pushed citizens out of the public square." They did this, she said, not out of spite or meanness or because of any lack of confidence in citizens, but rather "because we honestly believed we could and should fix their problems." *In truth, some problems are simply too large for government to solve alone.* It is time, Lemmie said, to reengage citizens in the work of government to solve the "wicked" problems of our times (Lemmie 2007).

To effectively address the challenges before us, government must move to a collaborative model. Fortunately, there is now a unique convergence between the acute need to do things in government in a fundamentally different way and our ability to use Web 2.0 and the collaboration it enables to achieve this. Collaborative technology has the potential to transform government in America, to tap into the expertise of people outside the hierarchy of any single agency or department, to make government more transparent, and to open the door to an array of experts or citizens to solve a problem or make government work better. This chapter examines the evolution of technology-enabled collaboration in government with the aim of capturing what works and suggesting what might be next.

Collaboration vs. Consultation: Classifying the Species

In an era where collaboration is required, public agencies may be tempted to label any consultation or communication with other federal agencies, stakeholder groups, or the public as "collaboration." So a clear understanding of the continuum of such activities is critical. Figure 21.1 is an illustration of the collaboration continuum. Definitions for each stage in the continuum follow:

- *Communication:* informing stakeholders, who may be internal or external, of activities or planned activities of the agency.
- *Consultation:* inviting interested parties to provide comments and input on the activities or planned activities of the agency.

Figure 21.1   **A Collaboration Continuum for the Public Sector**

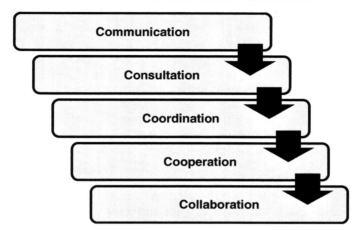

- *Coordination:* sharing information and organizing the activities of the agency in synchronization with other parties for public benefit.
- *Cooperation:* sharing information and resources, and organizing the activities of the agency in a shared endeavor with other parties toward a common goal in the public interest.
- *Collaboration:* sharing information, resources, and decision-making authority with other parties to co-create or co-deliver a product or service toward shared outcomes in the public interest.

In any stage short of collaboration, and regardless of the breadth and depth of the shared engagement, government agents retain decision-making authority, acting on behalf of the public. Collaboration, on the other hand, requires public officials to engage in shared decision making, or, as Frank Reeder terms it, "shared sovereignty" (Reeder 2010). Collaboration is further characterized by capacity-building outcomes in all parties.

As it turns out, governments in the United States are pretty well versed in consultation. Beginning in the 1940s, the federal government developed rules to integrate public participation into the process of governing. Written in recognition of the government's expanding functions and roles, the Administrative Procedures Act of 1946 (APA) standardized how federal agencies generated and promulgated new rules and regulations. It also established, for the first time, periods of public comment as part of this process. In the 60-plus years since the APA became law, agencies have consulted with the public by publishing proposed rules in the *Federal Register,* through which any member of the public can submit a written comment or response. Agencies then publish and publicly respond to these comments before issuing a final decision. Because government has "hard-wired" this capacity into how it makes rules, many interest groups and members of the public have come to depend upon this opportunity to participate in governance.

As information technology (IT) advanced, government has recognized the opportunity to use new tools to make consultation both more effective and more efficient. The hallmark law that enabled agencies to do this was the E-Government Act of 2002, which promoted the use of the Internet and other information technologies to enable broader citizen consultation. The act provided for greater use of IT in sharing information, such as enabling online applications for grants, increased transparency, and real-time online interaction between government and citizens.

Lemmie draws a clear line, however, between citizen participation (which she argues is relatively passive) and the more active role played by citizens when truly engaged in collaborative problem solving. It is through the act of engaging in shared responsibility for solving intractable problems that citizens establish what she calls an "adult-adult relationship" with their government, rather than one based on the parent-child paradigm. This equal footing is a necessary condition for successful collaboration (Lemmie 2007).

Tim O'Reilly, founder and CEO of O'Reilly Media, likens our ability to work together—not just to improve policy and regulation, but to deliver services—to an old-fashioned barn raising, and labels it "do it yourself" government. "Governments, like corporations," he says, "are vehicles for collective action. We pay a government, or a business, because it's an efficient way to tackle projects that are larger than a single person or group of friends can take on. But let's not forget that we ourselves are the raw material of collective action" (O'Reilly 2009). The good news is that although there are many barriers to overcome, citizens have proven themselves willing and able to collaborate effectively, and increasingly are leveraging technology in order to do so. Simply put, we have good genes. Collaboration is in our DNA.

The Early Days: Learning to Use Tools

As part of its Congressional Charter, the National Academy is charged with anticipating and examining emerging issues critical to the effective administration of public programs and formulating practical approaches to their resolution. In service of this mission, in 2007 we launched the Collaboration Project, a research program aimed at developing a deeper understanding of how collaborative "Web 2.0" tools could be used to improve the way government works and how it interacts with citizens and stakeholders. With the support of 10 federal agencies, and participation by National Academy fellows and other subject matter experts, the project convened in person and online to share best practices, produce research on the opportunities and challenges of collaboration, and assist agencies in implementing collaborative tools and approaches.

In the beginning, much of our work involved the identification and celebration of innovative uses of collaborative technology to improve government. The evaluation framework employed analyzed use cases along four dimensions, by asking the following questions:

1. What business problem were you trying to solve?
2. What approach did you use?
3. What results did you achieve?
4. What lessons did you learn?

In documenting these cases, we were energized by the sheer number of innovative efforts under way across federal, state, and local governments, as well as in the not-for-profit sector.

Example 1

Some of the most notable early successes were in the field of emergency response. Multiagency collaboration is vital to emergency response to ensure public safety before, during, and after an event. Yet governments at all levels failed to manage and share the critical information at their disposal when the Gulf Coast was hit by Hurricane Katrina. To fill the void, a powerful grassroots effort—modeled after a similar effort to assist in the aftermath of the tsunami in Indonesia—emerged immediately to reunite loved ones and to aggregate data regarding fund-raising efforts, refugee records, helpline numbers, volunteer opportunities, and government resources. Combined, the KatrinaHelp wiki and the Katrina PeopleFinder Project responded where traditional government structures could not, taking advantage of a collaborative Web-based network to produce one of the most quickly developed, comprehensive collections of information and online resources seen at that time.

Example 2

Other online networks also emerged, allowing people to engage anytime from anywhere in the world, enabling large and diverse communities to form quickly around issues as they arose. The National Academy, on behalf of the Office of Management and Budget and the federal Chief Information Officers Council hosted the first ever "National Dialogue," to explore how new information technology solutions could improve the delivery of health care while at the same time protecting patient privacy. Over the course of eight days, thousands of visitors from every U.S. state and territory, as well as 79 foreign nations, participated in an invigorating discussion. They contributed hundreds of ideas, comments, and insights about the debate over health IT and privacy. Some who engaged were informed professionals. Others were infrequent participants in policy discussions, with personal stories that illustrated how health policy affects citizens' daily lives. This diversity of voice provided insight that might have otherwise escaped the attention of stakeholders with key roles in health IT implementation. The dialogue demonstrated the viability of this kind of approach, and served as a model for similar efforts on a wide range of topics (Reeder 2008).

Example 3

True collaboration also sprang from the unlikeliest of places. One of the best examples of cross-disciplinary, multijurisdictional teamwork started out as an effort by a state governor to leverage a billion-dollar investment in maps. At the request of Governor Bob Riley, the Alabama Department of Homeland Security (AL DHS), created a comprehensive online database of satellite imagery and aerial photography by county. The goal was to find new ways to utilize the mapping data at their disposal. As AL DHS began engaging stakeholders at the local level, they overlaid Google maps with other pertinent information as well—budget data, crime statistics, urban planning information, and more—to provide a common operational picture across the state that first responders, county planners, and other officials could use. "Virtual Alabama" went live in August 2006. By November 2007, over 1,800 online users were contributing the best available data from each of Alabama's 67 counties. Powered by Google Earth Enterprise, the system was developed for a fraction of what such a powerful tool might traditionally have cost. The state has employed "Virtual Alabama" primarily to provide enhanced coordination and awareness to the state's first responders. It has also proved useful for economic development, law enforcement, education, and any other function that is made more effective through the aggregation of previously disparate data elements (AL DHS 2010).

Example 4

Web 2.0 also enables collaborative editing of a centralized work product. Everyone is familiar with Wikipedia, the pioneer of collaborative editing. Police in New Zealand, looking to raise awareness of and increase public participation in the redevelopment of New Zealand's Police Act of 1958, opened a wiki-based collaborative effort to rewrite the act. Thanks to timely media coverage, the New Zealand Police Act wiki drew a global audience and extensive participation, establishing a strong model of utilizing collaborative technologies in the writing of laws.

Without taking anything away from these pioneers, the unfortunate reality is that early initiatives were typically one-off experiments that utilized only a fraction of the power of collaborative technology. More to the point, these early days of trial and error, experimentation, and feedback revealed legitimate legal, policy, culture, and governance issues that needed to be addressed if technology-enabled collaboration is to scale successfully. General counsels, web managers, accessibility experts, and privacy officers convened at the National Academy to discuss barriers to Web 2.0 adoption, including: Section 508 of the Rehabilitation Act (which is aimed at ensuring equality of access to online government resources for people with disabilities); privacy concerns related to Internet "cookies" and collection of personally identifiable information; ethical and legal issues surrounding commercial advertising and endorsements; Freedom of Information Act and record-keeping implications; security risks; and management issues. Early successes demonstrated the unique, measurable value of collaborative approaches and encouraged people to work together to find ways to address these numerous and daunting barriers.

Today: A Great "Leap Forward"?

Thanks in large part to effective use of social media tools by the Obama campaign team, and ongoing use by the resulting administration, online collaboration in the public sector has become more widespread. On his first full day in office, President Obama issued a memorandum calling on executive agencies and departments to "ensure the public trust and establish a system of transparency, public participation, and collaboration" that would "strengthen our democracy and promote efficiency and effectiveness in Government" (Obama 2009). This was followed by the administration's Open Government Directive, released in December 2009. The formulation of the directive itself employed a first-of-its-kind effort by the White House to engage the public. The vision for this exercise, as described by Aneesh Chopra, the federal Chief Technology Officer, was to invert the policymaking process by enabling public dialogue to inform policymaking at the front end (Kundra and Chopra 2010). This is in contrast to the traditional model, where proposed policy is crafted by government representatives who, though knowledgeable, do not always have access to the best possible expertise and information, and subsequently post to invite public comment. The three-phase process employed by the Office of Science and Technology Policy (OSTP) in 2009 presented tremendous possibilities for real-time innovation.

In the first phase, OSTP asked the National Academy to host a civic engagement exercise—an online brainstorm, labeled the OpenGov Dialogue—then analyze the results and provide a synthesis of key themes. In this brainstorm, the public was invited to share ideas on how to make government more open, participatory, and collaborative, and to discuss and prioritize the ideas of others. OSTP hosted the second phase of the effort—a discussion phase—on their blog, where participants had the ability to dig deeper into the ideas and challenges identified during the brainstorming phase. The third, and final, phase leveraged the functionality of MixedInk, an online collaborative writing tool that allowed users to work collaboratively to craft constructive recommendations for an Open Government Directive.

The directive itself identifies three principles of open government: transparency (public access to government information), participation (engagement of stakeholders and the public in the policymaking process), and collaboration. In addressing collaboration, the directive sets out three broad goals: (1) collaborate better, (2) collaborate more, especially on core mission activities, and (3) propose management and policy changes that further support 1 and 2. Figuring out how best to accomplish those goals has been left to individual agencies to decide. This process is unique in that—with regard to collaboration—the directive has pushed agencies down a path, but has not defined the outcome. This allows for innovation and creativity. But it also means that, in responding, agencies will move in different directions and at different speeds. In a sense, this is entirely the point. The process is intended to be not only collaborative, but evolutionary, innovative, and continually improving as well, acknowledging that agencies are at various stages of capability in this regard.

It is not surprising that the resulting open government plans—and in particular the collaboration components thereof—were uneven. The White House review found that although agencies made good strides, all but three, "including our own offices of OSTP and OMB—have more work to do before the Plan fully satisfies every requirement in the Directive" (White House 2010). Furthermore, in the White House repository of open government plan "leading practices," the participation and collaboration categories were combined. All three practices listed were specific to participation:

- *Leading practice 1:* the plan creates multiple means of engagement.
- *Leading practice 2:* the agency commits to implementing at least one of the ideas emerging from public consultation.
- *Leading practice 3:* the plan commits to incorporating public input into the agency's core decision-making processes (White House 2010).

A review of the flagship initiatives—a component of the open government plans designed to highlight at least one priority initiative per agency—falls short in surfacing any examples of collaboration as "shared sovereignty." NASA's Open Source Software Development initiative comes close, however. NASA is planning to enable third-party developer access to software code, in the hope that it will significantly improve functionality. Still in its early stages, the project is showing promise. One program (www.worldwindcentral.com) allows users to study "virtual globes" of Earth and other planets, and add functionality. We are heartened to see resource and knowledge sharing taking place with universities and researchers in pursuit of shared goals, although for obvious safety and security reasons, decision-making authority rests with NASA.

Although not a product of the open government planning process, Manor Labs is a great example of collaboration at the local level. This innovation and idea-generation platform involves more than just consultation on government issues. Residents of Manor, Texas, can submit their ideas regarding community projects and problems, and the community of users can discuss them openly. The community plays an active role in guiding those ideas they like through a funneling process, with input from discussion moderators, all the way to implementation. Users can build a quantifiable "reputation" on the platform over time and can be rewarded with actual products donated by local partners. Manor, Texas, has implemented 84 ideas, with more working their way through the stages. This is one of the better examples of government ceding some decision-making authority to the public.

The poor showing on the collaboration front is not solely, or even primarily, a function of the process employed in creating open government plans. Successful collaboration requires an enabling environment that does not yet exist in the public sector, at least at the federal level. There are four elements of such an environment to consider:

- *Culture:* government is hierarchical and risk-averse.
- *Governance:* roles and responsibilities are clear in a traditional hierarchy; in a networked environment, they are uncertain.
- *Law and policy:* many laws and policies were written well before the advent of the Internet, or were designed to address a specific issue, and resulted in unintended consequences for others.
- *Skill and capability:* agencies lack people with an understanding of and experience in how to use these tools effectively, and when they do have those skills at their disposal, they are most often found in people who are new to the highly regulated and structured government environment.

Gaining widespread acceptance requires demonstrably successful cases of collaboration, which can pattern behavior for others. Fortunately, the four elements listed also provide the framework for a roadmap that can lead us forward.

Looking to the Future: Continuing to Evolve

It is difficult to imagine the outcomes of widespread collaboration in government. Will we end up with direct democracy, where a fully participating citizenry is closely engaged in the governing of the nation? Unlikely, I believe. Although there is opportunity for government to become more agile, responsive, efficient, and effective in addressing the problems of our nation, doing so requires an enabling environment for a collaborative government. Following is a roadmap to guide our efforts:

Create an Environment That Is Open and Networked

In most cases, agencies can provide immense value simply by providing a platform or framework in which their workforce or stakeholders can engage. Consider the National Oceanographic and Atmospheric Administration (NOAA). Their core activities of scientific research, data collection, and modeling related to oceans and the atmosphere are major tasks. Few resources are available to create products and services that are easily digestible by the public. Yet the citizenry has an insatiable appetite for weather information, and particularly for the informed decisions it enables. The answer for NOAA is not to build these services internally, but rather to tap the energy and expertise of the crowd to design and develop products and services that leverage government data and serve mission outcomes.

Develop Models for Collaborative Teams and Approaches

Governance in a hierarchy is clear; power and authority move upward. In a collaborative environment, however, it's not your grade level but your contributions that determine role and responsibilities. New models that provide guidance and suggest governance for collaborative activities are therefore required.

Update Laws and Policies

Impossible to accomplish on an agency-by-agency basis. Either the White House or the Congress will need to take action in this regard. Section 508 (accessibility), government use of cookies, the Paperwork Reduction Act (PRA), security concerns—and many other issues that commonly arise—all have at their heart a set of good government objectives, the spirit of which must be maintained. Yet these "rules of the road" must be updated, to reflect the fact that we are no longer driving on a country lane, but speeding along an interstate highway.

Learn by Doing, Smartly

Building skill and capability is not just a function of how well agencies recruit, although that is certainly important. Many current federal employees, in all age groups, are interested in better understanding how to apply collaborative tools and approaches to solve problems. Learning by doing is therefore a powerful means by which to build internal capacity. In choosing this path, agencies should remember that early adopters have blazed a trail with greater certainty that the desired outcomes will be achieved without the same risk.

Celebrate and Learn from Failure

Agencies must create space for their employees to experiment, innovate, and collaborate. Collaboration assumes the adage that "none of us is as smart as all of us" is true. Risk is inherent in a "shared sovereignty" model, if only because agencies are ceding full control of the achievement of mission objectives to stakeholders outside the hierarchy and beyond their control. But it is also true that without risk, there is no reward.

Conclusion

Creating a transparent, participatory, and collaborative government is a foundational shift. Success requires that we access the best and most creative ideas for accomplishing this goal, wherever they reside. Let's ensure that we prevail.

References

Alabama Department of Homeland Security (AL DHS). 2010. "Welcome to Virtual Alabama." http://www.dhs.alabama.gov/virtual_alabama/home.aspx.

Fields, W. C. n.d. "Failure." Wikipedia. http://en.wikiquote.org/wiki/Failure.

Goldsmith, Stephen, and William D. Eggers. 2004. *Governing by Network: The New Shape of the Public Sector.* Washington, DC: Brookings Institution Press.

Kundra, Vivek, and Aneesh Chopra. 2010. "An Initial Assessment of Open Government Plans." April 27. http://www.whitehouse.gov/blog/2010/04/26/honest-assessment-open-government-initiatives.

Lemmie, Valerie A. 2007. Monumental possibilities: Capitalizing on collaboration. Remarks made by Valerie A. Lemmie at the national conference of the American Society of Public Administrators, Washington, DC, March 25.

Obama, Barack. 2008. "Barack Obama's Acceptance Speech." *New York Times,* August 28. http://www.nytimes.com/2008/08/28/us/politics/28text-obama.html?_r=1.

———. 2009. "Transparency and Open Government." Memorandum for the heads of executive departments and agencies. http://www.whitehouse.gov/the_press_office/TransparencyandOpenGovernment/.

O'Reilly, Tim. 2009. "The Change We Need: DIY on a Civic Scale." O'Reilly Radar, April 17. http://radar.oreilly.com/2009/04/change-we-need-diy-civic-scale.html.

The Pew Research Center for the People and the Press. 2010. *The People and Their Government: Distrust, Discontent, Anger and Partisan Rancor.* April 18. http://people-press.org/reports/pdf/606.pdf.

Reeder, Franklin S. 2009. *A National Dialogue on Health Information Technology and Privacy.* February. Washington, DC: National Academy of Public Administration.

———. 2010. Interview with Lena Trudeau, Washington, DC.

The White House. 2010. "Open Government Dashboard 'Leading Practices' for Agency Open Government Plans." http://www.whitehouse.gov/open/documents/leading-practices-open-govt-plans.

Index

Italic page references indicate tables, charts, and graphs.

351

About the Editors and Contributors

Editors

Alan Balutis is a Distinguished Fellow and Senior Director, North American Public Sector for Cisco Systems' Internet Business Solutions Group, the firm's global strategy and consulting arm. Balutis joined the networking leader after more than 30 years in public service and industry leadership roles. Most recently, he was President and Chief Executive Officer, Government Strategies, of a leading market research firm, INPUT. Before that, he served as COO of a small minority-owned firm. From 2001 to 2003, he headed a major public sector IT industry association, the Industry Advisory Council (IAC), as well as its parent group, now known as the American Council for Technology. Balutis was a founding member of the Federal CIO Council. He led its strategic planning and outreach committees, helped create the council's e-government committee and served as its first chair. His 28 years in the federal sector were spent at the Department of Commerce, where he headed its management and budget office for over a decade and was its first CIO, and at the Department of Health, Education and Welfare (now the Department of Health and Human Services). Balutis is a five-time Federal Computer Week FED 100 winner, and a member of both the Government Computer News and Federal Computer Week halls of fame. He is also a Fellow of the National Academy of Public Administration.

Terry F. Buss, PhD, is Executive Director and Distinguished Professor of Public Policy at Carnegie Mellon University in Adelaide, Australia. Buss earned his doctorate in political science and mathematics at Ohio State University. He did so as an unprecedented two-time Fulbright Scholar winner in Hungary, working with the Minister of the Interior and Budapest University of Economic Science. He also received two fellowships with the Congressional Research Service, where he authored policy studies mandated by Congress. Buss has published 12 books and nearly 340 professional articles on a variety of policy issues. Buss has won numerous awards for research and public service, among them, Most Honored Professor of the Russian Federation. Over the years, Buss has worked overseas on major projects in England, Wales, Italy, Czech Republic, Slovakia, Hungary, Romania, Bulgaria, Albania, Ghana, Haiti, Canada, Colombia, Jamaica, Bahamas,

Vietnam, Taiwan, and Australia. He also directed projects in Iraq, South Africa, and Botswana from the United States.

Dwight Ink is President Emeritus of the Institute of Public Administration and a Fellow of the National Academy of Public Administration. An icon of government management, Mr. Ink began his career in local government and later served in senior federal policy positions under seven presidents, with responsibilities for a variety of national security and domestic activities. These ranged from national urban development, environmental protection, education, and antipoverty efforts to U.S. foreign assistance, international atomic weapons arrangements, disaster reconstruction, and energy conservation and development. He headed two independent agencies, chaired several presidential task forces, and was vice president of two public corporations. He is a past President of the American Society of Public Administration and served for many years as vice-chair of the National Advisory Council of the Center for the Study of the Presidency. Dubbed "Mr. Implementation" by William Eggers and John O'Leary in their book *If We Can Put a Man on the Moon . . .* Mr. Ink continues to write, lecture, and testify on government reform.

Contributors

Scott Blanchard is Executive Vice President of Client Solutions for the Ken Blanchard Companies, the company cofounded by his father, best-selling business author Ken Blanchard.

Nathaniel J. Buss is a doctoral student at the Center for Public Administration and Policy, School of Public and International Affairs, Virginia Tech, Blacksburg, Virginia.

John Callahan is Interim Executive Director of the School of Health and Human Services at the University of Baltimore and a former Assistant Secretary of Management and Budget at the U.S. Department of Health and Human Services.

Robert D. Childs is Chancellor of the iCollege at the National Defense University.

Gary A. Christopherson is developing policy and management models for creating and sustaining large-scale change.

Robert F. Durant is Professor of Public Administration and Chair of the Department of Public Administration and Policy in the School of Public Affairs at American University.

Vicky Essary is Director of Assessment Strategy for the Ken Blanchard Companies.

H. George Frederickson is Distinguished Professor in the Department of Public Administration at the University of Kansas.

Gerry Gingrich is Professor of Systems Management at the iCollege at the National Defense University.

Derek L. Hansen is an Assistant Professor at the University of Maryland's iSchool and Director for the Center for the Advanced Study of Communities and Information.

Dobie Houson is Director of Marketing Research for the Ken Blanchard Companies.

Norman Jacknis is a Director in Cisco's Business Solutions Group, the firm's global strategy and consulting arm.

Erik W. Johnston is an Assistant Professor in the School of Public Affairs at Arizona State University and the Co-Director of the Center for Policy Informatics.

Paul Johnston is a Director in Cisco's Business Solutions Group and head of their Europe Public Sector practice.

Donald F. Kettl is Dean of the School of Public Policy at the University of Maryland and author of the recent book, *The Next Government of the United States.*

John Kincaid is Director of the Meyner Center for the Study of State and Local Government at Lafayette College.

Alan Lyles is the Henry A. Rosenberg Professor of Public, Private and Nonprofit Partnerships at the School of Public Affairs of the University of Baltimore.

Terry M. McGovern is Professor of Systems Management at the iCollege, National Defense University.

Bradley H. Patterson Jr. is an author and a former senior member at The Brookings Institution and the White House.

F. Stevens Redburn is a consultant for the National Academy of Public Administration and a former senior executive at the Office of Management and Budget.

Thom Reilly is a Professor and Director at the School of Social Work at San Diego State University. He is the former county manager for Clark County, Nevada, and state child welfare administrator for Nevada.

Paulette Robinson is the Assistant Dean for Teaching, Learning, and Technology at the iCollege, part of the National Defense University.

Alan R. Shark is Executive Director of the Public Technology Institute.

Thomas H. Stanton is a Fellow of the Center for the Study of American Government at Johns Hopkins University.

Martin Stewart-Weeks is a Director in Cisco's Business Solutions Group and head of their Asia/Australia Public Sector practice.

Robert J. Tekniepe is an adjunct professor in the graduate program at the Department of Public Administration, Greenspur College of Urban Affairs, University of Nevada, Las Vegas. He is also a Principal Management Analyst for Clark County, Nevada.

W. Frederick Thompson is an independent consultant with extensive executive experience in the public, private, and nonprofit sectors.

Lena Trudeau is former Vice President at the National Academy of Public Administration and is a founder of the Collaboration Project, an independent forum of leaders committed to leveraging Web 2.0 and the benefits of collaborative technologies to solve government's complex problems.

Susan Urahn is Managing Director of the Pew Center on the States; she holds a doctorate in education policy and administration from the University of Minnesota.

Drea Zigarmi is an executive with the Ken Blanchard Companies and coauthor of *Leadership and the One Minute Manager,* the third book in Ken Blanchard's best-selling series.